SOCIO-ECONOMIC RIGHTS IN SOUTH AFRICA

edited by

Danie Brand and Christof Heyns

Centre for Human Rights
Faculty of Law

University of Pretoria

Pretoria University Law Press
——— PULP ———
2005

Socio-economic rights in South Africa

Published by PULP (Pretoria University Law Press)

The Pretoria University Law Press (PULP) is a publisher based in Africa, launched and managed by the Centre for Human Rights and the Faculty of Law, University of Pretoria, South Africa.

PULP endeavours to publish, and increase access to, innovative, high-quality and peer-reviewed texts with a focus on human rights and other aspects of public international law especially in Africa.

For more information on PULP see: www.chr.up.ac.za/pulp

To order, contact:
Centre for Human Rights
Faculty of Law
University of Pretoria
South Africa
0002
Tel: +27 12 420 4948
Fax: +27 12 362 5125
Email: pulp@up.ac.za
Website: www.chr.up.ac.za

Printed and bound by:
ABC Press
Cape Town

Cover illustration:
"Duduza", by Vusi Khumalo, used with permission of the artist and Murray Hofmeyer.

ISBN: 0-620-34086-X

© 2005
Copyright subsists in this work. It may be reproduced only with permission of the editors.

Abbreviated table of contents

Full table of contents	v
Foreword	xi
Contributors	xiii
One / Introduction to socio-economic rights in the South African Constitution Danie Brand	1
Two / The right to education Faranaaz Veriava and Fons Coomans	57
Three / The right to housing Pierre de Vos	85
Four / Rights concerning health Charles Ngwena and Rebecca Cook	107
Five / The right to food Danie Brand	153
Six / The right to water Anton Kok and Malcolm Langford	191
Seven / The right to social security and assistance Linda Jansen van Rensburg and Lucie Lamarche	209
Eight / Environmental rights Loretta A Feris and Dire Tladi	249
Table of cases	267
Table of statutes	274
Table of international instruments	283
Other international documents	288
Subject index	292
Bibliography	298

Full table of contents

Foreword	xi
Contributors	xiii

One / Introduction to socio-economic rights in South Africa — 1

1	Introduction	1
2	**Textual basis: The rights and related provisions**	3
	2.1 The rights	3
	2.2 The interpretation of socio-economic rights	6
	2.2.1 Section 39(1) – The role of international and foreign law	6
	2.2.2 Section 7(2) – Duties	9
3	**Processes of translation**	12
	3.1 Translation through legislation	12
	3.2 Translation through executive and administrative action	16
	3.3 Translation through adjudication	17
	3.3.1 Modes of adjudication: Sections 8 and 39(2)	18
	3.3.2 Constraint in the adjudication of socio-economic rights claims	20
4	**Results of translation: Concrete legal duties and entitlements**	30
	4.1 The duty to respect socio-economic rights	30
	4.1.1 Refraining from interfering with the existing exercise of socio-economic rights	30
	4.1.2 Mitigating the impact of interferences in the exercise of socio-economic rights	33
	4.1.3 Refraining from impairing access to socio-economic rights	36
	4.2 The duty to protect socio-economic rights	37
	4.2.1 Legislative and executive measures	37
	4.2.2 The judiciary	38
	4.3 The duty to fulfil socio-economic rights	42
	4.3.1 Background	42
	4.3.2 Reasonableness review	43
	4.3.3 Remedies	54

Two / The right to education   57

1	Introduction	57
2	International law	58
3	South African law	59
	3.1 The right to basic education	61
	3.1.1 Availability	66
	3.1.2 Accessibility	67
	3.1.3 Acceptability	71
	3.1.4 Adaptability	73
	3.2 The right to further and higher education	74
	3.3 The right to instruction in the official language of one's choice	77
	3.4 The right to establish private educational institutions	79
4	**Other provisions in the Bill of Rights**	81
	4.1 The principle of equality and equal access	81
	4.2 Freedom of choice	81
5	**Conclusion**	82

Three / The right to housing   85

1	**Introduction**	85
2	**Interpreting the right to housing**	87
	2.1 Rights must be interpreted contextually	88
	2.2 The role of international law in interpreting the right to housing	89
3	**International and South African law**	92
	3.1 Introduction	92
	3.2 Negative obligations on the state and other role-players to respect the right to housing	92
	3.2.1 General principles	92
	3.2.2 Evictions and South African law	93
	3.2.3 Evictions and international law	96
	3.3 Positive obligations	98
	3.3.1 Reasonable legislative and other measures	99
	3.3.2 Progressive realisation of the right	99
	3.3.3 Resource constraints	100
	3.4 Minimum core obligations	101
	3.5 International law and the concept of 'adequate' housing	102
	3.5.1 Legal security of tenure	102
	3.5.2 Availability of services, materials and infrastructure	102
	3.5.3 Affordable housing	103
	3.5.4 Habitable housing	103
	3.5.5 Accessible housing	103

		3.5.6 Location	103
		3.5.7 Culturally adequate housing	103
4		**Housing-related protection of vulnerable groups**	104
	4.1	Children's right to shelter	104
	4.2	Prisoners' rights to adequate accommodation	105
5		**Conclusion**	106

Four / Rights concerning health — 107

1		**Introduction**	107
2		**International law**	108
3		**State obligations in international law**	111
	3.1	The Universal Declaration of Human Rights	111
	3.2	The International Covenant on Economic, Social and Cultural Rights	112
	3.3	Interpreting the right to health under human rights treaties other than CESCR	120
	3.4	Ensuring equality in fact	121
	3.5	Possible limitations on rights	122
	3.6	Monitoring compliance	124
4		**South African law**	125
	4.1	Introduction	125
	4.2	A legacy of gross inequality	127
	4.3	Transformation through section 27 of the Constitution	131
	4.4	Other reforms that impact on the right of access to health care services	143
	4.5	Impeding factors	149
5		**Conclusion**	150

Five / The right to food — 153

1		**Introduction**	153
2		**International law**	154
	2.1	Sources	154
	2.2	Content	157
		2.2.1 The content of the right to food: Availability, accessibility, adequacy	157
		2.2.2 Duties	159
3		**South African law**	161
	3.1	Content	161
	3.2	Legal duties	163
		3.2.1 The duty to respect the right to food	165
		3.2.2 The duty to protect the right to food	170
		3.2.3 The duty to promote and fulfil the right to food	178
4		**Conclusion**	189

Six / The right to water — 191

1	Introduction	191
2	International, regional and comparable national law	192
	2.1 International law	192
	2.2 Regional law	195
	2.3 Comparable national law	197
3	**South African law**	197
	3.1 Recognition of the right in section 27	197
	3.1.1 'Sufficient'	197
	3.1.2 'Access'	200
	3.1.3 Obligations of the state	202
	3.2 Interrelationship with other rights	206
	3.3 General guidelines	207
4	**Basic sanitation**	208
5	**Conclusion**	208

Seven / The right to social security and assistance — 209

1	Introduction	209
2	Social security, social assistance and social protection	209
3	**International law**	213
	3.1 United Nations binding instruments	213
	3.1.1 The International Covenant on Economic, Social and Cultural Rights	213
	3.1.2 Convention on the Rights of the Child	217
	3.1.3 Convention on the Elimination of All Forms of Discrimination Against Women	221
	3.1.4 Convention on the Elimination of All Forms of Racial Discrimination	222
	3.1.5 Treaties on the protection of refugees and stateless persons	223
	3.2 International Labour Organisation instruments	225
	3.3 United Nations non-binding instruments	229
4	**Regional law**	231
	4.1 The African Charter on Human and Peoples' Rights	231
	4.2 The African Charter on the Rights and Welfare of the Child	232
5	**South African law**	233
	5.1 Introduction	233
	5.2 The constitutional scope of the right to social security	234
	5.2.1 The wording of section 27(1)(c)	234
	5.2.2 Underpinning values and aims of social	

		security rights	235
	5.2.3	*The duty to respect, protect, promote and fulfil*	238
6	Conclusion		247

Eight / Environmental rights 249

1	Introduction	249
2	Conceptual debates on human rights and the environment	250
3	International law	255
4	Regional systems	256
5	South African law	257
6	Conclusion	264

Table of cases	267
Table of statutes	274
Table of international instruments	283
Other international documents	288
Subject index	292
Bibliography	298

Foreword

This book is aimed at practicing lawyers, academics and other specialists interested in constitutional socio-economic rights, especially in South Africa. In most cases, South African as well as overseas authors worked together to write the different chapters. The authors were briefed to provide an overview and analysis of the available international and local legal materials on the various socio-economic rights recognised in the South African Constitution, and to introduce readers to current legal issues regarding these rights. At a minimum, the contributions reflect the law as at the end of January 2004.

Each of the contributions to the book was peer reviewed by an independent specialist prior to publication. Sandra Liebenberg reviewed the introduction chapter; Russel Wildeman the chapter on the right to education; André van der Walt the chapter on the right to housing; Karrisha Pillay the chapter on rights concerning health; Marie Ganier-Raymond the chapter on the right to food; Bronwen Morgan the chapter on the right to water; Nick de Villiers the chapter on the right to social security and assistance, and Michael Kidd the chapter on environmental rights.

In addition to the authors and reviewers, thanks are due to the following people: Lizette Besaans did the cover layout and was responsible for the task of formatting the manuscript. Waruguru Kaguongo spent considerable time assisting with double checking references and getting the manuscript ready for publication. Tina Rossouw and Liana Viljoen, working with Shirley Schröder from the Oliver R Tambo Law Library of the University of Pretoria, compiled the indexes. Help was also provided by the doctoral students of the Centre for Human Rights. Denise Fourie did most of the proofreading. John Adolph, Lawrence Mashava, Karen Stefiszyn and Matseleng Lekoane provided research assistance. Isabeau de Meyer assisted with formatting the text. We also thank Gill Jacot-Guillarmod. The Norwegian Centre for Human Rights generously financed the project.

This book builds on a series of publications on socio-economic rights edited by Gina Bekker and Lawrence Mashava, published by the Centre for Human Rights in 1999 and 2000. We also want to give recognition to the fact that some of the material published here was used in the *Ten Years Review of Democratic Governance* of the South African Human Rights Commission (2005).

This book is the first to be published by the Pretoria University Law Press (PULP). The objective of PULP is to produce high quality legal texts, focusing specifically (although not exclusively) on issues of public international law in Africa. One of the main driving forces behind PULP is Frans Viljoen, who contributed greatly to the production of this book, as a model for future PULP publications. Nick Grové and Duard Kleyn created the space in which PULP could be established. Marie Ferreira, Faculty Manager of the Faculty of Law of the University of Pretoria, manages PULP. We thank Pieter van der Spuy for his assistance on intellectual property issues.

Danie Brand
Christof Heyns

Pretoria, June 2005

Contributors

Danie Brand *(BLC LLB (Pretoria), LLM (Emory))* is a Senior Lecturer in the Department of Public Law and a Research Associate of the Centre for Human Rights at the University of Pretoria, South Africa. His area of research interest is socio-economic rights, in particular the right to food.

Rebecca Cook *(AB (Barnard), MA (Tufts), MPA (Harvard), JD (Georgetown), LLM (Columbia), JSD (Columbia), called to the Bar of Washington DC)* is a Professor in the Faculty of Law, the Faculty of Medicine and the Joint Centre for Bioethics at the University of Toronto, Canada, and Co-Director of the International Program on Reproductive and Sexual Health Law at the University of Toronto, Canada. She specialises in international human rights, the law relating to women's health and feminist ethics.

Fons Coomans *(MPol (Amsterdam), PhD (Maastricht))* is a Senior Researcher in the Centre for Human Rights at Maastricht University, The Netherlands. His area of research interest is the international protection of economic, social and cultural rights in general, and the right to education in particular.

Pierre de Vos *(BComm LLB LLM (Stellenbosch), LLM (Columbia), LLD (Western Cape))* is a Professor in the Faculty of Law at the University of the Western Cape, South Africa. His research focuses on constitutional law and theory, especially social and economic rights and the right to equality.

Loretta A Feris *(LLB (Stellenbosch), LLM (Georgetown), LLD (Stellenbosch))* is an Associate Professor of Law in the Department of Public Law and a Research Associate of the Centre for Human Rights at the University of Pretoria, South Africa. Her areas of research interest are environmental law and international trade and investment law.

Christof Heyns *(LLB MA (Pretoria), LLM (Yale), PhD (Witwatersrand))* is Professor of Human Rights Law and Director of the Centre for Human Rights at the Faculty of Law, University of Pretoria, South Africa and Academic Coordinator of the United Nations University for Peace, Addis Ababa, Ethiopia. He specialises in international human rights law, particularly in Africa.

Linda Jansen van Rensburg *(BComm LLB LLM (Potchefstroom), LLD (Rand Afrikaans))* is an Associate Professor in the Faculty of Law at the North-West University (Potchefstroom Campus), South Africa. Her areas of research interest are socio-economic rights, focusing on the rights of children and on social security.

Anton Kok *(BComm LLB LLM (Pretoria))* is a Senior Lecturer in the Department of Legal History, Jurisprudence and Comparative Law at the University of Pretoria and an attorney of the High Court of South Africa. His areas of research interest include human rights, with a particular focus on equality and anti-discrimination legislation, and legal skills education.

Lucie Lamarche *(Licence en droit, LLM (Montréal), LLD (Université libre de Bruxelles))* is a Professor in the Faculty of Law at the University of Québec in Montréal, Canada. Her areas of research interest are labour law, with a specific focus on women in work, and socio-economic rights, in particular the right to social security and assistance.

Malcolm Langford *(BComm LLB (New South Wales), LLM (European University Institute))* is a Senior Legal Officer in the Economic, Social and Cultural Rights Litigation Programme and Director of the Right to Water Programme at the Centre on Housing Rights and Evictions (COHRE), Switzerland. He specialises in the judicial enforcement of economic, social and cultural rights with a specific focus on the right to water and adequate sanitation, the right to social security and land rights in the South Pacific.

Charles Ngwena *(LLB LLM (Wales))* is a Professor in the Faculty of Law at the University of the Free State, South Africa. His area of research interest lies at the intersection between human rights, ethics and health care, including HIV/AIDS and reproductive and sexual health.

Dire Tladi *(BLC LLB (Pretoria) LLM (Connecticut))* is an Associate Professor in the Department of Constitutional, International and Indigenous Law at the University of South Africa. He specialises in international law, particularly relating to sustainable development, and international human rights law.

Faranaaz Veriava *(BA LLB (Witwatersrand), LLM (Pretoria))* is a Researcher in the Law and Transformation Programme of the Centre for Applied Legal Studies at the University of the Witwatersrand, South Africa and a part-time practising member of the Johannesburg Bar. Her areas of research interest are the role of law in social transformation and socio-economic rights, with a focus on education rights.

One / Introduction to socio-economic rights in the South African Constitution*

Danie Brand

1 Introduction

The South African Constitution[1] is known for its entrenchment of a range of socio-economic rights: environmental rights and rights to land, housing, health care, food, water, social assistance and education.[2] These rights, together with various other features in the Constitution, indicate that the South African Constitution differs from a traditional liberal model in that it is *transformative*, as it does not simply place limits on the exercise of collective power (it does that also), but requires collective power to be used to advance ideals of freedom, equality, dignity and social justice.[3]

---

* Parts of this introduction are derived from a paper co-authored with Christof Heyns ('Introduction to socio-economic rights in the South African Constitution', published in (1998) 2 *Law, Democracy and Development* 153 and G Bekker (ed) *A compilation of essential documents on economic, social and cultural rights* (1999) 1). My thanks also to Sandra Liebenberg, the external reviewer for this chapter, for her thoughtful suggestions. Mistakes are my own.

[1] Constitution of the Republic of South Africa of 1996 (Constitution), referred to as the 'final' Constitution to distinguish it from the 'interim' Constitution (Constitution of the Republic of South Africa Act 200 of 1993), which was in force from 1994 to 1997 as the framework for the election of a Constitutional Assembly to draft and adopt the 'final' Constitution.

[2] The irony of this fact should be noted. When the Universal Declaration of Human Rights (1948) was drafted, South Africa was one of the few countries that objected to the inclusion of socio-economic rights, arguing that 'a condition of existence does not constitute a fundamental right merely because it is eminently desirable for the fullest realisation of all human potentialities' and that recognition of socio-economic rights would make it 'necessary to resort to ... totalitarian control of the economic life of the country' (UN Doc E/CN 4/82/Add 4 (1948) 11 13 as quoted in HJ Steiner & P Alston *International human rights in context - Law, politics, morals* (1996) 260).

[3] The term 'transformative constitutionalism' is Karl Klare's. See K Klare 'Legal culture and transformative constitutionalism' (1998) 14 *South African Journal on Human Rights* 146 151-156. The theme has been explored by a number of South African scholars. See eg P de Vos '*Grootboom*, the right of access to housing and substantive equality as contextual fairness' (2001) 17 *South African Journal on Human Rights* 258 and AJ Van der Walt 'Tentative urgency: Sensitivity for the paradoxes of stability and change in social transformation decisions of the Constitutional Court' (2001) 16 *SA Public Law* 1.

In this respect, constitutional socio-economic rights play two roles. The Constitution first places a duty on the state actively to *implement* socio-economic rights. Section 2 requires the state to *fulfil* constitutional duties; section 7(2) requires the state to *respect, protect, promote* and *fulfil* rights; and a number of the socio-economic rights themselves indicate that affirmative steps must be taken to give effect to them.[4] In this sense, constitutional socio-economic rights are blueprints for the state's manifold activities that proactively guide and shape legislative action, policy formulation and executive and administrative decision-making. On the flip side, they are also tools of political struggle, rhetorical devices to be used in 'forms of political action, such as lobbying bureaucrats and legislators, campaigning for public support, or protest'.[5]

Apart from requiring their implementation, the Constitution enables the enforcement of socio-economic rights, creating avenues of redress through which complaints that the state or others have failed in their constitutional duties can be determined and constitutional duties can be enforced. In this sense, constitutional socio-economic rights operate reactively. They are translated into concrete legal entitlements that can be enforced against the state and society by the poor and otherwise marginalised to ensure that appropriate attention is given to their plight.

In this introduction I focus on the second role of socio-economic rights outlined above. My aim is to describe the different ways in which constitutional socio-economic rights can and have been translated into legally enforceable entitlements that can in particular cases be used, through the legal process, to advance social justice. In part 2 below, I identify the textual basis for this translation. I describe the socio-economic rights in the Constitution, together with other rights that could play a role in the protection and advancement of basic socio-economic interests. In part 3, I describe the processes of translation - the role of the legislature, the executive, the state administration and the courts in the creation of concrete legal entitlements on the basis of constitutional socio-economic rights. In part 4, I describe the results of the translation. I provide an overview of the different ways in which socio-economic rights have been translated into enforceable legal claims.

---

[4] Eg sec 25(5) ('[t]he state must take reasonable legislative and other measures' to make it possible for citizens to gain access to land) and sec 26(2) ('the state must take reasonable legislative and other measures' to realise the right to have access to adequate housing).

[5] S Wilson 'Taming the Constitution: Rights and reform in the South African education system' (2004) 20 *South African Journal on Human Rights* 418 421.

2 Textual basis: The rights and related provisions

2.1 The rights

Socio-economic rights create entitlements to material conditions for human welfare – they are rights to things such as food, water, health care services and shelter, rather than rights to vote, or speak, or associate. A number of such rights are found in the Constitution. Section 24 guarantees everyone's right to a safe and healthy environment and requires the state to protect the environment. Section 25(5) requires the state to enable citizens to gain equitable access to land. Section 26 provides for everyone the right to have access to adequate housing and prohibits arbitrary evictions. Section 27 guarantees everyone's right to have access to health care services, sufficient food and water and social security and assistance and prohibits the refusal of emergency medical treatment. Section 28(1)(c) entrenches children's rights to shelter and to basic nutrition, social services and health care services. Section 29 provides for everyone's right to basic education and to further education. Finally, section 35(2)(e) guarantees the right of detained persons to be provided with adequate nutrition, accommodation, medical care and reading material.

The precise formulation of these rights determines the duties they impose and entitlements they create. Three groups of socio-economic rights can be distinguished. First, some rights - the *'qualified* socio-economic rights' - follow a standard formulation, circumscribing the positive duties[6] they impose on the state. These rights (all rights of 'everyone') are formulated as 'access' rights rather than rights to a particular social good, and the positive duties they impose on the state are described as duties to take reasonable steps, within available resources, to achieve their progressive realisation. Standard examples are the section 26(1) right to 'have access to adequate housing' and the section 27(1) rights to 'have access to' health care services, including reproductive health care; sufficient food and water; and social security and assistance. The positive duties of these rights are explicitly described in subsections 26(2) and 27(2) respectively, so that the state is required to take 'reasonable legislative and other measures, within its available resources, to achieve ... [their] progressive realisation ...' Other qualified socio-economic rights are those in section 24(b) ('[e]veryone has the right to have the environment protected ... through *reasonable legislative and other measures*'); in section 25(5) ('[t]he state must take *reasonable legislative and other measures, within its available resources*, to foster conditions which enable citizens to *gain access* to land on an equitable basis'); and section 29(1)(b) ([e]veryone has the right 'to further education, which the state, *through reasonable*

---

[6] See sec 2.2.2 below regarding the viability of the distinction between positive and negative duties.

measures, must make *progressively* available and *accessible*') (my emphasis).

A second group - '*basic* socio-economic rights'[7] - are neither formulated as access rights, nor subjected to the qualifications of 'reasonableness', 'available resources' or 'progressive realisation'. These are the section 29(1)(a) right of everyone to 'basic education, including adult basic education'; the section 28(1)(c) rights of children to 'basic nutrition, shelter, basic health care services and social services', and the section 35(2)(e) rights of detained persons to 'the provision, at state expense, of adequate accommodation, nutrition, reading material and medical treatment'.

Third, sections 26(3) and 27(3) describe particular elements of the section 26(1) right to have access to adequate housing and the section 27(1)(a) right to have access to health care services respectively. These rights are formulated as prohibitions of certain forms of conduct, rather than rights to particular things. Section 26(3) prohibits arbitrary evictions and section 27(3) the refusal of emergency medical treatment. These two rights are also not explicitly subjected to any of the special qualifications that are typically attached to the qualified socio-economic rights.

In addition to the socio-economic rights themselves, other rights, not explicitly formulated as rights to material conditions for human welfare, but that can be interpreted to create entitlements to such things, should be noted. Examples are the section 11 right to life, the section 9 right to equality and the section 33 right to administrative justice. The right to life can be interpreted as not only requiring the state to refrain from killing, but also to protect and sustain life and to foster and maintain a certain quality of life.[8] The right to equality can ground claims that a socio-economic benefit provided to one class of needy people should be extended to others.[9]

---

[7] S Liebenberg 'The interpretation of socio-economic rights' in Chaskalson, M et al, *Constitutional law of South Africa* (2nd edition, Original Service, 12-03) (2003) ch 33 5.

[8] This argument featured in *Soobramoney v Minister of Health, KwaZulu-Natal* 1998 1 SA 765 (CC) to support a claim that a patient suffering renal failure was entitled to dialysis from a state hospital for free, but was rejected on the reasoning that the claim fell to be decided on the basis of secs 27(3) and 27(1). However, the Court did not deny that such an interpretation of the right to life was possible. For discussion of the space this leaves for claims for material conditions for welfare through the right to life, see M Pieterse 'A different shade of red: Socio-economic dimensions of the right to life in South Africa' (1999) 15 *South African Journal on Human Rights* 372 384.

[9] See eg *Khosa v Minister of Social Development* 2004 6 SA 505 (CC) (challenge against provisions of the Social Assistance Act 59 of 1992 excluding people with permanent residence status from access to social assistance upheld, both on the basis that the exclusion violated sec 27(1) and discriminated unfairly against permanent residents in violation of sec 9(3)).

In addition, a person's socio-economic status could be recognised as a ground for distinction analogous to the grounds explicitly listed in section 9(3), thus rendering distinctions made on the basis of socio-economic status actionable as unfair discrimination in terms of section 9(3) or 9(4).[10] Finally, equality is relevant to claims decided in terms of socio-economic rights in that a contextually fair[11] conception of equality is part and parcel of the review standard of reasonableness that the Constitutional Court has developed to determine whether state efforts to realise qualified socio-economic rights are constitutionally sound.[12]

Administrative justice rights in section 33 are also relevant. Most state decisions affecting access to health care, housing, education, social services, food and water qualify as administrative action and must comply with the standards of procedural fairness, lawfulness and reasonableness. Administrative law grounds of review are potent tools for the protection of socio-economic rights. Particularly in the field of social assistance, a large body of socio-economic rights case law based on administrative law principles has developed.[13]

Socio-economic rights are indirectly protected not only through other constitutional rights. Any number of non-rights related constitutional provisions that seemingly have nothing whatsoever to do with socio-economic rights can be used to protect and advance socio-economic rights. In *Mashava v President of the Republic of South Africa*, the validity of a presidential proclamation assigning administration of the Social Assistance Act from national government to the provincial governments was at issue.[14] The case was decided on the basis of a number of technical, non-rights related provisions of the interim Constitution regulating transitional arrangements and determining the relationship between the legislative power at national and provincial level. However, the mischief the case sought

---

[10] Sec 34(1)(a) of the Promotion of Equality and Prevention of Unfair Discrimination Act 4 of 2000 lists socio-economic status as one of a number of grounds that must be considered by the Equality Review Committee established in terms of sec 32 of the Act for future inclusion in the list of prohibited grounds. The special consideration accorded socio-economic status in sec 34 indicates that, at the very least, it will be regarded, for purposes of the Act, as a ground analogous to the listed grounds. This seems to indicate that the legislature regards it for constitutional purposes also to be a ground analogous to those listed in sec 9(3) of the Constitution. See, in general, P de Vos 'The Promotion of Equality and Prevention of Unfair Discrimination Act and socio-economic rights' (2004) 5(2) *ESR Review* 5.
[11] See, in general, De Vos (n 3 above).
[12] See Mokgoro J for the majority in *Khosa* (n 9 above) paras 42 & 44-45.
[13] See N de Villiers 'Social grants and the Promotion of Administrative Justice Act' (2002) 18 *South African Journal on Human Rights* 320; AJ van der Walt 'Sosiale geregtigheid, prosedurele billikheid, en eiendom: Alternatiewe perspektiewe op grondwetlike waarborge (Deel Een)' ('Social justice, procedural fairness, and property. Alternative perspectives on constitutional guarantees (Part One)') (2002) 13 *Stellenbosch Law Review* 59 and 'A South African reading of Frank Michelman's theory of social justice' in H Botha, AJ van der Walt & JC van der Walt *Rights and democracy in a transformative constitution* (2004) 163 172-174 187-189. The sec 33 administrative justice rights have been given effect in the Promotion of Administrative Justice Act 3 of 2000, which currently forms the basis for review of administrative action.
[14] *Mashava v President of the Republic of South Africa* 2004 12 BCLR 1243 (CC); the Social Assistance Act (n 9 above).

to address was the inability of provincial governments properly to administer the social grant system. This inability frustrated the access of people like the complainant to social assistance, such that the case was quite directly about the right of everyone to have access to social assistance.

2.2 The interpretation of socio-economic rights

The interpretation of socio-economic rights is conditioned by two generally applicable provisions of the Constitution: section 7(2) and section 39(1).

2.2.1 Section 39(1) - The role of international and foreign law

Section 39(1) obligates courts, in their interpretation of the Bill of Rights, to have regard to international law, and allows courts to have regard to foreign law.[15]

Socio-economic rights are protected as justiciable rights in many national constitutions.[16] However, apart from notable exceptions,[17] they have seldom formed the basis of constitutional litigation. The largest bodies of case law have developed in jurisdictions where socio-economic rights are indirectly recognised, through extended interpretation of other rights or application of broader constitutional norms. In India, courts have used so-called 'directive principles of state policy' to read basic socio-economic entitlements into civil and political rights such as the right to life.[18] The German Constitutional Court has used the constitutional 'social state' principle to insulate state conduct intended to protect access to basic socio-economic

---

[15] Section 39: When interpreting the Bill of Rights, a court, tribunal or forum ... must consider international law; and may consider foreign law.

[16] F Viljoen 'The justiciability of socio-economic and cultural rights: Experiences and problems' (2005) (unpublished paper on file with author) 6 notes that, on the African continent, 'only a handful of states, notably Botswana, Nigeria and Tunisia, ... do not ... guarantee any socio-economic ... rights' and that such rights are included in many Latin-American constitutions.

[17] See eg a Colombian decision which held, on the basis of the right to health care, that an AIDS sufferer was entitled to, at state expense, health services essential to keep him alive; Rights of sick persons/AIDS patients, Constitutional Court of Columbia, Judgment No T-505/92, 22 August 1992; and a Latvian decision holding legislation conditioning access to social security benefits on payment of employer contributions on behalf of employees invalid, on the basis of the right to social security (sec 109) in the Latvian Constitution; Constitutional Court of the Republic of Latvia, Case No 2000-08-0109. See Viljoen (n 16 above) 10-11 & 15.

[18] See eg *Paschim Banga Khet Mazdoor Samity & Others v State of West Bengal & Another* (1996) AIR SC 2426 (right to emergency medical treatment read into right to life)(see Constitutional Court's references in *Soobramoney* (n 8 above) para 18); and *Francis Coralie Mullin v The Administrator, Union Territory of Delhi* (1981) 2 SCR 516 529 (right to food read into right to life).

resources against challenge on the basis of, for instance, freedom of competition.[19] In other jurisdictions, the right to equality and due process guarantees have been used to protect or establish entitlements to basic socio-economic resources.[20]

Absent foreign jurisprudence on socio-economic rights, the focus in South Africa has been on international human rights law. The work of a variety of human rights treaty monitoring or enforcement bodies has been influential in shaping both the socio-economic rights provisions of the Constitution,[21] and the jurisprudence that has developed around them.[22] The primary United Nations (UN) instrument in this respect is the International Covenant on Economic, Social and Cultural Rights (CESCR) of 1966, which South Africa has signed but not ratified. In various respects, the socio-economic rights provisions of the Constitution are modelled on CESCR, and it is consequently particularly important as an interpretative source.

The international body that supervises compliance with CESCR is the Committee on Economic, Social and Cultural Rights (Committee on ESCR). This Committee receives regular reports from state parties on the realisation of socio-economic rights in their respective countries. In practice, non-governmental organisations (NGOs) also submit 'shadow' reports, which are considered alongside those of the states when performance of the state in question is evaluated. The Committee on ESCR also issues General Comments on CESCR, which are highly influential in the interpretation of socio-economic rights in general.[23] Other international instruments with strong socio-economic rights dimensions are the Universal Declaration on Human Rights (1948) (Universal Declaration),[24] the Convention on the Elimination of All Forms of Discrimination against Women (1979)[25] and the Convention on the Rights of the Child (1989).[26] South Africa is a state party to the latter two Conventions.

---

[19] *Milk and Butterfat* case, 18 BVerfGE 315, 1965 (price control regulations upheld against freedom of competition-based constitutional challenge because state, in terms of 'social state' principle, held to be obliged to combat high food prices so as to protect access to basic foodstuffs).
[20] See eg with respect to equality the Canadian case of *Eldridge v British Columbia (Attorney General)* 1997 151 DLR (4th) 577 SCC (state required to provide sign language interpretation to deaf patients as part of publicly funded health care system) and with respect to due process the US cases of *Goldberg v Kelly* 397 US 254 (1970) and *Sniadach v Family Finance Corp* 395 US 337 (1969) (hearing is required before access to welfare benefits is revoked). For a view that the latter two cases could, when they were decided, have been read to give expression to welfare rights in the US Constitution, see FI Michelman 'Formal and associational aims in procedural due process' in JR Pennock & JW Chapman (eds) *Due process (Nomos XVII)* (1977) 126.
[21] S Liebenberg 'The International Covenant on Economic, Social and Cultural Rights and its implications for South Africa' (1995) 11 *South African Journal on Human Rights* 359.
[22] *Government of the Republic of South Africa v Grootboom* 2001 1 SA 46 (CC) para 26 (court confirming the importance of international law in the interpretation of the Bill of Rights). See also eg references in *Grootboom* paras 28 & 45 to CESCR and the Committee on ESCR.
[23] The Committee has to date published 15 General Comments.
[24] Arts 22-26.
[25] Arts 3 & 10-14.
[26] Arts 4, 6(2), 19, 20, 24, 26-29 & 31.

On regional level, South Africa is a state party to the African Charter on Human and Peoples' Rights (African Charter). The African Charter contains civil and political and socio-economic rights, which, when the African Court on Human and Peoples' Rights is operational, will be justiciable. Currently, the African Commission on Human and Peoples' Rights (African Commission) deals with complaints in respect of the African Charter. The African Commission has decided few cases dealing with socio-economic rights.[27] Other regional instruments that deal with economic and social rights are the European Social Charter (1961) and the Additional Protocol to the American Convention on Human Rights in the area of Economic, Social and Cultural Rights (Protocol of San Salvador) (1988).

On a less formal level, bodies of experts have formulated guidelines that inform the interpretation of socio-economic rights, such as the Limburg Principles on the Implementation of the International Covenant on Economic, Social and Cultural Rights of 1986, the Maastricht Guidelines on Violations of Economic, Social and Cultural Rights of 1997[28] and the Bangalore Declaration and Plan of Action of 1995.

Despite the valuable guidance international law provides for the interpretation of socio-economic rights in the Constitution and the significant contribution it has made in this respect, the continued absence of case law from other domestic jurisdictions is problematic. The most important of the international socio-economic rights documents, CESCR, does not have an individual complaints mechanism through which complaints can be laid against states for violation of its provisions.[29]

---

[27] An exception is *Social and Economic Rights Action Centre (SERAC) and the Centre for Economic and Social Rights v Nigeria* Communication 155/96 (complaint against Nigeria for the destruction and wilful neglect, in collusion with an oil mining consortium, of natural resources, agricultural land and livestock on which the Ogoni people depended for their livelihood. The African Commission found Nigeria had a duty to protect socio-economic rights against private actors, that it had facilitated the invasion of these rights by allowing and participating in the actions of oil companies and that it was consequently in violation of arts 2, 4, 14, 16, 18(1), 21 & 24 of the African Charter). See C Mbazira 'Reading the right to food into the African Charter on Human and Peoples' Rights' (2004) 5:1 *ESR Review* 5. See also *Purohit and Moore v The Gambia* Communication 241/2000.

[28] The Maastricht Guidelines on Violations of Economic, Social and Cultural Rights' (1998) 20 *Human Rights Quarterly* 691.

[29] The creation of such a complaints mechanism through the adoption of an optional protocol to CESCR is under consideration. A working group established by the UN Commission on Human Rights is due to report to the Commission at its 60th session with recommendations on such an optional protocol to CESCR (Commission on Human Rights Resolution 2003/18).

As a result, interpretations that the Committee on ESCR gives to the provisions of CESCR are not developed in the context of concrete disputes or complaints, and often take the form of general guidelines.[30] In addition, the absence of any effective method for the actual *enforcement* of the norms developed by the Committee on ESCR has meant that little attention has been devoted in international law to the difficult issues of separation of powers and institutional capacity that arise at domestic level in the enforcement of court orders with respect to socio-economic rights.[31] Both these difficulties dilute the usefulness of international norms as interpretative sources for socio-economic rights at domestic level, particularly as the South African socio-economic rights jurisprudence develops and becomes more concrete and specific.

2.2.2 Section 7(2) - Duties

Section 7(2) determines that '[t]he state must respect, protect, promote and fulfil the rights in the Bill of Rights'. Section 7(2) is central to the transformative ethos of the Constitution. It explicitly conveys the idea that the state must not only refrain from interfering with the enjoyment of rights, but must act so as to protect, enhance and realise their enjoyment.[32] For practical purposes, this provision is important, as it indicates the scope and nature of the entitlements that socio-economic rights can create and so shows when and how they can be used to advance legal claims.

The *duty to respect* requires the state to refrain from interfering with the enjoyment of rights. The state must not limit or take away people's existing access to, for instance, housing, without good reason and without following proper legal procedure; where limitation or deprivation of existing access to housing is unavoidable, must take steps to mitigate that interference (in the context of state eviction, for example, must take steps to find alternative

---

[30] See D Brand 'The minimum core content of the right to food in context: A response to Rolf Künneman' in D Brand & S Russel (eds) *Exploring the core content of socio-economic rights: South African and international perspectives* (2002) 99 (Brand 2002) 100-102 for a discussion of this point. See also M Craven 'Introduction to the International Covenant on Economic, Social and Cultural Rights' in A Blyberg *et al Circle of rights. Economic, social and cultural rights: A training resource* (2000) 49 55. It has to be said that the approach that the Constitutional Court has adopted to the adjudication of socio-economic rights claims - its 'reasonableness review' approach - in many respects amounts to the same kind of generalised policy review method as that applied in the reporting system of the Committee on ESCR and as such to some extent obviates this particular difficulty with the use of international law norms.

[31] Viljoen (n 16 above) 3.

[32] The realisation that rights impose such different kinds of duties is usually attributed to Henry Shue (H Shue *Basic rights: Subsistence, affluence and US foreign policy* (1980)). His typology is widely adopted in international law circles; see eg GJH van Hoof 'The legal nature of economic, social and cultural rights: A rebuttal of some traditional views' in P Alston & K Tomasevski (eds) *The right to food* (1984) 97 99; Maastricht Guidelines (n 28 above) para 6; and Committee on ESCR General Comment No 12 (*The right to adequate food (art 11 of the Covenant)* UN Doc E/2000/22) para 15; General Comment No 14 (*The right to the highest attainable standard of health (art 12 of the Covenant)* UN Doc E/C 12/2000/4) paras 33-37; and General Comment No 15 (*The right to water (arts 11 and 12 of the Covenant)* UN Doc E/C 12/2002/11) paras 20-29.

accommodation for the evictees); and must not place undue obstacles in the way of people gaining access to housing.

The *duty to protect* requires the state to protect existing enjoyment of rights, and the capacity of people to enhance their enjoyment of rights or newly to gain access to the enjoyment of rights against third party interference. The state must, for instance, regulate private health care provision to protect against exploitation by private institutions and must, through such regulation, provide effective legal remedies where such exploitation or other forms of interference occur. An aspect of this duty that is often overlooked is the duty of courts, through their powers of developing the common law and interpreting legislation, to strengthen existing remedies or develop new remedies for protection against private interference in the enjoyment of rights.

The *duty to promote* is difficult to distinguish from the duty to fulfil. Liebenberg describes it as a duty to raise awareness of rights - to bring rights and the methods of accessing and enforcing them to the attention of right holders and to promote the most effective use of existing access to rights.[33] Budlender describes it as a duty on administrative bodies to use the promotion of socio-economic rights as a primary consideration in their discretionary decision-making, much like the constitutional injunction contained in section 28(2) requires that the best interest of the child be the primary consideration in any decision affecting a child.[34] In this chapter I discuss the duty to promote as part of the duty to fulfil.[35]

The *duty to fulfil* requires the state to act, to 'adopt appropriate legislative, administrative, budgetary, judicial, promotional and other measures'[36] so that those that do not currently enjoy access to rights can gain access and so that existing enjoyment of rights is enhanced.

A distinction is often made between positive duties (duties to do something) and negative duties (duties to refrain from doing something). The duty to respect is then classified as a negative duty, whereas the duties to protect, promote and fulfil are described as positive duties.[37] This distinction is presented in hierarchical fashion.

---

[33] Liebenberg (n 7 above) 6.
[34] G Budlender 'Justiciability of socio-economic rights: Some South African experiences' in YP Ghai & J Cottrell (eds) *Economic, social and cultural rights in practice. The role of judges in implementing economic, social and cultural rights* (2004) 33 37.
[35] See in this respect sec 4.3 below.
[36] Committee on ESCR General Comment No 14 (n 32 above) para 33.
[37] See eg *Jaftha v Schoeman; Van Rooyen v Stoltz* 2005 1 BCLR 78 (CC) paras 31-34, where the Constitutional Court discusses the distinction between the negative duty to respect the right to adequate housing and the positive duty to fulfil it. See also *Grootboom* (n 22 above) para 34.

The negative duty to respect is seen as more amenable to enforcement through adjudication than the positive duties to protect, promote and fulfil.[38] The argument is that enforcement of a positive duty, unlike enforcement of a negative duty, requires courts to interfere in allocational choices of the executive or legislature. It is also argued that the enforcement of a negative duty does not immerse courts in the fraught field of policy evaluation to the extent that the enforcement of positive duties does. However, in reality, the distinction between positive and negative duties is little more than a semantic distinction between acting and not acting.

First, often the same conduct of the state can be described both as a breach of the positive duty to fulfil a right and of the negative duty to respect it. As Liebenberg points out, in *Minister of Health v Treatment Action Campaign*, it was not clear whether the refusal to extend provision of Nevirapine to all public health facilities constituted a negative interference in or impairment of the right to have access to health care services, or a failure of the state positively to provide an essential health service. In effect, it could be characterised as both.[39] Similarly, an element of the supposedly negative duty to respect rights - the duty to mitigate interference in the exercise of a right where such interference is unavoidable - clearly requires the state to act, rather than to refrain from acting.

Second, the distinction in consequence does not hold up. Enforcement of a negative duty is as likely to have consequences for expenditure of resources as enforcement of a positive duty. Enforcement of a negative duty also potentially requires a court to interfere as deeply in policy-making powers as does enforcement of a positive duty. Suppose the state seeks to evict illegal occupants from state land to develop that land for low-cost housing, to be occupied by a different group of people, next in line on the waiting list. For a court to prevent the state from doing so (to enforce the negative duty to respect the right to housing) will have important resource consequences - the state will have to find alternative land and buy it, or use other state land, which itself might have been allocated for a different use. Equally, in enforcing the negative duty in this respect, a court would interfere directly in a complex, multi-faceted policy

---

[38] See eg the remarks of the Constitutional Court in *Ex parte Chairperson of the Constitutional Assembly: in re certification of the Constitution of the Republic of South Africa, 1996* 1996 4 SA 744 (CC) para 78: 'The objectors argued ... that socio-economic rights are not justiciable ... because of the budgetary issues their enforcement may raise. The fact that socio-economic rights will ... inevitably give rise to such implications does not seem ... to be a bar to their justiciability. At the very minimum, socio-economic rights can be negatively protected from improper invasion.'

[39] Liebenberg (n 7 above) 19, referring to *Minister of Health v Treatment Action Campaign* 2002 5 SA 721 (CC). By the same token, the provisions of the Social Assistance Act (n 9 above) that were challenged in *Khosa* (n 9 above) could be described as either negative or positive breaches of the right to have access to social assistance.

choice about how to decide who gets access to housing first, about where to situate low-cost housing development, etc.[40]

Nevertheless, despite its porousness, the distinction between positive and negative duties remains important for strategic reasons. As will become clear below, courts subject negative breaches of socio-economic rights to more robust scrutiny than failures to meet positive duties, both because the structure of the Constitution seems to demand it and because courts regard themselves as bound by separation of powers concerns to a lesser extent when dealing with negative breaches.[41]

3 Processes of translation

As with all constitutional rights, the translation of constitutional socio-economic rights from 'background moral claims'[42] into enforceable legal rights occurs through a variety of 'law-making processes and institutions'.[43] Not only courts, but at least also the legislature, the executive and the state administration play important roles in this respect.[44] In what follows, I briefly describe the respective roles of these institutions.

3.1 Translation through legislation

Socio-economic rights in South Africa are not only entrenched in the Constitution. They are also protected as statutory entitlements in national legislation. The Constitution is replete with commands to the legislature to enact legislation to give effect to constitutional rights. Examples are found in section 9, in relation to the prohibition on unfair discrimination; in section 32, in relation to the right to access

---

[40] With respect to the blurring of the distinction between positive and negative constitutional duties, see S Bandes 'The negative constitution: A critique' (1990) 88 *Michigan Law Review* 2271-2347.
[41] See sec 3.3 below.
[42] FI Michelman 'The constitution, social rights, and liberal political justification' (2003) 1 *International Journal of Constitutional Law* 13 14.
[43] Klare (n 3 above) 147.
[44] One possible law-making institution with respect to socio-economic rights that I do not focus on is the South African Human Rights Commission (SAHRC). The SAHRC has, in terms of sec 184(3) of the Constitution, a mandate to monitor the realisation of socio-economic rights. The Commission has developed this mandate into a reporting process, in terms of which organs of state report to it annually about steps they have taken to realise socio-economic rights, and the Commission then drafts a report evaluating the socio-economic rights performance of the state, which is tabled in parliament. This could be referred to as a mechanism for the 'soft protection' of socio-economic rights, emphasising the programmatic involvement of all sectors in government in the implementation of socio-economic rights. The SAHRC is also empowered to receive and deal with complaints of the infringement of socio-economic rights in an extra-judicial fashion. See J Kollapen 'Monitoring socio-economic rights. What has the SA Human Rights Commission done?' (1999) 1:4 *ESR Review* 18-20 and CV McClain 'The SA Human Rights Commission and socio-economic rights. Facing the challenges' (2002) 3:1 *ESR Review* 8-9. For critiques, see D Brand 'The South African Human Rights Commission: First economic and social rights report' (1999) 2:1 *ESR Review* 18-20; and D Brand & S Liebenberg 'The South African Human Rights Commission: The second economic and social rights report' (2000) 2:3 *ESR Review* 12-16.

to information; and in section 33, in relation to the right to administrative justice. Similarly, several of the socio-economic rights explicitly require legislation to be enacted to give effect to them. So, for instance, sections 26(2) and 27(2) require that the state take 'reasonable legislative ... measures', amongst other things, to realise the right to have access to adequate housing and the rights to have access to health care services, food, water and social security and assistance, respectively.[45] The legislature has given effect to these constitutional commands by enacting a wide range of legislation aimed at facilitating, providing and protecting access to basic resources.[46]

The statutory measures envisaged here include legislation creating and empowering structures and institutions and setting in place processes for the implementation of socio-economic rights.[47] However, an important aspect of such legislation is the creation of statutory socio-economic rights. Such statutory socio-economic rights can take the traditional form of subjective legal entitlements of particular persons to particular things. Examples are statutory entitlements to receive defined social assistance benefits if one meets certain eligibility conditions that can be enforced against the state[48] and entitlements to tenure on land exercised through legal protection against eviction that can be enforced against private persons.[49] Importantly, such statutory socio-economic rights include rights or entitlements of a less traditional nature. Given the liberalised law of standing that applies in Bill of Rights-related litigation in South Africa pursuant to section 38 of the Constitution, it is possible for individuals either on their own behalf, on behalf of a group or class of persons or in the public interest,[50] to enforce broadly phrased statutory duties, or statutory commands against the state - a person doing so would not so much be claiming something specific for him or herself (perhaps also that), but the performance of a public statutory duty or commitment on behalf of a larger collective.

---

[45] See also secs 24(b) & 25(5).
[46] Examples of such legislation with respect to specific socio-economic rights are discussed in detail in the various other chapters of this volume, and will not be listed here.
[47] See eg the Social Assistance Act (n 9 above), ch 3 & 4 and the South African Social Security Agency Act 9 of 2004.
[48] See ch 2 of the Social Assistance Act (n 9 above), which creates entitlements to a Child Support Grant, a Care Dependency Grant, a Foster Child Grant, a Disability Grant, a War Veteran's Grant, an Older Person's Grant, a Grant-in-Aid and a Social Relief in Distress Grant.
[49] See eg secs 8(1) & 11(1), (2) & (3) of the Extension of Security of Tenure Act 62 of 1997 (ESTA).
[50] Sec 38:
'Anyone listed in this section has the right to approach a competent court, alleging that a right in the Bill of Rights has been infringed or threatened, and the court may grant appropriate relief, including a declaration of rights. The persons who may approach a court are -
(a) anyone acting in their own interest;
(b) anyone acting on behalf of another person who cannot act in their own name;
(c) anyone acting as a member of, or in the interest of, a group or class of persons;
(d) anyone acting in the public interest; and
(e) an association acting in the interest of its members.'

In *Kutumela v Member of the Executive Committee for Social Services, Culture, Arts and Sport in the North West Province*,[51] the plaintiffs had applied for the Social Relief of Distress Grant, but despite clearly qualifying, did not receive it. Their complaint in response was not framed only as an application for each individual complainant to receive the social assistance grant for which they were eligible and to which they each had a subjective statutory right. Instead, the complaint alleged that, although, in terms of the Social Assistance Act[52] and its regulations, the state had statutorily committed itself to provide to eligible persons a Social Relief in Distress Grant and had placed a duty on provincial governments to do so, the province in question had not dedicated the necessary human, institutional and financial resources to do so. The case was settled and resulted in an order requiring relief specific to the parties, as well as various forms of general relief. Apart from requiring the provincial government to acknowledge its legal responsibility to provide Social Relief of Distress effectively to those eligible for it, the order requires it to devise a programme to ensure the effective implementation of Social Relief of Distress and to put in place the necessary infrastructure for the administration and payment of the grant. In essence, the state was ordered to make good on a statutory commitment to give effect to an aspect of the right to have access to social assistance, with the result that the grant would in future be available to all eligible persons, in addition to it being paid out to the individual complainants.

The enforcement of socio-economic rights through both kinds of statutory entitlements holds great promise. Statutory entitlements are likely to be more detailed and concrete in nature than the vaguely and generally phrased constitutional rights forming their background, and are consequently more direct in the access to resources that they enable people to leverage. In addition, courts are likely to enforce statutory entitlements more robustly than they would constitutional rights, because they are enforcing a right, duty or commitment defined by the legislature itself, rather than a broadly phrased constitutional right to which they have to give content. As such they are not to the same extent confronted with the concerns of separation of powers, institutional legitimacy and technical competence that have so directly shaped and limited their constitutional socio-economic rights jurisprudence.[53]

---

[51] *Kutumela v Member of the Executive Committee for Social Services, Culture, Arts and Sport in the North West Province* Case 671/2003 23 October 2003 (B). My thanks to Nick de Villiers, of the Legal Resources Centre in Pretoria, for providing me with a copy of the order.
[52] n 9 above.
[53] See sec 3.3 below where these limitations on the power of courts to develop concrete entitlements on the basis of constitutional socio-economic rights are discussed.

In many jurisdictions other than South Africa, where socio-economic rights do not enjoy constitutional status, they are protected as statutory entitlements in the ordinary law. Good examples are a number of the Scandinavian countries, in particular Finland, where rights such as the right to social assistance, the right to housing, the right to day-care for small children and rights of specified assistance for the severely handicapped are protected as subjective rights in national legislation.[54] For the same reasons that apply in the South African context, this form of protection of socio-economic rights has therefore been very effective. However, in the absence of constitutional socio-economic guarantees, the existence of statutory socio-economic entitlements is often precarious.

As has been shown in the United States with respect to statutory welfare entitlements at federal level, where broad social agreement that the state has a duty to protect against severe socio-economic deprivation does not exist, or dissipates, statutory entitlements that are not sourced in substantive constitutional guarantees are vulnerable to legislative interference.[55] In South Africa, statutory socio-economic rights are not subject to legislative *fiat* to the same extent as in other jurisdictions where constitutional socio-economic rights are absent. These rights in South Africa are enacted by the legislature to give effect to constitutional socio-economic rights.[56]

Legislative interference with a statutory socio-economic right – such as a restrictive legislative redefinition of a social assistance benefit – therefore breaches the constitutional socio-economic right that the statutory entitlement gives effect to and will only be constitutionally permissible if justifiable in terms of the appropriate standard of scrutiny. Similarly, a statutory scheme intended to give effect to a socio-economic right can be evaluated against that right to see whether or not it does adequately give effect to it.[57]

---

[54] See Viljoen (n 16 above) 12-13; M Scheinin 'Economic and social rights as legal rights' in A Eide, C Krause & A Rosas (eds) *Economic, social and cultural rights: A textbook* (1995) 41 61.

[55] See LA Williams 'Welfare and legal entitlements: The social roots of poverty' in D Kairys (ed) *The politics of law: A progressive critique* (1998) 569 570-571 and WH Simon 'Rights and redistribution in the welfare system' (1986) 38 *Stanford Law Review* 1431 1467-1477, both describing the gradual cutbacks in statutory welfare rights occasioned by changed public perceptions about the sustained viability of comprehensive welfare provision and by erosion of the idea that the state should provide in the basic needs of its people.

[56] Much of the social legislation so far enacted is explicit as to this purpose. See eg the Preamble of the Social Assistance Act (n 9 above), where it is stated that one purpose of the Act is to give effect to sec 27(1)(c) of the Constitution. Courts, in their interpretation of such legislation, have also emphasised the link between social legislation and the constitutional rights they are intended to give effect to; see eg with respect to the relationship between the Prevention of Illegal Eviction from and Unlawful Occupation of Land Act 19 of 1998 (PIE) and secs 26(3) & 25 of the Constitution, *Port Elizabeth Municipality v Various Occupiers* 2004 12 BCLR 1268 (CC) para 17 and *Cape Killarney Property Investments (Pty) Ltd v Mahamba* 2001 4 SA 1222 (SCA) para 21.

[57] So, eg in *Grootboom* (note 22 above), the Housing Act 107 of 1997, the statutory framework for the state's measures to give effect to the right to have access to adequate housing, was found to be lacking in that it made no provision for the shelter needs of those in housing crisis (para 52).

Apart from this corrective or protective role played by constitutional socio-economic rights *vis-à-vis* statutory socio-economic rights, constitutional socio-economic rights inform the interpretation of statutory socio-economic rights. Also, the fact that a statutory right or scheme is intended to give effect to a constitutional socio-economic right can in a rhetorical sense reinforce the enforcement of that statutory right or scheme.[58]

Finally, constitutional socio-economic rights protect statutory socio-economic rights from legal challenge on the basis of other constitutional rights. *City of Cape Town v Rudolph*[59] dealt with a constitutional challenge, brought on the basis of section 25 property rights, to provisions of the Prevention of Illegal Eviction from and Unlawful Occupation of Land Act (PIE).[60] The impugned provisions of PIE were intended to give effect to section 26(3) of the Constitution. The High Court relied on this fact to reject the challenge.[61]

3.2 Translation through executive and administrative action

Apart from the legislature, the executive and state administration can also, through adoption of policies or through executive or administrative decisions, interpret socio-economic rights and self-define the duties those rights impose on them. Courts can then enforce these self-defined duties against the executive or administration, as the case may be. The policy formulation or administrative decisions in some sense translate constitutional rights into enforceable legal duties or entitlements. In *B v Minister of Correctional Services*,[62] four HIV-positive prisoners approached the High Court with an application for an order that the state was constitutionally obliged to provide them with anti-retroviral treatment at its own expense. The case turned on the interpretation of the term 'adequate medical treatment' in section 35(2)(e) of the Constitution. The Court held that it did not have the requisite medical expertise to determine what adequate medical treatment for the applicants entailed and whether it included anti-retroviral medication. On this basis it held against two of the applicants.[63]

---

[58] In *Residents of Bon Vista Mansions v Southern Metropolitan Council* 2002 6 BCLR 625 (W) the High Court, on the basis of secs 4(1) & 4(3) of the Water Services Act 108 of 1997, gave an interim order that the plaintiff's water supply be reconnected. Although the decision was based on statutory entitlements, the court invoked the sec 27(1)(b) constitutional right to sufficient water to reinforce its finding. The Court proceeded from the assumption that disconnection of a household water supply was a *prima facie* infringement of the sec 27(1)(b) constitutional right, which had to be justified in order to be constitutionally sound (para 20). The Court then held that the provisions of the Water Services Act constituted 'a statutory framework within which such breaches may be justified' (para 21). Further, throughout the judgment the Court made reference to the fact that the Act was intended to give effect to the constitutional right and that non-compliance with its provisions constituted an infringement of the constitutional right (eg paras 28-30).
[59] 2004 5 SA 39 (C).
[60] n 56 above.
[61] *Rudolph* (n 59 above) 74H-75J.
[62] 1997 6 BCLR 789 (C).
[63] n 62 above, para 37.

However, the Court found in favour of the two applicants *to whom physicians had already prescribed anti-retroviral medication*. The Court's reasoning with respect to these prisoners was that, in their case, medical experts had through the prescription determined what 'adequate medical treatment' was. In doing so, they had translated the constitutional right to be provided with adequate medical treatment into a concrete legal entitlement that the Court was willing to enforce.[64]

The relationship between socio-economic rights defined through executive or administrative action, on the one hand, and constitutional socio-economic rights, on the other, is similar to that between constitutional and statutory socio-economic rights. Executive or administrative action defining duties and entitlements in terms of constitutional socio-economic rights gives effect to those rights. As such, they can be protected against challenge on other constitutional grounds.[65] Second, such executive or administrative definition of constitutional socio-economic rights has to comply with the requirements of the right it is intended to give effect to.[66]

3.3 Translation through adjudication

The socio-economic rights in the Constitution are *justiciable* – when breached, they can be enforced through the courts.[67] Courts in the first place exercise this role in the enforcement of the statutory socio-economic rights described above. In such cases they more or less mechanically enforce socio-economic rights as predefined by the legislature, often also through remedies determined by the legislature. Their law-making role here, although present, is

---

[64] n 62 above, paras 35, 36 & 60. See also *People's Union for Civil Liberties v Union of India* Writ Petition [Civil] 196 of 2001 (1997) 1 SCC 301, available at http://www.righttofoodindia.org/mdm/mdm_scorders.html (accessed 31 October 2004), in which the Indian Supreme Court heard an application in part for an order that existing national measures designed to address food insecurity and famine be adequately resourced and implemented at state level so as effectively to reach intended beneficiaries. The complaint alleged that, although massive food reserves existed in India and programmes existed both on an ongoing basis to address food insecurity of poor households and in specific instances to address famines, these policies were not implemented due to administrative inefficiency and because state governments diverted funds from national government, intended to implement them, to other needs. The Supreme Court has issued interim orders requiring, among other things, that the identification of beneficiaries qualifying for state assistance be standardised and completed; that the effectiveness of the current public distribution system for food be enhanced and that corruption in the process be rooted out; and that funds allocated from national level to state governments for use in public distribution of food and famine measures in fact be used for those purposes. For a discussion, see KB Mahabal 'Enforcing the right to food in India: The impact of social activism' (2004) 5(1) *ESR Review* 7.
[65] See *Minister of Public Works v Kyalami Ridge Environmental Association* 2001 3 SA 1151 (CC) (decision by appellant to house a group of flood victims on land belonging to it upheld against challenge on basis of administrative justice rights, partly because decision was taken to give effect to the right to have access to adequate housing).
[66] The complaint in *Treatment Action Campaign* (n 39 above) was in essence that the state's executive definition of its duties in terms of the right to have access to health care, in the context of prevention of mother-to-child transmission of HIV, fell short of the requirements of the right.
[67] Sec 172(1)(a) requires courts to declare law or conduct inconsistent with the Constitution invalid to the extent of its inconsistency.

restricted. However, courts also themselves translate constitutional socio-economic rights into enforceable legal claims. When adjudicating disputes on the basis of constitutional socio-economic rights, rather than statutory socio-economic rights, courts interpret these rights and give concrete expression to the duties they impose and entitlements they create in much the same way that the legislature does when giving effect to them through legislation. Courts also, through their orders, enforce the duties and entitlements that they define.

3.3.1 Modes of adjudication: Sections 8 and 39(2)

The power of courts to translate socio-economic rights into concrete legal claims is mediated through two provisions of the Constitution. Sections 8 and 39(2) regulate how and under what circumstances fundamental rights, including socio-economic rights interact with existing law and with conduct. As such, they indicate which kinds of legal claims can be launched through the courts on the basis of constitutional socio-economic rights, against whom and how such claims may be handled by courts. Section 8(1) declares that the Bill of Rights 'applies to all law'[68] and 'binds the legislature, the executive, the judiciary and all organs of state'. Section 8(2) extends the reach of the Bill of Rights to the private sphere, declaring that, if the 'nature of [a] right and the nature of any duty imposed by [that] right' allows, the right 'binds a natural or a juristic person'.

In terms of section 8(3), if a court finds in terms of section 8(2) that a right in the Bill of Rights is applicable in litigation between private parties and that the right has been limited by one of the parties, it must give effect to that right by applying an existing statutory or common law remedy. In the absence of an existing remedy, a court must develop the common law to create a remedy that will give effect to the right.[69] Finally, section 39(2) determines that a court, when interpreting legislation or developing the common law, 'must promote the *spirit, purport and objects of the Bill of Rights*', thus placing a general interpretive injunction on courts to infuse existing law with constitutional values.

What exactly these sections mean is uncertain.[70] In this chapter, I do not engage in an in-depth analysis of them. I am interested only in the different ways in which they allow the socio-economic rights in

---

[68] See *Du Plessis v De Klerk* 1996 5 BCLR 658 (CC) for a unanimous holding that the same term in sec 7(2) of the interim Constitution referred to statute, common law and customary law.

[69] A court can also develop a common law rule to limit the right, provided that such a rule would then have to be justifiable in terms of sec 36(1) of the Constitution.

[70] The application of rights in the Bill of Rights has been one of the most contentious issues in South African constitutional law scholarship over the last several years; see eg S Woolman 'Application' (forthcoming) in Chaskalson *et al* (n 7 above); ch 10 'Application of the Bill of Rights' in J de Waal *et al The Bill of Rights handbook* (2001) 35; MH Cheadle 'Application' in MH Cheadle *et al* (eds) *South African constitutional law: The Bill of Rights* (2002) 19.

the Bill of Rights to be used to challenge law and conduct. In this respect the application sections provide the following possibilities:

- One can challenge the constitutionality of *law* – a statutory, common law or customary law rule - whether the state or a private party relies on it.[71] The consequence of a successful challenge to legislation is that the legislation is overturned and the situation reverts to the common law position that existed before it was enacted. This should prompt the legislature to enact new legislation to regulate the same issues, but the court can also itself remedy the constitutional defect by reading words into the impugned provision. If a common law rule is successfully challenged, a court will develop the common law to change that rule, or develop new rules to make the common law consistent with the constitution.[72]

Legislation was challenged as inconsistent with a constitutional socio-economic right in *Khosa v Minister for Social Development*,[73] where provisions of the Social Assistance Act and the Welfare Laws Amendment Act[74] that excluded permanent residents and their children from access to social assistance were successfully challenged as inconsistent with the section 27(1) right of everyone to have access to social security and assistance and the section 9(3) prohibition on unfair discrimination.[75]

An example of where the common law was challenged as inconsistent with a constitutional socio-economic right occurred in *Brisley v Drotsky*,[76] where the common law regulating evictions was (unsuccessfully) challenged as inconsistent with the section 26(3) prohibition on arbitrary evictions. Had the challenge been successful, the court would have had to develop the common law to take adequate account of the section 26(3) injunction that courts consider 'all relevant factors' before issuing an eviction order, with the result that courts would have a discretion,

---

[71] The textual basis for a bill of rights challenge to a statutory or common law rule relied upon by the state as against a private entity is sec 8(1). Similarly, the textual basis for a bill of rights challenge to a statutory rule relied upon by one private entity against another is clearly sec 8(1). However, there is some controversy about whether the textual basis for a challenge to a common law rule relied upon by one private entity against another is sec 8(1) rather than sec 8(2) read with sec 8(3). The Constitutional Court in *Khumalo & Others v Holomisa* 2002 5 SA 401 (CC) rejected reliance on sec 8(1) in a challenge directed at the existing common law rules of defamation relied upon by a private party, opting instead to bring the Bill of Rights to bear through secs 8(2) & (3).

[72] It seems that this would be the case, irrespective of whether the Bill of Rights is brought to bear upon a dispute through sec 8(1) or secs 8(2) & (3).

[73] n 9 above. See also *Jaftha* (n 37 above) (provisions of the Magistrates' Courts Act 32 of 1944 allowing for the sale in execution of a debtor's home to satisfy a [debtor's] judgment debt found inconsistent with sec 26(1) of the Constitution; words read into the Act to remedy the defect.)

[74] Secs 3(c), 4(b)(ii) & 4B(b)(ii) of the Social Assistance Act (n 9 above) and sec 3 of the Welfare Laws Amendment Act 106 of 1997.

[75] The sections were found inconsistent with the Constitution, but were not invalidated. Instead, the Court read words into the sections to remedy the constitutional defect; *Khosa* (n 9 above) para 98.

[76] 2002 4 SA 1 (SCA).

exercised on the basis of their consideration of relevant circumstances, whether or not to grant the order.[77]

- One can challenge *conduct* as inconsistent with a constitutional right. If state conduct is successfully challenged, it would be invalid and the court will craft a constitutional remedy to vindicate the right in question. If private conduct is successfully challenged, a court will attempt to find a remedy in the existing statutory or common law that can be adapted to vindicate the right in question, and in the absence of such existing remedy, will develop the common law to provide such a remedy. An example of a successful challenge to state conduct as inconsistent with a constitutional socio-economic right is *Minister of Health v Treatment Action Campaign*,[78] where a policy position of the National Department of Health was challenged as inconsistent with the section 27(1) right to have access to health care services, with the result that the policy was invalidated and the government ordered to adopt and implement a policy that would be constitutionally sound. There has as yet not been an example of a challenge to private conduct as inconsistent with a constitutional socio-economic right.

- Finally, one can, in the course of litigation, argue that a rule of law that the other party to the litigation relies on is inconsistent, not with a particular right, but with the general tenor of the Bill of Rights, the 'objective value system' that underlies its particular provisions. A court that accepts such a proposition would interpret the statutory provision in question, or develop the common law rule to give effect to the 'spirit, purport and objects' of the Bill of Rights. An example of such interaction between the Bill of Rights and the existing law occurring in the context of socio-economic rights is *Afrox Health Care (Pty) Ltd v Strydom*,[79] where the Supreme Court of Appeal was (unsuccessfully) asked to develop the common law of contract, through the rule that contractual terms that conflict with the public interest are unenforceable, to render unenforceable disclaimers in contracts that indemnify hospitals from liability for damage negligently caused to patients.

3.3.2 Constraints in the adjudication of socio-economic rights claims

Particularly when they adjudicate claims on the basis of constitutional socio-economic rights, in any of the three ways described above, courts operate under the control of a set of unwritten constraints related to their institutional legitimacy, their constitutional place and their technical capacity - what can loosely be

---

[77] For a variety of reasons, the use of constitutional socio-economic rights in this indirect way to influence the existing law is potentially extremely important. See sec 4.2.2 below.
[78] n 38 above.
[79] 2002 6 SA 21 (SCA).

described as separation of powers concerns. Both in the international arena and, to a lesser extent in South Africa, the status of socio-economic rights as legal rights has long been questioned, mostly on the basis that these rights are not *justiciable*.[80] The arguments along this line proceed from the assumption that socio-economic rights uniquely create entitlements to affirmative state action and consequently require the expenditure of resources to be realised. Courts have neither the institutional and technical capacity to deal with the questions of social and economic policy that claims based on these affirmative rights will inevitably raise, nor the democratic legitimacy to question the socio-economic policy choices of the political branches of government that will be implicated.

Courts are further hampered by the fact that socio-economic rights do not pose justiciable legal standards according to which these assessments can be made. For courts to engage in the adjudication of socio-economic rights claims, the arguments proceed, could both erode the legitimacy of the judiciary and the idea of human rights as a whole if, by virtue of economic realities, the basic services that they require the state to provide cannot be delivered, whatever courts have to say,[81] and place courts in potentially damaging confrontation with the political branches of government.[82]

The most convincing response to these arguments does not deny that socio-economic rights present problems to the process of adjudication, but does deny that these problems mark them as *essentially different* from other rights. According to this argument, all rights impose both affirmative and negative duties on the state, depending on the circumstances under which they are enforced. Difficulties attending the judicial enforcement of the affirmative aspects of socio-economic rights also occur in the judicial enforcement of these aspects of other rights. The conclusion is that a rigid categorisation of rights into those that are justiciable and those

---

[80] Eide points out that the focus on *justiciability*, as if that determines the status of rights, diverts attention from the 'effective protection' of rights, something that occurs through different mechanisms, including adjudication; A Eide 'Future protection of economic and social rights in Europe' in A Bloed *et al* (eds) *Monitoring human rights in Europe: Comparing international procedures and mechanisms* (1993) 187 214. But see AA An-Na'im 'To affirm the full human rights standing of economic, social and cultural rights' in Ghai & Cottrell (n 34 above) 7 13, who recognises the limitations of the justiciability debate, but argues that 'the claim that judicial enforcement of [socio-economic rights] is not possible or desirable, *undermines the human rights standing of these rights*' (my emphasis) and, accordingly, remains an important focus.

[81] The idea of justiciable socio-economic rights is also criticised from a, for me more promising, radically democratic perspective. The argument is that the judicialisation of issues of socio-economic politics through entrenchment of justiciable socio-economic rights could stifle social action, impoverish politics and damage struggles for social justice – as Davis puts it, justiciable socio-economic rights might 'erode the possibility for meaningful public participation in the shaping of the societal good'; DM Davis 'The case against the inclusion of socio-economic demands in a bill of rights except as directive principles' (1992) 8 *South African Journal on Human Rights* 475 488-490. See also J Bakan 'What's wrong with social rights' in J Bakan & D Schneiderman (eds) *Social justice and the Constitution: Perspectives on a social union for Canada* (1992) 85; YP Ghai & J Cottrell 'The role of the courts in the protection of economic, social and cultural rights' in Ghai & Cottrell (n 34 above) 58 88.

[82] T Roux 'Legitimating transformation: Political resource allocation in the South African Constitutional Court' (2003) 10 *Democratisation* 92-93.

that are not is false. All rights instead fall somewhere along a 'justiciability spectrum', some more easily justiciable than others, and the 'possibility and role of judicial enforcement ... [should be] assessed and developed in relation to each human right',[83] instead of being denied a whole class or category of rights.

That socio-economic rights were eventually included in the Constitution in South Africa as justiciable rights shows that the latter, more nuanced argument regarding their justiciability won the day. Nevertheless an echo of the objection to their inclusion remains in their formulation - the careful limitation of the positive duties imposed by the qualified socio-economic rights described above[84] is aimed at mediating some of the difficulties with the judicial enforcement of socio-economic rights that those opposed to their entrenchment have raised. In their interpretation of socio-economic rights, our courts have been attuned to this echo. Although the Constitutional Court has always emphasised that socio-economic rights are indeed justiciable,[85] it has been at pains to show that it regards itself importantly bound by the unwritten 'separation of powers' constraints outlined above.[86]

The Court has variously justified what many have described as its restrained, respectful or deferential approach to deciding socio-economic rights cases[87] with reference to its lack of technical expertise in deciding the issues raised in socio-economic rights cases; its lack of democratic accountability, in distinction to the executive and legislative branches;[88] and its institutionally determined inability to access and process the essential information needed to decide the

---

[83] An-Na'im (n 80 above) 7.
[84] See sec 2.1 above.
[85] See the *Certification* case (n 38 above) paras 76-78.
[86] See Yacoob J in *Grootboom* (n 22 above) para 41: 'The precise contours and content of the measures to be adopted are primarily a matter for the Legislature and the Executive. They must, however, ensure that the measures they adopt are reasonable. In any challenge based on s 26 in which it is argued that the State has failed to meet the positive obligations imposed upon it by s 26(2), the question will be whether the legislative and other measures taken by the State are reasonable. A court considering reasonableness will not enquire whether other more desirable or favourable measures could have been adopted, or whether public money could have been better spent. The question would be whether the measures that have been adopted are reasonable. It is necessary to recognise that a wide range of possible measures could be adopted by the State to meet its obligations. Many of these would meet the requirement of reasonableness. Once it is shown that the measures do so, this requirement is met.'
[87] See eg CR Sunstein 'Social and economic rights? Lessons from South Africa' (2001) 11:4 *Constitutional Forum* 123 123.
[88] The following passage from *Soobramoney* (n 8 above) para 21 shows the Court's concern with both these issues: 'The provincial administration which is responsible for health services in KwaZulu-Natal has to make decisions about the funding that should be made available for health care and how such funds should be spent. These choices involve *difficult decisions to be taken at the political level in fixing the health budget, and at the functional level in deciding upon the priorities to be met*. A court will be slow to interfere with rational decisions taken in good faith by the political organs and medical authorities whose responsibility it is to deal with such matters' (my emphasis). See also Sachs J's concurring judgment in the same case at para 58: 'Courts are not the proper place to resolve the agonising personal and medical problems that underlie these choices. Important though our review functions are, there are areas where *institutional incapacity* and *appropriate constitutional modesty* require us to be especially cautious' (my emphasis).

policy evaluative questions that arise in such cases.[89] Commentators have also pointed out that the Court's concern for the maintenance of its own institutional integrity *vis-à-vis* the executive and legislature has had a constraining effect.[90]

The constraint of separation of powers concerns shows up at two points in the process of adjudicating socio-economic rights claims. First, it influences the willingness of the court, in the process of deciding a case, whether or not at all to entertain certain questions,[91] and determines the extent to and manner in which the court is willing to interrogate those questions that it does deal with.[92] Second, it constrains the court in fashioning orders to enforce its findings, where it has held against the state.[93] Clearly, the extent to which courts feel themselves bound by constraints in specific cases significantly determines the possible outcome of those cases. A number of factors related to the nature of specific cases and the manner in which they are argued influence the extent to which courts feel themselves bound by these constraints. Awareness of these factors would allow one to calibrate the constraint that could be expected to limit the courts' powers in specific cases, and to plan litigation accordingly. In this respect two general points can be made.[94]

Where the state has acted – legislative, executive and administrative self-definition of duties

Where courts are required simply to enforce socio-economic rights duties *as the legislature, the executive or the administration have themselves defined those duties*, rather than to interpret constitutional socio-economic rights, define duties on the basis of those rights and then to impose them on the state, there is less constraint. Arguing a case on the basis of such self-defined duties, rather than directly on the basis of a constitutional socio-economic right, is therefore generally to be preferred. The most obvious examples of the enforcement of self-defined duties are cases where

---

[89] *Grootboom* (n 22 above) para 32.
[90] Roux (n 82 above).
[91] See eg *Treatment Action Campaign* (n 39 above) para 128 (Court declining to consider question whether the state is under a duty to provide breast milk substitutes to HIV-positive mothers to prevent transmission of HIV to babies through breastfeeding, because this 'raises complex issues' that are best left to government and health professionals to deal with and because sufficient information was not at the disposal of the Court to make a finding in this respect).
[92] See eg *Grootboom* (n 22 above) para 41 with respect to the extent to which the Court is willing to interrogate the relative effectiveness of policy options in applying its 'reasonableness' test.
[93] See eg *Treatment Action Campaign* (n 39 above) paras 124-133, in particular para 129.
[94] I refer to two factors only that influence the extent to which courts feel themselves constrained in adjudicating socio-economic rights claims here. There are many other, more nuanced factors, such as the extent to which the adjudication of a particular case would involve a court in evaluating policy; the position of the claimants in society; and the degree of deprivation motivating a claim. See De Vos (n 3 above) 367; TJ Bollyky 'R if C>P+B: A paradigm for judicial remedies of socio-economic rights violations' (2002) 18 *South African Journal on Human Rights* 161 165.

courts enforce statutory socio-economic rights, in any one of the two senses described above.[95] In most such cases, constraint is diluted not only by the fact that courts are not faced with themselves having to define duties to impose on the state, but also because courts are able to make use of remedies from the existing law to enforce statutorily defined duties. The many instances where courts have enforced statutory entitlements to social assistance through administrative law remedies illustrate this point.[96]

Perhaps the most dramatic example of courts' preference for enforcing statutory entitlements, is the line of cases culminating in *Ndlovu v Ngcobo; Bekker v Jika*.[97] At common law, a court *must* grant an eviction order on a showing by the applicant of ownership and of the illegality of the evictee's occupation.[98] Section 26(3) of the Constitution, in distinction, determines that a court may only grant an eviction order *after considering all relevant circumstances*. Tenure security laws - most importantly PIE[99] - require courts in certain instances to consider all relevant circumstances before granting an eviction order and as such give effect to section 26(3).[100] However, conflicting decisions in the High Courts raised uncertainty over whether PIE applied also to cases of 'holding over' - cases where initially lawful occupation subsequently became unlawful.[101] In such cases, courts have consequently been faced with the question whether, in lieu of PIE, section 26(3) changed the common law rules of eviction to confer discretion on courts.

After a series of conflicting decisions in the High Courts,[102] the question reached the Supreme Court of Appeal in *Brisley v Drotsky*.[103] In *Brisley* the Court went to tortuous lengths to avoid itself developing the common law in line with section 26(3). It held that the section 26(3) 'relevant circumstances' could only be *legally* relevant circumstances. The only circumstances *legally* relevant to the question whether an eviction should be allowed were the common law requirements of whether the evictor was owner of the land in question and the evictee was occupying it unlawfully. As a result, it was held that section 26(3) did not change the rules of common law.[104] The only influence that section 26(3) exerted on the existing

---

[95] Either statutory subjective rights, or statutory commands/commitments. See sec 3.2.1 above.
[96] See De Villiers (n 13 above) for an overview.
[97] *Ndlovu v Ngcobo; Bekker & Another v Jika* 2003 1 SA 113 (SCA).
[98] *Graham v Ridley* 1931 TPD 476.
[99] n 56 above.
[100] See also ESTA (n 49 above) and the Land Reform (Labour Tenants) Act 3 of 1996 (Labour Tenants Act). See sec 3.2 above for a discussion of these laws.
[101] See eg *Ellis v Viljoen* 2001 4 SA 795 (C) (PIE does not apply); and *Bekker v Jika* [2001] 4 All SA 573 (SE) (PIE does apply).
[102] *Ross v South Peninsula Municipality* 2000 1 SA 589 (K) (sec 26(3) changed common law so that an applicant for an eviction order, in addition to the common law showing, had to raise circumstance that would persuade the court that it is just and equitable to grant the order); *Betta Eiendomme (Pty) Ltd v Ekple-Epoh* 2000 4 SA 486 (W). The court, at 473A-B, held that sec 26(3) only applied to evictions by the state and not to evictions by natural or juristic persons.
[103] *Brisley* (n 76 above).
[104] As above, para 42.

law remained that exerted through the tenure security laws, with the common law left intact with respect to those evictions to which these laws did not apply.

Five months after *Brisley*, the Court decided *Ndlovu*.[105] In this case, the Court had to decide whether or not the statutory entitlements to security of tenure created by the legislature in PIE applied also to evictions in cases of 'holding over'. The Court extended PIE to such evictions.[106] The result in practice was exactly the same as the result would have been had the Court decided *Brisley* differently: Also in cases of 'holding over', courts would now have a discretion, exercised after considering all relevant circumstances, whether or not to grant an eviction order.[107] What the Court was unwilling to do in *Brisley* on the basis of a constitutional right, it was happy to do in *Ndlovu* on the basis of PIE's statutory entitlements.

Courts will also be more comfortable with enforcing socio-economic rights as defined through executive or administrative action. In *B*,[108] the willingness of the Court to order the state to provide at its own cost anti-retroviral medication to the two applicants to whom it had been prescribed, in contrast to its refusal to do so with respect to the two applicants for whom it had not yet been prescribed, turned on the fact that the prescription of the medication to the first two applicants amounted to an expert self-definition of the state's duty. The Court was willing to enforce that duty because, in doing so, it was not required itself to determine what adequate medical treatment entailed, a task that it felt it did not have the requisite expertise to undertake.[109]

In *Treatment Action Campaign*[110] the relatively robust manner in which the Constitutional Court engaged with issues of AIDS policy and the willingness of the Court, as opposed to in other cases, to impose an intrusive directory order on the state can in part be explained by the fact that the Court was requiring the state to extend a policy decision that it had itself already taken (that Nevirapine was suitable to provide to mothers giving birth at select public health facilities and their new-born children to prevent transmission of HIV) to its logical conclusion (to extend the provision to all public health facilities for the same purpose).[111] Again, an element of self-definition of duties,

---

[105] *Ndlovu* (n 97 above).
[106] As above, para 23.
[107] In fact, the result was not exactly the same. Had the SCA developed the common law in line with sec 26(3) in *Brisley* (n 76 above), landowners seeking to evict unlawful occupiers 'holding over' would certainly have had to persuade courts to exercise their discretion in their favour, as they have to do in terms of PIE (n 56 above). However, landowners would then not have been subject to PIE's stringent procedural requirements. The SCA's decision in *Ndlovu* (n 97 above) has therefore in some respects made it more difficult for landowners to evict unlawful occupiers 'holding over' than it would have been for them had *Brisley* been decided differently.
[108] n 62 above.
[109] n 62 above, para 37. See also paras 35, 36 & 60.
[110] n 39 above.
[111] D Brand 'The proceduralisation of South African socio-economic rights jurisprudence, or "What are socio-economic rights for?"' in Botha *et al* (n 13 above) 33 53.

this time through an executive policy decision, influenced the Court's perception of constraint.

Negative rather than positive duties

As a general point of strategy it is preferable to characterise breaches of any of the socio-economic rights as negative rather than positive. As a rule, courts will scrutinise breaches of negative duties imposed by socio-economic rights more strictly than they would failures in meeting positive duties.

There is some evidence from the case law that this is a matter of judicial attitude - that courts simply 'feel' themselves less constrained when adjudicating negative infringements as the perception is that enforcing negative duties requires of them less interference in the sphere of power of the political branches than the enforcement of positive duties would.[112]

However, particularly with respect to the qualified socio-economic rights, the difference in degree of judicial constraint at play in cases of enforcement of positive as opposed to negative duties seems simply to be required by the way in which these rights are formulated and by the general structure of constitutional litigation.

Constitutional litigation in South Africa proceeds in two stages. The complainant bears the onus to persuade the court that a right in the Bill of Rights has been infringed. Should a court find that the right has in fact been infringed, the state (or where a constitutional duty has been infringed by a private party, the private party) bears the onus to justify and so render constitutionally sound its limitation of that right. In principle, the standard of scrutiny in terms of which courts decide whether any infringement of any constitutional right, including any socio-economic right, is justified is prescribed by section 36(1), which applies to all rights. However, despite the fact that section 36(1) in principle applies to all infringements of all constitutional rights, courts in practice do not apply section 36(1) when they must decide whether or not failures by the state to give effect to the *positive*

---

[112] See, eg the Constitutional Court's indication in *Grootboom* that retrogressive steps in the process of giving progressive realisation to socio-economic rights (negative infringements of such rights) 'require the most careful consideration and would need to be fully justified by reference to the totality of the rights provided for in the Covenant and in the context of the full use of the maximum available resources' - that is, that the Court would subject such negative interferences to especially robust scrutiny; Committee on ESCR General Comment 3 para 9 as quoted in *Grootboom* (n 22 above) para 45. See also *Jaftha* (n 37 above), where the Constitutional Court, having found that provisions of the Magistrates' Courts Act (n 73 above), allowing for the sale in execution of a person's home without adequate judicial oversight, violated the negative duty to respect the right to have access to adequate housing, proceeded to order the relatively intrusive remedy of reading words into the Act, in spite of submissions by the Minister of Justice that the order of invalidity be suspended to allow the legislature to remedy the constitutional defect in the Act (paras 61-64). See, further, my discussion of *Port Elizabeth Municipality* (n 56 above) and *Modderfontein Squatters v Modderklip Boerdery (Pty) Ltd* 2004 6 SA 40 in sec 4.1.2 below.

duties to protect, promote and fulfil the *qualified socio-economic rights* can be justified.[113] It will be recalled that the positive duties imposed by qualified socio-economic rights are explicitly described as duties to take reasonable legislative and other measures, within available resources, to achieve the progressive realisation of the rights in question.[114] The Constitutional Court has interpreted this phrase as an internal limitation clause - a standard of 'reasonableness' scrutiny, used instead of section 36(1), according to which to decide whether or not failures in meeting the positive duties imposed by qualified socio-economic rights can be justified.[115]

Whether or not the justification of an infringement of a socio-economic right is considered in terms of section 36(1) or in terms of the special limitation clause that applies to positive infringements of qualified socio-economic rights, significantly determines the degree of constraint under which a court operates. The standard of scrutiny that is applied under the two different tests is different. Section 36(1) poses both a threshold requirement that an infringement of a right must meet in order for it to be capable of justification - the infringement must have occurred in terms of 'law of general application'[116] to be at all justifiable - and a standard of justification that the infringement must satisfy once it has passed the threshold.

The standard of justification required by section 36(1) is relatively intrusive. It has been described by our courts as a *proportionality test*: A court weighs the purpose and benefits of the infringement against its nature, effect and severity, and considers the relative efficacy of the infringing measure in achieving its purpose, to decide whether or not it is justified. As such, it allows courts a fair amount of leeway to interrogate state conduct and to prescribe specific alternative options where state conduct is found to be unjustifiable. The reasonableness test that applies in cases of negative infringement of the qualified socio-economic rights, by contrast, is applied as a shifting standard of scrutiny. Usually it operates only at the intermediate level of a means-end effectiveness test[117] and only in

---

[113] M Pieterse 'Towards a useful role for section 36 of the Constitution in social rights cases? *Residents of Bon Vista Mansions v Southern Metropolitan Local Council*' (2003) 120 *South African Law Journal* 41. See also *Khosa* (n 9 above) paras 83 & 84.

[114] See sec 2.1 above.

[115] See sec 4.3.2 below for a description of this standard of scrutiny.

[116] This means the infringement must have occurred in terms of a rule (as opposed to a once-off decision) that is clear, precise and public and applies in equal measure to those it reaches; see Kriegler J in *President of the Republic of South Africa v Hugo* 1997 4 SA 1 (CC) 36 n 86. A breach occasioned by 'mere conduct', unrelated to law of general application, cannot be justified – if such a breach is shown, the conduct in question is unconstitutional.

[117] *Grootboom* (n 22 above) and *Treatment Action Campaign* (n 39 above) at paras 39-45; 38 & 123 respectively. In *Soobramoney* (n 8 above) paras 27 & 29, the Court applied an even more lenient basic rationality standard of scrutiny.

exceptional cases does it rise to the level of proportionality.[118] In particular, as a rule it does not allow courts explicitly to consider the relative efficacy of challenged state measures compared to other possible measures.[119] As a result, infringements of the positive duties imposed by qualified socio-economic rights are usually evaluated against a more lenient standard of scrutiny than that which applies to other infringements of rights in terms of section 36(1). Courts are, in other words, more constrained in their assessment of such infringements than they are with respect to others.

It is often possible to characterise the same infringement of a socio-economic right as an infringement of either the negative or the positive duties imposed by the right.[120] The special limitation clause that applies to the positive duties of the qualified socio-economic rights in lieu of section 36(1) does not also apply to the negative duty to respect those same qualified socio-economic rights[121] or to any of the negative or positive duties imposed by the basic socio-economic rights.[122] Infringements of these can still only be justified in terms of section 36(1). As a strategic matter, therefore, it is better to characterise a case brought on the basis of a qualified socio-economic right as a negative infringement of that right (where possible). This will draw the application of section 36(1) during the justification phase of the litigation and as such will significantly dilute the constraint under which the court will operate. By the same token, it is preferable to base a case on one of the unqualified (basic) socio-economic rights, whether a negative or a positive infringement is at play.

---

[118] In *Khosa* (n 9 above), the Constitutional Court confirmed a ruling that the exclusion of permanent residents from social assistance benefits violated the right to social assistance (sec 27(1)(c)). The measures were found unreasonable because the purpose of the exclusion (to prevent people immigrating to South Africa becoming a burden on the state) could be achieved through means less restrictive of permanent residents' rights (stricter control of access into the country) (at para 65) and because 'the importance of providing access to social assistance to all who live permanently in South Africa and the impact upon life and dignity that a denial of such access has far outweighs the financial and immigration considerations on which the state relies' (para 82).

[119] *Grootboom* (n 22 above) para 41: 'A court considering reasonableness will not enquire whether other more desirable or favourable measures could have been adopted, or whether public money could have been better spent. The question would be whether the measures that have been adopted are reasonable. It is necessary to recognise that a wide range of possible measures could be adopted by the state to meet its obligations. Many of these would meet the requirement of reasonableness. Once it is shown that the measures do so, this requirement is met.'

[120] See sec 2.2.2 above.

[121] *Jaftha* (n 37 above) para 34 (a measure negatively breaching the right to have access to adequate housing 'may ... be justified under section 36 of the Constitution'.

[122] As the basic socio-economic rights are not qualified by the same 'reasonable measures' phrase that applies to the qualified rights, the reasonableness analysis does not seem to apply to them and breaches of these rights fall to be justified in terms of sec 36(1); Liebenberg (n 7 above) 54. However, although this seems clear from the text, the Constitutional Court has been ambiguous in its application of these basic rights, in particular the rights of children, in this respect. In both *Grootboom* (n 22 above) and *Treatment Action Campaign* (n 39 above) the Court, despite being invited to do so, chose not to decide the dispute on the basis of children's socio-economic rights. Instead the Court relied on the fact that the state conduct in question breached also these rights, to bolster its eventual finding that the conduct was unreasonable in terms of secs 26(2) & 27(2) respectively; Brand (n 111 above) 48; Liebenberg (n 7 above) 51.

The question whether or not section 36(1) or the special 'reasonableness' limitation clause applies is in a strategic sense important for two further reasons, unrelated to judicial constraint. First, it has important consequences for the onus of persuasion facing litigants in socio-economic rights cases. As a rule, in Bill of Rights litigation a party that alleges that a right in the Bill has been infringed must persuade a court that this is indeed so - a complainant has to make a *prima facie* case that the conduct of the respondent has infringed a right in the Bill of Rights. Once such a *prima facie* case has been made, the respondent bears the onus to persuade the court that the infringement is justifiable.[123] The potential benefit of this structure is that it requires very little of a complainant in the way of establishing questions of fact - the complainant simply has to propose a certain interpretation of the right it alleges is being infringed and then has to show that the respondent's conduct infringes the right so described, an exercise that mostly involves arguing questions of law on an abstract level.

However, in the kinds of socio-economic rights cases referred to above, where the allegation is that the state has failed to take reasonable steps, within available resources to achieve the progressive realisation of a qualified socio-economic right, this structure is bedevilled. In such cases, for the complainant to show that the right has in fact been infringed involves making a *prima facie* case that the state's existing measures are unreasonable. The state then gets the opportunity to rebut this *prima facie* showing by arguing that its measures are in fact reasonable.[124] The difficulty is that, for a complainant to make a *prima facie* showing that the state's measures are unreasonable requires it to establish a range of factual questions, mostly relating to information that is uniquely in the knowledge of the state.[125] Often, of course, the typical socio-economic rights complainant would not have the required access to information and resources to do this.

Secondly, the special limitation clause that applies in cases of positive infringements of qualified socio-economic rights potentially allows for the justification of *all* positive infringements of qualified socio-economic rights, as it does not also impose a threshold requirement of law of general application as section 36(1) does. Certain infringements that would simply not be capable of justification in terms of section 36(1) - infringements that occur in terms of simple state conduct, for example, unrelated to any law of general application[126] - can be justified in terms of the reasonableness test that applies to the qualified rights. Both these

---

[123] *S v Zuma* 1995 2 SA 642 (CC) para 21.
[124] Liebenberg (n 7 above) 53.
[125] Liebenberg (n 7 above) 53-54; Brand (n 111 above) 52-53.
[126] *Per* Langa J in *City Council of Pretoria v Walker* 1998 2 SA 363 (CC) para 80: 'The rights guaranteed in Chapter 3 of the interim Constitution may be limited in terms of section 33(1) of the interim Constitution. A requirement of section 33(1) is that a right may only be limited by a law of general application. Since the respondent's challenge is directed at the conduct of the council, which was clearly not authorised, either expressly or by necessary implication by a law of general application, section 33(1) is not applicable to the present case.'

factors, although not related to constraint as such, additionally indicate a preference for arguing a case as a negative infringement rather than a positive one, or on the basis of a basic rather than a qualified socio-economic right.

4 Results of translation: Concrete legal duties and entitlements

In what follows, I provide an overview of the extent to which, and the different ways in which constitutional socio-economic rights have through legislation and adjudication been translated into concrete legal entitlements. The most useful way in which to do this is to use section 7(2)[127] as a framework and to describe how and to what extent the duties to respect, to protect and to promote and fulfil socio-economic rights have each been concretised. An overview of the various existing statutory and other entitlements that give expression to these duties illustrates the different ways in which constitutional socio-economic rights can be used as practical legal tools.

4.1 The duty to respect socio-economic rights

The duty to respect socio-economic rights requires the state and others to refrain from interfering with people's existing enjoyment of those rights; when such interference is unavoidable, to take steps to mitigate its impact; and to refrain from impairing access to socio-economic rights. As pointed out above, this 'negative' duty is potentially a potent tool with which to ensure people's adequate access to basic resources, as courts, for a variety of reasons, are more likely robustly to enforce the different elements of this duty than the duties to protect, promote and fulfil.

4.1.1 Refraining from interfering with the existing exercise of socio-economic rights

South Africa's apartheid history provides good examples of the violation of this element of the duty to respect socio-economic rights. The most obvious relate to the right to have access to land and housing. In terms of the spatial segregationist policies of grand apartheid, large numbers of people were dispossessed of and forcibly removed from productive land and housing. People were also routinely arbitrarily evicted from informal settlements as a result of so-called 'influx control' policies.[128] The statutory measures in terms of which these dispossessions and removals occurred have now been

---

[127] See sec 2.2.2 above.
[128] For an overview of the different ways in which people's access to land and housing was interfered with during this time, see D van der Merwe 'Land tenure in South Africa: A brief history and some reform proposals' (1989) *Journal for South African Law* 663.

repealed and new legal measures have been put in place preventing a recurrence of such practices. Apart from the fact that dispossession of land by the state is now regulated by section 25 of the Constitution,[129] eviction of people from state land is heavily regulated.

Two examples are the Extension of Security of Tenure Act (ESTA)[130] and PIE.[131] Both laws make eviction from land by the state in certain instances more difficult than it would ordinarily be, *inter alia* by requiring that a court, before granting an eviction order, consider whether an eviction would be just and equitable in the light of all relevant circumstances.[132] Both the repeal of the old laws and the new legal measures are examples of legislative translations of the duty to respect the rights to have equitable access to land and to housing, and particularly of the prohibition on arbitrary evictions, into concrete legal entitlements. Another example of such a legislative translation of this element of the duty to respect a constitutional socio-economic right is found in the Water Services Act,[133] which regulates the circumstances under which and the manner in which household water supply may be disconnected, also by the state. In much the same way as the tenure security laws referred to above give expression to constitutional rights to have access to land and housing, and to be protected against arbitrary eviction, the Water Services Act protects people's existing access to water for household purposes by prescribing certain conditions that have to be complied with before water supply may be disconnected for non-payment.[134] Importantly, section 4(3) of the Act determines that the procedures in terms of which water service providers effect disconnections of water supply may not result in the water supply of persons being disconnected for non-payment, where those persons are able to show, to the satisfaction of the service provider, that they are unable to pay their arrears.

Courts have been involved in the translation of this element of the duty to respect socio-economic rights in different ways. First, of course,

---

[129] Secs 25(2) & (3) of the Constitution. This means it can only occur through regular expropriation, for a public purpose, following the payment of 'just and equitable' compensation, the amount, and time and manner of payment of which must be determined after all relevant circumstances have been considered. The Expropriation Act 63 of 1975 further regulates expropriation.

[130] n 49 above. ESTA applies to rural land occupied with the tacit or explicit consent of the owner or person in charge; see sec 2(1) of ESTA and the definitions of 'occupier' and 'consent' in sec 1.

[131] n 55 above. PIE applies to all land, including state-owned land; see PIE secs 6 & 7. See also the Labour Tenants Act (n 100 above), which applies to rural land occupied and used in terms of a labour tenancy agreement; sec 1. This Act will in practice not apply to state land, as the labour tenancy agreements that it is intended to regulate are usually with private landowners. ESTA, PIE and the Labour Tenants Act are also instruments to regulate private evictions and as such give effect to the duty to protect the right to food; see sec 3.2.2 below.

[132] ESTA (n 49 above), secs 8(1) & 11(1), (2) & (3); PIE (n 56 above), secs 4(6) & (7), 5(1)(b) and 6(1) & (3). State sponsored eviction from private land or state eviction from state land in terms of PIE secs 4 or 6 have been heavily litigated. See eg *Rudolph* (n 59 above).

[133] n 58 above.

[134] n 58 above, sec 4(3).

courts have enforced legislative translations in this respect. One thinks of the large body of case law that has already developed around the eviction provisions of a statute such as PIE[135] and the enforcement of the statutory entitlements protecting against water disconnection created in the Water Services Act.[136] However, courts have also directly enforced this element of the duty to respect socio-economic rights to invalidate laws allowing interference in the existing enjoyment of socio-economic rights or to prevent state interference in the enjoyment of such rights.

In *Despatch Municipality v Sunridge Estate and Development Corporation*,[137] the High Court declared that, in light of section 26(3) of the Constitution, section 3B of the Prevention of Illegal Squatting Act,[138] which permitted the demolition and removal, also by the state, without a court order of shelters illegally erected on land, was 'no longer of application'.[139] In *Jaftha v Schoeman; Van Rooyen v Stoltz*,[140] the Constitutional Court found that provisions of the Magistrates' Courts Act[141] that allowed, without adequate judicial oversight, the sale in execution of a person's home to make good a judgment debt, breached[142] the negative duty to respect the right of everyone to have access to adequate housing. The Court proceeded to read words into the statute to make provision for appropriate judicial oversight.[143] Finally, in *Ross v South Peninsula Municipality*[144] - an example of a case where state *conduct* was challenged as in breach of the duty to respect a socio-economic right - the Cape High Court relied directly on section 26(3) of the Constitution to deny a local authority an eviction order, as the granting of such an order would not have been just and equitable in all the circumstances.[145]

Section 27(3), the right not to be refused emergency medical treatment, can perhaps also be interpreted to give expression to the state's duty to respect socio-economic rights by refraining from interfering in their existing exercise. In *Soobramoney*,[146] the Constitutional Court held this right only required the state not to refuse arbitrarily emergency medical treatment where it exists[147] - an

---

[135] n 56 above. See eg *Port Elizabeth Municipality* (n 56 above).
[136] *Bon Vista* (n 58 above).
[137] 1997 4 SA 596 (SE).
[138] Act 52 of 1951.
[139] *Despatch* (n 137 above) 611B-C/D. The Prevention of Illegal Squatting Act has since been repealed in its entirety. See sec 11(1) read with Schedule I of PIE (n 56 above).
[140] n 37 above.
[141] Sec 66(1)(a) of the Magistrates' Courts Act (n 73 above).
[142] The possible justification of this breach was considered by the Court in terms of the sec 36(1) proportionality test; *Jaftha* (n 37 above) para 34. See in this respect sec 3.3.2 above.
[143] *Jaftha* (n 37 above) paras 61-64.
[144] n 102 above.
[145] As outlined above, *Ross* was overturned by the Supreme Court of Appeal in *Brisley* (n 76 above). However, it remains as one example where state conduct interfering in the existing enjoyment of a socio-economic right was tested against that right and found to be wanting.
[146] n 8 above.
[147] As above.

inordinately restrictive reading, which, as Alston and Scott have pointed out, renders the right virtually redundant.[148] A matter that remains unclear is the question whether or not section 27(3) could also be used to prohibit the state from disestablishing an emergency medical service at a public health institution to save costs.[149]

4.1.2 Mitigating the impact of interferences in the exercise of socio-economic rights

The duty to respect socio-economic rights does not absolutely prohibit the state from interfering in the existing exercise of such rights. In many instances it is unavoidable for the state to do so, often to advance the public interest or to protect the rights of others. In such cases, the duty to respect requires that an effort be made to mitigate the effect of the interference in the enjoyment of the right, by providing some form of alternative access to it. This element of the duty to respect socio-economic rights is potentially quite burdensome and often requires the expenditure of significant resources and significant adjustments in policy.

Nevertheless, our courts have shown themselves to be willing to enforce this duty robustly. The security of tenure laws again provide a good example of how this constitutional duty has been translated into a statutory entitlement of sorts. These laws, in some instances, require courts to consider to what extent suitable alternative land is available for evictees before granting an eviction order and an eviction order can be denied if such alternative is absent.[150] A recent case decided in terms of PIE illustrates this aspect of the duty to respect socio-economic rights in the context of statutory protection of those rights and indicates the robust manner in which courts will interrogate whether or not this duty has been met.

In *Port Elizabeth Municipality v Various Occupiers*,[151] the state had applied for an order to evict illegal occupants from privately owned land in terms of section 6 of PIE. Section 6 allows a court to grant such an order, but only if it is just and equitable to do so, taking into account various factors, including 'the availability to the unlawful occupier of suitable alternative accommodation or land'.[152] The Constitutional Court confirmed the Supreme Court of Appeal's decision denying the eviction order.[153]

The Court held that section 26(3) of the Constitution, mediated through section 6 of PIE, required the state, when it seeks to evict, to

---

[148] P Alston & C Scott 'Adjudicating constitutional priorities in a transnational context: A comment on *Soobramoney's* legacy and *Grootboom's* promise' (2000) 16 *South African Journal on Human Rights* 206 245-248.
[149] Liebenberg (n 7 above) 21.
[150] In respect of ESTA (n 49 above), see secs 9(3)(a), 10(2) & (3) & 11(3); in respect of PIE (n 56 above), see sec 6(3)(b).
[151] n 56 above.
[152] PIE (n 56 above), sec 6(3)(c).
[153] The Supreme Court of Appeal decision is reported as *Baartman v Port Elizabeth Municipality* 2004 1 SA 560 (SCA).

provide alternative accommodation to the evictees. This duty would not be operative in all cases of state sponsored eviction.[154] A court would have to decide whether or not to enforce this duty on the basis of a consideration of each case's 'own dynamics, its own intractable elements that have to be lived with (at least for the time being), and its own creative possibilities that have to be explored as far as reasonably possible'.[155] To decide whether or not the duty applies, the Court looked at the position and the conduct of the occupiers, at the conduct of the municipality in its management of the matter and at the conduct of the landowners in question. The fact that the occupiers had lived on the land in question for a long period of time;[156] that they would be severely affected by any eviction;[157] that they had occupied the land not to force the municipality to provide to them, in preference to others, alternative land, but because they had been evicted from elsewhere and had nowhere to go;[158] that there was 'no evidence that either the municipality or the owners of the land need to evict the occupiers in order to put the land to some other productive use';[159] and that the municipality had made no serious effort to reach an amicable conclusion to the matter, but had rushed to apply for an eviction order and had acted unilaterally,[160] drove the Court to conclude that an eviction order could not be granted unless suitable alternative land was provided.

The municipality had indeed offered to allow the occupiers to move to two possible alternative sites. However, the Court went as far as to find that neither of those sites were suitable, most importantly because the municipality could not guarantee to the evictees security of tenure if they were moved there.[161] As a result, the occupiers were allowed to remain on the land in question.[162]

The robust manner in which the Constitutional Court saw fit to deal with this element of the duty to respect socio-economic rights in *Port Elizabeth Municipality* could certainly in part be explained by the fact that the Court was enforcing a statutory duty in terms of PIE. However, there are indications in the case law that courts are willing to enforce this burdensome element of the duty to respect against the state even where a statutory duty to this effect does not apply. In *Modderfontein Squatters v Modderklip Boerdery (Pty) Ltd*,[163] the Supreme Court of Appeal dealt with a claim of a private landowner

---

[154] *Port Elizabeth Municipality* (n 56 above), para 58: 'The availability of suitable alternative accommodation is a consideration in determining whether it is just and equitable to evict the occupiers, it is not determinative of that question.' See also para 28: 'There is therefore no unqualified duty on local authorities to ensure that in no circumstances should a home be destroyed unless alternative accommodation or land is made available.'
[155] n 56 above, para 31.
[156] n 56 above, paras 27, 28, 49 & 59.
[157] n 56 above, paras 30 & 59.
[158] n 56 above, paras 49 & 55.
[159] n 56 above, para 59.
[160] n 56 above, paras 45, 55-57 & 59.
[161] n 56 above, para 58.
[162] n 56 above, para 59.
[163] n 112 above.

that the state was constitutionally obliged, in order to protect his constitutional right to property, to enforce an eviction order he had obtained in terms of section 4 of PIE against squatters illegally occupying his land. The Court held that the state was indeed obliged to protect the claimant's right to property against invasion by unlawful occupiers.[164] However, at the same time, the state was obliged to protect the right of the squatters to have access to adequate housing.[165] The Court held that this meant that the state, were it to execute the eviction order against the squatters, would have to act 'humanely'. This meant *inter alia* that the state could not evict the squatters unless it 'provide[d] some [alternative] land'.[166] This conclusion led to the Court eventually ordering the state to pay damages to Modderklip to make good the breach of its right to property and the state's failure to protect against that breach,[167] and to allow the squatters to remain on Modderklip's land until alternative land is made available to them.[168]

In effect, the order required the state to buy the land so that the squatters could remain there, without continuing to infringe Modderklip Boerdery's property rights.[169] The Court made this intrusive order without considering the substantial resource consequences that its decision would have for the state and the extent to which its order prescribes a particular policy option to the state, in preference to others. This robust approach, as in *Port Elizabeth Municipality*, is justified by the Court with reference to the conduct of the state, the landowner and the squatters during the course of the dispute. The Court points out that the state, despite the holding in *Grootboom*[170] that it must introduce measures to take account of the needs of those in housing crisis, still had no measures in place to deal with the plight of people such as the Modderfontein squatters.[171] The Court also highlights the fact that the state had, despite various opportunities to do so, not attempted to solve the dispute between the squatters, the landowner and itself. The state had failed diligently to pursue a settlement and had reneged on agreements reached,[172] despite the fact that it had itself caused the predicament of the squatters and the landowner, by previously evicting the squatters from state land without providing alternative

---

[164] n 112 above, para 21.
[165] n 112 above, para 22.
[166] n 112 above, para 26.
[167] n 112 above, paras 43 & 52. The amount of damages would be determined at a separate inquiry into damages (para 44).
[168] n 112 above, paras 43 & 52. The case is no appeal to the Constitutional Court.
[169] Although expressly indicating that it would not be proper for it to order the state to expropriate the land in question (n 112 above, para 41), the Court does point out that, in light of its order, it would be the sensible thing for the state to do indeed to expropriate the land (para 43).
[170] n 22 above.
[171] n 22 above, para 22. See also *Rudolph* (n 59 above) 77B-84H. See further sec 4.2.2 below.
[172] n 22 above, paras 35-38.

accommodation.[173] As such, to some extent, it had made its own bed and now had to lie in it.

The conduct of both the squatters and the landowner had, in contrast to the state's, been exemplary. The landowner had at all times acted within the law and had throughout sought to effect an amicable solution that would vindicate both his and the occupiers' rights.[174] The squatters had not occupied the land to force the hand of the state to provide them with land in preference to others and had also sought to reach an amicable solution, both with the landowner and the state.[175]

4.1.3 Refraining from impairing access to socio-economic rights

The duty to respect socio-economic rights is also violated if the state obstructs people's access to basic resources or their efforts to enhance their existing access to such resources. The most obvious way in which the state can fail in this duty is if it arbitrarily refuses to provide access to a basic resource that it has the capacity to provide. In, for example, *Soobramoney*,[176] the Constitutional Court held section 27(3) of the Constitution, the right not to be refused emergency medical treatment, to impose a duty on the state not arbitrarily to refuse access to such treatment where it exists.[177]

Both *Treatment Action Campaign*[178] and *Khosa*,[179] decided as cases of infringements of the positive duty to fulfil the rights to have access to health care services and to social assistance respectively, are in fact also examples of the state breaching the duty to respect those rights by refusing to allow access to a basic resource. In *Treatment Action Campaign*, the policy decision not to make Nevirapine available generally at public health facilities to prevent mother-to-child transmission of HIV at birth was in fact a refusal by the state to provide essential health care to pregnant, HIV-positive women, and not only a failure by the state suitably to extend health care provision to those women.[180] Equally, in *Khosa*, the provisions of the Social Assistance Act[181] excluding permanent residents and their children from access to social assistance constituted a legislative obstacle to them gaining access to these benefits.

A less obvious way in which this element of the duty to respect can be breached by the state is where the state impairs access to a basic resource through administrative inefficiency. In *Mashava v The*

---

[173] n 22 above, para 35.
[174] n 22 above, paras 33, 37 & 38.
[175] n 22 above, para 25.
[176] n 8 above.
[177] This interpretation leaves little work for sec 27(3) that other rights (eg the prohibition on unfair discrimination) and other ordinary remedies (eg the administrative law) do not do; see Alston & Scott (n 148 above).
[178] n 39 above.
[179] n 9 above.
[180] Liebenberg (n 7 above) 19.
[181] n 9 above.

President of the Republic of South Africa,[182] the Constitutional Court confirmed a High Court order that a presidential proclamation[183] assigning the administration of the Social Assistance Act[184] to provincial governments was invalid.

Although the validity of the proclamation was challenged on the argument that the President, in terms of the transitional arrangements in the interim Constitution and the allocation of powers between provinces and national government, was not competent to make the assignment,[185] the case was motivated by the fact that the assignment resulted in the right of access to social assistance of persons eligible for social assistance grants being impaired. The plaintiff was an indigent disabled person who had applied for and been awarded a disability grant, but who, for a period of more than a year after his successful application, did not receive the grant from the Limpopo Department of Health and Welfare.[186]

It was clear that the failure to pay to the plaintiff the grant to which he was entitled was caused by the administrative incapacity of the provincial Department of Health and Welfare and by the fact that the administration of the social welfare system in the province was woefully under-resourced, due to 'demands for the reallocation of social assistance monies to other [provincial] purposes'.[187] The plaintiff contended that the Social Assistance Act could be administered more efficiently and equitably by the national government than by the provinces. As a result, the assignment of the administration of the Social Assistance Act to the provinces constituted a negative impairment of the right to have access to social assistance. In effect, therefore, the decision of the Constitutional Court invalidating the assignment is a decision that the state must give effect to the duty to respect the right to have access to social assistance, by removing an impediment to its effective exercise.

4.2 The duty to protect socio-economic rights

The duty to protect socio-economic rights requires the state to protect existing enjoyment of these rights, and the capacity of people to enhance or newly to gain access to the enjoyment of these rights, against third party interference.

4.2.1 Legislative and executive measures

The state most obviously carries out the duty to protect socio-economic rights by regulating, through legislation or executive/

---

[182] n 14 above.
[183] Proclamation R7 of 1996, *Government Gazette* 16992 GN R7, 23 February 1996. The assignment was made in terms of sec 235 of the interim Constitution.
[184] n 9 above.
[185] *Mashava* (n 14 above), para 1.
[186] n 14 above, para 9.
[187] n 14 above, para 10.

administrative conduct, those instances in which private entities control access to basic resources such as housing, health care services, food, water and education. Such regulation could first be aimed at opening up access to these resources - current state regulation of rental housing[188] and land development[189] provide examples. The state can also protect access to socio-economic rights through standard setting in respect of safety and quality in the provision of services and products. An example, with respect to the right to adequate food, is the Foodstuffs, Cosmetics and Disinfectants Act (FCDA),[190] which is intended to regulate fungicide and pesticide residue and additive and preservative levels in food, by setting standards and creating mechanisms for the monitoring of these levels in foodstuffs.

Finally, the state can exercise its duty to protect socio-economic rights by regulating instances in which private parties can interfere in the existing enjoyment of socio-economic rights. The tenure security laws discussed above[191] provide an example. These laws protect informal rights to housing also against private interference just as it protects these rights against the state: by making eviction more difficult than it would otherwise be through imposing procedural and substantive safeguards that have to be met before an eviction order can be granted.

4.2.2 The judiciary

Courts can also act so as to protect socio-economic rights. In the first place, courts can protect socio-economic rights by adjudicating constitutional and other challenges to state measures that are intended to advance those rights.[192] This protective role of courts has been illustrated in *Minister of Public Works v Kyalami Ridge Environmental Association*.[193] In this case, a state decision temporarily to house destitute flood victims on the (state-owned) grounds of a prison, was challenged by surrounding property owners as in breach of administrative justice rights. The challenge was in part based on the argument that the decision was unlawful, as the Minister of Public Works had no statutory authority to take such a decision. The Court rejected this argument, primarily because it held that the Minister had the requisite power to take the decision by virtue of the state's common law rights as property owner,[194] but also because the decision was taken in furtherance of a constitutional duty to provide

---

[188] See the Rental Housing Act 50 of 1999.
[189] See eg the Development Facilitation Act 67 of 1995, which, amongst other things, is intended to simplify and so speed up private development of land for purposes of low cost housing provision.
[190] 54 of 1972.
[191] PIE (n 56 above) and ESTA (n 49 above). See also the Labour Tenants Act (n 100 above). See secs 4.1.1 and 4.2.2 above.
[192] See, in general, CH Heyns 'Extended medical training and the Constitution: Balancing civil and political rights and socio-economic rights' (1997) 30 *De Jure* 1.
[193] n 65 above. See in this respect Budlender (n 34 above) 36.
[194] n 65 above, para 40.

shelter to those in dire straits.[195] Through its decision, the Court effectively protected the right to adequate housing of the flood victims against private interference. Similarly, in *City of Cape Town v Rudolph*,[196] the Cape High Court rejected a property-based constitutional challenge to the security of tenure law PIE.[197] The Court held that PIE authorised neither the arbitrary deprivation[198] nor the expropriation of property,[199] and as such did not infringe property rights. The decision was partly based on the finding that the state was at the very least authorised, but probably obliged by the Constitution to enact legislation such as PIE to give effect to the right to housing and the prohibition on arbitrary evictions.[200]

Courts can also protect socio-economic rights through their law-making powers of interpreting legislation and developing the rules of common law. Courts are constitutionally obliged to interpret legislation and develop rules of common law so as to promote the 'spirit, purport and objects' of the Bill of Rights.[201] Courts are in other words required to infuse legislation and the common law with the value system underlying the Constitution - to read the rights in the Bill of Rights and the values underlying them into the existing law. This power of courts to engage constitutionally with the existing law is, particularly with respect to the common law, an extremely important, but as yet much neglected way in which socio-economic rights can be advanced. In a private ownership economy such as ours, common law background rules of property and transaction centrally determine access to and distribution of basic resources.[202] Although the development of constitutional socio-economic rights to establish new and unique constitutionally based remedies is an important endeavour on its own, to explore the full transformative potential of socio-economic rights, sustained critical engagement also with these common law background rules is crucial.

Experience with welfare rights campaigning in the United States, for example, has shown how a focus on the development of constitutional protection for welfare rights[203] at the expense of an adequately critical engagement with the common law background rules has, in the struggle for social justice, been counter-productive

---

[195] n 65 above, paras 37-40.
[196] n 59 above.
[197] n 56 above.
[198] *Rudolph* (n 59 above) 72J & 74G.
[199] n 59 above, 73F.
[200] n 59 above, 74H-75J.
[201] See sec 39(1) of the Constitution. See also sec 3.3.1 above.
[202] Simon (n 55 above)) 1433-1436; Williams (n 55 above) 575-577. See in this respect also A Sen *Poverty and famines. An essay on entitlement and deprivation* (1981) 166, who writes that access to food (I would add other basic resources) is determined by 'a system of legal relations (ownership rights, contractual obligations, legal exchanges, etc)', and that these legal relations, or the law itself quite literally 'stand between' such resources and those in desperate need of them.
[203] The focus of this movement, which reached its zenith in the Supreme Court decision of *Goldberg v Kelly* (n 20 above), was obtaining for statutory welfare rights the same kind of due process protection as that afforded property and other basic personal rights. See Williams (n 55 above) 571-575 for an overview.

in the longer term, because it sublimates deep political questions regarding distribution of basic resources.[204] In South Africa, some of these common law background rules have of course been significantly adapted through legislation - the impact of the different security of tenure laws on private property rights is a case in point.[205] However, courts retain an important responsibility to extend the protection afforded socio-economic rights in the 'ordinary' law, through their powers of interpretation of legislation and development of common law.

Courts have readily engaged with legislation in attempts to broaden the protection of socio-economic rights. So, for instance, the Labour Tenants Act[206] and ESTA,[207] both primarily intended to protect informal rights to land against private interference, have in various respects been interpreted by courts so that their protection also extends to other rights, such as the right to food.[208] In addition, the decision of the Constitutional Court in *Jaftha v Schoeman*[209] provides an interesting example of how courts can, when dealing with legislation, advance the duty to protect socio-economic rights. In *Jaftha*, the Court considered provisions of the Magistrates' Courts Act[210] that authorised, without proper judicial oversight, the sale in execution of the home of a debtor to satisfy a judgment debt. On the basis of the section 26(1) right to adequate housing, the Court, through a combination of interpretation and of reading words into the Act, adapted the Act so that a judgment debtor's home can only be sold in execution if a court has ordered so after considering all relevant circumstances.[211]

Jaftha was argued and decided on the basis of the negative duty to respect the right to have access to adequate housing.[212] However, the Court's order also amounts to interpretative lawmaking through

---

[204] Williams (n 55 above) 581-582; Simon (n 55 above), 1486-1489.
[205] See secs 4.1.1 & 4.1.2 above. See also AJ Van der Walt 'Exclusivity of ownership, security of tenure, and eviction orders: A model to evaluate South African land reform legislation' 2002 *Journal for South African Law* 254.
[206] n 100 above.
[207] n 49 above.
[208] The Land Claims Court has in a number of cases, dealing with either ESTA (n 49 above) or the Labour Tenants Act (n 100 above), eg interpreted the term 'eviction' broadly, to extend not only to interference with occupation of land for purposes of shelter, but also to landowner interference with activities on land through which people gain access to food (eg grazing and watering rights). See eg re ESTA, *Ntshangase v The Trustees of the Terblanché Gesin Familie Trust* [2003] JOL 10996 (LCC) para 4; and, re the Labour Tenants Act, *Van der Walt v Lang* 1999 1 SA 189 (LCC) para 13 and *Zulu v Van Rensburg* 1996 4 SA 1236 (LCC) 1259. See also *In re Kranspoort Community* 2000 2 SA 124 (LCC) (Land Claims Court interpreting the term 'rights in land' in the Restitution of Land Rights Act 22 of 1994 to include also 'beneficial occupation', so that the use of land for grazing and cultivation also constitutes such a right in land that can be reclaimed).
[209] n 37 above.
[210] n 73 above. See sec 66(1)(a).
[211] *Jaftha* (n 37 above) paras 61-64 & 67. The factors the Court lists are: 'circumstances in which the debt was incurred; ... attempts ... by the debtor to pay off the debt; the financial situation of the parties; the amount of the debt; whether the debtor is employed or has a source of income to pay off the debt and any other factor relevant to the ... facts of the case ...' (para 60).
[212] n 37 above, paras 17, 31-34 & 52. See also the discussion in sec 4.1.1 above.

which the court introduces into the Magistrates' Courts Act a measure of *protection* for the right to housing - the Court gave effect to its duty to protect that right. In addition, the judgment has opened the door for further court driven development in this respect. Although *Jaftha* involved only the protection of a judgment debtor's home against sale in execution, in future cases where a creditor seeks the sale in execution of immovable property that a judgment debtor uses, for example, to produce food, courts can extend the Constitutional Court's reasoning. The fact that the immovable property is the debtor's means with which to exercise the right to food must also be considered relevant to the decision whether or not to allow its sale in execution. In this way courts could further develop the law to protect judgment debtors' right to food against interference from creditors.[213]

Courts have been less active in engaging with the common law to enhance protection of socio-economic rights than they have been with respect to legislation.[214] In those cases where the courts have been asked to develop the common law so as better to give effect to socio-economic rights, they have declined. In *Afrox Healthcare (Pty) Ltd v Strydom*,[215] the Supreme Court of Appeal was invited to develop the law of contract so that disclaimers in hospital admission contracts indemnifying hospitals against damages claims on the basis of the negligence of their staff would be seen as in conflict with the public interest and consequently unenforceable. The argument was that such disclaimers had the effect that patients were not adequately protected against unprofessional conduct at private hospitals and as such impaired access to health care services.[216] This argument was rejected and the common law position remained intact.[217] Equally, in

---

[213] The judgment suggests this possibility. The list of factors provided by the Court to take account of when considering whether to allow sale in execution of immovable property is not exclusive. The Court stated that any other factor that, on the facts of the case before it, is relevant, must be considered (para 60). The Court also emphasised that the severe impact that the execution process could have on the human dignity of a judgment debtor and on a judgment debtor's capacity to have access to the basic necessities of life importantly influenced its decision (paras 21, 25-30, 39 & 43). Certainly, the impact on an indigent person's dignity and survival interests of the attachment and sale in execution of immovable property that the person uses to produce food for own use is comparable to the impact of the sale in execution of such a person's home.

[214] This is certainly due in the first place to the fact that, except in the area of eviction law (see eg *Brisley* (n 76 above)), few such cases have been brought to court. Second, courts have in those few cases where the development of the common law to protect socio-economic rights did come into play, readily deferred to the legislature rather than drive the development themselves; as pointed out above (section 3.2.2), whereas in *Brisley* the Supreme Court of Appeal was unwilling itself to develop the common law so as to extend the protection of sec 26(3) to unlawful occupants who 'hold over', it was willing to do so in *Ndlovu* (n 97 above) by extending the legislative protection afforded other unlawful occupiers.

[215] n 79 above.

[216] n 79 above, para 21.

[217] For critiques of this aspect of the judgment, see D Brand 'Disclaimers in hospital admission contracts and constitutional health rights' (2002) 3:2 *ESR Review* 17-18; PA Carstens & JA Kok 'An assessment of the use of disclaimers against medical negligence by South African hospitals in view of constitutional demands, foreign law and medico-legal considerations' (2003) 18 *SA Public Law* 430; D Tladi 'One step forward, two steps back for constitutionalising the common law: *Afrox Health Care v Strydom*' (2002) 17 *SA Public Law* 473.

Brisley,[218] the Court declined to develop the common law of eviction in line with section 26(3) of the Constitution.

One example where courts were willing to develop the common law to protect socio-economic rights is *Permanent Secretary, Department of Welfare, Eastern Cape v Ngxuza*.[219] *Ngxuza* dealt with a class action claim brought in terms of section 38 of the Constitution by social assistance grantees for the reinstatement of disability grants unlawfully terminated by the Eastern Cape Province. The respondents had been granted leave to proceed with such a class action claim by the court *a quo*. The province appealed against this grant of leave to the Supreme Court of Appeal. The Supreme Court of Appeal, in the absence of any legislative form having been given to section 38's provision for class actions, developed the common law of standing to make provision for such claims. Although the decision certainly opens the door for all kinds of class action claims, at least where any constitutional right is at play, it is centrally important for the protection of particularly socio-economic rights. As Cameron JA (as he then was) states for the Court: 'The law is a scarce resource in South Africa. This case shows that justice is even harder to come by. It concerns the way in which the poorest of the poor are to be permitted access to both.'[220]

4.3 The duty to fulfil socio-economic rights[221]

4.3.1 Background

The duty to fulfil socio-economic rights requires the state to act affirmatively to realise the rights.[222] The state breaches the duty to fulfil not when it invades the existing exercise of socio-economic rights, but when it does not do enough, or does not do the appropriate things fully to realise those rights. For courts to enforce the duty to fulfil requires them directly to evaluate state policy and practice, to decide whether or not those are adequate measures to realise the socio-economic rights in question. Courts are constrained in this evaluation by concerns about technical capacity and institutional legitimacy and by a perceived absence of justiciable standards against which to assess state performance.[223] To deal with these difficulties, the Constitutional Court has used a traditional model of judicial review,[224] but has given it new content.

---

[218] n 76 above.
[219] 2001 4 SA 1184 (SCA).
[220] n 219 above, para 1.
[221] I discuss the duties to promote and fulfil as one duty although various understandings of the duty to promote as distinct from the duty to fulfil have been proposed (see sec 2.2.2 above).
[222] Committee on ESCR General Comment No 14 (n 32 above) para 33.
[223] See sec 3.3.2 above.
[224] As suggested by Mureinik in an early article; E Mureinik 'Beyond a charter of luxuries: Economic rights in the Constitution' (1992) 8 *South African Journal on Human Rights* 464.

As with any breach of any other right, when it is alleged that the duty to fulfil a socio-economic right has been breached, where *prima facie* such a breach is established, the Court considers whether or not it can be justified. However, the Court has developed a special test or standard against which to evaluate the justifiability of state measures to fulfil socio-economic rights that allows it to mediate its concerns with capacity and legitimacy. Which standard of scrutiny applies to breaches of the duty to fulfil socio-economic rights depends on which socio-economic rights are at issue.[225] If the duty to fulfil a *basic socio-economic right* (children's rights, rights of detainees, or the right to basic education) is breached, the section 36(1) proportionality standard, one would hope, applies.[226] As the Court has as yet decided no case on the basis of a basic socio-economic right,[227] it is unclear how this standard will operate in the context of socio-economic rights.[228] If the duty to fulfil a *qualified socio-economic right* is breached, that breach can be justified only in terms of a special standard of scrutiny - the Court's 'reasonableness' standard - developed on the basis of the internal limitation clause attached to these rights.[229]

4.3.2 Reasonableness review

The Constitutional Court has described its 'reasonableness' standard of scrutiny in four cases. In *Soobramoney v Minister of Health, KwaZulu-Natal*,[230] it denied an application for an order that a state hospital provide dialysis treatment to the applicant, finding that the guidelines according to which the hospital decided whether to provide the treatment were not unreasonable[231] and were applied rationally and in good faith to the applicant.[232] As such, the Court was asked to

---

[225] See sec 3.3.2 above.
[226] See n 120 above and the caution expressed about this conclusion there.
[227] It could, but did not do so in *Grootboom* (n 22 above) and *Treatment Action Campaign* (n 39 above).
[228] In *B* (n 62 above), although finding detainees' right to adequate medical treatment (a basic socio-economic right) had been breached, the High Court did not explicitly consider the justification for that breach (but see paras 48-58, where the Court considers whether the breach can be condoned due to resource constraints). See further in this respect Liebenberg (n 7 above) 55-57.
[229] This seems to be so also where a positive duty to fulfil is sourced in sec 27(3), ie where an argument is made that in terms of this right, emergency medical services have to be established at an institution where they do not exist. In *Soobramoney* (n 8 above), the Court held that sec 27(3) only entitled one not to be refused treatment *where it is available* (see n 227 above). However, the Court intimated that, should a positive duty be read into this right, it would be subject to the sec 27(2) internal limitation; para 11; see also Liebenberg (n 7 above) 20.
[230] n 8 above.
[231] n 8 above, paras 24-28.
[232] n 8 above, para 29.

consider whether the denial of treatment did not breach the section 27(1) right of everyone to have access to health care services.[233] In *Government of the Republic of South Africa v Grootboom and Others*,[234] the Court heard a claim that the state was obliged to provide homeless people with shelter. It declared the state's housing programme inconsistent with section 26(1) of the Constitution.[235] In *Minister of Health v Treatment Action Campaign*,[236] the Court was asked to consider whether the state's policy not to provide Nevirapine at all public health facilities to prevent the mother-to-child transmission (MTCT) of HIV at birth, as well as the general failure by the state to adopt an adequate plan to combat MTCT of HIV breached sections 27(1) and 28(1)(c) of the Constitution. The Court held that the state's measures to prevent MTCT of HIV breached its duties in terms of section 27(1) of the Constitution,[237] declared as much and directed the state to remedy its programme.[238] In *Khosa v Minister of Social Development*,[239] the Court held sections of the Social Assistance Act[240] excluding permanent residents from access to social assistance grants inconsistent with section 9(3) (the prohibition on unfair discrimination)[241] and section 27(1)(c) (the right to have access to social assistance)[242] of the Constitution. The Court read words into the Act to remedy the constitutional defect.[243]

Although the Court has as yet not been explicit about this, it is clear from these cases that the reasonableness standard is a shifting standard of scrutiny. In *Soobramoney*, the Court applied a basic rationality and good faith test to the decision of the state not to provide renal dialysis treatment to the claimant.[244]

---

[233] n 8 above, para 36. The application was argued around the sec 27(3) right not to be refused emergency medical treatment and a reading of the right to life in terms of which the state is required to keep the applicant alive. The court denied the application in these respects, holding that, because health care rights were explicitly protected in the Constitution, it was unnecessary to give such an interpretation to the right to life (para 19) (see Pieterse (n 8 above)) and that sec 27(3) did not apply to the applicant's case, because his was not an emergency situation (para 21) and sec 27(3) was a right not arbitrarily to be refused emergency medical treatment *where it was available*, instead of a positive right to make available emergency medical treatment where it was not (para 20) (see Alston & Scott (n 148 above)). Having disposed of these two arguments, the Court on its own initiative proceeded to consider the claim on the basis of sec 27(1) (para 22).
[234] n 22 above.
[235] n 22 above, para 95.
[236] n 39 above.
[237] n 39 above, para 95.
[238] n 39 above, para 135.
[239] n 9 above.
[240] As above.
[241] n 9 above, para 77.
[242] n 9 above, para 85.
[243] n 9 above, paras 89 & 98.
[244] With respect to its evaluation of the guidelines according to which the state made this decision, the Court applied a stricter reasonableness test; *Soobramoney* (n 8 above) paras 23-28.

In *Grootboom*[245] and *Treatment Action Campaign*,[246] the Court applied a more stringent means-end effectiveness test.[247] In *Khosa*,[248] in turn, the Court applied a yet stricter proportionality test. The Court has not been explicit about which factors determine the strictness of its scrutiny,[249] but the cases indicate that the position of the claimants in society;[250] the degree of deprivation they complain of and the extent to which the breach of right in question affects their dignity;[251] the extent to which the breach in question involves undetermined, complex policy questions;[252] and whether or not the breach also amounts to a breach of other rights,[253] all play a role.

The Court derives its reasonableness standard from the state's duty to take reasonable legislative and other measures, within its available resources, to achieve the progressive realisation of socio-economic rights. In describing this duty, the Court has described the standards against which to evaluate the state's measures. The Court has presented its reasonableness test as a means-end effectiveness test: In *Grootboom*, the Court indicated that measures are evaluated to determine whether they are 'capable of facilitating the realisation of the right'.[254] The Court has been at pains in all its judgments to emphasise that it does not test relative effectiveness, that it 'will not enquire whether other more desirable or favourable measures could have been adopted, or whether public money could have been better spent', but will leave the 'precise contours and content of the measures to be adopted [to render a programme reasonable] ... [to] the legislature and the executive.'[255] The Court adopts this distinction between testing effectiveness and relative effectiveness to mediate its concerns with institutional capacity and legitimacy and to manage its relationship with the executive and the legislature.

---

[245] n 22 above.

[246] n 39 above.

[247] It is also clear that in *Treatment Action Campaign*, although the standard of scrutiny applied by the court was in formal terms the same as in *Grootboom*, the Court in fact scrutinised the state policy at issue there more rigorously than it did in *Grootboom*; Brand (n 111 above).

[248] n 9 above.

[249] See for comparison *Bel Porto School Governing Body v Premier of the Western Cape Province* 2002 3 SA 265 (CC) para 127, where the Court lists factors that could play a role in determining the strictness of its scrutiny with respect to administrative law reasonableness review.

[250] Whether they are a marginalised or especially vulnerable group; De Vos (n 3 above) 266.

[251] *Khosa* (n 9 above) para 80.

[252] In *Grootboom* (n 22 above), the issues were much less clearly delineated than in either *Treatment Action Campaign* (n 39 above) or *Khosa* (n 9 above). Also, in *Treatment Action Campaign*, many of the complex issues the Court had to consider (ie the safety/efficacy of Nevirapine and the availability of the necessary infrastructure to provide it properly) had either been determined by specialised bodies empowered to decide such issues (ie the Medicines Control Council), or the Court had dispositive evidence at its disposal with which to decide. In both the latter cases a stricter scrutiny was applied than in *Grootboom*.

[253] In *Khosa*, the impugned provisions also breached sec 9(3). In applying this section, the Court uses a standard of scrutiny rising to the level of proportionality. It would make little sense to apply sec 27(2) to the same breach using a more lenient standard.

[254] *Grootboom* (n 22 above) para 41.

[255] As above.

However, the distinction is in many cases a fiction. In *Grootboom*, the Court could maintain it. The policy issue in question (how best to provide for the needs of the 'absolutely homeless') allowed for a wide variety of different possible solutions, so that the Court could simply declare that the housing programme was inconsistent with the Constitution to the extent that it made no provision for the 'absolutely homeless', and leave the choice of specific solution to the state. By contrast, in *Treatment Action Campaign*,[256] and particularly in *Khosa*,[257] the specificity of the policy issue that the Court evaluated was such that it did not allow this scope. The Court's finding in *Treatment Action Campaign* that the state's restriction of the provision of Nevirapine to the designated pilot sites breached section 27(1), ineluctably led to the state having to provide Nevirapine elsewhere, despite its unwillingness to do so.[258] By the same token, in *Khosa*, the Court's finding of unreasonableness left no option but that permanent residents should be included in the social assistance scheme. Indeed the Court itself read words to this effect into the Social Assistance Act.[259] However, this fiction is useful as it allows the Court to enforce rights, without it having to admit to prescribing directly to the state. As such, it helps the Court avoid direct confrontation with the political branches.[260]

The Court's reasonableness standard requires first that the state indeed act to give effect to socio-economic rights, and then requires that what the state does, meets a standard of reasonableness.

Having a plan

The Court's standard requires that the state must devise and implement measures to realise socio-economic rights - it cannot do nothing.[261] Although these measures need realise the rights only *progressively* - the need for full realisation is deferred[262] - the state must have measures in place to realise these rights and must implement them.

In addition, the state must show progress in implementing these measures and be able to explain lack of progress or retrogression.

---

[256] n 39 above.
[257] n 9 above.
[258] The Court did soften the prescriptive edge of its finding, by directing that Nevirapine be provided only there where the attending physician and the superintendent of the facility in question opined that it was indicated; *Treatment Action Campaign* (n 39 above) para 135, para 3(b) of the order.
[259] *Khosa* (n 9 above) para 98.
[260] See, with respect to a similar fiction operating in the context of the Court's engagement with resource allocation issues, Roux (n 82 above) 9.
[261] Secs 26(2) & 27(2) are clearly mandatory provisions with respect to this basic point - 'the state *must* take ... measures ... to achieve the ... realisation of these rights' (my emphasis).
[262] *Grootboom* (n 22 above) para 45.

Particularly any deliberate retrogression would be a *prima facie* breach, requiring convincing justification.[263]

Reasonableness

Those measures that the state does adopt must be reasonably capable of achieving the realisation of the right in question.[264] To be judged as reasonable in this sense, the state's measures must meet at least the following basic standards:

- *The measures must be comprehensive and co-ordinated.*[265] This means first that the state's programme with respect to a right must address 'critical issues and measures in regard to *all* aspects' of the realisation of that right.[266] Using the right to food as an example, the Committee on ESCR has said this requires the state to adopt measures with respect to the 'production, processing, distribution, marketing and consumption of safe food, as well as parallel measures in the fields of health, education, employment and social security', whilst at the same time taking care 'to ensure the most sustainable management and use of natural and other resources for food at the national, regional, local and household levels'.[267]

  Grootboom, although decided on another basis, is an example of a case where the state's measures to fulfil the right to housing were not sufficiently comprehensive to be reasonable. The state's mistake in *Grootboom* was that, despite having a programme to provide access to housing that the Constitutional Court described as 'a major achievement',[268] it had done nothing with respect to a critical aspect of the right to housing - it had no measures in place with which to provide shelter to people with no roof over their heads. As such, its housing programme was not comprehensive.[269] The requirement of co-ordination holds that a programme must as a whole be coherent, such that responsibilities are allocated to different spheres and institutions within government. To ensure that state measures are comprehensive and co-ordinated, the Committee on ESCR

---

[263] As above. Deliberate retrogression can be argued to breach the negative duty to respect rights. As such it would be subject for its justification to sec 36(1) rather than to the reasonableness scrutiny that applies uniquely to the positive duties imposed by qualified rights; see secs 3.3.2 & 4.1.1 above.
[264] n 22 above, para 41.
[265] n 22 above, para 39.
[266] Committee on ESCR General Comment No12 (n 32 above) para 25.
[267] As above.
[268] *Grootboom* (n 22 above) para 53.
[269] And, according to the various courts' remarks in *Modderklip* (n 112 above), para 22 and *Rudolph* (n 59 above) 77B-84H, still is not.

has suggested that states adopt national strategies or plans of action,[270] which may or may not be presented in national framework laws, through which to give effect to particular socio-economic rights.[271] The Constitutional Court's references in *Grootboom* to the need for a 'national framework' with respect to housing, embodied in 'framework legislation'[272] and to the need for a 'coherent public housing programme'[273] seem to endorse this suggestion by the Committee.[274]

- *Financial and human resources to implement measures must be made available*. In *Grootboom* the Court stated that, for a programme to be reasonable, 'appropriate financial and human resources [must be] available'.[275] The Court has as yet not elaborated on this tantalising phrase. It is clear that the Court is loath to prescribe to the state how and on what it must spend its money - to tell it that it must expend resources so as to do something it did not plan on doing and does not want to do.[276] However, this phrase does seem to indicate that the Court will not allow the state to adopt mere token measures: *Where the state has itself decided and so undertaken to do something*, it is under a legal duty, which the Court would be able to enforce, to allocate the resources reasonably necessary to execute its plans.

In *Kutumela v Member of the Executive Committee for Social Services, Culture, Arts and Sport in the North West Province*,[277] the plaintiffs had applied for the Social Relief of Distress Grant, but despite clearly qualifying for it, did not receive it. Their complaint was that although, in terms of the Social Assistance Act[278] and its regulations, provincial governments were required to provide the grant to qualifying individuals upon successful application, the North West Province had not dedicated the necessary human, institutional and financial resources to do so. The grant was consequently available on paper only, and not in practice. The case resulted in a settlement order that in essence required the province to dedicate the necessary human, institutional and financial resources to provide the grant.

---

[270] See eg Committee on ESCR General Comment No 12 (n 32 above) paras 21-30; General Comment 14 (n 32 above) para 43; General Comment No 15 (n 32 above) paras 37 and 46-54.

[271] See Committee on ESCR, specifically General Comment No 12 (n 32 above) para 29 and General Comment No 15 (n 32 above) para 50.

[272] *Grootboom* (n 22 above) para 40.

[273] n 22 above, para 41.

[274] The South African government also seems to understand its duty to fulfil socio-economic rights in this manner. See eg the recent adoption by the Department of Agriculture, reacting to criticism from various quarters that no coherent and comprehensive plan through which to fulfil the right to food existed in South Africa, of the Integrated Food Security Strategy (a framework document seeking to create institutions through which the fulfilment of the right to food can be co-ordinated), coupled with its ongoing efforts to enact framework legislation in this respect.

[275] n 22 above, para 39.

[276] See below for a discussion of the court's approach to scrutinising the state's budgetary choices.

[277] n 51 above.

[278] n 9 above.

Specifically, it requires the province to acknowledge its legal responsibility to provide Social Relief of Distress effectively to those eligible for it and then to devise a programme to ensure its effective provision. This programme must enable it to process applications for Social Relief of Distress on the same day that they are received, must enable its officials appropriately to assess and evaluate such applications and must enable the eventual payment of the grant. Importantly, the province was ordered to put in place the necessary infrastructure for the administration and payment of the grant, *inter alia* by training officials in the welfare administration in the province.[279]

- *The state's measures must be both reasonably conceived and reasonably implemented.*[280] This element of the Court's reasonableness test is closely related to the requirement of 'reasonable resourcing' outlined above. Of course (also in terms of the understanding of 'progressive realisation' outlined above) it is not sufficient for the state merely to adopt measures on paper. These measures must also in fact be implemented effectively. The *Kutumela* case, described above in the context of adequate resourcing, also illustrates this element of the Court's reasonableness standard. In effect, the Court in *Kutumela* ordered the provincial government to implement a measure that existed in concept but not in practice.

- *The state's measures must be 'balanced and flexible', capable of responding to intermittent crises and to short-, medium- and long-term needs,*[281] *may not exclude 'a significant segment of society',*[282] *may not 'leave out of account the degree and extent of the denial' of the right in question and must respond to the extreme levels of deprivation of people in desperate situations.*[283] These related requirements of flexibility and 'reasonable inclusion'[284] formed the basis for the Constitutional Court's decisions in both *Grootboom* and *Treatment Action Campaign*. In *Grootboom*, the Court found that the state's housing programme was inconsistent with sections 26(1) and (2) because

---

[279] See in this respect also *People's Union for Civil Liberties v Union of India* (n 64 above).
[280] *Grootboom* (n 22 above) para 42.
[281] n 22 above, para 43.
[282] As above.
[283] n 22 above, para 44.
[284] See T Roux 'Understanding *Grootboom* – A response to Cass R Sunstein' (2002) 12:2 *Constitutional Forum* 41 49.

it 'failed to recognise that the state must provide relief for those in desperate need'.[285]

In *Treatment Action Campaign*, the Court held the state's measures to prevent MTCT of HIV to be inconsistent with the Constitution because they 'failed to address the needs of mothers and their newborn children who do not have access'[286] to the pilot sites where Nevirapine was provided, and because the programme as a whole was 'inflexible'.[287] In one sense, these different requirements all relate to the idea that the state's programmes must be *comprehensive*. Any state programme designed to fulfil a socio-economic right, will be incomplete (and as such unreasonable) unless it includes measures through which short term crises in access to the right can be addressed and measures that 'provide relief for those in desperate need'.[288] However, the intriguing question raised by these requirements related to flexibility and reasonable inclusion, and particularly the Constitutional Court's phrase in *Grootboom*, that a programme must take account of the degree and the extent of deprivation with respect to a right,[289] is whether the Court's reasonableness test in this respect requires state measures to prioritise its efforts, both with respect to temporal order and resource allocation, according to different degrees of need.

Does the test require the state to engage in 'sensible priority-setting, with particular attention to the plight of those in greatest need'?[290] Roux has made a strong argument that it does not. He points out that the Court's finding in *Grootboom* requires 'merely *inclusion*' and that 'a government programme that is subject to socio-economic rights will [in terms of this finding] be unreasonable if it fails to *cater* to a significant segment of society.'[291] With respect to the finding in *Grootboom*, Roux's reading is correct: The Court there clearly simply required the state to *take account of* the needs of those most desperate, without at the same time suggesting that the needs of such people should in any concrete way take precedence over other needs.[292] However, it has been suggested that the Court's reasonableness test can take account of a prioritisation according to need, by varying the standard of scrutiny that it applies to particular alleged breaches of socio-economic rights *according to*

---

[285] *Grootboom* (n 22 above) para 66.
[286] *Treatment Action Campaign* (n 39 above) para 67.
[287] n 39 above, para 80.
[288] *Grootboom* (n 22 above) para 66.
[289] n 22 above, para 44.
[290] CR Sunstein 'Social and economic rights? Lessons from South Africa' (2001) 11:4 *Constitutional Forum* 123 127.
[291] Roux (n 284 above) 49.
[292] Brand (n 111 above) 50.

the degree of deprivation suffered by those affected by the breach.[293] According to this view, a court would scrutinise state measures more rigorously where those complaining of their impact are desperately deprived.

This idea has recently been given credence in *Khosa*.[294] As pointed out above, the Court in *Khosa*, possibly for a variety of reasons, applied a substantially stricter standard of scrutiny to the state's exclusion of permanent residents than it applied to the state's HIV prevention policy in *Treatment Action Campaign*,[295] or the state's housing programme in *Grootboom*.[296] The Court in *Khosa* applied a proportionality test, weighing the impact that the exclusion had on the dignity and practical circumstances of indigent permanent residents against the purposes for which the state had introduced the exclusion. The Court did not only find that the basic survival interests of the excluded permanent residents should take precedence over the legitimate purposes for their exclusion.[297] It also, particularly by rejecting the state's arguments that to include permanent residents in the social assistance scheme would place an undue financial burden on the state, potentially requiring the diversion of resources from other social assistance needs,[298] by implication held that the basic survival needs of the permanent residents should take precedence over further expansion of the social assistance system as it applies to South African citizens. The most important factor determining the Court's robust scrutiny in this respect was 'the severe impact [that the exclusion of permanent residents from the scheme was likely to have] on the dignity of the persons concerned, who, unable to sustain themselves, have to turn to others to enable them to meet the necessities of life and are thus cast in the role of supplicants'.[299]

- *The state's measures must be transparent in the sense that they must be made known both during their conception and once conceived to all affected.*[300] This final element of the Court's reasonableness test was added in *Treatment Action Campaign* where the Court held that, in order for it to be reasonable, a programme's 'contents must be made known appropriately'.[301] As *Treatment Action Campaign* itself illustrated, litigants in socio-economic rights cases face great difficulties if it is not possible to ascertain with certainty what the state's measures entail. In a very basic sense, in order to be able to challenge the state's

---

[293] See Brand (n 30 above) 108 and D Bilchitz 'Toward a reasonable approach to the minimum core. Laying the foundations for future socio-economic rights jurisprudence' (2003) 19 *South African Journal on Human Rights* 11 15-17.
[294] n 9 above.
[295] n 39 above.
[296] n 22 above.
[297] *Khosa* (n 9 above) para 82.
[298] n 9 above, paras 60-62.
[299] n 9 above, para 80.
[300] *Treatment Action Campaign* (n 39 above) para 123.
[301] n 39 above, para 123.

position, one has to be able to pinpoint what exactly it is. In this respect, the requirement of transparency is practically very important.[302]

Within available resources

The state's duty to fulfil socio-economic rights must be exercised 'within available resources'. Liebenberg points out that this phrase both provides an excuse to and imposes a duty on the state: It allows the state to attribute its failure to realise a socio-economic right to budgetary constraints; and requires the state in fact to make resources available with which to realise a right.[303]

The Constitutional Court has been circumspect in scrutinising budgetary issues. In some cases it has avoided them altogether. In *Soobramoney*, the Court simply accepted the state's contention that resources were limited as a given, and allowed that fact to determine its decision. The Court interrogated neither the allocation for health purposes from national government, nor in any rigorous way the manner in which it was used at provincial level.[304] In *Grootboom*, resource constraints were not a direct issue. Equally, in *Treatment Action Campaign*,[305] with respect to the question whether provision of Nevirapine should be extended to public health facilities *where the necessary counselling and monitoring infrastructure already existed*, the question of availability of resources was obviated. The manufacturers of Nevirapine had undertaken to provide it for free for five years and no additional infrastructural spending was required to proceed with the extension to such facilities.[306]

In those instances where budgetary issues could not be avoided, the Court has required the state to persuade it of its financial constraint.[307] It has then proceeded to scrutinise the state's assertions in this respect, but on its own terms - that is, taking the limits of the existing budget allocations as a given. The Court has not scrutinised initial budgetary decisions at macro-economic level. In *Treatment Action Campaign*,[308] with respect to the extension of the programme to prevent MTCT of HIV to facilities *without the necessary counselling and monitoring infrastructure*, the state indeed objected that it did not have requisite resources. The Court engaged with and rejected this argument. First, since the litigation between the Treatment Action Campaign and the state had commenced, some provincial governments had proceeded with extending provision of

---

[302] See also Liebenberg (n 7 above) 38.
[303] n 7 above, 44, quoting from *Grootboom* (n 22 above) para 46.
[304] n 8 above, paras 24-28.
[305] n 39 above.
[306] n 39 above, para 19. This prompted the Court to hold that the extension of the programme to these sites 'will not attract any significant additional costs' (para 71).
[307] That the onus in this respect is indeed on the state, rather than on the claimant (see sec 3.3.2 above) is most clearly established in *Khosa* (n 9 above). See in this respect n 316 below.
[308] n 39 above.

Nevirapine to facilities other than the pilot sites,[309] despite the asserted resource constraints. This demonstrated to the Court that in fact 'the requisite political will', rather than resources, was lacking.[310] In addition, whilst the case was heard, the state announced that significant additional resources had been allocated to deal with the HIV pandemic.[311] The Court could therefore find that whatever resource constraints had existed previously, existed no longer.[312]

Also in *Khosa*, the state objected that it would not have the resources with which to extend social assistance grants to indigent permanent residents.[313] Again, the Court considered and rejected this argument.[314] It could do so first because the state had not provided 'clear evidence to show what the additional cost of providing social grants to ... permanent residents would be'.[315] As a result, the Court could not assess whether the additional cost would place an untenable burden on the state.[316] In addition, the state provided the Court with evidence of current spending on and projected increases in spending on social assistance.[317] This enabled the Court to point out that, even at the most pessimistic estimate of the additional cost occasioned by an extension of social assistance to permanent residents,[318] the additional burden on the state would in relative terms be very small.[319]

The Court's approach to scrutinising budgetary issues and to the consequences of that scrutiny is captured in a remark from *Treatment Action Campaign*, where the Court indicates that its scrutiny is not in itself 'directed at rearranging budgets', but that its scrutiny 'may in fact have budgetary implications'.[320] This remark indicates that the Court will neither directly interrogate, nor prescribe the state's initial allocational decisions at macro-economic level. At the same time, it

---

[309] n 39 above, para 118.
[310] n 39 above, para 119.
[311] n 39 above, para 120.
[312] As above.
[313] *Khosa* (n 9 above) paras 60 & 61.
[314] The Court's willingness to do so is not insignificant. See by way of contrast Ncgobo J, dissenting in *Khosa* at para 128: 'Mr Kruger ... estimates that the annual cost of including permanent residents could range between R243 million and R672 million. Policymakers have the expertise ... to present a ... prediction about future social conditions. That is ... the work that policymakers are supposed to do. Unless there is evidence to the contrary, courts should be slow to reject reasonable estimates made by policymakers.'
[315] n 9 above, para 62.
[316] *Khosa* establishes that it is not for the claimant in a socio-economic rights case to show the state is not constrained by lack of resources, but for the state to show it is so constrained (paras 60-62). Because the state couldn't make this showing satisfactorily, the Court rejected its objection, without requiring the claimants to make a contrary showing (para 62). See sec 3.3.2 above.
[317] n 9 above, para 60.
[318] The state estimated that the additional cost would be between R243 million and R672 million. The wide range itself indicated to the Court the absence of clear evidence as to the possible resource consequences of a finding of inconsistency (n 9 above, para 62).
[319] As above.
[320] *Treatment Action Campaign* (n 39 above) para 38.

will not be discouraged to interrogate the reasonableness of state measures, even if a finding of unreasonableness would have the consequence that the state would itself have to rearrange its budget.[321]

This distinction between itself rearranging budgets and taking decisions that have the consequence that budgets must be rearranged by the state is - as with the distinction between effectiveness and relative effectiveness - at least sometimes a fiction. The effect of the decision in *Khosa*, although the Court does not directly 'rearrang[e] budgets', is that the state has to allocate additional resources (however slight an amount in relative terms) to an item that it did not want to finance. However, as Roux has argued, this is perhaps a useful fiction, as it has the virtue of allowing the Court to interfere in allocational choices to the extent required to enforce a right, without admitting to it. As such, it avoids confrontation with the executive.[322]

4.3.3 Remedies

In constitutional matters, including matters dealing with socio-economic rights, courts have wide remedial powers. Section 38 determines that courts must provide 'appropriate relief, including a declaration of rights', whilst section 167 empowers courts to declare invalid law or conduct inconsistent with the Constitution, and in addition to provide any order that is 'just and equitable'.[323] The Constitutional Court has been clear that these powers allow it to fashion new remedies where necessary to 'protect and enforce the Constitution'.[324] An important consideration for the Court in this respect is that its remedies, whether new or existing, must be effective.[325]

In most socio-economic rights cases, providing 'appropriate relief' is unproblematic, requiring courts to do little else than they are used to do in cases decided on the basis of other rights or indeed cases decided on the basis of the common law or ordinary legislation. However, when courts are required to provide relief in cases where the state has been found to breach the duty to fulfil socio-economic rights, or where the state has been found to have interfered in the existing exercise of a socio-economic right and is under a duty to mitigate the impact of that interference, their position is often more difficult. In these cases, the Court's finding requires the state to act affirmatively in order to remedy its breach of the right; to amend its policy or adopt a new policy, or to provide a service that it is not

---

[321] In *Khosa* (n 9 above), the Court did so. Its finding of unreasonableness forces the state to expend resources on providing to permanent residents access to social assistance benefits, something it has not budgeted for itself.
[322] Roux (n 82 above) 9.
[323] Such 'just and equitable' orders include but are not limited to orders limiting the retrospective effect of an order of invalidity or suspending an order of invalidity; sec 172(1)(b)(i) & (ii).
[324] *Fose v Minister of Safety and Security* 1997 3 SA 786 (CC) para 19.
[325] n 324 above, para 69.

currently providing or extend a service to people who do not currently qualify for it.

Such cases necessarily involve 'amorphous, sprawling party structures, allegations broadly implicating the operations of large public institutions such as schools systems ... mental health authorities ... and public housing authorities, and remedies requiring long term restructuring and monitoring of these institutions' policies and programmes.[326] Courts are consequently faced with having to decide to what extent to prescribe directly to the state what it must do, and to what extent and in what manner to retain control of the implementation of their orders, to see that indeed they will be effective.

An obvious way for courts to retain control of the implementation of their orders is through structural or supervisory interdicts.[327] Such interdicts usually require the state to draft a plan for its implementation of the order, which could then be submitted to the court and the other party for approval, and then periodically to report back to the court and the other party with respect to its implementation of that plan. The court could manage the supervision on its own, through the other party to the litigation or through a court-appointed supervisor.[328] In the two cases where a supervisory interdict could have been used, the Constitutional Court elected not to make use of it. In *Grootboom*, the Court issued a simple declaratory order, leaving the remedy of the constitutional defect in its housing programme entirely to the state.[329] In *Treatment Action Campaign*, the Court similarly issued a declarator, coupled with a mandatory order requiring the state to remedy the constitutional defect in its programme for prevention of MTCT of HIV.[330] However, despite confirming that it did indeed have the power to do so, the Court again declined issuing a supervisory interdict, holding that there was no indication that the state would not implement its order properly.[331]

Although the Court's failure in *Grootboom* to use a supervisory interdict certainly trenched on the effectiveness of its order,[332] it is understandable that the Court is circumspect in its use of these

---

[326] CF Sabel & WH Simon 'Destabilisation rights: How public law litigation succeeds' (2004) 117 *Harvard Law Review* 1016 1017.

[327] See, in this respect, W Trengove 'Judicial remedies for violations of socio-economic rights' (1999) 1(4) *ESR Review* 8-11 9-10 and, in general, Sabel & Simon (n 326 above).

[328] The Constitutional Court used such a structural interdict in *August v Electoral Commission* 1999 3 SA 1 (CC), to ensure the state takes steps to make it possible for prisoners to vote in general elections. The various High Courts have made quite regular use of such interdicts in socio-economic rights cases. See eg *Grootboom v Oostenberg Municipality* 2000 3 BCLR 277 (C).

[329] *Grootboom* (n 22 above) para 99.

[330] *Treatment Action Campaign* (n 39 above) para 135.

[331] n 39 above, para 129.

[332] Recently courts have pointed out that the state has for all intents and purposes simply ignored the order in *Grootboom* and has put in place few effective measures to take account of the plight of those in housing crises. See eg *Modderklip* (n 112 above) para 22 and *Rudolph* (n 59 above) paras 77B-84H. See also K Pillay 'Implementation of *Grootboom*: Implications for the enforcement of socio-economic rights' (2002) 6 *Law, Democracy and Development* 255.

remedies. Structural interdicts have to be carefully crafted indeed to be effective.[333] More importantly, structural interdicts have the potential to erode the legitimacy of the Court, both because they directly and on an ongoing basis place the Court in confrontation with the executive, and can involve the Court in the day to day management of public institutions, something at which it is almost bound to fail.[334]

Whether or not a structural interdict would be appropriate in a given case would depend on the nature of the breach in question and particularly on the nature of that which is required for the remedy of that breach.[335]

---

[333] Sabel & Simon (n 326 above) 1017.
[334] n 326 above, 1017-1018.
[335] It is, eg an open question whether a structural interdict would have led to the findings in *Grootboom* being implemented effectively, or whether the policy issue in *Grootboom* was so wide and required such wide-ranging and complex adjustment on the side of the state, that the Court would simply have become bogged down in debilitating detail had it retained jurisdiction.

Two / The right to education

Faranaaz Veriava
Fons Coomans

1 Introduction

The right to education is entrenched at the international and regional level as a fundamental human right. The right to education has also been included in the constitutions of at least 59 countries.[1] Furthermore, the right has, even in countries such as India[2] or the United States of America,[3] where it has not been constitutionally entrenched, nevertheless been recognised as a legal right of fundamental importance.

The importance of entrenching the right to education is based on certain premises.[4] Firstly, it is a precondition for the exercise and understanding of other rights. That is, the enjoyment of a number of civil and political rights, such as freedom of information and the right to vote depend on a minimum level of education, including literacy. Economic, social and cultural rights, such as the right to choose work or to take part in cultural life, can also only be exercised meaningfully once a minimum level of education has been achieved. Secondly, through education individuals can be taught values such as tolerance and respect for human rights. Education therefore can strengthen a culture of human rights within and amongst nations.

---

[1] C Dlamini 'Culture, education, and religion' in D van Wyk *et al* (eds) *Rights and constitutionalism: The new South African legal order* (1994) 580.

[2] In *Unni Krishnan JP v State of AP* AIR 1993 2178 SC, the Indian Supreme Court considered whether the right to education was guaranteed under the Indian Constitution. The right to education in the Indian Constitution (like other socio-economic rights) is listed as a non-justiciable directive principle of state policy, rather than being entrenched as a fundamental right. However, following established interpretative practice, the Court held that fundamental rights and the directive principles are supplementary and complementary to each other and accordingly rendered the right to education justiciable.

[3] In *Brown v Board of Education of Topeka* 347 US 438 (1954) the Court said: 'Today education is perhaps the most important function of state and local governments. Compulsory school attendance laws and the great expenditures for education both demonstrate our recognition of the importance of education to our democratic society. It is required in the performance of our most basic public responsibilities, even service in the armed forces. It is the very foundation of good citizenship. Today it is a principal instrument in awakening the child to cultural values, in preparing him for later professional training, and in helping him to adjust normally to his environment. In these days it is doubtful that any child may reasonably be expected to succeed in life if he is denied the opportunity of an education. Such an opportunity, where the state has undertaken to provide it, is a right that must be made available to all on equal terms.

[4] M Nowak 'The right to education' in A Eide *et al* (eds) *Economic, social and cultural rights: A textbook* (2001) 245. See also K Tomasevski 'Removing obstacles in the way of the right to education' *Right to Education Primers No 1*, 8-9; http://www.right-to-education.org (accessed 31 May 2002).

2   International law

The right to education is recognised in article 26 of the Universal Declaration of Human Rights (1948) (Universal Declaration)[5] and articles 13 and 14 of the International Covenant on Economic, Social and Cultural Rights (1966) (CESCR).[6] The Committee on Economic, Social and Cultural Rights (Committee on ESCR), created in terms of CESCR, has prime responsibility for monitoring socio-economic rights, including the right to education. The Committee has, to this end, issued a number of General Comments in which the rights enumerated in CESCR are given content. The most relevant for the right to education are General Comments No 3,[7] No 11[8] and No 13.[9]

The right to education is widely recognised in regional instruments. The right is included in the European Convention for the Protection of Human Rights and Fundamental Freedoms (European Convention) (1953).[10] It is also included in the American Declaration of the Rights and Duties of Man (1948)[11] and the Protocol of San Salvador to the American Convention on Human Rights (1988).[12] In the African region, the right to education is entrenched in article 17 of the African Charter on Human and Peoples' Rights (African Charter) (1981). Article 11 of the African Charter on the Rights and Welfare of the Child (1990)[13] also provides for the right to education.

The right is also recognised in a number of international instruments dealing with the rights of specific vulnerable groups.[14] In particular, articles 23(3) and (4), 28 and 29 of the Convention on the Rights of the Child (1989) (CRC) contain extensive provisions with regard to the progressive realisation of the right of the child to education and the aims of education. A final relevant document ratified by South Africa is the UNESCO Convention Against Discrimination in Education (1960).

---

[5] See art 26.
[6] See arts 13 & 14.
[7] General Comment No 3 *The nature of states parties' obligations (art 2, para 1 of the Covenant)* (5th session, 1990) [UN Doc E/1991/23]. This General Comment explains terms such as 'to the maximum of available resources', 'achieving progressively the full realisation of the rights' and 'all appropriate means'.
[8] General Comment No 11 *Plans of action for primary education* (21st session, 1999) [UN Doc E/C 12/1999/4]. This General Comment deals with the provisions in art 14.
[9] General Comment No 13 *The right to education (art 13 of the Covenant)* (21st session, 1999) [UN Doc E/C 12/1999/10]. This General Comment deals with the provisions in art 13.
[10] See art 2 Protocol 1.
[11] See art 12.
[12] See art 13.
[13] Art 11 sets out the purposes of education and the duties of state parties with regard to achieving the full realisation of the child's right to education.
[14] See eg art 10 of the Convention on the Elimination of Discrimination Against Women (1979).

3   South African law

Section 29 of the South African Constitution of 1996 provides as follows:

> (1)Everyone has the right -
> (a)to a basic education, including adult basic education, and
> (b)to further education, which the state through reasonable measures, must make progressively available and accessible.
> (2)Everyone has the right to receive education in the official language or languages of their choice in public educational institutions where that education is reasonably practicable. In order to ensure the effective access to, and implementation of, this right, the state must consider all reasonable educational alternatives, including single medium institutions, taking into account -
> (a)equity;
> (b)practicability; and
> (c)the need to redress the results of past racially discriminatory laws and practices.
> (3)Everyone has the right to establish and maintain, at their own expense, independent educational institutions that -
> (a)do not discriminate on the basis of race;
> (b)are registered with the state; and
> (c)maintain standards that are not inferior to standards at comparable public educational institutions.
> (4)Subsection (3) does not preclude state subsidies for independent educational institutions.

Section 29 is consequently made up of a bundle of education rights that are divided into subsections. Each of the subsections confers specific and separate entitlements on right-holders and the different subsections place concomitant obligations on the state that vary in nature and degree. That is, section 29 is a socio-economic right that obliges the state to make education accessible and available for all, but it is also a civil and political right as it contains freedom of choice guarantees, such as language choice in schools and the freedom to establish and maintain independent educational institutions and hence the freedom of individuals to choose between state organised and private education. The socio-economic entitlements under section 29 are also distinguishable from each other. That is, section 29(1)(a) has been described as a 'strong positive right' and section 29(1)(b) has been described as 'a weak positive right'.[15]

Section 29 therefore resists neat categorisation. This seems inevitable: The hybrid nature of section 29 is a demonstration of the interdependence and indivisibility of all human rights. This chapter is an attempt at an analysis of the nature and scope of each of the subsections of section 29 rights, having regard to South Africa's obligations under international law and South Africa's developing constitutional jurisprudence.

The approach to the interpretation of rights, and in particular of socio-economic rights, in the South African Constitution is discussed

---

[15]   R Kriel 'Education' in M Chaskalson *et al* (eds) *Constitutional law of South Africa* (RS 5, 1999) 38-1.

in depth in chapter 1 of this volume.[16] Some aspects of that approach are particularly important in interpreting the right to education.

Rights must be interpreted in their context. In *Government of the Republic of South Africa v Grootboom*, Yacoob J stated:[17]

> Interpreting a right in its context requires the consideration of two types of context. On the one hand, rights must be understood in their textual setting. This will require a consideration of chapter 2 and the Constitution as a whole. On the other hand, rights must also be understood in their social and historical context.

One implication of this excerpt is that all rights in the Bill of Rights should be seen as interrelated and mutually supporting. As stated, education is a precondition for the exercise of other rights. Therefore, the denial of access to education is also the denial of the full enjoyment of other rights that enable an individual to develop to his or her full potential and participate meaningfully in society.

A second implication is that a right must also be interpreted in its social and historical context.[18] In addition, rights must be interpreted with a historically conscious transformative vision in mind.[19]

The apartheid state legislated for a racially separate and unequal system of education.[20] One of the things that characterised apartheid education was gross inequality in the financing of education, with the African population receiving the least. This, in particular for Africans, manifested in high teacher-pupil ratios; unqualified and under-qualified teachers; lack of books, libraries and laboratories; and a curriculum that perpetuated the myth of white superiority and black inferiority.[21]

---

[16] See sec 2.2, chapter 1 of this publication.
[17] 2001 1 SA 46 (CC) para 22.
[18] As above, para 25.
[19] See P de Vos '*Grootboom*, the right of access to housing and substantive equality as contextual fairness' (2001) 17 *South African Journal on Human Rights* 258; A Chaskalson 'The third Bram Fischer memorial lecture: Human dignity as a foundational value of our constitutional order' (2000) 16 *South African Journal on Human Rights* 193.
[20] In the words of HF Verwoerd: 'Racial relations cannot improve if the wrong type of education is given to Natives. They cannot improve if the result of the Native education is the creation of frustrated people who, as a result of the education they received, have expectations of life which circumstances in South Africa do not allow to be fulfilled immediately, when it creates people who are trained for professions not open to them, when there are people who have received a form of cultural training which strengthens their desire for white-collar occupations to such an extent that there are more such people than openings available. Therefore, good racial relations are spoilt when the correct education is not given. Above all, good racial relations cannot exist when the education is given under the control of people who create wrong expectations on the part of the Native himself.' Dlamini (n 1 above) 589.
[21] Dlamini (n 1 above) 590.

Today, despite the existence of an innovative and rights-based curriculum and a policy framework for the transformation of education, the legacy of this inherited system continues to exist.[22] Any interpretation of section 29 must therefore be geared towards redressing this historical disparity.[23]

With these principles in mind, we now proceed to a discussion of each of the subsections of section 29.

3.1 The right to basic education

Section 29(1)(a) states: 'Everyone has the right to a basic education, including adult basic education.'

In the case of *Ex parte Gauteng Provincial Legislature: In re Dispute Concerning the Constitutionality of Certain Provisions of the Gauteng School Education Bill of 1995*,[24] which dealt with the equivalent provision under the interim Constitution,[25] the Court held:

> [This provision] creates a positive right that basic education be provided for every person and not merely a negative right that such a person should not be obstructed in pursuing his or her basic education.

Thus, the state is not only required not to interfere with an individual's enjoyment of the right, but the state is also obliged to provide basic education.[26] Save for acknowledging this positive obligation in the provision of basic education, our courts have to date

---

[22] The extent to which our schools continue to be riddled with such historic inequalities may be best surmised from details about the lack of basic facilities disclosed by the Minister of Education, Kader Asmal, in parliament in May 2001, namely that 45% (12 257) of the country's 27 148 schools remained without electricity, 27% (7 409) were without clean water, 66% (17 907) of schools were without adequate sanitation, 11,7% (3 188) did not have any sanitation at all and 34% did not have telephones. In the same address, the Minister also noted that none of the nine provinces had completed the delivery of learning materials by the first day of the 2001 school year, and that by early May 2001 most provinces had still not yet completed delivery of learning materials. He also stated that in 2000 there were 67 000 unqualified or under-qualified teachers in South African schools. *Mail & Guardian* (2002-01-11).

[23] Such an approach will give effect to the values as set out in sec 39(1)(a) as well as the Preamble to the Constitution, which recognises the need to 'heal the divisions of the past and establish a society based on democratic values, social justice and fundamental rights; [and] improve the quality of life of all citizens and free the potential of each person'. In *S v Mhlungu* 1995 7 BCLR 793 (CC) para 112, the Court acknowledged the interpretive value of the Preamble.

[24] *In re School Education Bill of 1995 (Gauteng)* 1996 4 BCLR 537 para 9. The main issue in this case was whether or not sec 32(c) of the interim Constitution, which guaranteed every person the right 'to establish where practicable, educational institutions based on a common culture, language or religion, provided that there shall be no discrimination on the ground of race', entailed a positive obligation on the state to accord to every person the right to require the state to establish educational institutions based on a common culture, language or religion as long as there is no discrimination on the ground of race. The Court held that no such positive obligation in respect of sec 32(c) existed. This is discussed in greater detail below.

[25] Sec 32 Constitution of the Republic of South Africa Act 200 of 1993.

[26] Compare with the interpretation of the European Court of Human Rights of art 2 of the European Convention. In the *Belgian Linguistic Cases* 1 EHRR 241 and 1 EHRR 252, the Court found that the negative formulation of the right indicates that state parties do not recognise such a right to education as would require them to establish, at their own expense, a particular type of education or education at any particular level; rather it guaranteed a right of access to existing institutions at a given time.

not had the opportunity to comment on the scope and content of the right to basic education and the extent and nature of the state's obligations in respect thereof.

The obligations engendered by section 29(1)(a) are distinguishable from other socio-economic rights in the Constitution. These rights - such as the rights of access to housing and health care services and the rights to food, water and social security - are qualified to the extent that they are made subject to the adoption of 'reasonable legislative and other measures' and 'progressive realisation' ... 'within [the state's] available resources'. The right to basic education, including adult basic education, is by contrast unqualified and is therefore an absolute right.[27] In *Grootboom*, the standard of review established in respect of the qualified rights was to determine whether or not state measures were *reasonable* in progressively facilitating access to the right in question.[28]

This was confirmed in the recent case of *Minister of Health & Others v Treatment Action Campaign & Others* (the *TAC* case).[29]

From a textual reading of section 29(1)(a), when compared to these other socio-economic rights in the Constitution, the unqualified and absolute nature of the right to basic education requires a standard of review higher than that used in respect of the qualified rights to determine the extent of the state's obligations in respect of the right to basic education. It is submitted that this higher standard requires that the state implement measures to give effect to the right as a matter of absolute priority. This would require that the state prioritise those programmes, in its policies and budgetary allocations that seek to give effect to the right over its other spending requirements. Thus, where the state fails to allocate resources for the building of a primary school in a particular area, an individual learner from that area may have a direct claim against the state to provide adequate primary school facilities. An inquiry as to whether or not the state has with absolute priority sought to give effect to the right for all entitled to enjoyment of the right requires an understanding of the scope and content of the right to basic education and an evaluation of the extent to which state policies and practice actually seek to give effect to the right.

The language of prioritisation of the right to basic education under section 29(1)(a), over and above the other socio-economic rights mentioned above, and the inclusion of the right to further education in terms of section 29(1)(b) may be compared to the prioritisation of the right to free primary education in terms of article 13(2)(a) of CESCR over the other education rights listed under article 13 of

---

[27] See *Grootboom* (n 17 above) para 38, where the Court confirmed that socio-economic rights imposed obligations on the state, but stated that those obligations were in certain instances, such as housing, not absolute or unqualified, but had to be defined by these three key elements.

[28] As above, paras 39-44, where the Court set out some of the criteria for evaluating whether measures are reasonable. Such review need not necessarily require an inquiry into the content of the right or whether the measures were the most desirable under the circumstances.

[29] 2002 (5) SA 721 (CC) para 38.

CESCR. That is, the text of article 13(2)(a) that 'primary education shall be free and available to all' is also unconditional, absolute and without a reference to progressiveness. Subsections (b) and (c), by way of contrast, make reference to the progressive introduction of free secondary and higher education.[30] The interpretation accorded to the differences in the texts of these subsections confirms that state parties are to prioritise primary education over and above secondary and higher education and to take immediate steps to secure the former.[31]

The meaning of the term 'basic education' has yet to be decided by South African courts. When the opportunity does finally present itself, the courts should be guided by the objectives to be achieved from the guarantee of the right when defining the scope of the right. The World Declaration on Education for All states that:[32]

> [T]he focus of basic education must, therefore, be on actual learning acquisition and outcome rather than exclusively upon enrolment, continued participation in organised programmes and completion of certification requirements.

'Basic education' is accordingly viewed in the Declaration in terms of meeting basic learning needs (these needs include both essential learning tools such as literacy, oral expression, numeracy, problem-solving skills and basic learning content such as knowledge, skills, values, and attitudes) which essentially empower individuals to participate in and interact in the societies in which they live with dignity and with equal opportunities for employment in pursuing their life's vocations. Similarly, what constitutes basic education in the South African context cannot be arbitrarily defined in terms of age or the completion of a particular level of schooling but should be determined in accordance with the educational interest to be achieved by the guarantee of the right. The meaning should therefore be wider than that of only primary education, or compulsory education in terms of the South African Schools Act (Schools Act)[33] and should include secondary education, without which an individual's access to the full enjoyment of other rights, such as the freedom to choose a trade, occupation or profession (section 22) would be severely limited. Such a purposive understanding of the term is also strengthened by the inclusion in the right of the guarantee to provide adult basic education (ABE) so as to ensure the development of all individuals in society.[34]

---

[30] F Coomans 'In search of the core content of the right to education' in D Brand & S Russel (eds) *Exploring the core content of socio-economic rights: South African and international perspectives* (2002) 163.
[31] General Comment No 13 (n 9 above) paras 14, 51 & 57.
[32] Adopted in Jomtien in 1990; art 4. See also arts 1 & 5. This document is not a legally binding document.
[33] 84 of 1996. In terms of sec 3(1) of the Schools Act, it is compulsory for a learner to attend school from the age of seven until the age of 15 or the ninth grade, whichever comes first.
[34] The National Department of Education's Policy Document on Adult Basic Education and Training (1997) 5 defines adult basic education as education that 'subsumes both literacy and post-literacy as it seeks to connect literacy with basic (general) adult education on the one hand and with training for income generation on the other hand'.

As stated above, an inquiry into whether or not the state has met its obligations in respect of the right to basic education, as an unqualified right, necessitates a determination of the scope and content of the right in order to determine whether the state has with absolute priority sought to give effect to the right. Thus, unlike as in the *Grootboom* and *TAC* cases, where the Court was able to avoid an inquiry into the content of the rights to housing and health respectively, it is essential in respect of the right to basic education to determine the nature of the entitlements which make up the content of the right and which would achieve the basic learning needs secured by the right.

The interpretation of the 'core content' of socio-economic rights in the General Comments to CESCR is generally employed in international human rights law in respect of those rights which are subject to the qualifiers - 'reasonable legislative and other measures' and 'progressive realisation' ... 'within [the state's] available resources' - so as to ensure that nation states do provide for at least the minimum essential levels in respect of those rights and do not just attribute failures in respect thereof to a lack of resources. The unqualified nature of section 29(1)(a) obviates the necessity of setting minimum obligations in respect of the right to basic education. However, the identification of the core content of basic education as well as other qualified and unqualified rights in international human rights law is nevertheless extremely useful as such interpretations assist in defining the entitlements which make up the content of the rights and in so doing establish the broad principles against which to measure state compliance with its obligations in terms of the right.[35]

The notion of a 'core content' of the right of access to adequate housing as defined in the General Comments to CESCR was rejected in *Grootboom*.[36] The gist of the Court's reasoning in *Grootboom* was that there is a wide range of diversity as to what would constitute adequate housing, given the variations in housing needs, and that, based on the available information in that case, it was unable to determine the content of the right of access to adequate housing within a South African context. However, the Court stated explicitly that 'there may be cases where it may be possible and appropriate to have regard to the content of minimum core obligations to determine whether the measures taken by the state are reasonable'. This approach in *Grootboom* was confirmed in the *TAC* case.[37] The Court in doing this has left the door open for defining the content of socio-economic rights, in respect of a reasonableness inquiry for those

---

[35] For a similar argument, see F Viljoen 'Children's rights: A response from a South African perspective' in Brand & Russel (n 30 above) 201. According to Viljoen, the argument in favour of clarifying core content in respect of unqualified rights such as children's rights in sec 28 is the need to clarify vague terms.
[36] *Grootboom* (n 17 above) paras 29-33.
[37] *TAC* (n 29 above) para 34.

socio-economic rights that are qualified, but only in so far as a country-specific core is capable of being ascertained.[38]

To the extent, therefore, that the identification of the content of the socio-economic rights and the state obligations in terms of such rights remains a part of South African jurisprudence, the identification of the content of the right to basic education is not only appropriate, but also necessary in respect of the right to basic education. The identification of the content of the right to basic education is also possible in a South African context, in that learning outcomes for meeting basic learning needs are not diverse but are consistent for all learners and given the availability of statistical and other information relating to current provisioning for learners in South Africa, it is possible to determine the exact basic learning needs for learners in South Africa.[39]

General Comment No 13 of the Committee on ESCR defines article 13(2) of CESCR as the right to receive an education. It states that, while the exact standard secured by the right to basic education may vary according to conditions within a particular state, education must exhibit the following features: availability, accessibility, acceptability and adaptability.[40] This four 'A' scheme is a useful device to analyse the content of the right to basic education in terms of section 29(1)(a), and the reciprocal obligations deriving from this unqualified right. The extent to which these criteria are being met in South Africa through the existing policy framework, that is, the Schools Act[41] and the National Education Policy Act[42] and their accompanying regulations, as well as the case law, is analysed briefly below.

---

[38] *Grootboom* (n 17 above) paras 32-33. Compare with the view of Coomans, who argues that the core content of a right should be universal; and that a country-dependant core would undermine the concept of the universality of human rights (Coomans (n 30 above) 180). See also General Comment No 13 (n 9 above) para 57, which defines the elements of the core content of the right to education. In General Comment No 3 (n 7 above), the Committee confirms that state parties have 'a minimum core obligation to ensure the satisfaction of, at the very least, minimum essential levels of each of the rights enunciated in the Covenant, including 'the most basic forms of education'. In the context of art 13, this core includes an obligation to ensure the right of access to public educational institutions and programmes on a non-discriminatory basis; to ensure education conforms to the objectives set out in art 13(1); to provide primary education for all in accordance with art 13(2)(a); to adopt and implement a national strategy which includes provision for secondary, higher and fundamental education; and to ensure free choice of education without interference from the state or third parties, subject to conformity with 'minimum educational standards' (arts 13(3) & (4)).

[39] See eg National Department of Education/Human Sciences Research Council (HSRC) *School Register of Needs Surveys* (1996 & 2000) HSRC, Pretoria. These surveys collate the data as to the infrastructure provisioning of all schools in South Africa.

[40] General Comment No 13 (n 9 above) para 6. See also Preliminary Report of the Special Rapporteur on the Right to Education, Katarina Tomasevski, submitted in accordance with the Commission on Human Rights resolution 1998/33 Doc E/CN 4/1999/49; http://www.right-to-education.org (accessed 31 May 2002).

[41] n 33 above.

[42] 27 of 1996.

3.1.1 Availability

Availability relates broadly to the availability of functioning education institutions and programmes. Provisioning for basic infrastructure for schools is guided by the principles set out in the Norms and Standards for School Funding.[43] This funding policy aims primarily at providing redress to the most underdeveloped and the very poor schools and communities by directing that capital expenditure targets those in 'need', that is, those areas where no schools exist or where schools are overcrowded, and by directing that 60% of available recurrent, non-personnel expenditure should go to 40% of the poorest schools in each provincial education department.[44] Allocation for such recurrent expenditure is made by ranking schools from the poorest to the least poor and subsequent resource allocation is made according to the position of a school on the poverty index.

While this funding policy is clearly premised on a recognition by the state of the need to redress the historical unequal financing for basic infrastructure provisioning, the wording of the funding policy[45] and its practical impact suggest that state provisioning for basic infrastructure in terms of this policy is based on an interpretation of the right to basic education as a right that may be progressively realised, rather than as an unqualified right which the state must provide for as a matter of absolute priority. That is, the policy directs that funding for basic infrastructure targets those schools that are desperately lacking in facilities and prioritises those schools when allocating resources.

However, if the state is to comply with its obligations in terms of the right and provide for the right as a matter of absolute priority it should determine the standard of provisioning which would provide adequate facilities for all schools and allocate resources in terms of this standard of provisioning.[46] The effect of the provisioning in terms of the current approach is that the state is failing to provide facilities for all learners of a sufficient standard necessary to meet the basic learning needs of all learners. The impact of the funding policy is felt most by the so-called 'middle schools' that in terms of the current funding policy qualify for less state funding and, in the absence of

---

[43] General Notice 2362 (*Government Gazette* 19347) October 1998. These regulations have been developed pursuant to sec 35 of the Schools Act (n 33 above) and sec (3)(4)(g) of the Education Policy Act (n 42 above).

[44] Capital expenditure relates to the building of classrooms and other construction, while non-personnel expenditure is described as maintenance of school buildings, municipal services and utilities, and learner support materials.

[45] Para 44 states that '[a]n important assumption underlying these national norms is that the national and provincial levels of government will honour the state's duty, in terms of the Constitution and the SASA [Schools Act], to *progressively* provide resources to safeguard the right to education of all South Africans. However, educational needs are always greater than the budgetary provision for education. To effect redress and improve equity, therefore, public spending on schools must be specifically targeted to the needs of the poorest' (our emphasis).

[46] An example of what is available is that provided by para 6a of General Comment No 13 of the Committee on ESCR (n 9 above), in terms of which 'all institutions and programmes are likely to require buildings or other protection from the elements, sanitation facilities for both sexes, safe drinking water, trained teachers receiving domestically competitive salaries, teaching materials and so on'.

strong socio-economic parent communities, face the danger of real financial deterioration.[47] Also, where, as described above, an alarmingly high percentage of schools remain dysfunctional because of a lack of basic infrastructure such as classrooms, sanitation, clean water and electricity, the funding available in terms of the targeting model remains inadequate.

3.1.2 Accessibility

Accessibility relates to education being available to all on the basis of the principle of non-discrimination, economic accessibility as well as physical accessibility. In terms of the latter, where learners continue to walk distances of up to eight kilometres a day to get to school,[48] whether the state is providing schools that are physically accessible is questionable.

Accessibility of education is also premised on the principle of non-discrimination. The Schools Act has a general prohibition against unfair discrimination.[49] It also prohibits excluding a learner from admission to a school on certain specified grounds, such as the administering of an entrance examination as a basis for admission, failure to subscribe to the mission statement of a school, parental inability to pay schools fees, (this is dealt with in more detail below) and the refusal by parents to sign a waiver in respect of future liability by the school. The case of *Matukane & Others v Laerskool Potgietersrus*[50] dealt with discrimination on the basis of race. In this case the High Court held that black learners had been unfairly discriminated against when their application to a dual medium school had been rejected on the basis that the school had an exclusively Afrikaans culture and ethos, which would be detrimentally affected by admitting learners from a different cultural background.[51]

---

[47] 'Middle schools, as schools that do not exist in abject poverty, but which nevertheless lack stable income from user fees, become financially vulnerable because of insufficient funds, and are therefore unable to provide adequate services to learners. Middle schools fall in the per learner range of between R127 and R207 per year in terms of funding received, while it costs R300 per learner to maintain an ordinary school.' RA Wildeman 'School funding norms 2001: Are more learners benefiting?' (2001) *IDASA Budget Information Service* 7, 79.
[48] *The Star* (2002-01-17).
[49] Sec 5.
[50] 1996 3 SA 223 (WLD).
[51] The issue of discrimination on the basis of age was also raised in the case of *Minister of Education v Harris* 2001 4 SA 1297(CC), but the case was not decided on that basis. The case dealt with the legality of a notice, which stated that a learner might only be admitted to grade one at an independent school if he or she turns seven in the course of that calendar year. The applicant's parents challenged the validity of the notice on a variety of grounds, *inter alia* that it unfairly discriminated against children on the grounds of age and was against the best interests of children such as their daughter. The Constitutional Court in this case found that the matter was best decided not on the broad constitutional questions raised, but on whether the Minister had the power under the National Education Policy Act (n 42 above) to issue the notice he did. The Court held that that Act only gave the Minister powers to determine policy and not to impose binding law.

A more complex issue is that of the economic accessibility of basic education within the current regulatory framework that allows school fees to be charged but which at the same time provides for a system of exemptions from the payment of school fees for those learners who cannot afford to pay school fees.

In terms of the Schools Act, once state allocations to schools are made, the remaining financial requirements in school budgets, in particular deficiencies in basic provisioning and personnel, can only be provided through the charging of school fees or through private fund raising.[52] The regulatory framework attempts to alleviate the financial burden of the charging of school fees for parents who cannot afford to pay school fees in two ways. First, it makes the determination whether or not fees should be charged at a particular school an issue of individual school governance. Second, it allows parents who cannot afford to pay school fees to apply for exemptions from the payment of schools fees at schools where fees are charged.

Thus, the Schools Act provides that a school may only charge school fees when a majority of parents attending the annual budget meeting adopts a resolution to do so. It then provides that parents must at this meeting determine the amount of fees to be charged and the criteria to exempt those parents who are unable to pay fees.[53] The Exemption of Parents from the Payment of School Fees Regulations set the parameters for these exemptions.[54] A school must fully exempt parents whose annual incomes are less than the annual school fees times ten, and partially exempt those whose annual incomes are less than 30 times but more than 10 times the annual school fees. Partial exemptions are subject to the discretion of the school governing body.[55] These regulations also set out the procedures for making an application for exemption and for appealing the decision of the school governing body in this respect. Finally, the Schools Act provides that where parents have not applied for exemptions and have failed to pay the fees set by a school, the school can sue the parents for the school fees.[56] No compensation is provided to schools that grant exemptions to parents.

It has been suggested that the protection afforded to basic education in the South African Constitution - which does not explicitly guarantee free education - does not preclude a system that permits the charging of school fees, but does imply that no one should be

---

[52] In particular, sec 34(1) states that '[t]he State must fund public schools from public revenue on an equitable basis in order to ensure the proper exercise of the rights of learners to education and the redress of past inequalities in education provision', and sec 36 states that '[a] governing body of a public school must take all reasonable measures within its means to supplement the resources supplied by the State in order to improve the quality of education provided by the school to all learners at the school'. Sec 39 regulates the procedure for charging school fees. This is discussed in more detail below.

[53] Sec 39.

[54] Government Notice 1293 (*Government Gazette* 19347) October 1998. These regulations have been developed pursuant to sec 39(4) and sec 61 of the Schools Act (n 33 above).

[55] Reg 3.

[56] Secs 40-41.

denied a basic education owing to lack of resources.[57] In terms of this approach, the issue is whether or not the regulatory framework, in particular the exemption system that attempts to ameliorate the economic hardships associated with the charging school, is effective in guaranteeing all learners access to education. Increasingly there are concerns that the current system does not facilitate access for learners who cannot afford to pay school fees as incidents are documented that suggest that many schools are reluctant to implement exemptions laws and are unlawfully excluding learners from school if their parents are unable to pay the fees charged at the school.[58] Perhaps an explanation for this is that for as long as schools are reliant on school fees to supplement school budgets, and in the absence of the state compensating schools for granting exemptions to parents who cannot afford to pay school fees, schools will remain without an incentive to abide by the regulatory framework, thus rendering it ineffective.

Other factors that impede a learner's access to education within the current regulatory framework and which militate against the efficacy of the current system have also been documented. These have been summarised as follows:[59]

> First, many families who would be eligible for exemptions do not apply because of the burden it imposes - ie the process is too time-consuming, the cost in dignity or in spending time to acquire information is too high, or because the school discriminates unfairly against those who are granted exemptions. Second the statutory exemption system in many instances does not cover secondary fees, like uniforms and transport. Third, the exemption scheme is insufficiently broad to adequately cover those at the margins who do not qualify for any sort of exemption, but for whom school fees would be an unconstitutionally heavy burden. Finally, some evidence indicates that school governing bodies abuse their discretion by significantly restricting partial exemptions to a small percentage of the fee, or arbitrarily denying those who have applied for a partial exemption.

---

[57] See S Liebenberg 'Education' in D Davis *et al* (eds) *Fundamental rights in the Constitution: Commentary and cases* (1997) 536.

[58] On 16 September 2002, the Minister of Education, Kader Asmal, announced a review of all mechanisms and policies related to school funding. In a press release he said: 'I am concerned about reports of inadequate resourcing of many poor schools and the rising financial burden for education that poor parents are expected to bear. My information suggests that rising school fees and the cost of items such as transport; uniforms and books appear to be the main contributory factors. I am also disturbed by reports of poor learners being forced to pay school fees or face exclusion. The law stipulates that parents or guardians who do not have sufficient income relative to the school fees are automatically exempted from paying fees. Sadly, many schools are breaking the law.' Press Statement, Department of Education (16 September 2002). The Education Rights Project (ERP) has also dealt with complaints from parents where schools are failing to adopt and implement exemption policies at their schools. These schools deny learners access in various ways, by, for example withholding of their report cards or sending them home until school fees have been paid. See in this regard F Veriava & B Ramadiro 'Education is a right' *Sowetan* (2003-01-17). See also K Porteus 'Education financing: Framing inclusion or exclusion' in S Vally (ed) *Quarterly review of education and training in South Africa* (2002) 10.

[59] D Roithmayr 'The constitutionality of school fees in public education' *ERP Issue Paper 1* 17; http://www.law.wits.ac.za/cals/lt (accessed 30 September 2002).

Another argument challenging the constitutionality of the regulatory framework is that the system of charging school fees *per se* discriminates against poor learners on the basis of race and class and accordingly violates these learners' rights to equality. That is, since schools are reliant on school fees to supplement school budgets, those schools in wealthier communities are able to raise funds through school fees that will be able to provide learners with the sufficient facilities necessary for a basic education, while those schools situated in poor communities where parents cannot pay school fees will not be able to provide such facilities. This, it is argued, has resulted in the 're-stratification' of public schools because it creates and reinforces apartheid era class and racial inequalities. Accordingly the system constitutes unfair discrimination against learners in fee-poor schools.[60]

The final issue in respect of the regulatory framework is the extent to which it complies with South Africa's obligations in terms of international law. That education, at least at primary level, should be free and compulsory is entrenched at an international and regional level.[61] The current regulatory framework that provides for exemptions cannot be deemed to be 'free' education within the international understanding of the term. Article 28(1)(a) of CRC (which has been ratified by South Africa) requires that state parties 'make primary education compulsory and available free to all'. Article 28(1)(b), by contrast, provides that state parties should make secondary education 'available and accessible to every child, and take appropriate steps such as the introduction of free education and offering financial assistance in the case of need', thus suggesting that state parties take steps such as those in terms of the above-mentioned exemption provisions only with regard to secondary and not primary education, which should be free.[62] South Africa is accordingly not meeting its international obligations in terms of the provision of 'free education'. Finally, while education in South Africa is in most cases not free, it is compulsory until the age of 15 or the ninth grade, whichever comes first.[63] It has been argued that such a

---

[60] As above, 20-31.
[61] Art 26(1) of the Universal Declaration guarantees that education shall be free, at least in the elementary stages. Elementary education is also compulsory. Art 13(2)(a) of CESCR guarantees free and compulsory primary education and art 13(2)(b) makes provision for the progressive introduction of free secondary education. Art 28(1)(a) of CRC also guarantees free and compulsory primary education and art 28(1)(b) obliges state parties to make secondary education 'available and accessible to every child, and take appropriate steps such as the introduction of free education and offering financial assistance in the case of need'. Art 11(3)(a) of the African Charter on the Rights and Welfare of the Child requires state parties to take all appropriate measures to 'provide free and compulsory basic education.'
[62] See also para 7 of General Comment No 11 (n 8 above) for the interpretation given to the term 'free of charge' in art 14 of CESCR. See also the observations of the UN Committee on the Rights of the Child when examining South Africa's initial report on the implementation of CRC. The Committee, 'while noting that the law provides for compulsory education between the ages of 7 and 15, is concerned that education is not free'. UN Doc CRC/C/15/Add.122 para 34 (23-2-2000).
[63] Sec 3(1) of the Schools Act (n 33 above).

provision making education compulsory is irreconcilable with the payment of fees. That is:[64]

> Nobody can be required to do the impossible and thus parents cannot be obliged to ensure that their children attend school if they cannot afford the cost of schooling. Making education compulsory was thus contingent on making it free.
>
> ...
>
> The human rights obligation of Government to adequately fund education exists so that children would not have to pay for their schooling or remain deprived of it when they cannot afford the cost. Children cannot wait to grow, hence their prioritized right to education in international human rights law. The damage of denied education while they are growing up cannot be retroactively remedied.

The Department of Education, acknowledging some of these problems, has published a Plan of Action for 'Improving Access to Free and Quality Basic Education'.[65] This Plan is vague as to the precise nature of the proposed reforms, but nevertheless promises an array of reforms to facilitate better access to schools that include *inter alia* the regulation of the cost of uniforms and books and improved systems for schools to administer their budgets. The Plan also suggests that school fees will be abolished in the very poorest schools, and that these schools will be obliged to seek departmental approval before charging school fees. It then suggests a system for the closer monitoring and enforcement of the exemption policy for the majority of schools where school fees will continue to be charged. It also suggests a 'basic minimum package' of state funding to bring about adequate funding of schools. The Department of Education was to begin its implementation of the plan by 2004. To date, however, this has not happened.

3.1.3 Acceptability

Acceptability in basic education relates to whether or not curricula and teaching methods are sufficient to meet basic learning needs such as literacy, oral expression or numeracy. The scope of the acceptability of basic education has been broadened in international human rights jurisprudence to include a system of education that seeks to protect the individual rights of learners on issues such as language rights, parental choice and discipline of learners.[66]

---

[64] K Tomasevski 'Free and compulsory education for all children: The gap between promise and performance' *Right to Education Primers, Primer 2* 13; http://www.right-to-education.org (accessed 31 May 2002) and K Tomasevski 'The right to education' Report submitted by the Special Rapporteur, UN Doc E/CN.4/2004/45 para 8. See also K Tomasevski *Education denied - Costs and remedies* (2003).

[65] Department of Education (2003) *Plan of Action - Improving access to free and quality education for all* http://education.pwv.gov.za/DOE_sites (accessed 30 June 2003).

[66] K Tomasevski 'Human rights obligations: Making education available, accessible and adaptable' *Right to Education Primers, Primer No 3* 13-16; http://www.right-to-education.org (accessed 31 May 2002).

The Schools Act addresses the rights of learners when schools sanction their behaviour in detail.[67] In the case of *Antonie v Governing Body, Settlers High School, and Others*,[68] a Rastafarian learner challenged the School Governing Body's decision which found her guilty of serious misconduct and suspended her for five days for wearing a dreadlock hairstyle and covering her head with a cap. The learner was found to have violated the school's code of conduct that contained a prohibition pertaining to the appearance of learners. The Court set aside the decision of the School Governing Body on the basis that the learner's failure to comply with the prohibition was assessed in a 'rigid manner'. This, according to the Court, made 'nonsense' of the values and principles developed in accordance with the National Guidelines for the Consideration of Governing Bodies in Adopting a Code for Learners Guidelines as well as the Constitution, in terms of which the School Governing Body ought to have given 'adequate recognition' to the learner's need to indulge in freedom of expression.

The Schools Act also includes a ban on corporal punishment in schools.[69] This was the subject of an unsuccessful challenge in *Christian Education South Africa v Minister of Education*.[70] The case was brought by a group of independent Christian schools. They contended that 'corporal correction' was an integral part of the Christian ethos in these schools, and hence the blanket prohibition imposed by section 10 of the Schools Act should be declared invalid as it limited the individual, parental and community rights of the parents to practise their religion. The Court found that to the extent that the ban on corporal punishment was a restriction on the ability of parents to practise their religion and culture, this was justifiable as the practice of corporal punishment was inconsistent with the values underlying the Bill of Rights. Language and parental choice rights are dealt with later in this chapter.

---

[67] Sec 8 together with the Regulations on the 'Guidelines for the Consideration of Governing Bodies in Adopting a Code for Learners' sets the parameters for defining which conduct on the part of learners will be sanctioned and what such sanctions should entail. Sec 9 includes the due process provisions for the discipline of learners.
[68] 2002 4 SA 738 CPD.
[69] Sec 10.
[70] 2000 10 BCLR 1051.

3.1.4 Adaptability

Adaptability in basic education relates to the flexibility of the system of education to adapt to the changing needs in society, and to respond to the diverse needs of learners within their diverse social and cultural settings, most particularly the needs of the more vulnerable segments of society.[71]

The state's attempt to address this is reflected in its policy framework. The Admission Policy for Ordinary Schools Act[72] makes provision for non-citizens to be treated in the same way as other learners,[73] and for learners with special needs to be accommodated in ordinary schools where 'reasonably practical'.[74] The National Policy on HIV/AIDS for Learners and Educators in Public Schools and Students and Educators in Further Education and Training Institutions[75] makes provision for the increasing need to manage this pandemic in schools and to guarantee the rights of learners and educators living with HIV/AIDS.

In respect of Adult Basic Education (ABE), according to the state's policy document, there are approximately 9,4 million potential ABE learners,[76] yet, according to the South African Human Rights Commission's (SAHRC) 2001 socio-economic rights report, the National Department of Education has indicated that ABE as a budgetary line item for education began only in the year 2000/2001, thus accounting for the very low to non-existent spending on ABE in the provinces. Some provinces reported to the SAHRC that they had suspended ABE to give priority to other programmes.[77] Such an approach is obviously contrary to the absolute priority obligation imposed on the state by the inclusion of ABE in section 29(1)(a) of the Constitution.

A final note in respect of section 29(1)(a) is that, while it is not subject to any internal limitations and is in that sense 'absolute', it is nevertheless subject to the general limitations clause in terms of section 36, as with all other rights in the Bill of Rights. Therefore any claim to the right may nevertheless become subject to 'limited resources' arguments under the limitation clause. Such arguments

---

[71] *Grootboom* (n 17 above) para 44. One of the requirements for evaluating whether or not a programme is reasonable is to evaluate to what extent such a programme responds to the needs of the most desperate in society.

[72] 27 of 1996.

[73] See secs 19-21. In terms of sec 21, the admission of children of 'illegal aliens' to schools is dependent on such parents showing that they are in the process of legalising their stay. Such a provision is only workable in the context of liberal immigration policies and practices committed to assisting such persons, as opposed to deporting them once identified.

[74] See secs 22-25. See also White Paper 6: Special Needs Education July 2001, for a detailed and critical analysis of the state's policy provisioning for learners with special needs. See S Vally 'Special needs education - Building an inclusive education and training system' in M Tshoane (ed) *Quarterly Review of Education and Training in South Africa* (2001) 7.

[75] General Notice 1926 (*Government Gazette* 20372) August 1999.

[76] n 34 above, para 1.3.

[77] South African Human Rights Commission *Economic and social rights report* (2001) 120.

would of course be subject to the stringent requirements imposed by the balancing test of the limitations clause.[78]

3.2 The right to further and higher education

Section 29(1)(b) states: 'Everyone has the right to further education, which the state, through reasonable measures, must make progressively available and accessible.'

This right, unlike the right to basic education, does not place an absolute obligation on the state to provide further education since it is subject to certain of the qualifiers employed in respect of the other socio-economic rights in the Constitution. The term 'progressively' suggests that it is a right that may be realised over time. In *Grootboom* the Court stated:[79]

> The term 'progressive realisation' shows that it was contemplated that the right could not be realised immediately. But the goal of the Constitution is that the basic needs of all in our society be effectively met and the requirement of progressive realisation means that the state must take steps to achieve this goal. It means that accessibility should be progressively facilitated: legal, administrative, operational and financial hurdles should be examined and, where possible, lowered over time.

The text of section 29(1)(b) also suggests that the standard of review in respect of this section (as in *Grootboom*) is likely to be whether the measures taken to make further education available and accessible are 'reasonable'. A feature of section 29(1)(b) that distinguishes it from the other qualified socio-economic rights is that the phrase 'within available resources' is omitted from the text of the clause. Thus, this could be interpreted to mean that where a state policy or programme is challenged in terms of this right, the criteria for assessing the reasonableness of the programme, could, in addition to those set out in *Grootboom*, also entail an evaluation of the sufficiency of funding available for the policy or programme's implementation.

The term 'further education' is not used in international legal instruments.[80] In South Africa, further education and training is defined in the Further Education and Training Act[81] as levels above 'general education' but below 'higher education',[82] while higher education is defined in terms of the Higher Education Act[83] as 'all learning programmes leading to qualifications higher than grade 12 or its equivalent in terms of the National Qualifications Framework'. This includes universities, technikons and colleges.[84] Despite this

---

[78] *S v Mhlungu* (n 23 above). Also see ch 1 of this volume at sec 3.3.2 for a discussion of this issue.
[79] *Grootboom* (n 17 above) para 45. See further General Comment No 3 (n 7 above) para 9 and General Comment No 13 (n 9 above) paras 43-48.
[80] These instruments distinguish between 'primary', 'secondary' and 'higher' education.
[81] 98 of 1998.
[82] Sec 1, general education being a reference to the compulsory phase of education as set out in sec 3 of the Schools Act.
[83] 101 of 1997.
[84] Sec 1.

legislative categorisation, further education in terms of the constitutional right should be read as referring to all education of a higher level than basic education, including higher education. Such an approach would be consistent with the international interpretation given to the meaning of the right,[85] and would be the only way to make sense of the constitutional distinction between basic and further education.

A comparison with article 13(2)(c) of CESCR reveals a significant textual difference with section 29(1)(b). According to article 13(2)(c) of CESCR, higher education shall be made equally accessible to all on the basis of 'capacity'. This CESCR provision suggests that demonstrated individual ability should determine an individual's eligibility for further education.[86] A determination of a student's ability is complex in a South African context in the light of the legacy of apartheid education since students from disadvantaged schools, which generally produce poor results, are less likely to meet the eligibility criteria for further education than their counterparts from better resourced schools.

This should not mean, however, that 'capacity' does not have a role to play in determining eligibility for further education, only that 'capacity' cannot be narrowly defined or assessed, for example by relying solely on a student's matriculation results as an indicator of that student's eligibility for further education. Instead, 'capacity' should be measured in a manner that acknowledges the history of apartheid education and its continuing legacy of socio-economic disadvantage along racial lines. Thus, a commitment to transformation of further education has to acknowledge that black South Africans were denied opportunities for education, and in doing this develop and implement policies and programmes that redress this legacy. An example of such programmes includes selection tests that have been developed at certain universities to assess the potential of students whose schooling results do not necessarily qualify them for university entrance but who nevertheless through these tests demonstrate an ability to succeed at university.

In the case of *Motala & Another v University of Natal*,[87] the university's admission policy was the subject of an equality challenge. In this case, the parents of an Indian student brought an application against the university after her application to medical school had been rejected, despite good academic results. The parents claimed that the university admission policy discriminated against their daughter and favoured African applicants. The Court found that the

---

[85] See art 13 of CESCR, art 28 of CRC and arts 11(3)(b) & (c) of the African Charter on the Rights and Welfare of the Child. See also Davis *et al* (n 57 above) 298.

[86] According to General Comment No 13 para 19, 'higher education is not to be "generally available", but only available on the basis of capacity'. The capacity of individuals should be assessed by reference to all their relevant expertise and experience. Art 13(2)(c) refers only to higher education. Art 13(2)(b), which deals with secondary education, does not include a reference to capacity. Accordingly, state parties are obliged to make secondary education progressively accessible and available to all.

[87] 1995 3 BCLR 374 (D) 383.

discrimination was not unfair and that the policy was within the meaning of section 8(3)(a) of the interim Constitution. The Court accepted that, although the Indian community had been decidedly disadvantaged under apartheid, the disadvantage suffered by African pupils under apartheid was significantly greater, and accordingly an admission policy that acknowledged this was not unfair.

Access to higher education is regulated in terms of the Higher Education Act, which establishes the 'legal basis of a single, national higher education system on the basis of the rights and freedoms in our Constitution'.[88] However, institutions maintain a degree of self-regulation in respect of 'student admissions, curriculum, methods of teaching and assessment, research, establishment of academic regulations and the internal management of resources'. Thus, there may be institutions reluctant to adopt a programme of institutional transformation, which facilitates access. The Act accordingly gives the Minister of Education a wide discretion to withhold state funds under such circumstances.[89]

Accessibility to further education, as with basic education, requires that education be economically accessible. However, unlike with basic education, there appears to be less support that further education should be free. A more likely interpretation is that further education must be affordable to all who meet the criteria for admission to an institution providing such education.[90] A student aid scheme has been established in terms of the National Student Aid Scheme Act 56 of 1999. The Act provides for the establishment of a board *inter alia* to allocate funds for loans and bursaries to eligible students and to develop the criteria and conditions for the granting and withdrawing of such loans and bursaries.[91] Funding in terms of the scheme is provided from various sources such as state allocations, private funding, and the repayment of loans.[92]

A scrutiny of the reasonableness of the Act would require an inquiry into whether or not the Act facilitates access to all students, particularly those from disadvantaged backgrounds, who meet the criteria for admission to institutions falling within the Act. A vexing issue in this regard is that of the financial exclusions of those students who initially receive assistance in terms of the Act, but then have such assistance withdrawn because of poor academic performance. Factors which therefore need to be considered when setting conditions for granting and withdrawing loans should include an assessment of the impact of economic hardship on an individual learner's academic

---

[88] Higher Education Act (n 83 above); Higher Education White Paper 3 of 1993; Higher Education White Paper (July 1997) 38.
[89] Sec 42.
[90] Neither art 28 (c) of CRC nor art 11(3)(c) of the African Charter on the Rights and Welfare of the Child require that higher education be free. Art 13(2)(c) of CESCR requires that state parties take appropriate measures to secure the progressive introduction of free higher education. General Comment No 13 to CESCR (n 9 above) in defining economic accessibility states that higher education 'has to be affordable to all'.
[91] See secs 3, 4 &19.
[92] Sec 14.

performance, and whether or not processes are in place to bridge the gap between the schooling received and the demands of the particular institution. As stated above, an inquiry into the reasonableness of the Act could also entail a scrutiny of sufficiency of the funding in facilitating access to all students who meet the criteria for admission to institutions falling within the Act. Thus, to the extent that the fund does not make sufficient provisioning for all eligible students, the Act may not be reasonable.

3.3 The right to instruction in the official language of one's choice

Section 29(2) states that:

> Everyone has the right to receive education in the official language or languages of their choice in public educational institutions where that education is reasonably practicable. In order to ensure the effective access to, and implementation of, this right, the state must consider all reasonable educational alternatives, including single medium institutions, taking into account -
> (a) equity;
> (b) practicability; and
> (c) the need to redress the results of past racially discriminatory laws and practices.

This protection of language rights in the education clause, as in certain other jurisdictions, arises out of a political compromise with particular minority lobbies for the protection of minority rights.[93] Protecting the right of an individual to learn in the language of his or her choice is nonetheless paramount in facilitating that individual's ability to learn and develop. The approach taken to this right through various processes such as the Constitution drafting process, interpretation by the courts and policy development, has been to balance the need to give effect to this right against the need to ensure broader access to education for all. These processes have accordingly framed the conditions for when the right may be asserted.

In *In re School Education Bill of 1995 (Gauteng)*,[94] the Court, in interpreting the meaning of the right under the equivalent provision under the interim Constitution,[95] confirmed that the right creates a

---

[93] The inclusion of language rights in the education clause has its origins in the former government's proposals for a bill of rights for the protection of minority interests. These included, among others, the right to mother tongue education where reasonably practicable and the rights of parents to determine the medium of instruction and the character of schools. Later, during the Constitutional Assembly negotiations for the drafting of the final Constitution, the National Party was insistent on the inclusion of single medium institutions as a right for the purposes of the preservation of the language and culture of minorities, while the ANC feared that the inclusion of such a right would be used to perpetuate inaccessibility along racial lines to better resourced schools. See in this regard *Matukane* (n 50 above). A compromise was reached, with the Constitution allowing single medium institutions as one alternative method that the state would consider when providing education in the language of one's choice. See EFJ Malherbe 'Reflections on the background and content of the education clause in the South African Bill of Rights' (1997) 1 *Journal of South African Law* 85 94. For a discussion of the evolution of language rights as a political compromise in Canada, see *Mahe et al v The Queen in the Right of Alberta et al* 68 DLR 9 (4th) 69 84.

[94] *In re School Education Bill of 1995 (Gauteng)* (n 24 above) paras 9 &16.

positive right for every person to instruction in the language of his or her choice, but stated that this right was qualified to the extent that it was 'reasonably practicable'. The Court did not define the meaning of this term. Under the final Constitution this right has been qualified further by stating explicitly that the entitlement to language choice applies to an official language of one's choice only, as opposed to mother tongue education.[96]

An individual's entitlement under the final Constitution is also further qualified by the inclusion of an internal balancing test when adjudicating on the possible alternatives that may give effect to the right. That is, while the state is obliged to consider all possible options that seek to give effect to the right, such as 'single medium institutions', these must be weighed against certain enumerated grounds, that is, 'equity', 'practicability' and 'the need to redress the results of past racially discriminatory laws and practices'. Therefore, to the extent that a claim is made for an Afrikaans single medium institution, which may have the effect of denying other learners in that area, in particular black learners who are not Afrikaans speaking, access to a school, the establishment of such a single medium institution may be justifiably denied.

A school could also potentially look at the option of having a dual medium of instruction. Again, this will have to be balanced against the enumerated grounds. In this instance 'practicability' may require an investigation into the availability of resources and teachers. The effect of such an internal balancing test is that where a right in terms of this section is asserted and denied, the state will have to show that all possible alternatives were considered and that the failure to accommodate a learner was justifiable on the basis of one or more of these enumerated grounds.

The document entitled Norms and Standards Regarding Language Policy in Public Schools[97] sets out how schools and education departments are to give effect to their obligations in terms of section 29(2) of the Constitution. It sets out the process whereby a learner's language of education may be chosen at a school, and furthermore sets out a process for the Department of Education to assist in the accommodation of a learner at another school in that area, if the school of choice is unable to accommodate the learner. The Norms and Standards document also provides that:

> It is reasonably practicable to provide education in a particular language of learning and teaching if at least 40 in grades 1 to grade 6 or 35 in Grades 7 to 12 learners in a particular grade request it in a particular school.

---

[95] Sec 32(b) of the interim Constitution reads: 'Every person shall have the right to instruction in the language of his or her choice where this is reasonably practicable.'

[96] Compare sec 29(2) with sec 23 of the Canadian Charter of Rights and Freedoms, which guarantees mother tongue education in French or English where such a guarantee is more easily realisable in bilingual and bicultural societies such as Canada, as opposed to a multilingual and multicultural society as in South Africa.

[97] Government Notice R1701 (*Government Gazette* 18546) December 1997, promulgated pursuant to sec 6(1) of the Schools Act.

A reading of the document suggests that the state must provide education in the language of choice if the criterion of 'reasonably practicable' is met, and only where there are fewer than those numbers in each grade, should the internal balancing test be applied when there is a request for a particular language of education.[98] Where there are sufficient numbers of learners in a grade requesting a particular language at a school, the duty to provide an education in the language of choice of necessity also implies a resultant duty on the state adequately to provide the resources which may include teachers, classrooms and learning materials that would enable the school to comply with the request.

3.4 The right to establish private educational institutions

Section 29(3) of the Constitution states that:

> Everyone has the right to establish and maintain, at their own expense, independent educational institutions that -
> (a) do not discriminate on the basis of race;
> (b) are registered with the state; and
> (c) maintain standards that are not inferior to standards at comparable public educational institutions.

Section 29(4) states that 'subsection (3) does not preclude state subsidies for independent educational institutions'.

In *In re School Education Bill of 1995 (Gauteng)*, the Court, interpreting the meaning of the equivalent provision under the interim Constitution,[99] defined the extent of the state's obligations in respect of private education institutions based on a common language and culture:[100]

> The submission that every person can demand from the state the right to have established schools based on a common culture, language or religion is not supported by the language of section 32(c). The section does not say that every person has the right to have established by the state educational institutions based on such a common culture, language or religion. What it provides is that every person shall have the right to establish such educational institutions. Linguistically and grammatically it provides a *defensive right* to a person who seeks to establish such educational institutions and it protects that right from invasion by the state, without conferring on the state an obligation to establish such educational institutions.

---

[98] Sec V(c)(2) read with sec V(d)(3). The policy also lists two additional factors to be considered when weighing up all possible alternatives to give effect to the learner's right to an education in a language of his or her choice. These are: '(a) the duty of the state and the right of the learners in terms the Constitution, and (e) the advice of the governing bodies and principals of the public schools concerned'. The policy also appears to be consistent with the sliding scale formula as outlined in *Mahe et al v The Queen in the Right of Alberta et al* (n 93 above) 100, in terms of which the greater the number of learners making a request, the greater the obligation of the state in accommodating the language rights of those learners.

[99] Sec 32(c) stated that 'every person shall have the right to establish, where practicable, educational institutions based on common culture, language or religion provided there shall be no discrimination on the ground of race'.

[100] n 24 above, para 7 (our emphasis). Compare *Belgian Linguistic Case No 2* (1968) Series A No 6 1 EHRR 252.7.

The Court thus emphasised that the state's obligations in respect of minority rights in this context were limited to the protection of the rights of minorities to exist as a group, and not to be discriminated against, but that it did not extend to funding the establishment of institutions for particular minority groups.[101] In other words, the Court identified obligations to respect and to protect, but no obligations to fulfil.

The right of educational institutions to exist independently is, in terms of this section, conditional on meeting established criteria. That is, independent institutions may not discriminate against learners on the basis of race. Independent schools are also subject to the norms and standards set by the Department of Education and may only qualify for registration once certain basic criteria have been met.[102]

The protection available in terms of equivalent provisions under the interim Constitution was available only to schools that were established in terms of a specific cultural or religious identity. The right in terms of the final Constitution applies to all private schools. Thus, even private schools that do not exist because of a specific cultural or religious affiliation, such as Waldorf schools, may demand the protection afforded by the right, provided of course that the schools meet the established criteria.

While the state is not obliged to fund independent institutions, in terms of section 29(4) nothing precludes the state from granting such schools a subsidy. Such allocations should, however, be guided by the values in the Constitution, in particular the principle of non-discrimination.[103] Eligibility for subsidies at such schools is currently governed by the Schools Act,[104] in terms of which schools are eligible depending on the socio-economic circumstances of the schools' clientele. This is assessed by the level of fees charged at the schools, that is, those schools charging very low or no fees are more likely to qualify for a subsidy. Thus, while some may argue that such allocations amount to discrimination against those groups not

---

[101] The reasoning of the Court was that such an approach was compatible with the international developments relating to the protection of minorities' rights. See *In re School Education Bill of* (n 24 above) paras 45-90. The Court also justified its reasoning as appropriate in a 'multi-cultural and multi-lingual society' where the principle of equality prescribed that all languages and cultures be treated equally. It said 'thus, the dominant theme of the Constitution is the achievement of equality, while considerable importance is also given to cultural diversity and language, so that the basic problem is to secure equality in a balanced way which shows maximum regard for diversity.' *In re School Education Bill of 1995 (Gauteng)* (n 24 above) paras 51-52. For an example of international developments in the field of the international protection of minorities, see the 1992 UN Declaration on the Rights of Persons Belonging to National or Ethnic, Religious and Linguistic Minorities.

[102] See also sec 46 of the Schools Act.

[103] See also General Comment No 13 (n 9 above) para 54. On the basis of international human rights law, there is no obligation on a state to provide financial support to private educational institutions. If it does, however, it should do so on a non-discriminatory basis. See the views of the UN Human Rights Committee in the case of *Arieh Hollis Waldman v Canada* (1999) UN Doc CCPR/C/67/D/1996.

[104] n 33 above; Norms and Standards for School Funding; secs 45 & 48 of the Schools Act developed in terms of secs 29(3) & (4) of the Constitution.

benefiting from the subsidies, such targeting in fact demonstrates a commitment to redress and the principle of substantive equality.

4 Other provisions in the Bill of Rights

In addition to the specific protection guaranteed by the different subsections of section 29, other provisions of the Bill of Rights also affect the rights and freedoms of learners and students while at educational institutions.

4.1 The principle of equality and equal access

Section 32(a) of the interim Constitution specifically provided for equal access to educational institutions. Such a provision is not included in the final Constitution, but the principle of equality remains central to the meaning of the different subsections of the educational clause. Also, as suggested above, the principle of non-discrimination is intrinsic to the notion of accessibility that forms part of the right to basic education and further education. In giving effect to the right to education in a language of one's choice, regard must be had to the broader principle of equity, and independent educational institutions may only exist on the basis that they do not discriminate on the grounds of race. Nothing precludes a learner or student from asserting his or her right to equal access to an institution in terms of section 9, where such a right has been denied.[105]

4.2 Freedom of choice

The basic freedoms in the education clause extend to language choice, and implied in section 29(3) is the freedom of an individual to attend the school of his or her choice. Other rights in the Constitution may also be asserted where these rights of learners and students are threatened within educational institutions. These rights could include, but are not limited to the freedom of religion (section 15) or

---

[105] In *Mfolo & Others v Minister of Education, Bophuthatswana* 1994 1 BCLR 136 (B), a group of pregnant female students alleged that their right to equality in terms of the Bophuthatswana Constitution Act 18 of 1977 had been infringed when they were expelled from college in terms of a college rule banning pregnant women from attending college. The rule was found to be arbitrary and was accordingly declared unconstitutional. See, for a similar line of reasoning with respect to a case in Botswana, EK Quansah 'Is the right to get pregnant a fundamental human right in Botswana?' (1995) 39 *Journal of African Law* 97-102. See also *Matukane* (n 50 above). Any determination as to whether or not there has been discrimination in education must also be informed by the definition of discrimination in art 1 of the UNESCO Convention Against Discrimination in Education.

the freedom of assembly (section 17).[106] It is worth noting that, unlike certain international treaties where parental choice is explicitly entrenched, the education clause does not expressly give parents the right to choose to have their children educated according to their own religious and philosophical convictions.[107] In fact the Constitutional Court has rejected parental choice where such choice was not in conformity with the broader values in the Constitution.[108]

Freedom of choice may therefore be curtailed to the extent that individual values conflict with broader societal values, in particular those set out in the Constitution, but freedom of choice may also be curtailed by circumstances. That is, a parent living in a particular area may prefer to send a child to a better resourced school in a different area, but may be constrained in his or her choice of school because of the un-affordability of transport costs and fees associated with sending a child to a better resourced school in a different area.

5 Conclusion

Education is, as has been stated above, necessary for the enjoyment of the other rights and freedoms in the Constitution. Therefore, the full realisation of the right to education also enhances opportunities for the enjoyment of other rights and freedoms. To this end this chapter has attempted to define the scope and content of each of the subsections of section 29 and to provide an overview of the most significant policies that have been developed to give effect to the rights under section 29. These policies appear to have as a main objective the creation of an education system that ensures equal access for all. However, to the extent that certain policies do not facilitate the full enjoyment of the rights under section 29, these

---

[106] *Witmann v Deutscher Schulverein, Pretoria & Others* 1999 1 BCLR 92 (T). In this case the custodian parent sought an order *inter alia* declaring that her minor child be excused from attendance at religious instruction classes and the school assembly prayers. In a controversial decision the Court held that included in the right to freedom of religion, belief and opinion was the principle that attendance at religious instruction classes be voluntary. However, in terms of the facts of this particular case, the Court held that the right had been waived. See also *Acting Superintendent-General of Education KwaZulu-Natal v Ngubo & Others* 1996 3 BCLR 369 (N). In a case interdicting student action at a university, the Court acknowledged the rights of the students to assemble and protest in terms of sec 17, but held that such a right entailed a core content with 'express limitations', which the behaviour of the students had in this case exceeded.

[107] In the case of *Newdow v United States Congress et al* CV-00-00495 292 F 3d 597 (9th Cir 26 June 2002) (unreported), a parent of a schoolchild brought a claim alleging that the words 'under God' in the 1954 revision of the Pledge of Allegiance is a violation of the Establishment Clause of the First Amendment of the United States Constitution. The Court, in asserting that the parent has standing to bring the claim, relied on previous case law stating that 'parents have a right to direct the religious upbringing of their children and on that basis have standing to protect their right'. The parent is an atheist whose daughter attends a public school where, in accordance with state law, teachers begin each school day by leading their students in a recitation of the Pledge of Allegiance. The Supreme Court held that the words 'under God' did violate the Establishment Clause. See also art 2 of the First Protocol of the European Convention on Human Rights and the case of *Kjeldsen, Busk Madsen & Pedersen* (1976) ECHR Ser A 23.

[108] *Christian Education* (n 70 above) paras 43-44; see also *In re School Education Bill of 1995 (Gauteng)* (n 24 above) paras 53-54.

policies should be revised to ensure constitutional compliance. The international treaty provisions and interpretative work by international supervisory bodies may provide guidance on this.

Three / The right to housing*

Pierre de Vos

1 Introduction

South Africa faces an acute housing shortage. Millions of South Africans in need of housing occupy rudimentary informal settlements providing only minimum shelter, while thousands of others have no access to housing or shelter of any kind. The cause of this acute housing shortage lies, at least partly, in the apartheid policy of influx control, which sought to limit African occupation of urban areas.[1]

The South African Constitution aims to address this stark reality, as it explicitly guarantees the right of access to housing,[2] children's rights to shelter[3] and prisoners' rights to accommodation.[4] It also places a duty on the state – in the context of protecting existing property rights – to take reasonable measures within its available resources, to foster conditions which enable citizens to gain access to land on an equitable basis.[5]

---

* This paper is partly based on an earlier paper with the same title written by Karrisha Pillay and published in G Bekker (ed) *A compilation of essential documents on the rights to accommodation, housing and shelter* (2000).

[1] See *Government of the Republic of South Africa v Grootboom* 2000 11 BCLR 1169 (CC) para 6.

[2] See Constitution of the Republic of South Africa of 1996, sec 26, which provides as follows:
 (1) Everyone has the right to have access to adequate housing.
 (2) The state must take reasonable legislative or other measures, within its available resources, to achieve the progressive realisation of this right.
 (3) No one may be evicted from their home, or have their home demolished, without an order of court made after considering all the relevant circumstances. No legislation may permit arbitrary evictions.

[3] Sec 28 provides as follows:
 (1) Every child has the right ....
 (c) to basic nutrition, shelter, basic health care services and social services; ....
 (3) In this section 'child' means a person under the age of 18 years.

[4] Section 35:
 (2) Everyone who is detained, including every sentenced prisoner, has the right ...
 (e) to conditions of detention that are consistent with human dignity, including ... the provision, at state expense, of adequate accommodation ...

[5] Section 25:
 (5) The state must take reasonable legislative and other measures within its available resources, to foster conditions which enable citizens to gain access to land on an equitable basis.

These rights – included in the Bill of Rights with other civil and political and social and economic rights – engender different kinds of obligations[6] and are all clearly justiciable,[7] despite the fact that they may sometimes give rise to budgetary implications.[8] The question is how any of these rights may be enforced in a given case.[9] Unlike some of the other rights contained in the Bill of Rights, the rights related to housing and shelter do not have a long history of judicial enforcement in domestic contexts and our courts are therefore still grappling with the exact scope and content of these rights. The right of access to housing and other related housing rights have, however, come under judicial scrutiny and are also widely discussed and commented upon in international human rights bodies. It is to these sources that I shall turn to assist with the interpretation of the rights at hand.

---

[6]   *In re: Certification of the Constitution of the Republic of South Africa 1996* (*First Certification* case) 1996 10 BCLR 1253 para 77, where the Court states: 'It is true that the inclusion of socio-economic rights may result in courts making orders which have direct implications for budgetary matters. However, even when a court enforces civil and political rights such as equality, freedom of speech and the right to a fair trial, the order it makes will often have such implications.'

[7]   See sec 38 of the Constitution; J de Waal *et al* (eds) *The Bill of Rights handbook* (2001) 81-84; P de Vos 'Pious wishes or directly enforceable human rights? Social and economic rights in South Africa's 1996 Constitution' (1997) 13 *South African Journal on Human Rights* 67 69-71; G van Bueren 'Alleviating poverty through the Constitutional Court' (1999) 15 *South African Journal on Human Rights* 52 57-59; C Scott & P Alston 'Adjudicating constitutional priorities in a transnational context: A comment on *Soobramoney's* legacy and *Grootboom's* promise' (2000) 16 *South African Journal on Human Rights* 206, 214-217; J Sloth-Nielsen 'The child's right to social services, the right to social security, and primary prevention of child abuse: Some conclusions in the aftermath of *Grootboom* (2001) 17 *South African Journal on Human Rights* 210 218-20; S Liebenberg 'The right to social assistance: The implications of *Grootboom* for policy reform in South Africa' (2001) 17 *South African Journal on Human Rights* 232 238-41; and P de Vos '*Grootboom*, the right of access to housing and substantive equality as contextual fairness' (2001) 17 *South African Journal on Human Rights* 258 259.

[8]   See *First Certification* case (n 6 above) para 77, where the Court states: '[W]e are of the view that these rights are, at least to some extent justiciable ... [M]any of the civil and political rights entrenched in the NT will give rise to similar budgetary implications without compromising their justiciability. The fact that socio-economic rights will almost inevitably give rise to such implications does not seem to us a bar to their justiciability.'

[9]   *Grootboom* (n 1 above) 1183 para 20; *Minister of Health & Others v Treatment Action Campaign & Others* 2002 10 BCLR 1033 (CC) para 99 where the Court states: 'Where state policy is challenged as inconsistent with the Constitution, courts have to consider whether in formulating and implementing such policy the state has given effect to its constitutional obligations. If it should hold in any given case that the state has failed to do so, it is obliged by the Constitution to say so. In so far as that constitutes an intrusion into the domain of the executive, that intrusion is mandated by the Constitution itself.'

2 Interpreting the right to housing

South Africa's Constitutional Court has now had the opportunity to consider the scope and content of the various social and economic rights in at least three different decisions.[10] These three decisions – *Soobramoney v Minister of Health, KwaZulu-Natal*,[11] *Government of the RSA & Others v Grootboom*[12] and *Minister of Health & Others v Treatment Action Campaign & Others*[13] – provide us with a framework within which the scope and content of the right of access to housing and shelter and the legal consequences of these rights can be evaluated. Moreover, the *Grootboom* judgment deals specifically with the right of access to housing and contains very specific pointers as to the nature and scope of the state's obligations engendered by section 26 of the Constitution.[14] In this section I shall set out the general principles guiding the interpretation of the various provisions before moving on in the subsequent section to a more detailed analysis of the scope and content of the rights under discussion.

---

[10] Some commentators add a fourth case, namely *Minister of Public Works & Others v Kyalami Ridge Environmental Association & Others* 2001 7 BCLR 652 (CC), where the Constitutional Court used sec 26 of the Constitution to justify action taken by the state to provide access to housing to people in need. The Constitutional Court held in this case that sec 26(3) of the Constitution was relevant when considering whether the state – as *landowner* – could justify the way in which it dealt with its property. It therefore established the principle that sec 26(3) would be relevant when deciding whether it had acted in a legally appropriate manner. In my opinion, however, it does not add anything fundamental to our understanding of the scope and content of the social and economic rights in general. Subsequent to the submission of this chapter to the editors, a further case dealing with the scope and content of a constitutional socio-economic right was decided by the Constitutional Court: *Khoza v Minister of Social Development* 2004 6 BCLR 569 (CC). The author could not consider this case in his analysis (eds).
[11] 1997 12 BCLR 1696 (CC).
[12] n 1 above.
[13] n 9 above.
[14] Academic writers have written extensively on the scope and content of the duties engendered by the social and economic rights contained in the Constitution. Apart from those articles mentioned in n 7 above, the following sources are also relevant. N Haysom 'Constitutionalism, majoritarian democracy and socio-economic rights' (1992) 8 *South African Journal on Human Rights* 451; E Mureinik 'Beyond a charter of luxuries: Economic rights in the Constitution' (1992) 8 *South African Journal on Human Rights* 464; D Davis 'The case against the inclusion of socio-economic demands in a bill of rights except as directive principles' (1992) 8 *South African Journal on Human Rights* 475; S Liebenberg 'Social and economic rights: A critical challenge' in S Liebenberg (ed) *The Constitution of South Africa from a gender perspective* (1995) 79; H Corder *et al A charter for social justice: A contribution to the South African Bill of Rights debate* (1992) 18; C Scott & P Macklem 'Constitutional ropes of sand or justiciable guarantees? Social rights in a new South African Constitution' (1992) 141 *University of Pennsylvania Law Review* 1; B de Villiers 'Social and economic rights' in D van Wyk *et al* (eds) *Rights and constitutionalism: The new South African legal order* (1994) 599; South African Law Commission *Final Report on Group and Human Rights* (Project 58, October 1994) 179.

2.1 Rights must be interpreted contextually

South Africa's Constitutional Court has now reiterated on several occasions that the rights in the Bill of Rights cannot be interpreted in the abstract, but must be interpreted in the light of their context. What is required is the consideration of two types of context. On the one hand, rights must be understood in their textual setting. This is because the rights in the Bill of Rights are interrelated and mutually supporting.[15] The interrelated nature of rights requires that any interpretation of sections 26, 28(1)(c) and 35(2)(e) of the Constitution must take heed of other important and interrelated rights such as the rights to equality, human dignity, and the other social and economic rights.[16] When interpreting any of these rights, one should furthermore do so with reference to the other social and economic rights contained in the Bill of Rights. I have argued elsewhere,[17] that social and economic rights and the right to equality are particularly closely connected, but this view is not necessarily shared by other commentators on the work of the Constitutional Court.

The textual context is also important in as much as it may reveal a 'carefully constructed constitutional scheme' within which the various sections of the Bill of Rights should be interpreted.[18] For example, in *Grootboom* the Constitutional Court found that the scope and content of the children's right to shelter set out in section 28(1)(c) can only properly be ascertained in the context of the rights and obligations created by sections 25(5), 26 and 27 (the relevant social and economic rights). This is because there is an apparent overlap of these rights, and this overlap clearly has consequences for any understanding of the scope and content of the section under discussion.[19]

Secondly, when interpreting the relevant provisions relating to access to housing and shelter, it is important to take into account the social and historical context in which the state's action is being judged.[20] What is important is to focus on the Constitutional Court's understanding of the inegalitarian context within which it is called

---

[15] As Yacoob J stated in *Grootboom* (n 1 above): 'There can be no doubt that human dignity, freedom and equality, the foundational values of our society, are denied those who have no food, clothing or shelter. Affording socio-economic rights to all people therefore enables them to enjoy the other rights enshrined in Chapter 2. The realisation of these rights is also the key to the advancement of race and gender equality and the evolution of a society in which men and women are equally able to achieve their full potential' (para 23). See also *Minister of Health & Others v Treatment Action Campaign* (n 9 above) para 24.

[16] See *Grootboom* (n 1 above) paras 70-79; *Treatment Action Campaign* (n 9 above) para 74.

[17] De Vos (2001) (n 7 above).

[18] *Grootboom* (n 1 above) para 71.

[19] As above, para 74. The consequences of this view for the actual scope and content of sec 28(1)(c) will be explored below.

[20] *Grootboom* (n 1 above) para 25; *Treatment Action Campaign* (n 9 above) para 24.

upon to interpret the Bill of Rights. The Constitutional Court in *Soobramoney* already accepted this view when Chaskalson stated:[21]

> We live in a society in which there are great disparities in wealth. Millions of people are living in deplorable conditions and great poverty. There is a high level of unemployment, inadequate social security, and many do not have access to clean water or to adequate health services. These conditions already existed when the Constitution was adopted and a commitment to address them, and to transform our society into one in which there will be human dignity, freedom and equality, lies at the heart of our new constitutional order. For as long as these conditions continue to exist that aspiration will have a hollow ring.

Thus, in evaluating whether government action or inaction in providing access to housing or other constitutionally guaranteed forms of shelter infringes any of the relevant provisions, one will have to take cognisance of the fact that many of South Africa's poorest citizens have either no access to housing and/or shelter, or they only have access to rudimentary forms of informal housing. One will also have to take into account that many people have no choice but to live in the most desperate conditions, often on private or state-owned land not originally earmarked for housing. In particular, one will have to take note of the especially vulnerable position in which both women and children find themselves where they have no access to adequate housing. Where a state policy fails to take cognisance of these factors and, say, completely ignores the plight of the most vulnerable sections of the community, it will be highly relevant when coming to a decision on whether the state policy is reasonable and therefore constitutionally valid or not.

2.2 The role of international law in interpreting the right to housing

Section 39(1)(b) of the Constitution recognises the importance of international law in the interpretation of the Bill of Rights and accordingly requires consideration of international law in the interpretation of the Bill of Rights.[22] Of course, this does not imply that judges must follow international law positions slavishly. It does mean, I would contend, that courts cannot completely disregard international law. This, in turn, requires that where courts decide not to follow the precedents of international law, they must at least give cogent and well argued reasons for why, after due consideration, they have decided not to follow international law. Moreover, international law will arguably be of particular importance in assisting with the interpretation of the social and economic rights provisions in the Bill of Rights because the international law relating to social and economic rights is often more developed and more nuanced than equivalent domestic law. In the context of the transitional Constitution, the term international law has been interpreted generously to allow recourse also to treaties such as the European

---

[21] *Soobramoney* (n 11 above) para 8.
[22] Sec 39(1)(b) states: 'When interpreting the Bill of Rights, a court, tribunal or forum - ... (b) must consider international law ...'

Convention on Human Rights, to which South Africa is not a party and cannot become a party.[23]

International law in this context includes those sources of international law recognised by article 38(1) of the Statute of the International Court of Justice, namely the international conventions, international custom, the general principles of law recognised by civilised nations, and judicial decisions and the teachings of the most highly qualified publicists of the various nations.[24] The latter includes sources arising out of the international human rights conventions such as the comments and opinions of the United Nations (UN) Human Rights Committee, General Comments of the Committee on Economic, Social and Cultural Rights (Committee on ESCR), the comments of the European Commission, judgments of the European Court of Human Rights and judgments of the Inter-American Court of Human Rights.[25] There are numerous other conventions that deal with the right to housing with reference to specific vulnerable groups. Examples of these are the Convention Relating to the Status of Refugees,[26] the Convention on the Elimination of All Forms of Racial Discrimination (CERD),[27] the Convention on the Elimination of All Forms of Discrimination Against Women (CEDAW)[28] and the Convention on the Rights of the Child (CRC).[29] In addition to these binding instruments, there are also a number of declarations that make reference to the right to housing. The most important of these

---

[23] J Dugard 'The role of international law in interpreting the Bill of Rights' (1994) 10 *South African Journal on Human Rights* 208 212; N Botha 'International law and the South African interim Constitution' (1994) 9 *South African Public Law* 245 248-252. In *S v Makwanyane & Another* 1995 6 BCLR 665 (CC) para 35, Chaskalson P ruled that public international law would include 'non-binding as well as binding law' and stated: 'In the context of s 35(1), public international law would include non-binding as well as binding law. They may both be used under the section as tools of interpretation. International agreements and customary international law accordingly provide a framework within which chap 3 can be evaluated and understood, and for that purpose decisions of tribunals dealing with comparable instruments, such as the United Nations Committee on Human Rights, the Inter-American Commission on Human Rights, the Inter-American Court of Human Rights, the European Commission on Human Rights, and the European Court of Human Rights, and in appropriate cases, reports of specialised agencies such as the International Labour Organisation, may provide guidance as to the correct interpretation of particular provisions of chap 3 [the Bill of Rights].' See also generally D Devine 'The relationship between international law and municipal law in the light of the interim South African Constitution 1993' (1995) 44 *International and Comparative Law Quarterly* 1; J Dugard 'International law and the "final" Constitution' (1995) 11 *South African Journal on Human Rights* 241 242; LM du Plessis & H Corder *Understanding South Africa's transitional Bill of Rights* (1994) 121.

[24] Dugard (1995) (n 23 above) 243.

[25] Botha (n 23 above) 248-252.

[26] GA Res 429 (V) 1950; 189 UNTS 150.

[27] GA Res 2106 (XX) 1965; 660 UNTS 195; 5 *International Legal* Materials 50 (1974).

[28] GA Res 34/180 1979; 19 *International Legal* Materials 33 (1980).

[29] GA Res 44/25 1989; 28 *International Legal* Materials 1448 (1989).

are the Istanbul Declaration on Human Settlements[30] and the Habitat Agenda.[31]

The Constitutional Court provided more clarity about the use of international law in interpreting the social and economic rights provisions of the Bill of Rights in the *Grootboom* and *Treatment Action Campaign* judgments. In *Grootboom*, the Court emphasised that the use of international law may be directly applicable where the particular principle or rule of international law binds South Africa directly. But where such a principle does not bind South Africa directly, its relevance would be limited.[32] In interpreting the social and economic rights provisions in the Bill of Rights, the influence of international law not directly binding on South Africa will be limited where significant differences exist in the wording of the provisions of an international treaty and the provisions of the South African Constitution.[33] Thus, while the interpretation of the provisions of the International Covenant on Economic, Social and Cultural Rights (CESCR),[34] as expressed in the General Comments issued by the Committee on ESCR, will be pertinent and helpful for the Court in interpreting the right of access to housing, the extent of the influence of the General Comments will largely depend on the specific context and on the texts of the provisions under discussion.[35] In *Grootboom*, the Court relied directly on General Comment 3 issued by the Committee on ESCR[36] to explain the parameters of the justiciability of social and economic rights, and explicitly endorsed a passage from General Comment 3 regarding the meaning of the term 'progressive realisation' in the context of the South African Constitution.[37]

---

[30] UNA/CONF 165/14(part) 7 August 1996.
[31] Adopted at the 18th plenary meeting, on 14 June 1996 of the UN Conference on Human Settlements.
[32] *Grootboom* (n 1 above) para 26.
[33] n 32 above, para 28.
[34] GA Res 2200A (XXI); 993 UNTS 3 (1967); 6 *International Legal Materials* 360 (1967).
[35] *Grootboom* (n 1 above) para 45.
[36] UN Committee on ESCR General Comment No 3 *The nature of state parties' obligations (art 2 para 1 of the Covenant)* (5th session, 1990) [UN Doc E/1991/23].
[37] *Grootboom* (n 1 above) para 45.

3 International and South African law

3.1 Introduction

The right of access to adequate housing protected in section 26 of the Constitution engenders both negative and positive obligations on the state and other relevant role-players. These obligations are spelt out in section 7(2) of the Bill of Rights, which states that the state must 'respect, protect, promote and fulfil the rights in the Bill of Rights'.[38] In the next section I shall summarise the duties engendered by this right, focusing on both the negative[39] and positive[40] obligations for the state and other relevant role-players in respect of the right to housing.[41] I shall also proceed to illustrate these general principles with reference to South African case law and the relevant international law provisions.

3.2 Negative obligations on the state and other role-players to respect the right to housing

3.2.1 General principles

Section 26 places a negative obligation on the state and other relevant role-players to desist from preventing or impairing the right of access to adequate housing.[42] Any action by the state that would take away existing access to adequate housing or would make it more difficult for an individual to gain access to existing housing would thus potentially result in an infringement of this right. This means that the state is required to *respect* the autonomy of the individual in his or her exercise of the right of access to adequate housing. This duty to respect human rights is easiest to grasp because it corresponds to the traditional view of the nature of the Bill of Rights as a shield against

---

[38] Sec 7(2). See also De Vos (n 7 above) for an exposition on what this section entails.
[39] *Grootboom* (n 1 above) paras 20 & 34.
[40] n 39 above, para 38.
[41] According to sec 8(2), the Bill of Rights may, in certain circumstances, also bind natural and juristic persons. Stephen Ellmann has argued that in the context of the HIV/AIDS crisis in South Africa, pharmaceutical companies might be bound by sec 27(1) of the Constitution. This is because most South Africans are being denied access (in the negative sense) to anti-retroviral drugs. Unless this denial can be justified by the pharmaceutical companies' legitimate interest, their actions that continue to deny individuals access to anti-retroviral drugs could be found to be unconstitutional. Ellmann argues that where it is feasible for companies to lower their prices without compromising their financial stability, then refusing to make such reductions could be unconstitutional. The same will hold for companies and private individuals when it comes to the right of access to adequate housing. Although access to housing is arguably a less pressing right than the right of access to health care in the context of the HIV/AIDS pandemic, it might still be true that in certain circumstances not only the state but also companies and private individuals will be under a constitutional duty not to infringe on the existing right of access to health care or not to act in a way that will make it more difficult for individuals to gain access to adequate housing. See P Andrews & S Ellmann *The post-apartheid constitutions: Perspectives on South Africa's basic law* (2001) 444 460-462. See also De Vos (n 7 above) 67 80.
[42] *First Certification* case (n 6 above) para 20; *Grootboom* (n 1 above) para 34.

government interference. It is a duty whose flipside is a right: Every individual has a constitutional right to enjoy unhindered access to housing and not to be disturbed in existing access to housing. Like all rights, this right is not absolute and might be limited in specific circumstances.

This negative duty on the state to respect the right of access to housing is further elaborated upon in section 26(3), which addresses the question of unlawful evictions. This section explicitly outlaws people being evicted or having their homes demolished without an order of court after due consideration has been accorded to all relevant circumstances. While certain criteria as to what constitutes 'all relevant circumstances' are required, it is clear that this subsection is significant in the sense that it is subject to immediate implementation and not qualified by the availability of resources. In addition, it unequivocally prohibits legislation that permits arbitrary evictions.

3.2.2 Evictions and South African law

To give effect to the positive constitutional obligation in section 26(1) to respect the right of access to housing,[43] the South African Parliament has adopted a number of laws aimed at protecting the rights of those who occupied land or had access to housing.[44] For example, the Rental Housing Act[45] protects the occupation rights of (lawful) occupiers of (rural and urban) residential property; the Land Reform (Labour Tenants) Act[46] protects (lawful) occupiers of agricultural (rural) land; the Extension of Security of Tenure Act (ESTA)[47] protects the occupation rights of persons who (lawfully) occupy (rural) land with consent of the landowner; the Interim Protection of Informal Land Rights Act[48] protects (lawful) occupiers of (rural and urban) land in terms of informal land rights; the Restitution

---

[43] This section must be read with sec 25 (6) of the Constitution which deals with property, and which explicitly provides that 'a person or community whose tenure of land is legally insecure as a result of past racially discriminatory laws or practices is entitled, to the extent provided by an Act of Parliament, either to tenure which is legally secure or to comparable redress'.

[44] For an excellent discussion and analysis of the legislation referred to here, see AJ van der Walt 'Exclusivity of ownership, security of tenure, and eviction orders: A model to evaluate South African land-reform legislation' (2002) *Journal of South African Law* 254-289. See also R Keightley 'The impact of the Extension of Security of Tenure Act on an owner's right to vindicate immovable property' (1999) 15 *South African Journal on Human Rights* 277; and AJ van der Walt 'Exclusivity of ownership, security of tenure and eviction orders: A critical evaluation of recent case law' (2002) 18 *South African Journal on Human Rights* 372.

[45] 50 of 1999.
[46] 3 of 1996.
[47] 62 of 1997.
[48] 31 of 1996.

of Land Rights Act[49] protects (lawful and unlawful) occupiers of (urban and rural) land who have instituted a restitution claim; and the Prevention of Illegal Eviction from and Unlawful Occupation of Land Act (PIE)[50] regulates eviction of unlawful occupiers (from urban and rural land) in order to give effect to the provisions of section 26(3). These Acts form a web of protection that has considerably improved the position of previously vulnerable groups whose legal rights to access to land and housing were weak or non-existent.[51]

From the perspective of the right of access to housing, one of the most important strands of this web is PIE. This Act becomes relevant in two distinct situations, namely, first, where evictions are aimed at the unlawful invaders and occupiers of land, and second, where evictions are aimed at occupiers whose lawful occupation turned unlawful through lapse of time or cancellation. I shall deal with these two situations separately.

This Act prohibits the eviction of the 'unlawful occupier' of land, unless the eviction is ordered by a court of law and unless certain procedures are followed.[52] It distinguishes between unlawful occupiers who have occupied the land for less than six months and those unlawful occupiers who have occupied the land for more than six months. In the first case, a court may grant an order for eviction if it is of the opinion that it is just and equitable to do so, after considering all the relevant circumstances, including the rights and needs of the elderly, children, disabled persons and households headed by women.[53] In latter cases, courts are given the same power to issue an eviction order and are also required to take into account relevant circumstances, including those set out in section 6(4). However, in the second set of circumstances, relevant circumstances are said also to include the question whether land has been made available or can reasonably be made available by a municipality or other organ of state or another landowner for the relocation of the unlawful occupier.[54]

These provisions radically changed the South African common law.[55] Previously the common law held that an owner could claim his or her property wherever he or she found it, from whomever was holding it. The owner therefore only needed to allege and prove that he or she was the owner of that property and that the defendant was holding the property before the onus would shift to the defendant to establish any common law right to continue holding the property.[56] Under PIE, the owner no longer has the right to evict the unwanted

---

[49] 22 of 1994.
[50] 19 of 1998.
[51] See Van der Walt *Journal of South African Law* (n 44 above) 265.
[52] n 50 above, sec 4.
[53] Sec 4(6).
[54] Sec 4(7).
[55] See Van der Walt *South African Journal on Human Rights* (n 44 above) 377. Sec 4(1) states: 'Notwithstanding anything to the contrary contained in any law or the common law, the provisions of this section apply to proceedings by an owner or person in charge of land for the eviction of an unlawful occupier.'
[56] *Chetty v Naidoo* 1974 3 SA 13 (A) 20A.

and unlawful occupier. This right is given to the court that has a wide discretion in terms of wide-ranging criteria to decide whether an eviction order would be just and equitable.[57]

In cases where the occupiers are seen as unlawful invaders who have settled on land without permission, the courts have generally had no problem with interpreting the Act to give effect to its provisions which override the common law protection of property.[58] It is therefore clear that PIE applies to and protects all people who have unlawfully occupied land or property and now resist eviction from that property.

However, there has been some considerable confusion about whether PIE also applies to individuals who occupied property lawfully but became unlawful occupiers through defaulting on rent or bond payments, or refusing to vacate premises after the expiry of a lease. The Act does not provide explicitly for the situation where lawful occupation becomes unlawful.[59]

Until 2002, the Transvaal High Court case of *ABSA Bank Ltd v Amod*[60] was generally considered to be the authoritative decision on this matter. In this case, the High Court decided that the prohibition against summary eviction contained in PIE applied only to persons who invaded vacant land and who occupied structures in informal settlements. It was thus held that the Act did not apply to the occupation of formal structures such as houses and flats occupied in terms of rent agreements as these were still governed by the common law.[61] Early in 2002, the Supreme Court of Appeal in the case of *Brisley v Drotsky*[62] seemed to endorse this view when it assumed that PIE did not apply to a situation where a lease agreement was validly terminated and the occupation thus became unlawful. The appellant had argued that section 26(3) of the Constitution precluded the granting of an ejectment order without taking into account all relevant circumstances, including the personal circumstances of the appellant.[63] The Court rejected an argument that they had to take into account the relevant circumstances set out in sec 4(6) and (7) of PIE when deciding whether to grant an ejectment order, as they assumed this Act did not apply to the present case.[64]

However, in August 2002, the Supreme Court of Appeal in the case of *Ndlovu v Ngcobo*[65] found that PIE indeed applied not only to cases where land or housing was unlawfully occupied, but also where

---

[57] See the minority decision in *Ndlovu v Ngcobo; Bekker & Another v Jika* 2003 1 SA 113 (SCA).
[58] Van der Walt *South African Journal on Human Rights* (n 44 above) 377. See eg *Port Elizabeth Municipality v Peoples Dialogue on Land and Shelter* 2000 2 SA 1074 (SEC); *Mkangeli v Joubert* 2002 4 SA 36 (SCA).
[59] Van der Walt (n 58 above, 385-86) elaborates on the various situations in which lawful occupation can become unlawful.
[60] (1999) 2 All SA 423 (W).
[61] n 60 above, 429c-30h.
[62] 2002 12 BCLR 1229 1229 (SCA).
[63] n 62 above, para 43.
[64] n 62 above, para 37.
[65] n 57 above.

occupation of land and housing became unlawful after a previous period of lawful occupation. Harms J argued that:[66]

> [H]aving regard to the history of the enactment with, as already pointed out, its roots in s 26(3) of the Constitution which is concerned with rights to one's home, the preamble to PIE which emphasises the right to one's home and the interests of vulnerable persons, the buildings listed and the fact that one is ultimately concerned with 'any other form of temporary or permanent dwelling or shelter', the ineluctable conclusion is that, subject to the *eiusdem generis* rule, the term was used exhaustively. It follows that buildings or structures that do not perform the function of a form of dwelling or shelter for humans do not fall under PIE and since juristic persons do not have dwellings, their unlawful possession is similarly not protected by PIE.

However, as Van der Walt points out, the situation remains somewhat murky as the *Ndlovu* decision is based on an interpretation of the relevant provisions of PIE and not on a jurisprudential analysis of the relationship between section 26(3) of the Constitution, land reform legislation and the common law.[67]

3.2.3 Evictions and international law

The various pieces of legislation adopted by the South African Parliament over the past five years seem to have come close to ensuring respect for the right of access to housing as envisaged by the Constitution. The strong emphasis on the protection of existing occupiers of land and housing, and the Supreme Court of Appeal's extension of PIE to those whose unlawful occupation stems from causes other than the initial unlawful occupation of land or housing suggests that it would mostly be possible for individuals to enjoy their access to housing without undue interference.[68] This is also in line with the various resolutions, opinions and treaty provisions addressing the issue of access to land and housing.

For example, the UN Sub-Commission on Human Rights has adopted a Resolution on Forced Evictions,[69] parts of which are worth referring to in the present section. It has urged governments to undertake immediate measures, at all levels, aimed at eliminating the practice of forced evictions. It has further urged governments to confer legal security of tenure to all persons currently threatened with forced evictions and to adopt all necessary measures giving full protection against forced evictions, based upon effective participation, consultation and negotiation with affected persons or groups. It has

---

[66] n 57 above, para 20.
[67] Van der Walt *South African Journal on Human Rights* (n 44 above) 404.
[68] This mostly positive assessment of legal trends towards the protection of access to housing and land may seem optimistic in the light of criticism of judicial responses to land issues. Van der Walt argues that attempts to rectify the apartheid legacy regarding land are often frustrated by courts which instinctively adhere to the common law position which favours existing property rights unless clearly instructed otherwise. See Van der Walt *South African Journal on Human Rights* (n 44 above) 411. Although I am generally in agreement with this assessment, I believe the influence of the Constitution - especially sec 26(3) - is gradually turning the tide even in the more traditional courts such as the Supreme Court of Appeal.
[69] Resolution 1992/14.

recommended that all governments provide immediate restitution, compensation and/or appropriate and sufficient alternative accommodation or land, consistent with their wishes or needs, to persons and communities who have been forcibly evicted, following mutually satisfactory negotiations with the affected persons or groups.

Furthermore, the UN Commission on Human Rights has adopted a further Resolution on Forced Evictions,[70] parts of which are applicable to the issue at hand, and will accordingly be referred to in the present section. It has recognised forced evictions to mean '[t]he involuntary removal of persons, families and groups from their homes and communities, resulting in increased levels of homelessness and in inadequate housing and living conditions'.[71] It has noted its concern with the fact that forced evictions and homelessness intensify social conflict and inequality and invariably affect the poorest, most socially, economically, environmentally and politically disadvantaged and vulnerable sectors of society. In addressing the prevalent issue of forced evictions, the UN Commission on Human Rights has emphasised that governments bear the ultimate legal responsibility for preventing forced evictions.[72]

The Committee on ESCR has placed considerable emphasis on forced evictions and has asserted that 'instances of forced evictions are *prima facie* incompatible with the requirements of the [CESCR] and can only be justified in the most exceptional circumstances and in accordance with the relevant principles of international law'.[73] Although the South African Constitution differs in the sense that it prohibits evictions without an order of court after all the relevant circumstances have been considered (as opposed to 'in the most exceptional circumstances'), the relevant factors considered by the Committee on ESCR when deciding whether evictions should be allowed might be of help to South African courts when interpreting section 26(3) as well as the provisions of section 4 of PIE.[74]

---

[70] Resolution 1993/77.
[71] As above preamble para 5.
[72] n 70 above, preamble para 8.
[73] General Comment No 4 *The right to adequate housing (art 11(1) of the Covenant)* (6th session, 1991) [UN Doc E/1992/23] para 18.
[74] Some examples of what have been considered to be 'the most exceptional circumstances' in the international realm include racist or other discriminatory statements, attacks or treatment by one tenant or resident against a neighbouring tenant; unjustifiable destruction of rented property; the persistent non-payment of rent despite a proven ability to pay and in the absence of unfulfilled duties of the landlord to ensure dwelling habitability; persistent anti-social behaviour which threatens, harasses or intimidates neighbours, persistent behaviour which threatens public health or safety; manifestly criminal behaviour, as defined by law, which threatens the rights of others; the illegal occupation of property which is inhabited at the time of occupation; and the occupation of land or homes of occupied populations by nationals of an occupying power. See eg Committee on ESCR General Comment No 7 *The right to adequate housing (art 11.1): Forced evictions* (16th session, 1997) para 11.

3.3 Positive obligations

Section 26 of the Constitution also places a positive obligation on the state and other relevant actors to 'protect, promote and fulfil' the right of access to housing.[75] This means, at the very least, that the state must take steps – including the enactment of legislation – to ensure that individuals can acquire access to housing without interference from private actors and institutions. It furthermore means that the state has a duty to devise and implement – progressively and within its available resources – a comprehensive plan to ensure the full realisation of the right of access to housing. This plan cannot merely be aimed at providing individuals with shelter or basic housing, but must be aimed at providing adequate housing.[76] What is required is a holistic approach aimed at providing all South Africans with access to adequate, comprehensive housing that will enable an individual to live a dignified and productive life. This means that the state has a duty to foster conditions to enable citizens to gain access to health care services on an equitable basis.[77] The state is required 'to devise a comprehensive and workable plan to meet its obligations' in terms of section 26.[78]

Implicit in this approach is the understanding that the right of access to housing does not entitle any applicant to *individual* relief, because the state's duty is not immediately to provide each and every South African with the best possible housing that money can buy, but to devise and implement a comprehensive plan that will achieve this goal over time.[79] When devising and implementing this plan, the state must take cognisance of the conditions and capabilities of people at all economic levels of our society.[80] Those who can afford to pay for housing should do so themselves, but where people have no money to pay, the state has a duty to take steps to unlock the system through legislation and other measures. The state must address the needs of those who can afford housing and those who cannot. More importantly, the 'poor are particularly vulnerable and their needs require special attention'.[81]

The crux of any inquiry about whether the state has met its obligations in terms of sections 26(1) and (2) will depend on what constitutes 'appropriate steps'. Steps will be appropriate if they meet three key elements set out in section 26(2), namely (a) whether they are reasonable legislative or other steps; (b) to achieve the progressive realisation of the right; and (c) within available resources.

---

[75] See sec 7(2), which states that the state 'must respect, protect, promote and fulfil the rights in the Bill of Rights'.
[76] *Grootboom* (n 1 above) para 35, where the court states that the right of access to housing 'requires more than brick and mortar'.
[77] n 76 above, para 93.
[78] n 76 above, para 38.
[79] n 76 above, paras 94-95.
[80] n 76 above, para 35.
[81] n 76 above, para 36. See also *Treatment Action Campaign* (n 9 above) para 70.

3.3.1 Reasonable legislative and other measures

The obligation on the state is firstly to act reasonably in pursuit of realising the goal of providing accessible and adequate housing for people from all economic spheres. To judge the reasonability of the steps taken, it must be determined whether there is a comprehensive policy, encompassing all three tiers of government, to realise the right of access to housing progressively.[82] Legislation in itself will not be sufficient. What is required is for the state to act in order to achieve the intended result according to comprehensive policies and programmes that are reasonable both in their conception and implementation.[83] To determine whether such measures are reasonable, it will be necessary to consider housing problems in their social, economic and historical context and to consider the capacity of institutions responsible for implementing the programme. The programme must be 'balanced and flexible' and a programme 'that excludes a significant segment of society cannot be said to be reasonable'.[84] More pertinently, those whose needs are the most urgent and whose ability to enjoy all rights are most in peril, must not be ignored by the measures aimed at achieving the realisation of the goal. Where measures, though statistically successful, fail to respond to those most desperate, they may not pass the test of reasonability.[85]

This signals the interrelated and mutually supporting nature of the right of access to housing and the right to equality and the overarching goal of striving for 'real' equality and a respect for dignity. State action or inaction that fails to take into account the structural inequalities in society and action that fails to take into account the impact of that action or inaction on the relevant groups who are most vulnerable and in greater need of state assistance will inevitably become difficult to be justified as reasonable.

3.3.2 Progressive realisation of the right

The second requirement of progressive realisation signals that the right cannot be realised immediately. Nevertheless, it establishes a clear obligation on the state to move towards realisation of the right. What is required is that the state immediately takes steps to facilitate access to adequate housing progressively.

---

[82] *Grootboom* (n 1 above) para 41.
[83] n 82 above, para 42.
[84] n 82 above, para 43. See also *Treatment Action Campaign* (n 9 above) para 68.
[85] *Grootboom* (n 1 above) para 44.

The state has a duty to move expeditiously and effectively towards that goal. Any deliberate retrogressive measures in that regard would require the most careful consideration and would need to be fully justified by reference to the totality of the rights provided in the Bill of Rights.[86] It is imperative to understand that the requirement of progressive realisation of rights does not mean the state can sit back and do nothing. It must take steps immediately, even if those steps will not provide every South African with immediate access to adequate, humane and effective housing. The Constitutional Court in *Grootboom* thus endorsed the understanding of 'progressive realisation' set out by the Committee on ESCR in General Comment 3.

3.3.3 Resource constraints

To determine whether the state's action or inaction is reasonable, one has to take into account the resources available to realise the right in question. There has to be a balance between goal and means. The measures have to be calculated to attain a goal expeditiously and effectively, but the availability of resources would always be an important factor in determining what was reasonable in a particular case.[87]

While it would be inappropriate for the court to make orders directed at rearranging budgets, a determination of the unreasonableness of government action or inaction might well have budgetary implications.[88]

Where resources are clearly insufficient to provide any meaningful access to adequate housing, a lack of action on the part of the state may be found to be more reasonable than in cases where the resource constraints are less severe.

When considering resource constraints, it may be kept in mind that resources here refer to both the resources within the state and those

---

[86] n 85 above, para 45, relying on para 9 of General Comment No 3 (n 36 above). See also The Limburg Principles (a set of interpretative principles concerning the implementation of CESCR developed by human rights scholars and representatives of several UN bodies), which has also accorded significant attention to the term 'progressive realisation', which warrants attention. Principle 16 notes that '[a]ll state parties have an obligation to begin immediately to take steps towards full realisation of the rights contained in the Covenant'. Principle 21 notes as follows: 'The obligation 'to achieve progressively the full realisation of the rights' requires state parties to move as expeditiously as possible towards the realisation of the rights. Under no circumstances shall this be interpreted as implying for States the right to defer indefinitely efforts to ensure full realisation. On the contrary, all state parties have the obligation to begin immediately to take steps to fulfil their obligations under the Covenant' (Limburg Principles on the Implementation of the International Covenant on Economic, Social and Cultural Rights [UN Doc E/CN 4/1987/17]).
[87] *Grootboom* (n 1 above) para 46.
[88] *Treatment Action Campaign* (n 9 above) para 38. See also the Limburg Principles (n 86 above). Eg, Principle 23 provides as follows: 'The obligation of progressive achievement exists independently of the increase in resources; it requires effective use of resources available.' Limburg Principle 24 provides as follows: 'Progressive implementation can be affected not only by increasing resources, but also by the development of societal resources necessary for the realisation by everyone of the rights recognised in the Covenant.'

available from the international community through international cooperation and assistance.[89]

3.4 Minimum core obligations

It is clear from the above that the right of access to housing does not provide individual claimants with an individual right to claim relief from the government in the form, say, of ordering the government to provide him or her with access to housing. The question arose in both *Grootboom* and the *Treatment Action Campaign* cases whether the rights set out in sections 26 and 27 nevertheless required the state to provide at least a 'minimum core' of these rights regardless of resource and other constraints. The concept of 'minimum core' was developed by the Committee on ESCR and constitutes an attempt to define more clearly a minimum floor of social and economic entitlements that each state must ensure for its inhabitants as a matter of priority: 'A state party in which any significant number of individuals is deprived of essential foodstuffs, of essential primary health care, of basic shelter and housing, or of the most basic forms of education is, *prima facie*, failing to discharge its obligations under the Covenant.'[90]

In *Grootboom*, the Court indicated that evidence in a particular case may show that there is a minimum core of a particular service that should be taken into account in determining whether measures adopted by the state are reasonable.[91] But this does not mean that the socio-economic rights of the Constitution should be construed as entitling everyone to demand that the minimum core be provided to them. Minimum core is therefore relevant to reasonableness under section 26(2), and not as a self-standing right conferred on everyone under section 26(1).[92] Section 26(1) can therefore not be read to establish a positive obligation on the state to provide a 'minimum core' regardless of the qualification set out in section 26(2).[93] Courts 'are not institutionally equipped to make the wide-ranging factual and political enquiries necessary for determining what the minimum-core standards' should be,[94] and the Constitution thus contemplates a rather restrained role for the courts, namely to require the state to take measures to meet its constitutional obligations and to subject the reasonableness of these measures to evaluation.[95] But despite the fact that individuals cannot invoke the concept of a 'minimum core' to demand specific performance from the government, the concept remains relevant when evaluating the reasonableness of government action or inaction.

---

[89] De Vos (n 7 above) 98.
[90] General Comment No 3 (n 36 above) para 10.
[91] *Grootboom* (n 1 above) para 33.
[92] As above. See also *Treatment Action Campaign & Others* (n 9 above) para 34.
[93] *Treatment Action Campaign* (n 9 above) para 34.
[94] n 93 above, para 37.
[95] n 93 above, para 38.

3.5 International law and the concept of 'adequate' housing

Section 26(1) of the Constitution provides for a right of access to *adequate* housing as opposed to a right to housing *per se* or a right to shelter. In *Grootboom,* the Constitutional Court did endorse the idea that adequate housing 'entails more than bricks and mortar ... For a person to have access to adequate housing all of these conditions need to be met: there must be land, there must be services, there must be a dwelling.'[96] But the Constitutional Court has not focused specifically on the concept of adequate housing and has not provided a detailed indication of what might constitute 'adequate' housing for the purposes of section 26. It is therefore relevant and appropriate to provide an overview of the very specific understanding provided by the Committee on ESCR in General Comment 4 regarding what constitutes adequate housing. In General Comment No 4,[97] the Committee commented that, while cultural, climatic and contextual factors are important in making a determination on the adequacy of the housing, there are certain core factors that are central to making this determination. These entitlements form the core guarantees that, under international law, are legally vested in all persons. They include the following:

3.5.1 Legal security of tenure

Legal security of tenure refers to the fact that all persons should possess a degree of security of tenure that guarantees legal protection against forced evictions, harassment and other threats. The Committee on ESCR has noted that, in ensuring legal security of tenure, governments are obliged to take measures aimed at conferring legal security of tenure upon those households currently lacking such protection. It has further noted that this should be undertaken in consultation with the affected groups or individuals.[98]

3.5.2 Availability of services, materials and infrastructure

The Committee on ESCR has noted that the availability of services, materials and infrastructure refers to the right of all beneficiaries of the right of access to adequate housing to have sustainable access to natural and common resources, clean drinking water, energy for cooking, heating, lighting, sanitation and washing facilities, food storage facilities, refuse disposal, site drainage and emergency services.[99]

---

[96] *Grootboom* (n 1 above) para 35.
[97] General Comment No 4 (n 73 above) para 8.
[98] n 97 above, para 8(a).
[99] n 97 above, para 8(b).

3.5.3 Affordable housing

The Committee has noted that costs associated with housing should be at such a level that the attainment and satisfaction of other basic needs are not threatened or compromised by efforts to acquire or maintain access to housing. It has further referred to the need for housing subsidies and protection from unreasonable rentals or sporadic rent increases.[100]

3.5.4 Habitable housing

Adequate housing should, according to the Committee, be habitable. It should provide the inhabitants with adequate space and protection from the cold, damp, heat, rain, wind or other threats to health, structural hazards and disease vectors. The physical safety of the occupants must be guaranteed.[101]

3.5.5 Accessible housing

Adequate housing must further be accessible to those entitled to it. The Committee has noted that disadvantaged groups must be accorded full and sustainable access to adequate housing resources. These would include groups such as the elderly, children, the physically disabled, the terminally ill, HIV positive individuals, the mentally ill, victims of natural disasters, people living in disease-prone areas and other vulnerable groups. Such groups should be ensured some degree of priority consideration in the housing sphere and their housing needs should be adequately reflected in laws and policies.[102]

3.5.6 Location

Adequate housing must, according to the Committee, be in a location that allows access to employment options, health care services, schools, child care centres and other social and recreational facilities. Furthermore, housing should not be built on polluted sites, nor in immediate proximity to pollution sources that threaten the right to health of the inhabitants.[103]

3.5.7 Culturally adequate housing

Finally, the Committee has commented that the way in which housing is constructed, the building materials used and the policies underlying

---

[100] n 97 above, para 8(c).
[101] n 97 above, para 8(d).
[102] n 97 above, para 8(e).
[103] n 97 above, para 8(f).

these must appropriately enable the expression of cultural identity and diversity.[104]

4 Housing-related protection of vulnerable groups

The Constitutional Court has set out general principles that allow us to understand – to some degree at least – the extent of the obligations engendered by the right of access to housing in general. However, as indicated above, the Constitution also contains housing-related protection for certain vulnerable groups, such as children and prisoners. Given the general principles set out by the Constitutional Court, I shall now turn to these issues.

4.1 Children's right to shelter

As has been noted, section 28(1)(c) of the Constitution accords every child the right to basic nutrition, shelter, basic health services and social services. This section can be distinguished textually from section 26. Firstly, it provides for a right to shelter as opposed to adequate housing. A definition of what constitutes shelter for the purposes of the section is accordingly required. Secondly, it provides for a right to shelter as opposed to a right of 'access' to shelter. Finally, children's rights to shelter are subject to neither the internal qualifier of 'progressive realisation' nor that of 'within its available resources'. Judging from these differences, it has been argued that children's right to shelter is subject to immediate implementation and resource limitations may not be used to justify a failure to implement the right.[105]

However, the Constitutional Court in *Grootboom* in essence held that parents bore the primary obligation to provide shelter for their children. Because section 28(1)(c) should be read with sections 28(1)(b) and 26, the 'carefully constructed constitutional scheme for progressive realisation of socio-economic rights would make little sense if it could be trumped in every case by the rights of children to get shelter from the state on demand'.[106]

The Constitutional Court decided that the right to provide shelter was primarily imposed on the parents or family and only alternatively on the state. It further stated that the state's obligation was to provide shelter to those children who were for example removed from their families.[107] Thus, the Court argued, section 28(1)(c) 'does not create any primary state obligation to provide shelter on demand to parents and their children if children are being cared for by their

---

[104] n 97 above, para 8(g).
[105] See the High Court judgment in *Grootboom v Oostenberg Municipality & Others* 2000 3 BCLR 277 (C).
[106] *Grootboom* (n 1 above) para 71.
[107] For a general discussion of children's rights to shelter, see *Grootboom* (n 1 above) paras 70-79 of the judgment.

parents or families'.[108] The Court held that this did not mean that the state was absolved from all responsibility. The state would have to provide the legal and administrative infrastructure necessary to ensure that children are accorded the protection contemplated by section 28. In addition, the state would be required to fulfil its obligations to provide families with access to land in terms of section 25, access to adequate housing in terms of section 26 as well as access to the rights enumerated in section 27.[109] As was reiterated in the *Treatment Action Campaign* case, the needs of children will often be 'most urgent' and their rights 'most in peril'[110] and this might require the state to take special cognisance of their needs when devising and implementing the progressive realisation of the right of access to housing.

4.2 Prisoners' rights to adequate accommodation

Section 35(2)(e) of the Constitution provides for prisoners' rights to adequate accommodation at state expense. Prisoners' rights to adequate accommodation are not qualified by the term 'access'. Unlike the right of children to shelter, which the Constitutional Court linked to the duty of parents to provide shelter, this right is clearly directly enforceable against the state. Prisoners are, by their very circumstances, charges of the state and are thus entitled to accommodation at state expense. The only qualification that is contained in the text of section 35(2)(e) itself is that such accommodation must be adequate. In determining adequacy in the South African context, cognisance should be taken of international standards as set out in documents such as the Standard Minimum Rules for the Treatment of Prisoners.[111] The emphasis both at international level as well as in the South African Constitution is that the conditions in which people are detained and accommodated need to be consistent with human dignity.

---

[108] n 107 above, para 77.
[109] n 107 above, para 78.
[110] *Treatment Action Campaign* (n 9 above) para 78.
[111] Adopted by the First United Nations Congress on the Prevention of Crime and the Treatment of Offenders, held at Geneva in August 1955, and approved by the Economic and Social Council by its Resolution 663 C (XXIV) of 31 July 1957 and 2076 (LXII) of 13 May 1977.

In *Strydom v Minister of Correctional Services & Others*,[112] the Witwatersrand Division of the High Court relied on section 35(2)(e), read with section 7(2) of the Constitution, and found that prisoners have a right to be housed in circumstances where they would be able to enjoy all the privileges recognised by the Department of Correctional Services and that some of these privileges require access to electricity. Where, as in the present case, prisoners were housed in cells with no access to electric sockets, the Department was under a constitutional duty to work towards the provision of this facility.[113] Given the fact that the Department had already allocated funds to provide the prisoners in this instant case with access to electricity, the court therefore directed the Department to report to it to set out a timetable for upgrading the electricity at Johannesburg Maximum Security Prison where the applicants had been held.[114] This case suggests that adequate facilities must at least encompass those facilities envisioned by the rules of the Department of Correctional Services itself.

5 Conclusion

The right of access to housing does not provide the individual with a right to demand that the government provides him or her with access to a house. However, it does begin to spell out the duties of the state in progressively realising the right of access to housing. It is clear that the exact duties of the state will depend on the specific context and that cases will have to be judged on the individual merits. This is a difficult task, but in attempts to elaborate on the actual constitutional duties placed on the state the provisions of international treaties and the opinions of the Committee on Economic, Social and Cultural Rights will be of specific importance.

---

[112] 1999 3 BCLR 342 (W).
[113] n 112 above, para 15.
[114] n 112 above, para 23.

Four / Rights concerning health

Charles Ngwena
Rebecca Cook

1   Introduction

As a preliminary issue, it is worth noting that different terms have been used to describe rights concerning health care.[1] The terms 'right to health care', 'right to health protection' or 'right to health' have all been advanced as sufficiently conveying the notion of entitlement to the protection of health and the provision of health care under international law and domestic legal systems. There is no necessary conflict between the terms 'right to health care', 'right to health protection' or 'right to health'. The ultimate objective behind these normative terms is the realisation of the highest attainable standard of health. However, depending on the context, there might be good reasons underlying the choice of a particular term.

Proponents of the terms 'right to health care' or 'right to health protection' have argued that these terms are more accurate and more realistic than 'right to health' in that health itself cannot be guaranteed. At best, the state can provide diagnostic, preventative, curative and rehabilitative services for the attainment of health.[2] However, at an international level, the tendency has been to prefer the term 'right to health' for the reason that it is more inclusive than 'right to health care' or 'right to health protection', and has acquired more common usage. Leary, for example, concedes that the term 'right to health' might seem strange and absurd to the extent that no government, international organisation or individual can muster the capacity to guarantee a person's good health.[3] However, 'right to health' is a more convenient shorthand to cover the detailed language and references to fundamental rights principles that are found in international treaties, including the Universal Declaration of Human Rights (Universal Declaration) and the International Covenant on Economic, Social and Cultural Rights (CESCR). Toebes echoes this point when she says that international provisions concerning health not only proclaim a right to health care, but also a right to other services such as environmental health protection and occupational health services.[4] The term 'right to health' is widely understood to cover not only access to a range of facilities, goods and services

---
[1]   B Toebes 'Towards an improved understanding of the international human right to health' (1999) 21 *Human Rights Quarterly* 661-663.
[2]   R Roemer 'The right to health care' in HL Fuenzalida-Puelma & SS Connor (eds) *The right to health in the Americas: A comparative constitutional study* (1989) 17-23; H Hannum 'The UDHR in national and international law' (1998) 3(2) *Health and Human Rights* 145 153.
[3]   V Leary 'The right to health in international human rights law' (1994) 1(1) *Health and Human Rights* 25 28-34.
[4]   Toebes (n 1 above) 662-663.

(including health services), but also the conditions necessary for the attainment of health, such as food, housing, safe water, sanitation, healthy working conditions and a healthy environment.[5] Indeed, this is how the right to health is understood by the Committee on Economic, Social and Cultural Rights (Committee on ESCR), which is the primary organ responsible for monitoring the implementation of rights under CESCR, including article 12 pertaining to the right to health.[6]

In this chapter, a bifurcated approach will be adopted to accommodate prevailing terminological usage as well as to reflect South African peculiarities. To complement common usage at an international level, the term 'right to health' will be used when discussing international instruments bearing on health. However, when discussing the South African situation, in particular constitutional provisions, the term 'right to health care' will generally be preferred unless qualified, not least because section 27, the main constitutional provision on rights concerning health, explicitly provides for a 'right of access to health care services' rather than a right to health or a right to health protection.[7] The choice of language in the Constitution has implications for judicial interpretation and application of section 27.[8]

2 International law

In modern times, the earliest conceptualisation of a right to health did not so much emanate from a human rights organ, but from an international health authority - the World Health Organisation (WHO).[9] In the Preamble to the Constitution of the WHO, which was written in 1946, the WHO proclaimed that '[t]he enjoyment of the highest attainable standard of living is one of the fundamental rights

---

[5] C Shinn 'The right to the highest attainable standard of health: Public health's opportunity to reframe a human rights debate in the United States' (1999) 4(1) *Health and Human Rights* 115 119.

[6] Committee on ESCR, General Comment No 14, *The right to the highest attainable standard of health (art 12 of the Covenant)* (22nd session, 2000) [UN Doc E/C 12/2000/4].

[7] AR Chapman 'Core obligations related to the right to health and their relevance for South Africa' (2002) in D Brand & S Russell (eds) *Exploring the core content of socio-economic rights: South African and international perspectives* (2002) 35 51-52.

[8] See, in general, C Ngwena 'Access to health care as a fundamental right: The scope and limits of section 27 of the Constitution' (2000) 25 *Journal for Juridical Science* 1.

[9] Chapman (n 7 above) 39.

of every human being, without distinction of race, religion, political belief, economic or social condition'.[10] The WHO's Constitution defines health as 'a state of complete physical, mental and social well-being and not merely the absence of disease or infirmity'.[11] The right to health has since become an integral part of a host of human rights instruments at both an international and regional level.

The array of human rights instruments and documents that deal with the right to health is vast. At an international level, the following treaties contain provisions that address the right to health:

- the Universal Declaration of Human Rights (1948);[12]
- the Standard Minimum Rules for the Treatment of Prisoners (1955);[13]
- the International Convention on the Elimination of All Forms of Racial Discrimination (1965) (CERD);[14]
- the International Covenant on Economic, Social and Cultural Rights (1966) (CESCR);[15]
- the International Convention on the Elimination of All Forms of Discrimination Against Women (1979) (CEDAW);[16]
- the Convention Concerning Indigenous and Tribal Peoples in Independent Countries (1989);[17]
- the Convention on the Rights of the Child (1989) (CRC);[18]
- the International Convention on the Protection of the Rights of All Migrant Workers and Members of their Families (1990).[19]

While the above instruments directly address the right to health, it is important to appreciate that because the right to health overlaps with other rights such as environmental rights and the rights to life, food, shelter, housing and so on, there is also a host of other international instruments with provisions that impact on the right to health, albeit indirectly or implicitly. An example is article 6 of the International Covenant on Civil and Political Rights (CCPR).[20] The Human Rights Committee, the United Nations organ that monitors compliance of states with CCPR, has interpreted the corresponding duty to the right to life in article 6 expansively, to include a duty to take positive measures to reduce infant mortality, increase life

---

[10] Constitution of the World Health Organisation, adopted by the International Health Conference on 22 July 1946, opened for signature on 22 July 1946, and entered into force on 7 April 1948, available at http://www.who.int/governance/en (accessed 31 July 2004).
[11] n 10 above, Preamble.
[12] Art 25.
[13] Arts 22-26 & 82.
[14] Art 5(e)(iv).
[15] Art 12.
[16] Art 12.
[17] Art 25.
[18] Art 24.
[19] Art 28.
[20] RJ Cook et al Reproductive health and human rights: Integrating medicine, ethics and law (2003) 160-164.

expectancy, and eliminate epidemics[21]. Another example is the Human Rights Committee's approach when interpreting article 7 of CCPR, which guarantees the right to be free from inhuman and degrading treatment.[22] The Human Rights Committee has interpreted article 7 generously, thus making it a duty to ensure that women have reasonable access to safe abortion services.[23]

Mainly as a result of the influence of the Universal Declaration, there are also regional human rights instruments. The following regional instruments, *inter alia*, address the right to health:

- the European Social Charter (1961);[24]
- the African Charter on Human and Peoples' Rights (1981);[25]
- the Additional Protocol to the American Convention on Human Rights in the Area of Economic, Social and Cultural Rights (1988);[26] and
- the African Charter on the Rights and Welfare of the Child (1990).[27]

In addition to human rights treaties, the right to health has also been addressed in international debates. Some of the debates have culminated in documented consensus statements that have come to be regarded as authoritative.[28] In this connection, special mention must be made of the Programme of Action of the International Conference on Population and Development (the Cairo Programme),[29] a follow-up to the Cairo Programme - Cairo Plus Five,[30] the Beijing Declaration and Platform of Action of the Fourth World Conference on Women (the Beijing Platform[31]), and a follow-up to the Beijing Platform - Beijing Plus[32] Five, that produced documented authoritative statements on the meaning and scope of the right to health especially as it applies to the health of women. States are slowly applying the right to health, whether found in national constitutions, international or regional human rights treaties or international consensus documents, to redress the inequities in health. As the evidence of inequities in health becomes more compelling,[33] health advocacy groups are increasingly turning to

---

[21] Human Rights Committee General Comment No 6 (16th session, 1982) [37 UN GAOR, Supplement No 40 (A/37/40), annex V] para 5.
[22] Cook *et al* (n 20 above) 170-175.
[23] Concluding Observations of the Human Rights Committee: Peru, 18/11/96, CCPR/C/79/Add 72, para 15.
[24] Arts 11 & 13.
[25] Art 16.
[26] Art 10.
[27] Art 14.
[28] Toebes (n 1 above) 664; Cook *et al* (n 20 above) 225-228.
[29] United Nations *Report of the International Conference on Population and Development* (1994).
[30] United Nations *Key actions for the further implementation of the programme of action of the International Conference on Population and Development* (1999).
[31] United Nations *Report of the Fourth World Conference on Women* (1995).
[32] United Nations *Report of the Ad Hoc Committee of the Whole of the Twenty-Third Special Session of the General Assembly* (2000).
[33] T Evans *et al* (eds) *Challenging inequities in health: From ethics to action* (2001).

human rights tribunals and national courts to achieve social justice in access to health resources and improved equity in health outcomes. The challenges of doing so are enormous in part because there is limited experience in applying human rights in the health care context. Nonetheless, the experience is growing, and is facilitated by research and scholarship in the area of health and human rights and the work of WHO.[34]

3 State obligations in international law

A criticism that has often been directed at socio-economic rights, including the right to health, is that, when they are contrasted with their civil and political counterparts, their content and parameters are not easily ascertainable.[35] It is said that such rights are characterised by vagueness, and that the individual entitlements they create as well as the corresponding obligations they place on the state are not clear.[36] But while these observations were true at the time that socio-economic rights were first conceived, there has, over the years, been tremendous conceptual and interpretive progress by treaty bodies as well as other agencies. According to Leckie, what is impeding the implementation of socio-economic rights is no longer the limitation of jurisprudence but problems of perception and resolve.[37] Despite the acceptance of the interdependence and indivisibility of rights, states and states bodies have, on the whole, continued to harbour a truncated view of human rights, in which civil and political rights are seen to stand not so much in juxtaposition with, as in a hierarchically superior order to, socio-economic rights.

3.1 The Universal Declaration of Human Rights

The earliest modern human rights instrument - the Universal Declaration of Human Rights - proclaims a right to health, but without mapping its normative content. Article 25 of the Universal Declaration says:

> (1) Everyone has the right to a standard of living adequate for the health and well-being of himself and his family, including food, clothing, housing, and medical care and necessary social services, and the right to security in the event of unemployment, sickness, disability, widowhood, old age or other lack of livelihood in circumstances beyond his control.
>
> (2) Motherhood and childhood are entitled to special care and assistance. All children, whether born in or out of wedlock, shall enjoy the same social protection.

---

[34] World Health Organisation *Twenty-five questions and answers on health and human rights* (2002).
[35] Toebes (n 1 above) 661-662.
[36] As above.
[37] S Leckie 'Another step towards indivisibility: Identifying key features of violations of economic, social and cultural rights' (1998) 20 *Human Rights Quarterly* 81 82.

The Universal Declaration sought to achieve 'a common standard of achievement for all peoples and all nations'.[38] Though the Universal Declaration has come to acquire significant moral and legal force, and to provide the inspiration of many domestic constitutions, it was, nonetheless, not intended to be a statement of law or legal obligations.[39] Because it was not a treaty, it lacked normative force. It was exhortatory, based on existing commitments in national laws, rather than binding on member states.[40] What was missing from the Universal Declaration was a provision for corresponding obligations on member states to not only protect and promote, but also fulfil the rights accorded to individuals. The Universal Declaration did not impose a new obligation on part of the state to take positive measures aimed at enabling and assisting individuals and communities to realise the rights that it had proclaimed. In respect of socio-economic rights, including the right to health, this lacuna has been primarily filled by CESCR.

3.2 The International Covenant on Economic, Social and Cultural Rights

CESCR put into normative form what the Universal Declaration had merely proclaimed. CESCR, which South Africa has signed but not yet ratified, binds ratifying states to discharge the obligations that they have undertaken. In this regard, article 2(1) of CESCR provides that:

> Each State party to the present Covenant undertakes to take steps, individually and through international assistance and co-operation, especially economic and technical, to the maximum of its available resources, with a view to achieving progressively the full realisation of the rights recognised in the present Covenant by all appropriate means, including particularly the adoption of legislative measures.

Article 12 of CESCR, which is arguably the most important international provision on the right to health,[41] is explicit about the recognition of the right to health and the attendant obligations on part of the state. The obligations are not only in respect of providing curative care, but also preventative care. It says:

> (1) The States Parties to the present Covenant recognise the right of everyone to the enjoyment of the highest attainable standard of physical and mental health.
>
> (2) The steps to be taken by the States Parties to the present Covenant to achieve the full realisation of this right shall include those necessary for:
>
> (a) the provision for the reduction of the stillbirth-rate and of infant mortality and for the healthy development of the child;
>
> (b) the improvement of all aspects of environmental and industrial hygiene;
>
> (c) the prevention, treatment and control of epidemic, endemic, occupational and other diseases;

---

[38] Preamble to the Universal Declaration.
[39] Hannum (n 2 above) 147.
[40] As above.
[41] Chapman (n 7 above) 40.

(d) the creation of conditions which would assure to all medical service and medical attention in the event of sickness.

The work of the Committee on ESCR has been particularly instrumental in promoting greater awareness of the import as well as tangibility of obligations imposed upon states by CESCR.[42] The Limburg Principles on the Implementation of CESCR and the Maastricht Guidelines on Violations of Economic, Social and Cultural Rights have also been very useful in clarifying the normative content of CESCR, and developing criteria for identifying violations of socio-economic rights in domestic legal spheres.[43]

In its General Comments as well as Concluding Observations, the Committee on ESCR has clarified and illuminated provisions of CESCR, including articles 2(1) and 12. In General Comment No 3, the Committee on ESCR emphasised that article 2 is central to the understanding of the nature and extent of states' obligations under the various provisions of CESCR.[44] Article 2 imposes obligations of conduct as well as result.[45] The obligation of conduct requires the state to take action reasonably calculated to realise the enjoyment of a particular right.[46] The obligation of result requires the state to achieve a specified target as a measure of the standard of realisation of a particular right.[47] It would be a mistake, however, to see the two kinds of obligations as mutually exclusive. Instead they overlap with one another.[48]

The obligation 'to take steps' in article 2(1) is mandatory.[49] It is not open to a state party to choose not to take steps. What the state has, however, is an appreciable margin of discretion in the choice of appropriate means for satisfying the right in question.[50] Though legislation will frequently be indispensable, it is not a mandatory means for realising rights under CESCR. Other appropriate measures include administrative, financial, educational, judicial and social measures.[51] What is crucial is not so much the form of the measure, but its effectiveness.

---

[42] Leckie (n 37 above) 82.
[43] The Limburg Principles were developed in 1986 by a group of experts in international law under the auspices of the International Commission of Jurists. The principles can be found in the 'Limburg Principles on the implementation of the International Covenant on Economic, Social and Cultural Rights' (1987) 9 *Human Rights Quarterly* 122. The Maastricht Guidelines were similarly developed in 1997 under the auspices of the International Commission of Jurists. They serve to elaborate on the Limburg Principles in respect of the nature and scope of state violations of economic, social and cultural rights, and appropriate responses and remedies. V Dankwa et al 'Commentary to the Maastricht Guidelines on Violations of Economic, Social and Cultural Rights' (1998) 20 *Human Rights Quarterly* 705. The Maastricht Guidelines can be found in 'The Maastricht Guidelines on Violations of Economic, Social and Cultural Rights' (1998) 20 *Human Rights Quarterly* 691.
[44] General Comment No 3 *The nature of states parties' obligations (art 2, para 1 of the Covenant)* (5th session, 1990) [UN Doc E/1991/23] para 1.
[45] As above.
[46] Maastricht Guidelines (n 43 above) para 7.
[47] As above.
[48] Leckie (n 37 above) 92.
[49] General Comment No 3 (n 44 above) para 2.
[50] n 49 above, para 4.
[51] n 49 above, paras 5 & 7.

Though the concept of 'progressive realisation' implies that the realisation of the right in question will not generally be achieved immediately or within a short period of time, rights under CESCR cannot be deferred indefinitely. Steps towards achieving their realisation must be taken before or within a reasonable time after ratification.[52] The steps must be targeted, concrete, and transparent in this regard.[53] The state has an obligation to move as 'expeditiously' and 'effectively' as possible towards full realisation of the rights, making maximum use of available resources.[54] However, because the Committee on ESCR has not defined what constitutes moving expeditiously and effectively, it means that 'progressive realisation' does not, by itself, provide a ready criterion by which to review the performance of state parties.[55]

In any event, it is important to note that notwithstanding the notion of progressive realisation, provisions on non-discrimination and equal treatment impose immediate rather than progressive obligations and are comparable to obligations under the International Covenant on Civil and Political Rights. Under articles 2(2) and 2(3) of CESCR, state parties implicitly undertake to guarantee the rights enunciated in article 12 of CESCR regardless, *inter alia*, of race, colour, sex, language, religion, political or other opinion, national or social origin, property, birth or other analogous grounds.

The Committee on ESCR has affirmed that obligations under CESCR are amenable to realisation under any particular form of government.[56] Thus, it matters little whether the state is of a capitalist or socialist or mixed political orientation. What is crucial is that governments must subscribe to democracy and respect for human rights, and there must be maximum deployment of available resources towards the realisation of socio-economic rights. However, it is a reality that economic constraints are endemic to all countries and that some countries are much poorer than others. Where a state cannot meet the full realisation of a right due to lack of resources, it must at least endeavour to meet a certain minimum-level content of the right.[57] Moreover, the state must demonstrate that it has deployed its available resources to the maximum extent with a view to at least satisfying, as a matter of priority, the minimum obligation. In the context of the right to health, essential primary health and

---

[52] P Alston & G Quinn 'The nature and scope of state parties' obligations under the International Covenant on Economic, Social and Cultural Rights' (1987) 9 *Human Rights Quarterly* 156 166.
[53] General Comment No 3 (n 44 above) para 2.
[54] n 53 above, para 9.
[55] AR Chapman 'A "violations approach" for monitoring the International Covenant on Economic, Social and Cultural Rights' (1996) 18 *Human Rights Quarterly* 23 32.
[56] General Comment No 3 (n 44 above) para 8. However, note that it has been argued that the egalitarian orientation of the rights conferred by CESCR requires significant economic intervention by the state, and for this reason might be incompatible with governments that have a capitalist economic orientation. However, such criticism, as Alston and Quinn have observed, does not seem to reflect the reality as it is a universally accepted practice for governments to be involved in economic and social planning, through taxation and other means, even in the most *laissez faire* countries: Alston & Quinn (n 52 above) 181-183.
[57] General Comment No 3 (n 44 above) para 10.

underlying determinants of health such as essential foodstuffs, and basic shelter and housing constitute minimum core obligations.[58] Where failure to discharge minimum core obligations is attributed to a lack of available resources, the onus is on the state to demonstrate that every effort has been made to use all the resources at its disposal to satisfy this obligation as a matter of priority.[59] Vulnerable individuals and populations can be protected by the adoption of 'low-cost targeted programmes' even in times of severe economic constraints.[60] General Comment No 14, which is discussed below, has further developed the concept of minimum core obligations in the particular circumstances of the right to health. Available resources are taken to mean all the resources that the state has at its disposal, including international assistance and not merely what the state chooses to appropriate.[61] When inquiring into whether a state has deployed the maximum of available resources, it is therefore important to go beyond official government budgetary allocations so as to look at the 'real' resources.[62]

General Comment No 14 of the Committee on ESCR has illuminated, to a significant degree, the obligations of state parties in respect of the right to health under article 12 of CESCR. Apart from imposing obligations of conduct and result, article 12 can also be characterised in terms of three other types of obligations - obligations to 'respect, protect and fulfil' the rights conferred therein. According to General Comment No 14, the obligation to respect the right to health in article 12 requires the state, in the main, to refrain from adversely interfering with the right to health by denying or limiting equal access for all persons to preventive, curative and palliative health services.[63] For example, denial of access to health facilities to particular individuals or groups based on a discriminatory practice constitutes a violation of the obligation to respect.[64]

The obligation to protect primarily requires the state to prevent violations of the right to health by third parties by, for example, ensuring that the private health sector does not become a threat to availability, accessibility, acceptability and quality of health care, or ensuring that health care professionals meet the appropriate standards of education and discharge their duties with the requisite skill and standard of care.[65] Failures to discourage production, marketing and consumption of harmful substances such as tobacco and narcotics, or to enact laws to prevent damage to the environment, exemplify instances of a violation of a duty to protect.[66]

---

[58] As above.
[59] As above.
[60] n 57 above, para 12.
[61] n 57 above, para 13; Alston & Quinn (n 52 above) 178; RE Robertson 'Measuring state compliance with the obligation to devote the maximum available resources to realising economic, social and cultural rights' (1994) 16 *Human Rights Quarterly* 693 698.
[62] Alston & Quinn (n 52 above) 178.
[63] General Comment No 14 (n 6 above) para 34.
[64] n 53 above, para 50.
[65] n 53 above, para 35.
[66] n 53 above, para 51.

The obligation to fulfil requires the state to take positive measures to assist individuals and communities in realising the right to health.[67] The adoption of legislation and policies for realising the right to health, the provision by the state of health care services, including immunisations, and ensuring access to underlying determinants of health such as nutritiously safe food, potable drinking water, basic sanitation and adequate housing and living standards are examples of the obligation to fulfil. Insufficient expenditure or the misallocation of public resources which results in the non-enjoyment of the right to health, particularly by vulnerable individuals and communities, and failure to take measures to ameliorate inequitable distribution of health services are likely to be the most widespread kinds of violations of the duty to fulfil, especially in countries with extreme disparities in wealth and living standards.

As alluded to earlier, the right to health is closely related to and dependent upon the realisation of other rights, such as the rights to food, housing, work and education.[68] The right to health is not about the right to be healthy as some of the factors that influence health, including heredity and adoption of unhealthy lifestyles, are beyond the control of the state.[69] According to the Committee on ESCR, the right to health means certain freedoms and certain entitlements.[70] On the freedom side, it means a negative right to determine one's health, free from undue interference from the state, such as the right to consent to medical treatment. On the entitlement side, it means a positive right to the enjoyment of a variety of facilities, goods, services and conditions necessary for the realisation of the highest attainable standard of health. In its positive sense, the right to health imposes affirmative obligations on the state.

The Committee on ESCR has said that the right to health has four interrelated elements- 'availability, accessibility, acceptability and quality'.[71] 'Availability' requires that the public health care facilities, goods and services be available in sufficient quantity. 'Accessibility' has four overlapping dimensions, namely non-discrimination, physical accessibility, economic accessibility and information accessibility. 'Acceptability' requires that the health care services that are offered be ethically and culturally acceptable. 'Quality' ensures that it is not mere quantity that matters. Services must also be medically appropriate and of good quality.

The requirements of 'availability, accessibility, acceptability and quality' clearly suggest that article 12 is egalitarian in orientation. Thus article 12 seeks to secure not only non-discrimination, but also substantive equality in terms of access to health care services. It is ultimately aimed at attaining equal health outcomes for all persons, irrespective of means. This is underscored by a reaffirmation by the Committee on ESCR of the observation it made in General Comment

[67] n 53 above, paras 36-37.
[68] n 53 above, para 3.
[69] n 53 above, paras 8 & 9.
[70] n 53 above, para 8.
[71] n 53 above, para 12.

No 3 that the state has certain core obligations so as to ensure that a minimum essential level of the right to health is satisfied.[72] Essential primary health care is seen as a core minimum, and should be interpreted in the light of instruments such as the Alma Ata Declaration,[73] and the Programme of Action of the International Conference on Population and Development.[74] According to CESCR, at the very minimum, core obligations in respect of the right to health include the following obligations:[75]

- ensuring the right of access to health facilities, goods and services on a non-discriminatory basis, especially for vulnerable or marginalised groups;
- ensuring access to minimum essential food which is nutritionally adequate and safe;
- ensuring access to basic shelter, housing and sanitation, and an adequate supply of safe and potable water;
- providing essential drugs as defined under the WHO Action Programme on Essential Drugs;[76]
- ensuring equitable distribution of all health facilities and goods;
- adopting and implementing a national public health strategy and plan of action, on the basis of epidemiological evidence, addressing the health concerns of the whole population.

General Comment No 14 treats core obligations as strict non-derogable obligations.[77] It emphasises that a state cannot, under any circumstances whatsoever, justify its non-compliance with core obligations.[78] Thus a state cannot attribute, at all, failure to comply to lack of resources. In this regard, General Comment No 14 is a departure from General Comment No 3 (discussed above), which treats core obligations as rebuttable rather than irrebuttable obligations. The Maastricht Guidelines have reiterated this strict approach.[79] The virtue of the strict approach is that it is strongly egalitarian. It takes the idea of substantive equality seriously by requiring states to provide a minimum floor of health services in a manner comparable to the immediate realisation of civil and political rights. The rationale of requiring every state to comply with the core

---

[72] n 53 above, para 43.
[73] World Health Organisation *Primary health care: Report of the International Conference on Primary Health Care* (1978).
[74] n 29 above.
[75] General Comment No 14 (n 6 above) para 43.
[76] Essential drugs are those medicines that satisfy the priority health care needs of a given population. They are selected with due regard to public relevance, efficacy, safety and comparative cost-effectiveness. Essential medicines are intended to be available at all times in adequate amounts, in appropriate dosage forms, with assured quality and adequate information, and at a price the individual and the community can afford. The implementation of the concept of essential medicines is intended to be flexible to accommodate different situations. Ultimately, to determine what constitutes an essential medicine is a national responsibility. World Health Organisation *The 12th WHO model list of essential medicines* (2002).
[77] General Comment No 14 (n 6 above) para 47.
[78] As above.
[79] Maastricht Guidelines (n 43 above) paras 9 & 10.

obligations is that they are relatively affordable and do not require a significant diversion of resources.[80]

However, to be workable universally, including in developing countries, minimum core obligations should not be interpreted literally, but purposively. A purposive interpretation should necessarily take into account circumstances beyond the reasonable control of the state or *force majeure*.[81] Also, it should necessarily distinguish between inability to comply and unwillingness to comply on the part of the state.[82]

The egalitarian orientation of article 12 is also evident from health indicators and benchmarks that the Committee on ESCR has said are appropriate for guiding as well as monitoring implementation at national and international levels.[83] These indicators and benchmarks include those that have been developed by United Nations (UN) agencies such as the WHO, United Nations Children's Fund (UNICEF) and the United Nations Population Fund (UNPFA). Others have been developed in documents representing international consensus such as the Cairo Programme,[84] the Cairo Plus Five,[85] the Beijing Platform,[86] and the Beijing Plus Five.[87]

Health and health-related indicators are regarded as germane in determining whether governments are meeting their obligations under CESCR. Thinking on health indicators, human rights indicators and human development indicators is evolving. A distinction that is often made is between those indicators that measure access to services, often called health service or health coverage indicators, and those that measure health status, often called health status indicators. An example of a health service indicator is the percentage of births attended by a skilled health attendant in a given year. An example of health status indicator is infant mortality rates, that is the percentage of infants under the age of one that die in a given year.

Some indicators are more developed than others. In the context of reproductive health, for example, global indicators that are reasonably precise and workable have been developed by the WHO and in international documents.[88] The WHO's indicators for reproductive health include the following:

- contraceptive prevalence rate;
- maternal mortality ratio;
- percentage of women attended, at least once during pregnancy, by skilled health personnel for reasons relating to pregnancy;
- percentage of births attended by skilled health personnel;

---

[80] Dankwa *et al* (n 43 above) 717.
[81] Maastricht Guidelines (n 43 above) para 13; Dankwa *et al* (n 43 above) 719.
[82] As above.
[83] General Comment No 14 (n 6 above) paras 57 & 58.
[84] n 29 above.
[85] United Nations (n 30 above).
[86] *Report of the Fourth World Conference on Women* (n 31 above).
[87] *Report of the Ad Hoc Committee of the Whole of the Twenty-Third Special Session of the General Assembly* (n 32 above).
[88] Cook *et al* (n 20 above) 225-228.

- number of facilities with functioning basic essential obstetrics care per 500 000 population;
- number of facilities with functioning comprehensive essential obstetric care per 500 000 population;
- percentage of live births of low birth weight (<2 500g);
- percentage of women of reproductive age (15-49) screened for haemoglobin levels who are anaemic;
- percentage of obstetrics and gynaecological admissions due to unsafe abortion;
- prevalence of fertility in women; and
- positive syphilis serology prevalence in pregnant women.[89]

For the indicators to work, they must be translated into a standard for measuring compliance according to agreed international standards. An example in this regard is the following standard for measuring compliance offered by Cairo Plus Five:[90]

> In order to monitor progress towards the achievement of the goals of the International Conference on Population and Development for maternal mortality, countries should use the proportion of births assisted by skilled attendants as a benchmark indicator. By 2005, where the maternal mortality rate is very high, at least 40 per cent of all births should be assisted by skilled attendants; by 2010, this figure should be at least 50 per cent and by 2015, at least 60 per cent. All countries should continue their efforts so that globally, by 2005, 80 per cent of all births should be assisted by skilled attendants, by 2010, 85 per cent and by 2015, 90 per cent.

However, as Yamin and Maine have noted, the indicators that have been developed are not without limitations.[91] The indicators assume a certain level of capacity on the part of the state in gathering and interpreting data, yet such capacity may be lacking. Developing countries, especially, lack adequate systems for gathering data about, for example, maternal mortality. Maternal deaths may go unreported in rural areas where health facilities are largely deficient due to the historical urban-rural chasm that still plagues many developing countries. But the problem of capacity is not peculiar to developing countries. Yamin and Maine point to a study in the United States, which found that as many as 50% of all pregnancy-related deaths may have gone unrecognised.[92] Another limitation of the indicators is that while, for example, an unfavourable maternal mortality rate is an indication that something is wrong, it does not at the same time spell out what precise remedial action or actions need to be taken.[93] For these reasons, the indicators should be used cautiously and in combination with other interpretive guidelines.

---

[89] World Health Organisation *Reproductive health indicators for global monitoring: Report of the Second Interagency Meeting* (2001).
[90] United Nations (n 30 above) para 64; Cook *et al* (n 20 above) 62-63.
[91] AE Yamin & DP Maine 'Maternal mortality as a human rights issue: Measuring compliance with international treaty obligations' (1999) 21 *Human Rights Quarterly* 574-576.
[92] As above, 574; C Berg *et al* 'Pregnancy-related mortality in the United States 1987-1990' (1996) 88 *Obstetrics and Gynaecology* 161.
[93] Yamin & Maine (n 91 above) 575-576.

3.3 Interpreting the right to health under human rights treaties other than CESCR

Though the right to health has primarily been developed under CESCR, other treaties have also facilitated the development of its normative content, and in particular, the nature and scope of state obligations. The Committee on the Elimination of Discrimination Against Women (Committee on CEDAW), in its General Recommendation 24, has contributed to the elucidation of the obligations imposed by the right to health in the particular context of article 12 of CEDAW.[94] Article 12 provides that:

> (1) States Parties shall take all appropriate measures to eliminate discrimination against women in the field of health care in order to ensure, on a basis of equality of men and women, access to health care services, including those related to family planning.
>
> (2) Notwithstanding the provisions of paragraph 1 of this article, States Parties shall ensure to women appropriate services in connection with pregnancy, confinement and the post-natal period, granting free services where necessary, as well as adequate nutrition during pregnancy and lactation.

General Recommendation 24 has reinforced the importance of the right to health in respect of the particular circumstances of women and their historically vulnerable position. Its focus is the elimination of discrimination and the achievement of equality for women in the sphere of health.[95] In the particular circumstances of women, services must respond to the specific needs of a vulnerable and marginalised group. States should take into account that women are disproportionately vulnerable to gender discrimination and gender violence among other social ills. Health care services must be consciously gender-sensitive so as to be able to, *inter alia*, undertake preventive, promotional and remedial action to shield women from the impact of harmful socio-cultural practices. An illustration of gender sensitivity is taking cognisance of traditional practices such as female genital cutting (circumcision/mutilation), polygamy and marital rape that render women more vulnerable to HIV and other sexually transmitted diseases.[96]

A gender-based approach in planning and implementing programmes is part of eliminating discrimination against, and realising substantive equality for, women. It requires disaggregation of health and socio-economic data according to sex so as to be able to identify and remedy inequalities in health.[97] Where necessary, the state should supply free services to ensure safe pregnancies, childbirth and post-partum periods for women. States have a duty to ensure that women realise the right to safe motherhood and

---

[94] CEDAW General Recommendation 24 (1999).
[95] Cook *et al* (n 20 above) 198-202.
[96] n 94 above, para 18.
[97] n 94 above, para 9.

emergency obstetric services, and should allocate these services to the maximum extent possible.[98]

In terms of concrete actions for discharging obligations pursuant to article 12, General Recommendation 24 has in essence recommended the following on the part of the state:[99]

- implementing a comprehensive national strategy to promote women's health throughout their lifespan;
- allocating adequate budgetary, human and administrative resources to ensure that women's health receives a share of the budget which is substantively equal to that of men;
- adopting a gender perspective in all policies and programmes affecting women's health;
- ensuring removal of all barriers to women's health;
- prioritising prevention of unwanted pregnancy through family planning and sexuality education;
- reducing maternal mortality through safe motherhood services;
- where possible decriminalising abortion to remove punitive provisions imposed on women who seek abortion;
- monitoring provision of health services to women by public, non-governmental and private organisations to ensure equal access and quality of care;
- ensuring that all health services are consistent with the human rights of women, including the rights to autonomy, confidentiality, and informed consent; and
- ensuring that the training curricula of health workers included comprehensive, mandatory, gender-sensitive courses on women's health and human rights.

3.4 Ensuring equality in fact

Various international human rights treaties enable the use of temporary special measures to achieve equality in fact. Sometimes known as affirmative action programmes, temporary special measures are aimed to achieve equality in fact or *de facto* equality. Such measures are used to go beyond the requirements of mere formal equality or equality of opportunity to ensure equality in particular contexts such as health care. Article 4(1) of CEDAW distinguishes as permissible temporary special measures aimed at achieving substantive equality between women and men from otherwise discriminatory measures. Similarly, CERD, in article 1, paragraph 4, explains that special measures taken to bring the status of a particular racial or ethnic group in line with other groups shall not be deemed discriminatory, provided they are discontinued after equality among the groups has been achieved.

There is scope for the application of temporary special measures to promote equality in the health care context. Where health service indicators, such as percentage of births attended by skilled

---

[98] n 94 above, para 27.
[99] n 94 above, paras 29-31.

attendants, show unreasonable disparities among racial/ethnic groups in access to health services, temporary measures might be called for to ensure improved equality in skilled attendance. Where health status indicators, such as infant mortality rates, show unreasonable disparities in infant death rates by sex, temporary special measures might well be necessary to improve infant survival rates of the infant group that is disadvantaged by sex.

CEDAW might mandate the adoption of temporary special measures in the health context when they are the most appropriate means of achieving *de facto* equality, because article 12 refers to 'all appropriate' measures in an obligatory manner. The mandate to adopt temporary special measures as the most appropriate means is underscored by CEDAW General Recommendation 25.[100]

The idea of temporary special measures might well be appropriate under article 3 of CESCR, requiring the equal enjoyment of economic, social and cultural rights, when the means employed are proportional to the end of achieving equality in the protection of a particular right, such as health under article 12.

3.5 Possible limitations on rights

Under international human rights law, limitations of some rights are permissible if such restrictions are necessary to achieve overriding objectives such as public health, the rights of others, commonly agreed morality, public order, the general welfare in a democratic society, and national security. There are some rights, such as the right to life and the right to be free from torture that are absolute and cannot be limited in any circumstances, even in times of emergency. Other rights, such as the right to health, can be limited. Article 4 of CESCR explains that 'the state may subject such rights only to such limitations as are determined by law only in so far as this may be compatible with the nature of these rights and solely for the purpose of promoting the general welfare in a democratic society'.

The Limburg Principles on the Implementation of Economic, Social and Cultural Rights explain that '[a]rticle 4 was primarily intended to be protective of the rights of individuals rather than permissive of the imposition of limitations by the state'.[101] Moreover, article 4 'was not meant to introduce limitations on rights affecting the subsistence or survival of the individual or integrity of the person'.[102] The Limburg Principles clarify the phrases of article 4 in the following ways:

- The phrase 'determined by law': The Principles explain that '[n]o limitation on the exercise of economic, social and cultural rights shall be made unless provided for by national law of general

---

[100] General Recommendation 25 on art 4(1) of the CEDAW Convention, on temporary special measures, advance unedited copy, CEDAW/C/2004/1/WP1/Rev 1; See I Boerefijn *et al* (eds) *Temporary special measures: Accelerating* de facto *equality of women under article 4(1) UN Convention on the Elimination of All Forms of Discrimination Against Women* (2003).
[101] Limburg Principles (n 43 above) para 46.
[102] n 101 above, para 47.

application which is consistent with the Covenant and is in force at the time the limitation is applied'.[103] In addition, the Principles explain that laws and rules imposing limitations on the exercise of such rights shall not be 'arbitrary or unreasonable or discriminatory',[104] they shall be 'clear and accessible to everyone',[105] and adequate safeguards and remedies 'shall be provided by law against illegal or abusive imposition' of such limitations.[106]
- The phrase 'promoting the general welfare' is to be 'construed to mean furthering the well-being of the people as a whole'.[107]
- The phrase 'in a democratic society' places a further restriction on the application of limitations by placing the burden on the state 'imposing limitations to demonstrate that the limitations do not impair the democratic functioning of the society'.[108]
- The restriction 'compatible with the nature of these rights' requires that 'a limitation shall not be interpreted or applied so as to jeopardise the essence of the right concerned'.[109]

For example, the right to certain kinds of health care, such as pain control through opiates such as marijuana, might be legitimately limited by law to serve a public interest in the regulation of addictive substances. In respect of cannabis, for example, despite its known medicinal effects, it is listed as an undesirable dependence-producing substance in Part III of Schedule 2 of the Drugs and Drug Trafficking Act 140 of 1992 (Drugs Act). Its use or possession is prohibited by section 4b of the Drugs Act, unless it has been duly acquired for medicinal purposes in accordance with the requirements under the Medicines and Related Substances Control Act 101 of 1965, and is being used for such medicinal purposes.

In *Prince v The President of the Law Society of the Cape of Good Hope*,[110] the Constitutional Court observed that legislative restrictions on the use and possession of cannabis are intended to protect the general public against the harm caused by the use of drugs. Another example is the right of confidentiality of a patient who is HIV positive that might be restricted in the situation where the right of another specifically identified individual is at imminent risk of harm. If it has been established that the HIV-positive patient refuses to inform his or her partner, and it is strictly necessary for the purpose of preserving the health of that identified person, the law and codes of medical ethics allow for protective disclosure of this otherwise confidential information. Limited disclosure is required for the

---

[103] n 101 above, para 48.
[104] n 101 above, para 49.
[105] n 101 above, para 50.
[106] n 101 above, para 51.
[107] n 101 above, para 52.
[108] n 101 above, paras 53-54.
[109] n 101 above, para 56.
[110] 2002 3 BCLR 231 (CC).

legitimate reason of preserving the life or health of an identifiable person.[111]

3.6 Monitoring compliance

The task of monitoring compliance with human rights treaties is the responsibility of a committee of the respective treaty.[112] In the case of CESCR, for example, it is the Committee on ESCR that is the monitoring body. In respect of CEDAW, it is the Committee on CEDAW. States that have ratified a treaty are obliged to provide, on a periodic basis, a report showing how the state has complied with treaty obligations in the domestic sphere.[113] Civil society organisations can play a significant role in complementing the reporting process through the submission of their own reports. In response to reports, the monitoring committee issues Concluding Observations which are statements indicating the achievements of the reporting state as well as any concerns that the committee might have.[114] The concerns often take the form of pointing out significant or serious shortcomings in the county's health care systems or health indicators, and imploring the state party to take action to address areas of need and deprivation. For example, in 2000, the Committee on ESCR said this of Congo:[115]

> the Committee expresses its grave concern regarding the decline of the standard of health in the Congo. The AIDS epidemic is taking a heavy toll on the country, while the ongoing financial crisis has resulted in a serious shortage of funds for public health services, and for improving the water and sanitation infrastructure in urban areas. The war has caused serious damage to health facilities in Brazzaville. According to a joint study of the WHO and UNAIDS, some 100 000 Congolese, including over 5 000 children were affected by HIV at the beginning of 1997. More than 80 000 people are thought to have died from AIDS, with 11 000 deaths reported in 1997 alone. Some 45 000 children are said to have lost either their mother or both parents as a result of the epidemic.
>
> The Committee strongly urges the State Party to pay immediate attention to and take action with respect to the grave health situation in its territory, with a view to restoring the basic health services, in both urban and rural areas, and to preventing and combatting HIV/AIDS and other communicable diseases such as cholera and diarrhoea. The Committee

---

[111] United Nations *HIV/AIDS and human rights: International guidelines* (1998) 42 (Restrictions and Limitations). By way of analogy, in an American case, *Tarasoff v Regents of the University of California* (1976) 551 P 2d 334, the California Supreme Court held that where a mentally disturbed student had confided in a university counsellor his intention to kill a girlfriend, notwithstanding the confidential nature of the information, there was a duty upon the counsellor to warn the girl or her parents about the danger as the danger of death of or serious injury to an identifiable person was foreseeable. The Court said: 'The protective privilege ends where public peril begins.'

[112] Cook *et al* (n 20 above) 153-154.

[113] See eg art 16 of CESCR which says that '[t]he States Parties to the present Covenant undertake to submit in conformity with this part of the Covenant reports on the measures which they have adopted and the progress made in achieving the observance of the rights recognised herein'.

[114] Cook *et al* (n 20 above) 154, 249-250.

[115] Concluding Observations of the Committee on ESCR: Congo 23/105/2000 E/C 12/1/Add 45 paras 21 & 28.

also encourages the Government to work closely with WHO and UNAIDS, in its efforts to cope with these problems.

Guidance about the nature and content of treaty duties is found in General Recommendations, General Comments and other guidelines that are developed by the committees from time to time.[116] Over and above clarifying the obligations of the state, General Comments also serve the purpose of promoting an understanding of human rights responses in the light of new challenges, such as the challenge posed by the AIDS pandemic. In this connection, for example, in 2003, the Committee on the Rights of the Child issued General Comments No 3 and No 4 which are ultimately aimed at promoting the realisation of human rights of children in the context of HIV/AIDS and adolescent health respectively, as guaranteed under the Convention on the Rights of the Child. Decisions of treaty bodies in respect of those treaties where complaints procedures are available also assist in the clarification of state duties under the treaties.

It should generally be conceded that the efficacy of the international human rights framework for protecting rights concerning health largely depends on co-operation rather than coercion. The Committee on ESCR, for example, does not have complaints procedures and institutions for adjudicating individual violations. Notwithstanding these limitations, international human rights law has the capacity to play a significant role in the application and interpretation of domestic law concerning health. In this regard, as will be elaborated upon in the next section, South Africa is a case in point.

4 South African law

4.1 Introduction

The discussion in this section will essentially revolve around section 27 of the Constitution, not least because it provides the most direct and universal statement about a right concerning health under the South African Constitution. However, in the course of discussing section 27, reference will be made to other pertinent constitutional rights.

---

[116] Thus far, General Recommendation 24 on CEDAW, General Comment No 14 on CESCR and General Comments Nos 3 and 4 on CRC have been the most important specific interpretative sources that have emanated from the treaty bodies in respect of the international human right to health.

South Africa is one of a variety of 109 jurisdictions, such as Brazil,[117] Chile[118] and Venezuela,[119] to have embraced the idea of providing for a right concerning health in a substantive and justiciable form, especially in terms of recognition in a national constitution.[120] The most direct expression of a fundamental right concerning health is found in the provisions of section 27 of the Constitution. Section 27 provides that:[121]

1 Everyone has the right to have access to
(a) health care services, including reproductive health care;
(b) sufficient food and water; and
(c) social security, including, if they are unable to support themselves and their dependants, appropriate social assistance.

2 The state must take reasonable legislative and other measures, within its available resources, to achieve the progressive realisation of each of these rights.

3 No one may be refused emergency medical treatment.

However, section 27 is not the only provision dealing with a right concerning health. Section 12 of the Constitution provides everyone with a right, *inter alia*, to bodily and psychological integrity including the right 'to make decisions concerning reproduction'[122] and 'not to be subjected to medical or scientific experiments without their informed consent'.[123] Children are guaranteed a right to 'basic health care services'.[124] Everyone has a right 'to an environment that is not harmful to their health'.[125] Everyone who is incarcerated by the state, including every sentenced prisoner, has a right to conditions of detention that are consistent with human dignity, including the provision 'at state expense' of 'adequate medical treatment'.[126] As with the international right to health, it must be noted that there are also constitutional provisions that have an indirect bearing on health

---

[117] Art 196 of the Constitution of the Federal Republic of Brazil of 1988 as amended in 1998 provides that '[h]ealth is the right of all persons and the duty of the state and is guaranteed by means of social and economic policies aimed at reducing the risk of illness and other hazards and of universal and equal access to all actions and services for the promotion, protection and recovery of health'; RJ Cook *et al Advancing safe motherhood through human rights* (2001) 42.

[118] Art 19 of the Constitution of Chile of 1980 provides that the right to health protection is guaranteed to all persons and that the state protects free and equal access to activities for the promotion, protection and recovery of health and for rehabilitation of the individual; Toebes (n 1 above) 665.

[119] Art 76 of the Venezuelan Constitution of 1961 says: 'All persons have a right to the protection of health. The authorities shall see to the maintenance of public health and shall provide the means of prevention and care for those who lack them.' Cook *et al* (n 117 above) 84.

[120] ED Kinney 'The international human right to health: What does this mean for our nation and world?' (2001) 34 *Indiana Law Review* 1457.

[121] Our emphasis.

[122] Sec 12(2)(a).

[123] Sec 12(2)(c).

[124] Sec 28(1)(c).

[125] Sec 24(a).

[126] Sec 35(2)(e).

such as the rights to equality,[127] human dignity,[128] life,[129] housing,[130] and food, water and social security.[131]

To understand the significance of section 27 as a fundamental right concerning health, it is essential to take cognisance of the country's historical circumstances, and the transformation process under the new democratic dispensation, including the move towards substantive equality under the Constitution.

4.2 A legacy of gross inequality

Historically, income, geographical location, and most importantly race or ethnicity, have been the arch determinants of the quantity and quality of health care received by South Africans for the greater part of the twentieth century.[132] The health care system that the African National Congress-led government inherited in 1994, following the first democratic elections, can scarcely be described as functional and much less as egalitarian. Instead, the Medical Research Council's description of the South African health care system a few years earlier as 'a bureaucratic entanglement of racially and ethnically fragmented services; wasteful, inefficient and neglectful of the health of more than two-thirds of the population' is more fitting.[133] The new government came to power at the tail end of a long period that through a combination of deliberate official policy, discriminatory legislation and at times benign neglect, had managed firmly to imprint on the country's health care system a number of chronic maladies.

Van Rensburg et al have described and analysed the maladies that have afflicted the South African health care system for the greater part of the last century.[134] They can be subsumed under five main categories. The first is the dominance of curative-orientated health care. On the one hand, the exponential growth of Western modern medicine in this century has been a boon. It has yielded real gains to the health of the populace, including the eradication or control of many infectious diseases. However, on the other hand, modern medicine has become a victim of its own success in that it has led to

---

[127] Sec 9.
[128] Sec 10.
[129] Sec 11.
[130] Sec 26.
[131] Sec 27.
[132] HCJ Van Rensburg et al Health care in South Africa: Structure and dynamics (1992) 56-94.
[133] Medical Research Council Changing health in South Africa: Towards new perspectives in research (1991).
[134] Van Rensburg et al (n 132 above) 56-94. See also C de Beer The South African disease: Apartheid health and health services (1984); M Savage & SR Benatar 'An analysis of health and health services' in RA Schrire (ed) Critical choices for South Africa: An agenda for the 1990s (1990) 147-167; HCJ van Rensburg & A Fourie 'Inequalities in South African health care. Part I: The problem - manifestation and origins' (1994) 84 South African Medical Journal 95-103; HCJ van Rensburg & SR Benatar 'The legacy of apartheid in health and health care' (1993) 24 South African Journal of Sociology 99-111; African National Congress National Health Plan South Africa (1994) 27-32.

over-dependence on massively expensive hospital-based care, at the expense of affordable, preventative, community-based care. A report published in 1995, for example, indicates that in the 1992/93 financial year, 81% of public health expenditure was towards curative hospital-based care of which 44% was allocated to tertiary or academic hospitals.[135]

The second is the intensification of racial segregation in the provision of services. Race or ethnicity rather than need has, indubitably, been the most important variable determining quantitative and qualitative access to health care. In colonial and apartheid South Africa in particular, health care also became an integral part of a system that was intended to maintain white supremacy.[136] At the height of apartheid, whites disproportionately enjoyed the bulk of public expenditure on health care and received four times more *per capita* than their African counterparts, while coloureds and Indians enjoyed a somewhat intermediate share.[137]

There was also a racial fragmentation of services which was taken to absurd heights by the creation of separate departments of health for each of the ten 'bantustans' serving the African population under the 'homelands' policy of the 1950s,[138] and separate departments for coloureds, Indians and whites under the tricameral Constitution of 1983.[139] It was not until 1990 that social amenities such as health care were desegregated on the statute book.[140] But by then, the die of pervading and lasting socially engineered inequality in health care had been firmly cast.[141]

Thirdly, even putting aside the element of racial segregation and fragmentation, another compounding factor has been the functional fragmentation of services, which has its origins in the Public Health Act of 1919.[142] The Act bequeathed to the country a three-tiered, uncoordinated and uncomplimentary system of organising and

---

[135] Health Systems Trust & World Bank *Health expenditure in South Africa* (1995); South African Institute of Race Relations *South Africa survey 1995/96* (1995) 208.

[136] M Price 'Health care as an instrument of apartheid policy in South Africa' (1986) 1(2) *Health Policy and Planning* 158-170.

[137] HCJ van Rensburg 'South African health care in change' (1991) 22 *South African Journal of Sociology* 1 5. The classification of South African population groups into 'Africans', 'coloureds', 'Indians' and 'whites' is a necessary consequence of the official government policy of apartheid (or separate development). Legislation such as the Group Areas Act 41 of 1950 recognised, but also required such classification. Notwithstanding the offensive nature of such classification, structural inequality in South Africa cannot be understood without its use.

[138] Van Rensburg *et al* (n 132 above) 65-68. The bantustans were 'mini states' created for Africans by the apartheid government so as to separate them from 'white' South Africa. Policy decreed that Africans residing in 'white' South Africa had to be linked by ethnic descent to a 'homeland' or 'bantustan' where they would claim political rights and citizenship, and, in consequence, relinquish any claims to citizenship in 'white' South Africa; Price (n 136 above).

[139] Constitution of the Republic of South Africa Act 110 of 1983; L Baxter *Administrative law* (1984) 103-112; Van Rensburg *et al* (n 132 above) 69-71.

[140] Most of the racially discriminatory laws were repealed by the Abolition of Racially Based Measures Act 108 of 1991 as part of the transition towards a constitutional democracy that culminated in the interim Constitution of 1994.

[141] Van Rensburg & Benatar (n 134 above) 99-111.

[142] Public Health Act 36 of 1919; Van Rensburg *et al* (n 132 above) 59-60.

dispensing health care services that was to be augmented by subsequent legislation.[143] It created the Department of Public Health, provincial authorities and local authorities. The rationale was that the Department of Public Health would function as a co-ordinating and advisory body for provincial and local authorities. Furthermore, it would have the responsibility over contagious diseases, protection of environmental health and provision of district surgeons and institutions for the mentally ill. Provincial authorities were principally assigned the responsibility of establishing and managing hospitals. Local authorities were conceived as agents of the Department of Public Health, with the responsibility of controlling contagious diseases.

However, little harmony was obtained under the tripartite structure of the 1919 Act, especially as between the Department of Public Health and the provincial authorities.[144] The latter tended to develop autonomously from, if not antagonistically to, the Department of Public Health. Provincial authorities unduly concentrated on the provision of urban curative hospital-based care. Primary and community health care were neglected. It is not without significance that the National Health Service Commission (the Gluckman Commission), which was appointed in 1944 to inquire into the country's health services, found a system that was not only fragmented, but also lacking in community-based care.[145]

The paradigm of a fragmented system that was lacking in cohesion and community-based care continued largely unmitigated until the current government assumed office. Earlier attempts to reform the system so as to introduce cohesion, including the enactment of the Health Act of 1977,[146] did little to change to any substantial degree the reality of a system that was biased towards urban, curative hospital-based care. The 1977 Act repealed and supplanted the 1919 Act. Although it was intended to reform the 1919 Act in a fundamental way, including reorganising health care services and bringing about greater co-ordination of health services, its impact was, nevertheless, meagre. The primary failure of the 1977 Act was that it still operated within the tripartite structure of its predecessor - the 1919 Act - and an overarching apartheid superstructure in which the primary beneficiaries of health care were intended to be whites.

A fourth malady is the accentuation of rural-urban discrepancies and inequalities in the provision of services. For two main reasons, urban areas have historically consumed a preponderant share of health care services, but at the expense of rural areas. Firstly, the establishment and location of health care facilities essentially adhered to the country's pattern of urbanisation, which in turn was a consequence of the development of the mining industry and industrialisation. Secondly, and equally important, successive

[143] Van Rensburg *et al* (n 132 above) 71-88.
[144] n 143 above, 60.
[145] *Report of the National Health Services Commission* (Gluckman Commission) UG 30/1944 (1944).
[146] Health Act 63 of 1977.

governments were primarily preoccupied with establishing facilities to serve the white population concentrated in urban areas. The 'homelands' policy served to accentuate the chasm between rural and urban areas.

Last, but not least, is the growth of a pluralistic structure of health care in which the private sector was repeatedly augmented at the expense of the public sector. A perverse asymmetry has historically existed between the private and the public sector in terms of resources and health coverage.[147] The private sector commands 60% of the resources that are spent on health care, yet it provides coverage for a mere 20% of the population. With the exception of nursing staff, the private sector employs the majority of health care professionals. Some 62% of general practitioners, 66% of specialist practitioners, 93% of dentists and 89% of pharmacists serve the private sector.[148]

The National Party government during the 1970s and 1980s through privatisation policies particularly facilitated the proliferation of the private sector.[149] Privatisation was regarded as indispensable to achieving efficiency, devolving responsibility to the individual and reducing the state's financial burden.[150] However, paradoxically privatisation accentuated rather than ameliorated the state's burden in the provision of health care.[151] The private sector, prompted by a profit motive, devised exorbitantly expensive medical schemes that were focused on curative care and were heavily biased against the chronically sick, elderly, and poorly remunerated sections of the population. The preferred class became the younger, healthier and better remunerated section of the population. It was the state that ended up as the poorer and more burdened partner with the responsibility for providing care to 80% of the population that the private sector regarded as uninsurable.

---

[147] Van Rensburg *et al* (n 132 above) 202-207.
[148] Health Systems Trust & World Bank (n 135 above); Van Rensburg *et al* (n 132 above) 256-261.
[149] Van Rensburg *et al* (n 132 above) 71 371-380.
[150] Directorate of Social Planning *Report on an Investigation into the Present Welfare Policy in the Republic of South Africa* (1995); A Rycroft *Welfare rights: Policy and discretion* (1987) 367-373.
[151] HCJ van Rensburg & A Fourie 'Privatisation of South African health care: In whose interest?' (1988) 11 *Curationis* 1.

4.3 Transformation through section 27 of the Constitution

Section 27 translates to the health care sector the values of social justice, equality under the law and respect for human rights that underpin the Constitution. By conferring on everyone a right of access to health care services, the section is designed to provide a legal foundation for a liberal as well as egalitarian health care system. If diligently applied, it should secure for patients both formal and substantive equality in access to health care services.[152]

Like any provision of the Bill of Rights, section 27 confers relative rather than absolute rights. It is subject to section 36 of the Constitution - the limitation clause. Section 27 is about freedoms and entitlements. On the freedom side, it is about conferring formal equality to those who wish to access health care services. It ensures that in a liberal democracy, everyone, irrespective of personal attributes, can exercise what can be described as a negative right to pursue rather than receive health care services in the state and private sectors. In this sense, the right of access to health care is integral not only to the idea of self-determination or autonomy, but also to the rights to equality and human dignity. In consonance with section 9 of the Constitution, access to health care services must be provided in a manner that is free from any form of direct or indirect discrimination. Thus, personal attributes or characteristics such as race, gender, religion or HIV status cannot *per se* be relied upon by health care providers as a basis for denying treatment, as that would constitute unfair discrimination under section 9(3).

The intention to provide a right of access to health care services, free from unfair discrimination or any other undue interference, is even more apparent in the inclusive reference to 'reproductive services' in section 27(1)(a). The reference to reproductive services is significant in that such services are essentially accessed by women who, historically, have constituted a vulnerable and disadvantaged class, not least in respect of access to abortion. The overly restrictive tone of the Abortion and Sterilization Act of 1975 is in practice a form of unfair discrimination against women. The 1975 Act caused

---

[152] The Constitutional Court has made it abundantly clear that the goal of equality must go beyond merely achieving formal equality so as to achieve substantive equality. See, eg, *Brink v Kitshoff* 1996 6 BCLR 752 (CC); *Prinsloo v Van Der Linde* 1997 6 BCLR 759 (CC); *President of the Republic of South Africa & Another v Hugo* 1997 6 BCLR 708 (CC); *Harksen v Lane* 1997 11 BCLR 1489 (CC); *The City Council of Pretoria v Walker* 1998 3 BCLR 257 (CC); *National Coalition of Gay and Lesbian Equality v Minister of Justice* 1999 1 SA 6 (CC) 6; 1998 12 BCLR 1517 (CC) para 74. Substantive equality entails being alive to socio-economic inequalities and other disadvantages that have the effect of preventing equality of opportunity and equality of outcome. In the South African context, especially, it means acknowledging historical inequalities and disadvantages that were generated by colonialism, apartheid and patriarchy, and taking restitutionary or remedial steps: F Freedman 'Understanding the right to equality' (1998) 115 *South African Law Journal* 243; C Albertyn & J Kentridge 'Introducing the right to equality in the interim Constitution' (1994) 10 *South African Journal on Human Rights* 124; GE Devenish 'The legal significance of the right to equality clause in the interim Constitution' (1996) 1 *Stellenbosch Law Review* 92; C Albertyn & B Goldblatt 'Facing the challenge of transformation: The difficulties in the development of an indigenous jurisprudence of equality' (1998) 14 *South African Journal on Human Rights* 248 249.

thousands of women to resort to backstreet abortion, with an inevitable toll on health and mortality.[153] The 1975 Act has since been reformed by the Choice on Termination of Pregnancy Act of 1996. Section 27, thus, reinforces the right to equality in section 9 of the Constitution by ensuring that reproductive health services, including abortion, are treated like any other services. Such services are entitled to their legitimate share of resources and ought to be accessible to everyone, free from unfair discrimination. It is also worth noting that section 27 is a complement to section 12(2)(a), which accords everyone a right to bodily and psychological integrity including a right to make a decision concerning reproduction, which perforce includes a right to decide about abortion.[154] The fundamental right to make decisions concerning reproduction means little if it is not underpinned by a right of access to complementary services.[155]

Section 27 does not merely enjoin the state to refrain from unfairly interfering with the right of an individual to pursue health care services in a liberal state. Its broader significance lies in the fact that it imposes upon the state a positive duty to provide care according to need rather than ability to pay. This is made abundantly clear in section 27(2), which enjoins the state to take reasonable legislative and other measures, within its available resources, to achieve the progressive realisation of each of the rights in section 27(1). Thus, section 27 is also an economic right that is aimed at achieving substantive equality in respect of access to health care.[156] As a socio-economic right, it poses a challenge to the courts, not least because the development of socio-economic rights jurisprudence in South Africa is still in its infancy. To the extent that section 27 seeks to achieve substantive equality in access to health care, it should be seen as a compliment to section 9 – the equality clause of the Constitution.

The Constitutional Court has affirmed that socio-economic rights are justiciable and that the principle of separation of powers does not have the effect of depriving courts of competence over such rights. During the certification process that preceded the adoption of the final Constitution, it was contended before the Constitutional Court that socio-economic rights should not be included in the Constitution because they are not justiciable, not least because their adjudication

---

[153] C Ngwena 'The history and transformation of abortion law in South Africa' (1998) 30 *Acta Academica* 32.
[154] n 153 above, 28; *Christian Lawyers Association of South Africa & Others v Minister of Health & Others* 1998 11 BCLR 1434 (T).
[155] C Ngwena 'Accessing abortion under the Choice on Termination of Pregnancy Act: Realising substantive equality (2000) 25 *Journal for Juridical Science* 19; J Berger 'Taking responsibilities seriously: The role of the state in preventing transmission from mother to child' (2001) 2 *Law, Democracy and Development* 163 166.
[156] C Ngwena 'Substantive equality in South African health care: The limits of law' (2000) 4 *Medical Law International* 2.

might impact on the budget.[157] The Court rejected this argument and said:[158]

> These rights are, at least to some extent, justiciable. As we have stated in the previous paragraph, many of the civil and political rights entrenched in the NT [new text] will give rise to similar budgetary implications without compromising their justiciability. The fact that socio-economic rights will almost inevitably give rise to such implications does not seem to us to be a bar to their justiciability.

South African courts have substantively determined the violation of a socio-economic right in the context of rights concerning health in three cases only. The earliest case is *B and Others v Minister of Correctional Services and Others* which came before the High Court.[159] The issue was whether refusal by the Department of Correctional Services to pay for the cost of anti-retroviral therapy for four applicant prisoners who were HIV positive was a breach of section 35(2)(e) which, *inter alia*, guarantees a person who is incarcerated a right to 'adequate medical treatment' in the form of anti-retroviral therapy. Anti-retroviral therapy had been medically prescribed for two of the applicants. The Court held that the state had a constitutional duty to provide anti-retroviral therapy but only in respect of the two applicants for whom it had been medically prescribed.[160]

The judicial approach in *B and Others* has a number of shortcomings. One shortcoming is that the court did not invoke any jurisprudence on socio-economic rights or refer to any international law. The case was resolved on the narrow point that the Department of Correctional Services had pleaded lack of resources, but had failed to submit convincing supporting evidence. The Department failed to persuade the court that the treatment in question would be unaffordable. Also, a good portion of the case was taken up with determining whether anti-retroviral therapy was within the ambit of adequate medical treatment given its costly nature. The court could have turned to international human rights jurisprudence on this point but did not do so, save to observe that the term 'adequate' was relative and that its meaning could only be determined according to a given context, taking into account available resources. In this case, the court was satisfied that the treatment the prisoners were seeking was no more than adequate.[161] However, it did not seem to trouble the court that the treatment in question was, on account of cost, neither available for public health sector patients nor affordable to millions of South Africans living with HIV/AIDS.[162]

In any event, even if it is accepted that the court was correct in regarding anti-retroviral therapy as adequate medical treatment

---

[157] *Ex parte Chairperson of the Constitutional Assembly: In re Certification of the Constitution of the Republic of South Africa* 1996 10 BCLR 1253 (CC).
[158] n 157 above, para 78.
[159] 1997 6 BCLR 789 (C).
[160] Para 61.
[161] Para 60.
[162] C Ngwena 'AIDS in Africa: Access to health care as a fundamental right' (2000) 15 *SA Public Law* 1 17.

within the meaning of section 35(2)(e) of the Constitution, another shortcoming with the approach of the court is that the order to provide anti-retroviral therapy was only made in respect of two of the applicants for whom such therapy had been prescribed by doctors. The court did not stop to consider whether anti-retroviral therapy would also constitute adequate treatment for other prisoners for whom it had not been prescribed, but were nonetheless living with HIV/AIDS. Brand J, the trial judge, said this in respect of the applicants for whom anti-retroviral therapy had not been prescribed:[163]

> In respect of the third and fourth applicant, no medical practitioner has thus far prescribed anti-retroviral treatment for them. An order to the effect that they are entitled to be provided with the drugs that they claim, would, therefore, in my view, again amount to an instruction to a medical doctor as to what he should prescribe ... I do not believe that this court is empowered to grant such an order.

Brand J seems to have equated granting an order that there is a constitutional entitlement to receive anti-retroviral therapy with positively obliging doctors to prescribe those entitlements. As the decision of the Constitutional Court in *Minister of Health and Others v Treatment Action Campaign and Others* (which is discussed below) clearly shows, the two are not necessarily the same.[164] It would have been possible for the court to grant a wider order to the effect that where anti-retroviral therapy is medically indicated for prisoners living with HIV/AIDS, there is a constitutional duty to provide it on the part of the state, but subject to available resources, especially as the court accepted unequivocally that anti-retroviral therapy had prophylactic benefits.[165] That way, the decision of the court would have assisted other prisoners falling in the same class as the successful applicants but without the need for further litigation. Moreover, such an order would not have amounted to depriving doctors of independent clinical judgment about when to prescribe anti-retroviral therapy. Instead, it would have provided clearer guidance to those doctors who are consulted by prisoners living with HIV/AIDS but refrain from prescribing anti-retroviral therapy in the belief that the state will, in any event, not provide it. To the extent that the court refrained from inquiring into the appropriateness of anti-retroviral therapy for prisoners with the same medical condition as the successful applicants, the court abdicated its constitutional obligation under section 35(2)(e). For these reasons, *B and Others* is of limited value as a precedent.

The second case is *Soobramoney v Minister of Health, KwaZulu-Natal* that was decided by the Constitutional Court.[166] The applicant, a 41 year-old man, was seeking to compel the respondent to provide him with renal dialysis. He suffered from chronic renal failure. He had been receiving dialysis through private care, but his funds had run

---

[163] *B & Others* (n 159 above) para 37.
[164] 2002 10 BCLR 1033 (CC).
[165] *B & Others* (n 159 above) para 60.
[166] 1997 12 BCLR 1696 (CC).

out. He sought to have dialysis provided to him, at state expense, by a renal unit of a state hospital. He would otherwise die without dialysis. His request was declined for the reasons that due to scarcity of resources, access to renal dialysis was rationed and that he did not meet the medical criteria for providing dialysis at state expense.

The renal unit could only meet 30% of the demand for renal dialysis. It could only provide renal dialysis to patients who were candidates for renal transplantation. Thus, it could only provide dialysis to those patients who needed it not as lifelong therapy but as short-term therapy. The applicant, because he also suffered from other diseases, was not a candidate for transplantation. He suffered from ischaemic heart disease and was a diabetic with peripheral vascular disease. In the previous year, he had suffered a stroke. Indeed, his medical history placed him well outside eligibility for renal dialysis at state expense.

Though the applicant canvassed several grounds in support of his application, in the main, he contended that the respondent's decision had infringed his right to life under section 11 of the Constitution and his right not to be refused emergency medical treatment under section 27(3) of the same. The applicant was unsuccessful. The Court was of the view that the right to life argument was inappropriate as the Constitution provided explicitly for rights concerning access to health care services. In respect of section 27(3), the Court held, though the section was capable of a broader meaning to include ongoing treatment for chronic conditions, it had a narrower meaning. It was not intended for a condition such as chronic renal failure. Instead it was intended for a sudden catastrophe or unexpected trauma. The Court was also of the view that even if chronic renal failure constituted an emergency, the state was not violating its obligations when it declined to provide renal dialysis, as its resources were scarce.

Although the applicant had not raised the issue, the Court also took the opportunity to consider the application of sections 27(1) and (2) to the facts of the case. Indeed, the Court suggested that these sections were more appropriate to the facts of the case than sections 11 or 27(3) of the Constitution. The Court held, unanimously, that on account of scarcity of resources, it could not be said that the state had failed to discharge its obligations under section 27(2).[167]

From the standpoint of judicial precedent, *Soobramoney* did not contribute much to the understanding of socio-economic rights.[168] A number of criticisms can be levelled at the approach of the Court. The criticisms are not to do with the outcome of the case, but the judicial reasoning. The outcome of the case itself was correct given the prevailing scarcity of resources to provide lifelong renal dialysis at a

---

[167] Chaskalson P delivered the leading judgment.
[168] Ngwena (n 162 above) 13-15; C Scott & P Alston 'Adjudicating constitutional priorities in a transnational context: A comment on *Soobramoney's* legacy and *Grootboom's* promise' (2000) 16 *South African Journal on Human Rights* 206; P de Vos '*Grootboom*, the right of access to housing and substantive equality as contextual fairness' (2001) 17 *South African Journal on Human Rights* 258-259.

time that the state health sector could meet only 30% of the demand for renal dialysis.[169] Under the guidelines that had been worked out by the state renal unit, priority was given to patients who were candidates for renal transplant and, thus, did not require lifelong dialysis.[170] In this case, the applicant was in chronic renal failure. On account of his poor medical history and prognosis, he was not a candidate for a kidney transplant. Instead, he required lifelong dialysis whose cost could not be met under the rationed system.

One of the shortcomings with *Soobramoney* is the restrictive manner in which the Court interpreted section 27(3). It had been argued by the appellant that section 11 of the Constitution guaranteeing a right to life was relevant to the interpretation of section 27(3) to the extent that refusal to provide renal dialysis meant that the right to life would be nullified. In retort, the Court took the view that the right to life argument was inappropriate, as the Constitution had expressly provided provisions governing issues of access to health care services. In adopting this approach, the Court unduly minimised the relevance of section 11. Even conceding that chronic renal failure of the type that the appellant was afflicted with did not constitute a medical emergency as contemplated by section 27(3), the effect of the Court's interpretation was to cast the provisions of the Bill of Rights as atomistic elements rather than units of an interconnected web. Indeed, it is not inappropriate to interpret the Court's approach to section 27(3) as legalistic to the extent that it detracted from the generous purposive/contextual approach to constitutional interpretation. This is out of sync with the Court's own professed approach or human rights jurisprudence in general.[171] Fear that a holistic line of interpretation might lead to consumers of health care services making additional demands on the state should not have dissuaded the Court from interpreting section 27(3) as a positive right that is in part animated by section 11 – the right to life.

The Court also categorically interpreted section 27(3) as a negative rather than a positive right.[172] In the view of the Court, section 27(3) created a negative right only - the right not to be turned away arbitrarily by an institution or facility that is able to provide emergency treatment.[173] To the extent that the Court's approach can be construed as imposing no obligation upon the state, especially, to develop and make available emergency services, the Court undermined the import of the duties of health care providers.[174] Socio-economic rights draw sustenance from the imposition of positive obligations. It means precious little to say that no one may be refused emergency medical treatment and yet to decline to impose on health care providers a positive duty to make such treatment

---

[169] *Soobramoney* (n 166 above) para 26.
[170] As above.
[171] *S v Makwanyane & Another* 1995 6 BCLR 665 (CC) para 9; J de Waal *et al The Bill of Rights handbook* (2001) 130-135.
[172] *Soobramoney* (n 166 above) para 20.
[173] As above.
[174] Scott & Alston (n 168 above) 235-237.

available. Scott and Alston have described the Court's approach as constituting 'negative textual inferentialism'.[175] The proper way to limit the appellant's demand for renal dialysis should not have been an attempt to resurrect a literal approach but an application of section 27(2) which renders the provision of health care resources subject to available resources.

Another shortcoming with *Soobramoney* is that the Court seemed to paint an unduly limited role for the courts in decisions on allocation of health care resources and in the protection of socio-economic rights in general. Moellendorf's argument that the Court's approach has the unfortunate consequence of making socio-economic rights wholly dependent on, rather than informative of, executive policy, has much cogency.[176] The Court took, as its starting point, that once it is asserted by a provincial or national health care provider that resources are unavailable, then that *per se* limits the realisation of a right of access to the service sought. There is no promise in the judgment that the Court would be keen to inquire into whether the state and the province were in fact according due priority to the realisation of the right sought, by making available resources that *ought* to be available and utilising such resources effectively. It seems enough for the health care provider to 'toll the bell of tight resources'.[177] The task of the Court seems to have been limited to conducting judicial review in the traditional sense and to inquire only into the form rather than the substance of the decision to ensure that it is taken without bias, after weighing all relevant factors and excluding all extraneous factors.[178] Ultimately, what is intended to be a justiciable right may unwittingly be effectively reduced to the status of a directive. Indeed, Madala J, in his supporting judgment, did in fact make the error of describing some of the socio-economic rights in the Constitution as mere aspirations to strive for, rather than rights proper.[179]

Moreover, what is missing from *Soobramoney* is a systematic approach to the determination of a socio-economic right and a clear articulation of the normative content of the right to health care services.[180] *Soobramoney* did not really lay down any guidelines that could be followed when interpreting socio-economic rights so as to illuminate and indigenise jurisprudence on socio-economic rights, and also to guide lower courts with jurisdiction to determine constitutional matters. The Court did not consider how the right to health or the right of access to health care has been interpreted under

---

[175] n 174 above, 237.
[176] D Moellendorf 'Reasoning about resources: *Soobramoney* and the future of economic rights claims' (1998) 14 *South African Journal on Human Rights* 327 332.
[177] *R v Cambridge Health Authority, ex Pb (a minor)* (QBD) 25 BMLR 5 17, *per* Laws J; *Soobramoney* (n 166 above) para 52 *per* Sachs J where, drawing from *Cambridge Health Authority*, the learned judge said that '[i]n a case as the present which engages our compassion to the full, I feel it necessary to underline the fact that Chaskalson P's judgment, as I understand it, does not "merely toll the bell of lack of resources".'
[178] Baxter (n 139 above) 475-534.
[179] *Soobramoney* (n 166 above) para 42.
[180] Ngwena (n 162 above) 13-15.

international human rights instruments. In particular, the Court failed to make use of jurisprudence that has been developed by the Committee on ESCR. Thus, while the Court arrived at the correct conclusion, its approach fell short of a diligent consideration of relevant law. This was a serious shortcoming on the part of the Court, not least because the Constitution enjoins the courts to consider any relevant international law, and to adopt an approach that is consistent with international law where that is possible.[181]

The third case to raise an issue of the enforcement of a socio-economic right concerning health is *Minister of Health and Others v Treatment Action Campaign and Others*.[182] This was an appeal by the government against the decision of the High Court in *Treatment Action Campaign and Others v Minister of Health and Others*.[183] The applicants had challenged the decision of government to confine the dispensation of Nevirapine to 18 pilot sites only (two in each of the country's nine provinces) for the purpose of prevention of mother-to-child transmission of HIV (PMTCT).

The main argument of the applicants was that the government's failure to provide universal access to anti-retroviral therapy in the public health sector to prevent mother-to-child transmission of HIV, constituted a series of breaches of provisions of the Constitution, namely section 7(2) which enjoins the state to respect, protect, promote and fulfil the rights in the Bill of Rights; section 10 which guarantees everyone a right to human dignity; section 12(2)(a) which guarantees everyone a right to bodily and psychological integrity, including the right to make decisions about reproduction; section 27 which guarantees everyone a right of access to health care services, including reproductive health care; section 28(1)(c) which, *inter alia*, guarantees a child a right to basic health care; section 195 which, *inter alia*, requires that public administration must be governed by democratic values enshrined in the Constitution and that a high standard of professional ethics must be promoted and maintained; and section 237 which provides that all constitutional obligations must be performed diligently and without delay.

The reasons why government had confined Nevirapine to the 18 sites are twofold. Firstly, government had reservations about the safety of Nevirapine.[184] It wished to monitor the possible side effects of Nevirapine. Secondly, government wished to study the social, economic and public health implications of providing a nationwide programme.[185] This was with a view to enabling government to develop and monitor human and material resources for the provision of a comprehensive package, including the following services: voluntary testing and counselling; follow-up services; provision of formula milk where it is substituted for breastfeeding; and provision of antibiotics and vitamin supplements. Thus the pilot sites were

---

[181] Secs 39 & 233 respectively.
[182] *TAC* (n 164 above).
[183] 2002 4 BCLR 356 (T).
[184] *TAC* (n 164 above) para 11.
[185] n 184 above, para 14.

intended to serve the purpose of monitoring safety and generating information for developing capacity for the best prevention programme that would eventually be extended to all public facilities. However, government did not indicate as to when the programme would be extended to hospitals and clinics outside the pilot sites.

The applicants were successful before the High Court. Although the applicants had relied on several constitutional provisions, the case essentially turned on the interpretation and application of sections 27(1) and 27(2) of the Constitution. Botha J, the trial judge, held that the programme adopted by government fell short of a reasonable measure to realise the right of access to health care under section 27. The learned judge granted an order requiring the respondent health authorities to make Nevirapine available to all pregnant women who give birth in the public sector and to their babies, providing that the attending doctor, acting in consultation with the medical superintendent of the facility concerned, is of the opinion that Nevirapine is medically indicated, and that the woman concerned has been appropriately tested and counselled for HIV. Moreover, the court declared that the respondents had an obligation forthwith to plan and implement a comprehensive national programme to prevent mother-to-child transmission of HIV. The government appealed to the Constitutional Court against the decision.

The appeal was determined by the application of section 27. The Constitutional Court upheld the decision of the High Court but modified the order. Applying the principles it had formulated in *Government of the Republic of South Africa v Grootboom*[186] for the determination of socio-economic rights, the Court held that while government was better placed than the courts to formulate and implement policy on HIV, including measures for PMTCT, it had, nonetheless, failed to adopt a reasonable measure to achieve the progressive realisation of the right of access to health care services in accordance with section 27(2) read with section 27(1).[187] The decision to confine Nevirapine to the 18 pilot sites was unreasonable and thus constituted a breach of the state's obligations under sections 27(1) and (2) to the extent that it was rigid and inflexible.[188] The policy denied mothers and their newborn babies outside the pilot sites the opportunity of receiving a potentially life-saving drug that could

---

[186] 2000 3 BCLR 227 (C). The *Grootboom* case concerned the application of sec 26 that guarantees the right to have access to adequate housing and sec 28(1)(c), *inter alia*, guaranteeing every child a right to basic shelter. What is instructive about *Grootboom* is the approach adopted by the Constitutional Court to determine the right to have access to adequate housing in sec 26. The Court considered international human rights jurisprudence and drew particular assistance from the provisions of CESCR and their interpretation by the Committee on ESCR. The *Grootboom* case has been hailed as a meaningful step forward and a positive precedent for the judicial enforcement of socio-economic rights under the South African Constitution; P de Vos (n 168 above) 258; S Liebenberg 'The right to social assistance: The implications of *Grootboom* for policy reform in South Africa' (2001) 17 *South African Journal on Human Rights* 232; J Sloth-Nielsen 'The child's right to social services, the right to social security, and primary prevention of child abuse. Some conclusions in the aftermath of *Grootboom*' (2001) 17 *South African Journal on Human Rights* 224.
[187] TAC (n 164 above) para 80.
[188] As above.

have been administered within the available resources of the state. According to the Court, the reasons given by government to justify limiting its Nevirapine programme to the pilot sites had failed to distinguish between the need to evaluate a programme for PMTCT, and the need to provide access to health care services required by those who did not have access to the pilot sites.[189]

Given the Court's commendable reliance on international human rights jurisprudence in the *Grootboom* case, it is surprising that the Court did not take advantage of General Comment No 14 on the right to the highest attainable state of health under CESCR. As discussed above, the Committee on ESCR has substantially developed the normative content of the right to health in General Comment No 14. Perhaps it was not used in the arguments before the Court as it was only adopted in 2000. Had General Comment No 14 been argued, the Court might have found it useful to reinforce its reasoning about the compelling need to make Nevirapine available to pregnant mothers with HIV and their babies.

The Court also indicated, albeit implicitly, that it would have reached the same conclusion had the matter been determined according to the state's obligation under section 28 of the Constitution. The section, *inter alia*, guarantees every child a right to basic health services.[190] In the Court's view, the provision of Nevirapine to prevent transmission of HIV could be considered 'essential' to the child.[191] The needs of the children were 'most urgent'.[192] The right conferred on children by section 28 had been imperilled by the state's rigid and inflexible policy that excluded children outside the pilot sites from having access to Nevirapine.[193] Moreover, the children concerned were on the whole born to mothers who were indigent and relied on public health sector facilities as private care was beyond their means.[194]

By way of remedy, the Court modified the order of the High Court, and in essence ordered government without delay to:[195]

- remove the restrictions that prevent Nevirapine from being made available for the purpose of PMTCT at public health facilities outside the pilot sites;
- permit, facilitate and expedite use of Nevirapine for PMTCT at public health facilities when, in the judgment of the attending medical practitioner acting in consultation with the medical superintendent of the facility, Nevirapine is medically indicated, and if necessary, the mother concerned has been appropriately tested and counselled;

---

[189] n 164 above, para 67.
[190] Sec 28(1)(c).
[191] n 164 above, para 78.
[192] As above.
[193] As above.
[194] n 164 above, para 79.
[195] n 164 above, para 135.

- make provision, if necessary, for training of counsellors for counselling for PMTCT outside the pilot sites.

While the order was prescriptive, the Court said that government had the discretion to adapt the order if equally appropriate or better methods for PMTCT became available.

The finding that government had violated the right of access to health care under section 27 of the Constitution was perhaps inevitable for a number of reasons. Nevirapine had been recommended for PMTCT without qualification by an international health authority - the World Health Organisation.[196] The state's own licensing authority - the Medicines Control Council - had registered Nevirapine for PMTCT.[197] Thus, prevailing medical evidence and drug regulatory practice did not support the arguments about withholding extension of the programme for safety reasons. The government's pilot sites only covered 10% of the population of women who access antenatal care at public health facilities. Thus the needs of a large majority of patients (90%) were not catered for. According to the principles that were formulated in *Grootboom*, a programme that leaves out of account a significant section of the community cannot pass constitutional muster unless the cost of the programme is not within the available resources of the state. In this case the Court found that Nevirapine was easy to administer. Its cost (R10 per treatment) was patently within the means of the state as the budget for HIV/AIDS had been substantially augmented.

The state is not at liberty to ignore the needs of those who are in a crisis and in desperate need in favour of longer-term strategies.[198] The overwhelming picture in *Treatment Action Campaign* is that of a government proceeding in a tardy, rigid, unduly cautious and economical manner in the face of a gigantic and lethal epidemic. South Africa is experiencing a severe and sustained HIV/AIDS epidemic. An estimated four to five million people are living with HIV/AIDS.[199] HIV/AIDS is now the biggest contributor to morbidity and mortality.[200] Women and children are particularly vulnerable to HIV/AIDS. The average HIV prevalence for women attending antenatal clinics in the public sector is 24%.[201] Consequently, a significant proportion of the infections is on account of mother-to-child transmission. In 2001, an estimated 83 581 babies contracted HIV as a result of mother-to-child transmission.[202] Lifelong anti-retroviral therapy is unaffordable in the state sector at current pharmaceutical prices. However, anti-retroviral therapy for PMTCT opens a significant window of opportunity. Nevirapine has been established to reduce

---

[196] n 164 above, para 12.
[197] As above.
[198] *Grootboom* (n 186 above) para 68; Liebenberg (n 186 above) 254.
[199] Department of Health *National HIV and syphilis sero-prevalence survey of women attending antenatal clinics in South Africa 2001* (2000).
[200] Medical Research Council *The impact of HIV/AIDS on adult mortality in South Africa* (2001).
[201] Department of Health (n 199 above).
[202] As above.

PMTCT by as much as 50%. It costs far more to treat babies that are born HIV positive than to prevent the mother-to-child transmission in the first place. Against this backdrop, the government's programme and supporting reasons were untenable and the applicants had a compelling case.

The decision of the Court in *Treatment Action Campaign* demonstrates that government, to sanction breaches of socio-economic rights, cannot rely upon the doctrine of separation of powers. The decision of the court and the remedy it granted effectively countermanded existing government policy on HIV/AIDS. The court conceded that the matter of health policy was pre-eminently within the domain of government as the executive, and that all arms of government should be sensitive to and respect the separation of powers.[203] At the same time, the court was at pains to emphasise that the Constitution requires the state to 'respect, protect, promote and fulfil the rights in the Bill of Rights'.[204] Courts have competence over socio-economic rights. In appropriate cases courts are bound to pronounce that the state has, through the formulation or implementation of its policies, failed to respect, protect, promote and fulfil the rights in the Bill of Rights. Upon finding an infringement of a fundamental right, courts have competence to grant appropriate relief, including making orders that are just and equitable.[205]

Treatment Action Campaign was, as alluded to earlier, a beneficiary of the jurisprudence that the Constitutional Court had developed in *Grootboom*. The Court demonstrated a willingness to impugn executive policy making. Indeed, the effect of the Court's decision was not only to censure government policy on HIV/AIDS, but also to rewrite it in unambiguous terms. As with *Grootboom*, the Court went beyond rationality and good faith to inquire into the substantive reasonableness of the decision of government as measured against the egalitarian values of the Constitution. However, in following *Grootboom*, the Court perpetuated an understanding of the concept of minimum core rights and obligations, which is at variance with the approach of the Committee on ESCR.

In *Grootboom*, the Court rejected the idea of minimum core obligations if they were to be understood as founding freestanding minimum core rights.[206] However, the Court left the door open in those cases where sufficient information was made available to the Court to enable it to decide on a minimum core obligation.[207] The concern of the Court in *Grootboom* was that courts are generally not competent to undertake the complex, time-consuming inquiry that would enable them to determine minimum core obligations. In *Treatment Action Campaign*, the Court distanced itself even further

---

[203] *TAC* (n 164 above) para 98.
[204] n 203 above, para 99; sec 7(2) Constitution.
[205] *TAC* (n 164 above) paras 98-101; secs 38 & 172(1)(a) of the Constitution.
[206] *Grootboom* (n 186 above) para 33.
[207] As above.

from the justiciability of minimum core obligations.[208] The Court said that 'courts are not institutionally equipped to make the wide-ranging factual and political enquiries necessary for determining what the minimum standards ... should be'.[209] The Court concluded unequivocally that section 27(1) does not create a 'self-standing and independent positive right enforceable irrespective of the considerations mentioned in section 27(2)'.[210] Unlike the position in *Grootboom*, the Court did not seem to leave a possibility of finding minimum core obligations in appropriate cases.

The approach of the Court in *Treatment Action Campaign* is clearly that the idea of a minimum core should be seen as integral to rather than independent from the question whether the state has taken reasonable legislative and other measures to discharge its duty. To this extent, the Court has not really embraced the approach of the Committee on ESCR in General Comment No 14. While the approach of the Court has the advantage of flexibility and allows determinations to be made on a case-by-case basis, it may have the effect of inadvertently failing sufficiently to impress upon the state the compelling nature of socio-economic rights obligations. Indeed, *Treatment Action Campaign* itself is an instance where the state lost sight of its obligations concerning protecting health and the notion of providing a minimum floor of protection that was easily within its reach.

4.4 Other reforms that impact on the right of access to health care services

Numerous other reforms of an indubitably fundamental and positive nature have been taking place under the hegemony of the African National Congress-led government since its assumption of office in May 1994.[211] Over and above complementing the values of equality, human dignity and freedom under the Constitution,[212] the reforms are anchored in the overall reconstruction of the South African economic, social and political order as espoused in the Reconstruction and Development Programme of the ANC.[213] Also, the ANC's National Health Plan was instrumental in identifying and delineating the broad parameters of fundamental reform in the health care sector prior to constitutional reform.[214] In many ways, therefore, section 27 of the

---

[208] *TAC* (n 164 above) para 39; J Fitzpatrick & RC Slye '*Republic of South Africa v Grootboom. Minister of Health v Treatment Action Campaign*' (2003) 97 *The American Journal of International Law* 669 677.
[209] *TAC* (n 164 above) para 37.
[210] n 209 above, para 39.
[211] HCJ van Rensburg 'Health and health care in South Africa in transition' (1999) 31 *Acta Academica* 1; SR Benatar 'Health care reform in the new South Africa' (1997) 336 *The New England Journal of Medicine* 881.
[212] Sec 7 Constitution.
[213] African National Congress *The Reconstruction and Development Programme - A policy framework* (1994).
[214] African National Congress *National Health Plan for South Africa* (1994).

Constitution is serving as a constitutional basis for prior and ongoing reforms.

In the White Paper for the Transformation of the Health System of South Africa,[215] the government comprehensively articulated its various strategies for reforming the health care system. Over and above creating a single national ministry to direct and co-ordinate health policy in place of the erstwhile 14 health authorities, two main strategies stand out as the linchpins. One is a paradigm shift towards Primary Health Care. The other is the introduction of the District Health System.

The concept of Primary Health Care was born out of the World Health Organisation's Alma Ata Declaration.[216] Although the concept of Primary Health Care has many tenets, its central one is equitable access to a package of *essential* health services.[217] The Declaration of Alma Ata lists such services as the following: promotion of food supply and nutrition; adequate supply of safe water and sanitation; maternal and child health care, including family planning; immunisation against the major infectious diseases; prevention and control of locally endemic diseases; appropriate treatment of common diseases and injuries; and the provision of essential drugs. The government, through the Department of Health, has adopted Primary Health Care as the most effective means of improving the nation's health. It has developed a medium-term expenditure framework for the implementation of a package of services that go with Primary Health Care over a ten-year time scale.[218]

Primary Health Care is a broad philosophy and strategy for attaining accessible health care for all, which has been embraced by developing countries especially.[219] In many ways, Primary Health Care represents recognition of the inappropriateness of the health care structures inherited by developing countries following political emancipation from unrepresentative regimes. In South Africa's case, the implementation of Primary Health Care calls for a fundamental shift in the organisation and dispensation of health care services bequeathed from the colonial and apartheid eras. To this end, a redistribution of public health resources is taking place. The historically created urban-biased care described earlier is being dismantled in favour of equitable geographical allocations. Equally, there is now a de-emphasis of high technology care in urban and teaching hospitals in favour of providing Primary Health Care to historically underserved areas. In this connection, an extensive clinic-building programme in rural areas is underway.[220] The District Health System is becoming the vehicle for organising and dispensing health care services.

---

[215] Notice 667 of 1997 No 17910.
[216] Green *An introduction to health planning in developing countries* (1992) 43.
[217] n 216 above, 53-59.
[218] n 216 above, 36-41.
[219] n 216 above, 5.
[220] Benatar (n 211 above) 892.

The District Health System is an instrument for decentralising and regionalising health care. It is designed to bring health care services as close as possible to the consumers. Moreover, if diligently implemented, it should democratise health services and dilute substantially the dominance of the Department of Health and the provinces in the organisation and dispensation of services. The District Health System should provide an antidote to the dysfunctional structural fragmentation of services that was bequeathed by the Public Health Act of 1919 and its successors, which, as described earlier, were responsible for ills such as over-dependence on hospital-based care and the urban and rural chasm. Though Primary Health Care and the District Health System are being implemented, they have yet to be put on a statutory footing. To fill this gap, as will be elaborated below, plans are underway to enact a National Health Act that will, *inter alia*, provide a statutory recognition of Primary Health Care and the District Health System.[221]

A Patient's Rights Charter (Charter) has also been adopted by the Department of Health.[222] The Charter is intended to function as a discrete tool for improving the quality of care and raising awareness among users about rights concerning access to health care services. The Charter contains information on rights and responsibilities concerning access to health care services, including rights to access health care, choose health care services and complain if the service provided is perceived to be of a poor quality. The Charter has a complaints mechanism. The efficacy of the Charter in raising awareness about rights concerning health and improving services has yet to be established. Thus far there has been a baseline study that has demonstrated low levels of awareness and inconsistent implementation of the rights in the Charter.[223]

On the legislative front, one of the earliest measures was a decree by the President in 1994 to the effect that all children under the age of six and all pregnant mothers were entitled to free health care services.[224] The decree was in consonance with the international recognition that mothers, women and children are not only particularly vulnerable to disease, but also constitute vulnerable classes socio-economically. Other measures have followed.

The Choice on Termination of Pregnancy Act of 1996 has radically reformed the abortion law to provide relatively easy access to abortion, particularly in early pregnancy.[225] In the first 12 weeks of pregnancy, abortion is obtainable on request, without the need to provide a reason.[226] The state has committed resources to ensure that abortion services are easily available and obtainable on the basis of

---

[221] In 2002, the Minister of Health tabled the National Health Bill 2001.
[222] Department of Health *Patients' Rights Charter* (2002).
[223] K Block *Epidemiological study on the quality of care pertaining to the Patients' Rights Charter in the Browns farm community* (2001).
[224] *Government Gazette* Notice 657 (1994); D McCoy & S Khosa 'Free health policies' in Health Systems Trust *South African Health Review* 157-159 (1996).
[225] Act 92 of 1996; Ngwena (n 153 above).
[226] Sec 2(1)(a).

need rather than means, thereby removing erstwhile class and racial barriers.[227] Notwithstanding early problems in the implementation of the Act, it is evidently impacting positively on access to abortion. Vast numbers of women, who would have found their way to backstreet abortion under the extremely restrictive regime of the Act's predecessor, have been granted access to safe and legal abortion.[228] At the same time, it is important to note that a number of obstacles, including the urban-rural divide in the provision of health services, are still impeding access.[229]

The Pharmacy Amendment Act[230] and the Medicines and Related Substances Control Amendment Act[231] are, *inter alia*, designed to render medicines more accessible and affordable. Previously, ownership of pharmacies was restricted to pharmacists. The Pharmacy Amendment Act extends ownership to non-pharmacists, providing that prescribed medicines are dispensed under the supervision of a pharmacist. It is envisaged that this measure will encourage the setting up of pharmacies in rural and other locations that, hitherto, have been underserved.[232] Medicine prices are generally exorbitant in South Africa.[233] The Medicines and Related Substances Control Amendment Act is intended to provide cheaper medicines through a variety of ways, some of which are highly contentious. These include parallel importation of medicines; compulsory licensing; institution of price controls through the establishment of a pricing committee; promotion of generic substitution; and the prohibition of bonusing and rebates which drug manufacturers use to offer discounts to dispensers of medicines.[234] This Act, which has yet to be implemented, has met with vociferous opposition by the pharmaceutical industry.[235] The pharmaceutical industry brought an action to challenge the validity of the Act in the High Court.[236] However, the action was later withdrawn when the

---

[227] During the period of the Act's predecessor - the Abortion and Sterilisation Act 2 of 1975 - an average of 800 to 1 200 women per year 'qualified' for abortion. Well over 66% of the women were white from an urban middle-class background at a time that whites constituted 16% of the general population. On the other hand, upwards of 44 000 mainly black and poor women had recourse to 'backstreet' abortion. Unofficial estimates put the number of illegal abortions much higher, at 120 000 or more per year; South African Institute of Race Relations South Africa survey 1996/1997 (1997) 492; Ngwena (n 153 above).

[228] Ngwena (n 153 above). The 1996 Act took effect from 1 February 1997. Between February and July 1997, a total of 13 102 abortions were performed; from August 1997 to January 1998, 16 273 abortions were performed; Reproductive Rights Alliance *National terminations of pregnancy statistics* (2000) 5.

[229] Ngwena (n 156 above).

[230] 88 of 1997.

[231] 90 of 1997.

[232] A Gray 'Equity and the provision of pharmaceutical services' in Health Systems Trust *South African Health Review* (1998) 103; S Harrison & M Qose 'Health legislation' in Health Systems Trust *South African Health Review* (1998) 17 20.

[233] It has been alleged by the Department of Health that some South African drug prices are 4 000 times higher than elsewhere; 'Zuma vows to bring down cost of drugs' *The Star* (1997-03-22); 'Untangling the medicines tussle' *Sunday Times* (1997-10-12).

[234] Act 90 of 1997; Gray (n 232 above).

[235] Harrison & Qose (n 232 above) 17.

[236] *Pharmaceutical Manufacturers Association of SA & Another: In re Ex Parte President of the Republic of South Africa & Others* 1999 4 SA 788 (T).

pharmaceutical industry agreed to reach a negotiated settlement with the government.

The most contested provision is that relating to parallel importation and compulsory licensing. On the ground of necessity to protect the health of the public, section 15 of the Act permits the Minister of Health to authorise the importation of medicines, which have the same proprietary name as those already registered in South Africa from companies in countries other than the country of origin.[237] In doing so, it ostensibly disregards obligations towards the manufacturer's patent rights. Government has given assurances that it would honour patent rights, and invoke the provision in emergencies only. The Pharmaceutical Manufacturers' Association has alleged that as the provision stands, it effectively breaches patent rights.[238] The United States and European governments have alleged that the Act violates the Trade Agreement on Intellectual Property Rights and threatened to apply sanctions against South Africa if it is implemented.[239] Because of fear of a negative impact on investment, it is unlikely that section 15 will be implemented as it stands.

The Medical Schemes Act[240] is challenging the relative inaccessibility of private insurance cover to some extent. As mentioned earlier, over the years, medical schemes have increasingly cherry-picked the healthiest clients to eliminate, among others, the aged and chronically sick. The Act outlaws unfair discrimination in the provision of cover. The prohibited grounds include *disability* and *state of health*.[241] The Act also requires medical schemes to offer a prescribed minimum of benefits to all members irrespective of *age*, *sex* or *state of health*.[242] It is envisaged that the Act will increase access to private health cover, but there will be a cost. What the Act effectively does is to impose a shift in actuarial rating from experience to community rating. This should entail a greater element

---

[237] Sec 15 of the Act provides, *inter alia*, that '[t]he Minister may prescribe conditions for the supply of more affordable medicines in certain circumstances so as to protect the health of the public, and in particular may (a) notwithstanding anything to the contrary contained in the Patents Act 1978 (Act 57 of 1978), determine that the rights with regard to any medicine under a patent granted in the Republic shall not extend to acts in respect of such medicine which has been put onto the market by the owner of the medicine, or with his or her consent'.

[238] South African Institute of Race Relations *South African Survey 1997/98* (1998) 217-218.

[239] The Act prompted the United States to place South Africa on a 'watch list' of 32 countries that appear to violate intellectual property rights. This action was interpreted as an ultimatum to the South African government which would among other consequences lead to disinvestment by United States companies: 'Zuma Act puts SA on "watch list" *Sunday Argus* (1998-05-02)'. In 1999, the United States Congress passed legislation in response to the Act. US Public Law 105-277 established that '... none of the funds appropriated under this heading may be available for assistance for the central government of the Republic of South Africa, until the Secretary of State reports in writing to the appropriate Committees of the Congress the steps being taken by the United States Government to work with the Government of the Republic of South Africa to negotiate the repeal, suspension, or termination of section 15(c) of South Africa's Medicine and Related Substances Control Amendment Act 90 of 1997'.

[240] 131 of 1998.
[241] Sec 24(2)(e).
[242] Sec 29(1)(n).

of cross-subsidy among clients, but with a prospect of contributions rising across the board.

As alluded to earlier, legislation that puts on a statutory footing some of the major policy reforms that have taken place, including the establishment of Primary Health Care and the District Health System, is not in place. In this regard, a bill - the National Health Bill - that will eventually become the National Health Act is currently before parliament.[243] The Bill subscribes to constitutional objects, including the universal provision of access to health care and the deployment of state resources to this effect in accordance with section 27 of the Constitution.[244] It establishes a national health system.[245] It also provides for the decentralisation of health services to provinces and districts primarily through the establishment of provincial health authorities[246] and district health authorities.[247] The Bill espouses democratic governance of health care structures, including especially the active involvement of the community at a local level.[248] The Bill is comprehensive in the sense that it is not only aimed at the organisation and governance of health care services, but also at assuring quality and delivery of services within an institutional framework that recognises the respect for human rights. In this regard, the Bill explicitly recognises, *inter alia*, users' rights to informed consent,[249] confidentiality,[250] access to health records,[251] and their right to lay a complaint about treatment and care.[252] It is significant that while the Bill recognises that users have certain rights, they also have certain duties. The duties of users include treating health workers with dignity and respect, and refraining from using tobacco products and non-prescribed alcohol products while on the premises of the health facility.[253]

There is little doubt that current reforms in the health sector have yielded many positive benefits.[254] There has been a steady move away from racial discrimination in the provision of services. There is greater integration of formerly segregated facilities and services. As a result of the introduction of the Primary Health Care system, there is greater accessibility of health care for disadvantaged groups, including women and children. Health care professionals are now being trained with an orientation towards delivering efficient and effective care in Primary Health Care settings, and serving in remote

---

[243] National Health Bill 2001*Government Gazette* 9 November 2001 No 22824.
[244] n 243 above; Preamble to the Bill.
[245] n 243 above, clauses 25-32.
[246] n 243 above, clauses 33-39.
[247] n 243 above, clauses 40-46.
[248] n 243 above, clause 54.
[249] n 243 above, clauses 8-11.
[250] n 243 above, clause 14.
[251] n 243 above, clauses 15-19.
[252] n 243 above, clauses 20-21.
[253] n 243 above, clause 22.
[254] Van Rensburg (n 211 above) 11-13; HCJ van Rensburg & C Ngwena 'Health and health care in South Africa against an African background' in WC Cockeram (ed) *The Blackwell companion to medical sociology* (2001) 365 374-377.

rural areas. Many health initiatives have been implemented to target in particular the most acute health problems such as HIV/AIDS, TB and malnutrition. There have been significant strides towards interprovincial and intraprovincial equity.

However, the transformation of the health sector has not been an unqualified good. The process of transformation has not been smooth, and has, indeed, created problems of its own.[255] The large-scale restructuring of health departments and units has had a detrimental effect on continuity of service. The move towards 'free' health care has proceeded at a much faster pace than the development of capacity. Consequently, services in the public sector are overburdened. In many cases there is overcrowding, shortage of supplies and equipment and poor working conditions at clinics leading to deterioration in the quality of care. Health care personnel are disillusioned by the seemingly endless changes to the extent that dysfunction and inefficiency are building up and, thus, frustrating otherwise laudable changes. The public sector is still offering a 'second-class' service, and has remained much inferior to the private sector.[256]

4.5 Impeding factors

The ultimate objective of substantive equality in access to health care must be to ensure, as much as possible, equality in health outcomes. It would serve little to focus only on equality in access and then be oblivious to extreme differentials in health outcomes as demonstrated by traditional indicators such as morbidity rates and mortality rates. Health outcomes are closely linked to socio-economic status.[257] Health status is less an outcome of access to discrete health service than it is of general human and economic development. Factors such as income, nutrition, clean water, sanitation, housing, education and general living standards have a greater impact on health outcomes than access to health care services alone.

In the short term, South Africa's material conditions are not favourable to the attainment of equity in health status. In South Africa one finds extensive poverty, and extreme income differentials and living standards.[258] The old racial classification of the population into Africans, coloureds, Indians and whites explains the persistence of structural inequality in health care and health outcomes. However, with the realisation of formal equality, class will increasingly replace race as the ultimate factor in determining health outcomes.

---

[255] Van Rensburg (n 211 above) 13-23; Van Rensburg & Ngwena (n 254 above) 377-380.
[256] Van Rensburg (n 211 above) 15; Van Rensburg & Ngwena (n 254 above) 378.
[257] P Townsend *et al Inequalities in health: The Black report and the health divide* (1992).
[258] Office of the Deputy President *Poverty and inequality in South Africa* (1998).

The HIV/AIDS epidemic is putting a strain on the provision of health care services. With close to five million people (or approximately 12% of the population) living with HIV/AIDS,[259] the epidemic constitutes a national calamity and a major impediment towards equity in health status. More and more bed space is being taken by HIV-related admissions. It is estimated that in the next decade, it is likely to consume at least a third and possibly as much as 75% of the health budget.[260] For the greater part of the epidemic, the position of government has been that at current pharmaceutical prices, it cannot afford anti-retroviral therapy and that it can commit itself to symptomatic treatment of opportunistic infections.[261] However, the position has changed of late. In November 2003, government committed itself to establishing a comprehensive treatment plan for rendering anti-retroviral therapy at every service point in every district within a year, and a service point in every municipality within five years.[262] The challenge of providing universal anti-retroviral therapy is mammoth, to say the least. It requires major capacity building in the public health service sector, including the recruitment and training of thousands more health care professionals so as to ensure the delivery of safe, effective and ethical treatment. If the plan to render universal anti-retroviral treatment succeeds, it will be a welcome complement to the programme for the provision of Nevirapine for pregnant mothers and their babies. As discussed earlier, in *Treatment Action Campaign*, the Constitutional Court ordered government to expand its Nevirapine programme.[263]

5 Conclusion

An understanding of the sociological dimension to structural inequality and the economic limitations of remedial action must supplement a meaningful legal discourse on equality in access to health care as a fundamental right. Now that formal equality has been guaranteed and realised in democratic South Africa, the eradication of poverty, levelling of income disparities and general economic growth hold the key to the enhancement of equality of opportunity and choice in health care. The Constitution, law in general and health care sector reforms will be of little avail unless they are accompanied by socio-economic empowerment. Sustainable human development is a prerequisite to the attainment of equality in health outcomes.[264] The demands on the economy are enormous. Health care is competing with other sectors such as education and social welfare where there

---

[259] n 199 above.
[260] M Steinberg *et al* 'HIV/AIDS - Facts, figures and the future' in Health Systems Trust *South African Health Review 2000* (2000) 301.
[261] A Grimwood *et al* 'HIV/AIDS - Current issues' in Health Systems Trust *South African Health Review 2000* (2000) 287.
[262] Department of Health *Operational plan for comprehensive HIV and AIDS care, management and treatment for South Africa* (2004).
[263] n 164 above, para 135.
[264] United Nations Development Programme (UNDP) *Human development report 1996* (1996).

was equally a legacy of long years of neglect and gross inequality. However committed the state might be in effecting radical transformation on egalitarian lines, in the short term, it must be conceded that the South African economy does not have the capacity to render a comprehensive and universal system of health care delivery. Gross inequalities will continue to persist, but this time without the offensive element of state-spawned racial privileges that marked the colonial and apartheid eras. Long-standing extreme differentials in income and standard of living, combined with pervasive poverty will need to be substantially ameliorated before substantive equality in access to health care services can be achieved.

The lesson CESCR has for South Africa is that section 27(2) of the Constitution is not meaningless. Like its counterparts under international human rights instruments, it imposes ascertainable and time-laden duties, albeit within a framework that accommodates South Africa's peculiar economic circumstances, political orientation and history. South Africa must move towards horizontal equity in the provision of health care services and guarantee its people services that are accessible, affordable, available and effective. Within its scarce resources and taking into account other competing needs, South Africa must ultimately secure, or at least demonstrate a plan to secure, a minimum content of health services for everyone. Need, rather than the ability to pay, or one's phenotype or geographical location should become one of the newfound values in post-apartheid health care dispensation. Disadvantaged and vulnerable groups, including women, children, blacks, the disabled, elderly and chronically sick, should be given due priority. The dominance of the private sector and its inaccessibility to the chronically sick and the poor must be challenged. The cost of medicines should not be allowed to remain exorbitant, and beyond the reach of the majority of South Africa's people. But while the courts may be able to provide a yardstick for guiding health care policies towards a more equitable goal, the onus for rectifying gross disparities in respect of access to health care and health status rests primarily on the state and its policies.[265]

To succeed, South Africa must undertake her constitutional obligations with decisive vigour. The legacy of gross inequality and malaise in the health care system enjoins the state to focus on section 27(2) attentively and constantly, with reaffirmation and commitment so as to make the right of access to health care a reality. This requires no less than an urgent and sustained fundamental transformation of the health care system.

---

[265] Chapman (n 7 above) 60.

Five / The right to food*

Danie Brand

1   Introduction

In terms of section 27(1)(b) of the South African Constitution,[1] everyone has the right to have access to sufficient food. Section 28(1)(c) also guarantees for children the right to basic nutrition and section 35(2)(e) for detainees the right to the provision, at state expense, of adequate nutrition. Collectively these provisions proclaim for everyone, with varying degrees of intensity, a constitutional right to food.

In South Africa, where, despite an adequate national food supply,[2] 14,3 million people are food-insecure,[3] 21,6% of children under nine are stunted, 10,3% are underweight and 3,7% experience wasting,[4] and a staggering 43% of households suffer from food poverty,[5] this constitutional right is potentially an important tool for poor people with which to secure regular and sustainable access to food.

---

*   My thanks to Marie Ganier-Raymond, reviewer of this chapter, for her comments, to Annette Christmas and Moeniba Isaacs for answering questions about security of tenure and subsistence fishing and to Len de Vries and Etienne Fourie for research assistance. Mistakes are my own.

[1]   Constitution of the Republic of South Africa of 1996 (Constitution).

[2]   Meaning that there is enough food in South Africa for the population. Department of Agriculture *Integrated food security strategy for South Africa* (2002) 19-20. As a recent study puts it: 'Despite its comparatively unfavourable natural resource base, [South Africa] is a net exporter of agricultural commodities. Its *per capita* income is high for a developing country. It does not have a tight foreign exchange constraint. It is not landlocked. Its transport infrastructure is generally good ... Clearly, food ought always to be available in South Africa.' M de Klerk *et al Food security in South Africa: Key policy issues for the medium term* (2004) 3.

[3]   Food Pricing Monitoring Committee *Final report* (2003) (relying on data from Statistics South Africa). The United Nations Food and Agriculture Organisation (FAO) defines food security as access by all people at all times to the food needed for a healthy and active life; FAO *The right to food in theory and practice* (1998) 32.

[4]   D Labadarios (ed) *The national food consumption survey* (1999) 167-169. *Underweight* indicates a weight-for-age ratio under two standard deviations from the norm; *stunting* a height-for-age ratio under two standard deviations from the norm; and *wasting* (an indicator of severe current malnutrition) a weight-for-height ratio under two standard deviations from the norm.

[5]   Meaning they earn too little to afford a basic adequate diet; De Klerk *et al* (n 2 above) 25.

In this chapter, I explore the different ways in which the right to food can be used as such a tool, by illustrating the concrete legal duties that it imposes. First, in part 2, I provide an overview of the protection afforded the right in international law. Then, in part 3, I turn to the right as it is entrenched in the South African Constitution and describe the different ways in which it has been and can in future be given concrete expression in South African law, through legislation and judicial decisions. In the process I briefly consider the extent to which the South African government's existing responses to the country's food security problems meet its constitutional duties, in the light of current nutritional conditions in South Africa.

2 International law

Because of the continuing dearth of jurisprudence in respect of the right to food at domestic level,[6] international law remains a useful source for interpreting and developing the content of the right to food in South Africa, particularly because much work has been done there to describe the content of the right to food and to translate that content into duties – into things that states must do. It is useful both to know which sources regarding the right to food are available at international level, and what content the right has been given there.

2.1 Sources

The right to food is widely recognised in international law.[7] First, some international and regional human rights documents of general scope proclaim the right explicitly.

At international level the most important are the Universal Declaration of Human Rights (Universal Declaration), which proclaims a right of everyone to 'a standard of living adequate for the health and well-being of himself and his family, including food ...';[8] the International Covenant on Economic, Social and Cultural Rights (CESCR), which proclaims both a right to adequate food and a right to freedom from hunger;[9] and the Universal Declaration on the Eradication

---

[6] The right to food is not widely protected in domestic legal systems. In some systems it is recognised indirectly, through interpretation of other rights or application of broader legal norms. In Germany, price control regulations were upheld against freedom of competition-based constitutional challenge because the state, in terms of the 'social state' principle, was held to be obliged to combat high food prices; *Milk and Butterfat* case 18 BVerfGE 315, 1965 (see sec 3.2.2 below). In India, the right to basic nutrition has been read into the right to life; *Francis Coralie Mullin v The Administrator, Union Territory of Delhi* (1981) 2 SCR 516 529; see also the interim orders resulting from the current case of *People's Union for Civil Liberties v Union of India* Writ Petition [Civil] 196 of 2001, available at http://www.righttofoodindia.org/mdm/mdm_scorders.html (accessed 31 October 2004); see sec 3.2.3 below).
[7] On recent developments in international law relating to the right to food, see A Eide *The right to adequate food and to be free from hunger* (1999) E/CN 4/Sub 2/1999/12 paras 31-43 & 55-57.
[8] 1948. South Africa voted in favour. See art 25.
[9] 1966. Signed but not ratified by South Africa. See arts 11(1) & (2).

of Hunger and Malnutrition (UDEHM).[10] In addition, the right to food has been read into human rights documents of general scope where it is not explicitly proclaimed: Article 6 (the right to life) of the International Covenant on Civil and Political Rights (CCPR)[11] has been interpreted by the Human Rights Committee, in its General Comment No 6, to impose a duty on state parties to take measures to 'reduce infant mortality and to increase life expectancy, especially in adopting measures to *eliminate malnutrition* and epidemics'.[12]

At regional level, the right to food is, as a rule, not explicitly protected. Neither the European Convention on Human Rights,[13] nor the European Social Charter,[14] nor the African Charter on Human and Peoples' Rights (African Charter)[15] explicitly guarantees this right. Only article 12(1) of the Additional Protocol to the American Convention on Human Rights in the Area of Economic, Social and Cultural Rights (Protocol of San Salvador)[16] provides that 'everyone has the right to adequate nutrition which guarantees the possibility of enjoying the highest level of physical, intellectual and emotional development'. However, the right to food has been read into the African Charter: in the case of *Social and Economic Rights Action Centre (SERAC) and the Centre for Economic and Social Rights v Nigeria*,[17] the African Commission on Human and Peoples' Rights (African Commission) interpreted the rights to life,[18] to health[19] and to development[20] in the African Charter to require state parties not to interfere with access to food and to protect access to food from interference by powerful third parties.[21]

Apart from these provisions in documents of general scope, the right to food is also found in context-specific documents that deal, for instance, with the rights of vulnerable groups, or with human rights as they apply under specific circumstances. The Convention on the Rights of the Child (CRC)[22] requires state parties, in respect of children, to 'combat disease and malnutrition ... through, *inter alia*... the provision of adequate nutritious foods ...'[23] and, in case

---

[10] Adopted at the first World Food Conference, held in Rome, 1974. See para 1 of the Declaration.
[11] 1966. Ratified by South Africa.
[12] Human Rights Committee General Comment No 6 (1982) *The right to life (art 6)* para 5 (my emphasis).
[13] 1950.
[14] 1961.
[15] 1981. Ratified by South Africa.
[16] 1988.
[17] Communication 155/96. See C Mbazira 'Reading the right to food into the African Charter on Human and Peoples' Rights' (2004) 5(1) *ESR Review* 5.
[18] Art 4 African Charter.
[19] Art 16 African Charter.
[20] Art 22 African Charter.
[21] *SERAC* (n 17 above) paras 64-66.
[22] 1989. Ratified by South Africa.
[23] Art 24(2)(c).

of need, to '... provide material assistance and support programmes, particularly with regard to nutrition ...'[24] Furthermore, the (United Nations) Standard Minimum Rules for the Treatment of Prisoners[25] require that prisoners 'be provided ... with food of nutritional value adequate for health and strength, of wholesome quality and well-prepared and served'.[26] The Convention on the Elimination of All Forms of Discrimination against Women (CEDAW) refers to a right to adequate nutrition.[27] A number of documents also protect the right to food in case of armed conflict,[28] in case of natural disaster[29] and with respect to refugees.[30]

In the last instance, a number of documents describe policies and practices in respect of the right to food, or provide benchmarks against which the realisation of the right to food can be tested. Examples are the Rome Declaration on Food Security and the World Food Summit Plan of Action, both adopted at the 1996 World Food Summit in Rome. The Rome Declaration expresses commitments of world leaders in respect of the eradication of hunger and malnutrition and the Plan of Action translates these into practice by listing follow-up actions for the international community, international civil society and individual states.

The Plan of Action requires that steps be taken to clarify the content of the right to food and freedom from hunger. This commitment has led to at least two important initiatives that provide a better understanding of the right to food.[31] First, after an expert consultation on the right to food held in 1997, it was recommended that the United Nations (UN) Committee on Economic, Social and Cultural Rights (Committee on ESCR) draft a General Comment on the right to food. This the Committee did in 1999.[32] Second, it has led to a coalition of international non-governmental organisations (NGOs)[33] developing voluntary guidelines on the right to food. This culminated in the Food and Agriculture Organisation (FAO), through its Inter-

[24] Art 27(3). See also art 24(2)(e), requiring state parties to ensure that parents and children are informed about child nutrition. See also the African Charter on the Rights and Welfare of the Child (African Children's Charter) (1990), requiring states to provide to children adequate nutrition (art 14(2)(c)).
[25] 1957.
[26] Art 20(1).
[27] 1979. Ratified by South Africa. Art 12(2) reads as follows: ' ... States Parties shall ensure to women ... adequate nutrition during pregnancy and lactation.'
[28] Eg arts 26 & 51 of the Geneva Convention Relative to the Treatment of Prisoners of War (1949); and arts 23 & 55 of the Geneva Convention Relative to the Treatment of Civilian Persons in Time of War (1949). Using starvation as a weapon is a crime in international law; art 8(2)(b)(xxv) of the Rome Statute of the International Criminal Court (1998).
[29] Eg UN General Assembly Resolutions 2816(XXVI) of 14 December 1971 and 36/225 of 17 December 1981.
[30] Convention Relating to the Status of Refugees (1951) ch IV.
[31] For an overview of the Rome Declaration and the Plan of Action, see Eide (n 7 above) paras 31-43.
[32] Committee on ESCR General Comment No 12 (1999) *Substantive issues arising in the implementation of the International Covenant on Economic, Social and Cultural Rights: The right to adequate food (art 11 of the Covenant)*. See sec 2.2 below.
[33] Food First Information and Action Network (FIAN); the World Alliance on Nutrition and Human Rights; and the Jacques Maritain Institute.

Governmental Working Group on the Right to Food (IGWG) producing draft Voluntary Guidelines on the Progressive Realisation of the Right to Food. In July 2004, negotiations for the adoption of these guidelines started and it is expected that they will be adopted during October/November 2004.[34]

2.2 Content

Although all the international documents referred to above are important for understanding the right to food, the Committee on ESCR's General Comment No 12, interpreting article 11 of CESCR, is the most comprehensive description of the right to food in international law. The description that follows is mostly based on it.[35] In the General Comment the Committee first describes the content of the right to food and then the duties incumbent on states to realise the right.

2.2.1 The content of the right to food: Availability, accessibility, adequacy

Article 11 of CESCR entrenches a right of everyone to adequate food and a right to be free from hunger. The purpose of this right is clear: It is a legal guarantee that food security must be achieved and maintained for everyone.[36] However, the causes of hunger and malnutrition are complex and multifaceted[37] – it is necessary to describe the content of the right to food in more detail, so as to be able to translate the right into concrete legal duties.

When people go hungry on a large scale, or serious malnutrition exists, it is easy to say that food security has failed because there is not enough food. The solution would then be straightforward: produce more food or acquire more food through trade.[38] However, people do not usually go hungry because there is not enough food available. Rather, they go hungry because they cannot get their hands on the food that is available.[39] Achieving food security therefore depends both on the existence of a sufficient supply of food and on

---

[34] See M Windfuhr 'No masterpiece of political will: The last stage of negotiations on voluntary guidelines on the right to food' (2004) 5(2) *ESR Review* 11; M Vidar 'Towards voluntary guidelines on the right to adequate food' (2004) 5(1) *ESR Review* 11.

[35] General Comment No 12 (n 32 above). See also Eide (n 7 above).

[36] See n 3 above for the FAO's definition of food security.

[37] Eide (n 7 above) para 14.

[38] This analysis both oversimplifies and obscures responsibility for failures in food security. It is easy to 'naturalise' hunger when focusing on food supply - inadequate national food supply is caused by what are perceived as uncontrollable 'natural' factors such as drought or market forces. It is more difficult to explain a situation where there is enough food in a country, but people still regularly go hungry. Such food insecurity is caused by factors much more clearly controllable: distribution of wealth and background rules of contract and property; J Drèze & A Sen *Hunger and public action* (1989) 20. Failure to deal with these controllable causes indicates choice, and so responsibility.

[39] A Sen *Poverty and famines: An essay on entitlement and deprivation* (1981) 1. See also R Ravindran & A Blyberg (eds) *A circle of rights. Economic, social and cultural rights activism: A training resource* (2000) 222; and General Comment No 12 (n 32 above) para 5.

the ability of people to acquire that food. The Committee on ESCR has translated these two elements of food security into the core content of the right to food, in terms of which the right to food is intended to ensure:[40]

> [t]he *availability* of food in a quantity and quality sufficient to satisfy the dietary needs of individuals, free from adverse substances, and acceptable within a given culture; [and]
>
> [t]he *accessibility* of such food in ways that are sustainable and that do not interfere with the enjoyment of other human rights.

Availability of food refers to *national food security* – the existence of a national supply of food sufficient to meet the nutritional needs of all the people in the country and geographically distributed in such a way that it is physically available to everyone, and the existence of opportunities for production of food for own use.[41]

Accessibility of food in turn refers to *household food security* - it requires that people be able to acquire the food that is available or to make use of available opportunities to produce food for own use. This capacity exists if people exercise some entitlement over food or its means of production: they earn income by selling labour or other commodities, which they use to buy food; they have an entitlement to monetary or in-kind social assistance from the state with which they acquire food; or they own, or exercise some other form of legal control over means of food production (land, implements, water, etc) so that they can produce food for own use.[42] In the words of the Committee:[43]

> [A]ccessibility applies to any acquisition pattern or entitlement through which people procure their food and is a measure of the extent to which it is satisfactory for the enjoyment of the right to adequate food.

For the right to food to be realised, availability and accessibility of food must be sustainable – food must also be available for and accessible to future generations.[44]

---

[40] General Comment No 12 (n 32 above) para 8 (my emphasis).
[41] n 40 above, para 12.
[42] Drèze & Sen (n 38 above) 20: '[C]ommand over food can be established by ... growing food oneself and having property rights over what is grown, or selling other commodities and buying food with the proceeds. The third alternative ... is to receive free food or supplementary income from the state.'
[43] General Comment No 12 (n 32 above) para 13 distinguishes *economic* and *physical* accessibility. Economic accessibility refers to entitlements self-sufficient people require to gain access to food (income, control of means of food production). Physical accessibility refers to those who are not self-sufficient and have to receive state assistance to gain access to food. The distinction emphasises that states must both facilitate access to food for those who are reasonably self-sufficient and provide food or the means to acquire it directly to those who are not.
[44] n 40 above, para 7.

The Committee also emphasises that *adequate food* – food of adequate quantity, quality and nature – must be available and accessible. People must have access to *nutritionally adequate* food – to enough food, with the right amounts and balance of nutrients 'for physical and mental growth, development and maintenance, and physical activity ... in compliance with human physiological needs ... throughout the life cycle ...'[45] It also means food must be *safe* – free from adverse substances, and stored and handled such that it is not contaminated or spoiled.[46] It finally means food must be *culturally adequate* – must satisfy cultural preferences and practices.[47] Importantly, nutritional adequacy, safety and cultural adequacy are relative to conditions in different countries – what is adequate food in a given country is determined by a range of factors, such as climate, endemic disease, prevalent body type of population and traditional dietary patterns.[48]

2.2.2 Duties

What must the state do under international law to realise the right to food? The overarching duty is that described in article 2(1) of CESCR: the duty to take steps, to the maximum of available resources, progressively to achieve the full realisation of the rights,[49] which in this case means that the state must take steps to ensure that a sufficient supply of nutritionally adequate, safe and culturally acceptable food is available and is accessible to everyone on a sustainable basis. Concretely, the Committee on ESCR has said that this means the right to food must be *respected, protected,* and *fulfilled.*[50] These terms are by now familiar:[51]

- To respect the right to food, the state must refrain from impairing existing access to adequate food; must, where such impairment is unavoidable, take steps to mitigate its impact; and must refrain from placing undue burdens in the way of people gaining or enhancing access to food.
- To protect the right food, the state must take steps to protect people's existing access to food and their capacity to enhance their existing access to food and newly to gain access to food, against third party interference.
- To fulfil the right to food, the state must take steps so that those that do not currently enjoy access to food can gain such access, and that for those whose access is insufficient, it is enhanced. The Committee distinguishes between a duty to fulfil (facilitate),

---

[45] n 40 above, para 9.
[46] n 40 above, para 10.
[47] n 40 above, para 11.
[48] n 40 above, para 7; Eide (n 7 above) para 49.
[49] This over-arching duty has been described by the Committee on ESCR in its General Comment No 3 (1990) *The nature of States Parties' obligations (art 2(1) of the Covenant).*
[50] General Comment No 12 (n 32 above) para 15.
[51] See sec 7(2) of the Constitution. See also, in the context of the right to food particularly, Eide (n 7 above) paras 52-53.

which requires the state to act so as to enhance the opportunities for self-sufficient people to gain access to adequate food or to enhance their existing access, and a duty to fulfil (provide), which requires the state to take steps to make it possible for people who are unable to make use of existing opportunities, to gain access to food – in short, a duty to provide directly to such people food or the means with which to acquire it.

The right to food does not require states to adopt specific measures to achieve its realisation:[52]

> The most appropriate ways and means of [respecting, protecting, promoting and fulfilling] the right to adequate food will inevitably vary significantly from one state party to another [and] [e]very state will have a margin of discretion in choosing its own approaches.

States must simply adopt whichever measures will lead to both the availability and accessibility of adequate food under conditions prevalent in their countries. However, states must adopt measures that address *all* elements of food security[53] – measures to ensure the creation and maintenance of a sufficient supply of food (agricultural production planning and subsidisation, food import and export planning and sustainable management and use of natural and other resources for food production); measures to ensure that standards of nutritional adequacy, safety and cultural acceptability of food are maintained (nutritional supplementation of basic foodstuffs and regulation pertaining to toxicity, storage and handling of foodstuffs); measures facilitating access to food (tax zero-rating of basic foodstuffs, food price monitoring, market regulation, subsidisation or actual price control); measures actually providing food or the means to acquire it to those who are deprived (programmes to provide food directly to disaster victims; food stamp or other social assistance programmes to help indigent people gain access to food); measures to monitor the nutritional situation in the country so as to inform policy formulation and implementation; measures to prevent discrimination in access to food;[54] and measures particularly ensuring the fulfilment of the right to food for vulnerable groups even in those conditions where the state faces severe resource constraints.[55]

The Committee suggests that states adopt a 'national strategy',[56] preferably set out in a 'framework law',[57] to achieve the realisation of the right to food. This national strategy should be developed in a systematic fashion, to ensure that it is such as to ensure proper co-ordination of functions and responsibilities in respect of the right to food between different sectors and levels in government and contains measures addressing all issues relative to food security as listed above.[58] The strategy should also be developed by way of a

---

[52] General Comment No 12 (n 32 above) para 21.
[53] n 52 above, para 25.
[54] n 52 above, para 26.
[55] n 52 above, para 28.
[56] n 52 above, para 21.
[57] n 52 above, para 29.
[58] n 52 above, para 22.

transparent and participatory process and should ensure transparency and accountability in its implementation.[59]

As with all the other rights protected in CESCR, the state's duty to achieve the realisation of the right to food is subject to the proviso that it need be done only 'progressively' and 'to the maximum of available resources'. Obviously these two conditions on the duty imposed by the right are intended to avoid the absurdity of asserting a legal right to an impossibility - to avoid saying that the right to food creates a claim for food to be provided by a state even there where it is manifestly unable to do so. However, CESCR distinguishes in article 11 between two different degrees of deprivation in respect of food: full-blown hunger on the one hand, and inadequate access to food on the other.[60] The Committee on ESCR has made it clear that the duty to avoid hunger is a priority duty and that failure to meet that duty will attract heightened scrutiny - 'when a state fails to ensure the satisfaction of ... the minimum essential level required to be free from hunger', it 'has to demonstrate that *every effort* has been made to use *all the resources at its disposal* ... to satisfy, *as a matter of priority*, those minimum obligations'.[61]

3 South African law

3.1 Content

The right to food is guaranteed in the South African Constitution in various provisions. The central provision is section 27(1)(b), which provides that: '[e]veryone has the right to have access to ... (b) sufficient food ...' The right to food is furthermore guaranteed specifically to children and to detained persons: Section 28(1)(c) determines that '[e]very child has the right ... (c) to basic nutrition ...' and section 35(2)(e), which deals with conditions of detention, determines, amongst other things, that detained persons are entitled to the 'provision, at state expense, of adequate ... nutrition'.

These rights are entrenched in the Constitution along the same lines as all other socio-economic rights. All three nutrition-related provisions require, in terms of section 7(2) of the Constitution, that the state 'respect, protect, promote and fulfil' them. As is the case in international law,[62] this means that the state must refrain from interfering with the exercise of these rights, must adopt measures to

---

[59] n 52 above, paras 23 & 24.
[60] This distinction mirrors the distinction made in a scientific context between *nutritional deprivation* (a condition of not receiving enough food to avoid stunting, wasting and other serious health risks); and *under-nourishment* (a condition of not receiving enough food to live a normal, active working life, without, however, facing serious and long-term health risks); Drèze & Sen (n 38 above) 35. This is - politically, ethically and analytically - a difficult distinction to make; K Van Marle '"No last word" - Reflections on the imaginary domain, dignity and intrinsic worth' (2002) 13 *Stellenbosch Law Review* 307); Drèze & Sen (n 38 above) 35-45.
[61] General Comment No 12 (n 32 above) para 17 (my emphasis).
[62] See sec 2.2.2 above.

protect their exercise against interference from private sources and must take steps to extend access to them to everyone.

However, some of these duties differ in relation to the three different food-related provisions. In respect of the latter three of the section 7(2) duties (the duties to protect and to promote and fulfil), section 27(1)(b) proclaims a *qualified* right to sufficient food for everyone. The duty on the state to take steps to protect, promote and fulfil the section 27(1) right is explicitly described in section 27(2) in such a way that it is limited – the state must take *reasonable* steps, *within available resources*, to achieve the *progressive realisation* of the right of everyone to have access to sufficient food.

This qualification has been interpreted by the Constitutional Court, in the context of the rights to adequate housing,[63] health care services[64] and social assistance,[65] to mean that the state's measures to give effect to a socio-economic right can be subjected to a test of reasonableness. Although specific measures cannot as a rule be prescribed to the state, it must indeed take measures to give effect to these rights and those must be reasonably capable of achieving the realisation of the rights in question over time, subject to the resources at its disposal.[66] This test is applied by the Court with varying degrees of scrutiny, depending on the circumstances of each case – the Court has tested the state's conduct against standards ranging from basic rationality and good faith at the one end of the spectrum[67] to full-blown proportionality at the other.[68] A wide variety of factors play a role in determining the intensity of scrutiny in a given case, but an important factor is the position in society of those affected by the failure of the state to give effect to the right in question and the impact such failure has on them.[69]

---

[63] *Government of the Republic of South Africa v Grootboom* 2001 1 SA 46 (CC).
[64] *Minister of Health v Treatment Action Campaign* 2002 5 SA 721 (CC).
[65] *Khosa v Minister of Social Development* 2004 6 SA 505 (CC).
[66] *Grootboom* (n 63 above) para 41; *Treatment Action Campaign* (n 64 above) para 38; *Khosa* (n 65 above) para 43. See the discussion of this reasonableness test in sec 3.2.3 below.
[67] *Soobramoney v Minister of Health, KwaZulu-Natal* 1998 1 SA 765 (CC) paras 27 & 29, where the Court upheld a decision by a state hospital to refuse life-prolonging renal dialysis treatment to a patient, because the decision was made rationally and in good faith, in terms of a reasonable policy.
[68] Proportionality requires that the public interest advanced by the limitation of a right is weighed up against the harmful impact the limitation has on that right and the claimants before the court and that a court considers whether means are available to achieve the purpose of the limitation that are less restrictive of the right and the interests of the claimants. In *Khosa* (n 65 above), the Court confirmed a High Court ruling that the exclusion of permanent residents from social assistance benefits violated the right to have access to social assistance (sec 27(1)(c) of the Constitution) – the measures were found unreasonable because the purpose of the exclusion (to prevent people immigrating to South Africa becoming a burden on the state) could be achieved through means less restrictive of permanent residents' rights (stricter control of access into the country) (para 65) and because 'the importance of providing access to social assistance to all who live permanently in South Africa and the impact upon life and dignity that a denial of such access has far outweighs the financial and immigration considerations on which the state relies' (para 82).
[69] See P de Vos '*Grootboom*, the right of access to housing and substantive equality as contextual fairness' (2001) 17 *South African Journal on Human Rights* 258, in general.

The duties to protect and to promote and fulfil the nutritional rights of children and detainees, by contrast, are not subject to the same qualification, creating the impression that those duties in respect of these rights are more direct than in respect of the section 27 right of everyone. The Constitutional Court has acknowledged this in respect of children's rights, although it has not as yet explained what the implication is in practical terms.[70] Most likely it will mean that the state's efforts to protect and to promote and fulfil the nutritional rights of children and of prisoners are subject to a higher standard of scrutiny than its efforts to do the same in respect of the right of everyone to adequate food. Specifically the proportionality test required by the general limitation clause, section 36(1) of the Constitution, will apply in cases where it is found that the realisation of these rights has failed – it will be more difficult for the state to justify a failure in giving effect to the right to basic nutrition of children or the right to adequate nutrition of prisoners than a failure to give effect to the right to have access to food for everyone.[71]

3.2 Legal duties

A useful way in which to describe the concrete legal duties that the Constitution's nutritional rights impose on the state and others is to follow the framework of section 7(2), and to describe the duties to respect, to protect and to promote and fulfil those rights. An overview of the various existing statutory and other entitlements that give expression to these duties, together with an indication of instances where these duties are, *prima facie*, violated, illustrates the different ways in which the right to food can be used as a practical legal tool.

It is important here to take into account that the right to food is interlinked with, or interdependent on, other rights. Enjoyment of the right to food both depends on and makes possible the enjoyment of other rights, and other rights can be used to protect or advance the enjoyment of the right to food.[72] The most obvious such right is the section 27(1)(b) right to have access to water. Not only is access to water essential for someone producing food for own use – water, an essential element of a nutritious diet, is intrinsically linked to the right to food. Other rights are relevant in the sense that they

---

[70] *Grootboom* (n 63 above) para 77; *Treatment Action Campaign* (n 64 above) para 79. See also B Goldblatt & S Liebenberg 'Giving money to children: The state's constitutional obligation to provide child support grants to child headed households' (2004) 20 *South African Journal on Human Rights* 151 160.

[71] See n 68 above.

[72] Although all rights are interdependent, this is often emphasised in respect of the right to food. Eide notes a trend in international law to see the right to food, with the rights to education and health care, as elements of a broader right to nutrition, which is again a component of a right to an adequate standard of living; Eide (n 7 above) para 44. In CRC, the right to food is not guaranteed as a free-standing right, but in conjunction with the rights to health care and education: Art 24(2)(c) requires state parties to take 'measures to combat disease and malnutrition, including ... the provision of nutritious foods ...'; and art 24(2)(e) requires state parties to ensure that 'parents and children are informed about child health and nutrition ...' In most international documents, the right to food is an element of the right to an adequate standard of living; see eg art 11(1) of CESCR.

guarantee an environment conducive to production of food for own use: One thinks here of the provisions in respect of tenure security and access to land in section 25,[73] the prohibition on arbitrary eviction in section 26 and the section 24 environmental rights.[74] Still other rights are relevant to the realisation of the right to food in the sense that they create entitlements to an income, or to the freedom to earn an income with which to acquire food: Examples are section 22, guaranteeing freedom of choice of trade, occupation and profession, section 23, which deals with labour relations, and section 27(1)(c), which guarantees the right of everyone to have access to social security and assistance.[75]

The rights to health care (section 27(1)(a)) and education (section 29) are especially important to the right to food. Education is important for the realisation of the right to food not only because being educated increases the capacity of people to earn income with which to gain access to food, but also because a person educated about the nutritional value of different foods and about food storage and preparation can derive more nutritional benefit from food than others. The right to food is also a precondition for proper exercise of the right to education: One's capacity effectively to participate in education is centrally determined by one's nutritional status.[76]

The relationship between the right to health care and the right to food is similarly inter-linked: One's health determines one's nutritional requirements, and nutritional status is an important determinant of health. Finally, the right to equality and the prohibition on unfair discrimination (section 9)[77] and the administrative justice rights (section 33) are important channels through which the right to food can be protected.

In short, the right to food is more or less embedded in other rights - measures to give effect to it are intertwined with measures to give effect to other rights, and its violation is often inseparable from the violation of a range of other rights. As a consequence, the right to food is seldom directly protected, whether through legislation or adjudication. More often it is indirectly protected through another

---

[73] Sec 25(5) (State must 'take reasonable legislative and other measures, within its available resources, to foster conditions which enable citizens to gain access to land on an equitable basis') and sec 25(6) ('[a] person or community whose tenure of land is legally insecure as a result of past racially discriminatory practices is entitled ... to tenure which is legally secure or to comparable redress').

[74] Sec 24(b) (State must take reasonable measures to prevent 'pollution and ecological degradation' and 'secure ecologically sustainable development and use of natural resources while promoting justifiable economic and social development'). On the importance of sustainable environmental management to the right to food, see General Comment No 12 (n 32 above) para 4.

[75] Most South African households acquire food through exchange, rather than production (only 5% of households nationally - 600 000 households – rely on farming as their main source of food); E Watkinson & N Makgetla *South Africa's food security crisis* (2002) 2. This illustrates the importance of income, whether generated through employment or social assistance, to gain access to food.

[76] D McCoy et al (eds) *An evaluation of South Africa's primary school nutrition programme* (1997) 8.

[77] About the intersection between equality and socio-economic rights, see *Khosa* (n 65 above) para 42.

constitutional right or lower level entitlement – to see the right to food in operation, one also has to look there.

3.2.1 The duty to respect the right to food

The duty to respect the right to food requires the state:
- to refrain from impairing people's existing access to adequate food;
- when such impairment is unavoidable, to take steps to mitigate its impact; and
- to refrain from placing obstacles in the way of people newly gaining access or enhancing existing access to food.

Refraining from impairing existing access to food

The clearest example of this element of the duty to respect the right to food being violated occurs where food is intentionally and actively destroyed by the state, such as happened in the *SERAC* case.[78] In this case, Nigerian military forces, in an attempt to quell opposition to uncontrolled development of oil fields, intentionally destroyed crops and killed animals in attacks on Ogoni villages. This led to malnutrition and starvation. The African Commission found that these actions violated the duty to respect the right to food of the Ogoni people.[79] The intentional use of the destruction of food, resulting in starvation as a weapon of war has happily not occurred in South Africa for a long time – should it happen again that would constitute a clear violation of the right to food that would be very difficult to justify.[80]

More commonly, this first element of the duty to respect the right to food is violated indirectly - the state interferes with the entitlements that people use to produce food, thus making it impossible, or very difficult for people to continue producing food. South Africa's apartheid history provides a particularly good example – in terms of the segregationist 'homeland' policies, large numbers of people were dispossessed of and forcibly removed from productive agricultural land by the state and dumped in overcrowded 'native reserves' or 'homelands' that were most often unsuited to agricultural use and particularly unsuitable for subsistence farming. In this way, people who used to be food self-sufficient were rendered

---

[78] *SERAC* (n 17 above).
[79] n 78 above, para 64-66. Use of starvation as a weapon is a crime in international law; n 28 above. *SERAC* also illustrates a violation of the right to food through destruction not only of food, but also of the means for and environment conducive to its production. Nigerian forces also destroyed farmland and implements; para 9. In addition, the Nigerian government participated in irresponsible development of oil fields, '[poisoning] much of the soil and water upon which ... farming and fishing depended'; para 9. The African Commission found that both the military's destruction of the means for food production and the government's wilful neglect violated the duty to respect the right to food; para 66.
[80] Intentional destruction of food was last used as a weapon of war in South Africa during the Anglo-Boer War, when British forces instituted a 'scorched earth' policy, systematically destroying herds, crops, food stores and farmsteads to deprive Boer fighters of food and other resources.

food insecure.[81] Recurrence of this kind of large-scale interference by the state in people's access to the resources with which to produce food is unlikely, as the statutory measures in terms of which these dispossessions occurred have been repealed and new legal measures have been put in place preventing such a recurrence. Although the best examples of these new legal measures focus explicitly on protecting property rights or housing and security of tenure rights rather than the right to food, they can be, and in some cases have already been developed to operationalise also the duty to respect the right to food. A few examples: Dispossession of land by the state can now only occur within the limits of section 25 of the Constitution, through regular expropriation, for a public purpose, following the payment of 'just and equitable' compensation, the amount, and time and manner of payment of which must be determined after all relevant circumstances have been considered.[82] In those cases where a dispossession of land used for subsistence farming is unavoidable, an argument can be made that the fact that the land was used to exercise the constitutional right to food is a circumstance that is eminently relevant to the determination of the amount of 'just and equitable' compensation.[83]

In addition, eviction of people from state land is heavily regulated through a raft of new laws that seek to improve security of tenure of people who exercise informal rights to land. These laws are clearly not aimed only at protecting people's rights to housing, but also at seeking to protect people's ability to use land as a resource with which to produce food and generate income. The two most important examples of such legislation in the context of state-owned land are the Extension of Security of Tenure Act (ESTA)[84] and the Prevention of Illegal Eviction from and Unlawful Occupation of Land Act (PIE).[85] These laws protect informal rights of not only residence on, but also

---

[81] On this history's impact on black farmers' capacity to produce food for own use, see C van Onselen *The seed is mine: The life of Kas Maine, a South African sharecropper, 1894-1985* (1996).

[82] Secs 25(2) & (3) of the Constitution. The Expropriation Act 63 of 1975 further regulates expropriation.

[83] See *In re Kranspoort Community* 2000 2 SA 124 (LCC) for an analogous description of 'just and equitable compensation' supporting this argument. Here the validity of a restitution claim in terms of the Restitution of Land Rights Act 22 of 1994 was challenged on the basis that the claimant community had been compensated for its loss of rights in land at the time of dispossession. Sec 2(2) of the Act determines that a claim will only be successful if the claimant can show it did not receive just and equitable compensation for the dispossession. The Court found that the compensation that was received covered only improvements to the land, and not the loss of 'beneficial occupation': The community's loss of grazing and cultivation rights - their entitlements to food - had not been compensated. As such the compensation was not 'just and equitable'; para 78.

[84] Act 62 of 1997. ESTA applies to rural land occupied with the tacit or explicit consent of the owner or person in charge; see sec 2(1) of ESTA and the definitions of 'occupier' and 'consent' in sec 1.

[85] Act 19 of 1998. PIE applies to all land, including state-owned land; see PIE secs 6 & 7. See also the Land Reform (Labour Tenants) Act 3 of 1996 (Labour Tenants Act), which applies to rural land occupied and used in terms of a labour tenancy agreement; sec 1. This Act will in practice not apply to state land, as the labour tenancy agreements that it is intended to regulate are usually with private landowners. ESTA, PIE and the Labour Tenants Act are also instruments to regulate private evictions and as such give effect to the duty to protect the right to food; see sec 3.2.2 below.

use of land,[86] by making eviction from land in certain instances more difficult than it would ordinarily be, *inter alia* by requiring that a court, before granting an eviction order, consider whether an eviction would be just and equitable in the light of all relevant circumstances.[87] Although none of the laws state this explicitly, where the land in question is used to produce food, the exercise of this discretion by a court should surely include a consideration of the extent to which the granting of an eviction order would impact on the exercise by the evictee of the constitutional right to food.[88] In this way the state's duty to respect existing exercise of the right to food is enforced.

People's ability to produce food for own use and for sale was during apartheid times also diminished in more insidious ways than through dispossession of and eviction from land. One example is the statutory prohibition imposed on share-cropping, a practice in terms of which black farmers were allowed by white landowners to cultivate part of their land, in return for a share in the resultant crop.[89]

---

[86] In terms of ESTA (n 84 above) (sec 1), a restriction of grazing or cultivation rights can be an eviction for its purposes; *Ntshangase v The Trustees of the Terblanché Gesin Familie Trust* [2003] JOL 10996 (LCC) para 4 (obstruction of the applicant's access to portions of a farm that she had used to graze and to water her cattle held to constitute an eviction for purposes of ESTA); *Van der Walt v Lang* 1999 1 SA 189 (LCC) para 13 (held that, in respect of the similar definition of 'eviction' in sec 1 of the Labour Tenants Act (n 85 above), a limitation on the number of cattle that may graze on land constitutes an eviction; and *Zulu v Van Rensburg* 1996 4 SA 1236 (LCC) 1259 (in respect of the Labour Tenants Act, the respondent's impounding of the applicant's cattle was an eviction subject to the Act).

[87] ESTA (n 84 above), secs 8(1) & 11(1), (2) & (3); PIE (n 85 above), secs 4(6) & (7), 5(1)(b) and 6(1) & (3).

[88] Both in ESTA (n 84 above) and PIE (n 85 above), the list of factors relevant to a decision whether a termination of an occupier's residence was lawful or an eviction order should be granted is not exclusive. In addition, some of the factors listed explicitly in eg ESTA sec 8(1) clearly require, in cases where land is used to produce food, a consideration of the impact that a termination of residence would have on the occupier's right to food (eg subsec (c), which requires a consideration of the comparative hardship to the owner or person in charge and the occupier if the right to residence is terminated or not terminated). See also sec 9(3), which requires a court under some circumstances to consider a report of a probation officer that must amongst other things indicate how an eviction will affect the constitutional rights (which would presumably include the right to food) of the occupier, before granting an eviction order. See also *City of Cape Town v Rudolph* 2004 5 SA 39 (C) para 48 where Selikowitz J describes the discretion whether to grant an eviction order that PIE affords a court as 'wide and open', and goes further to say that the 'circumstances to be taken into account by the court ... are also wide-ranging'.

[89] See Van Onselen (n 81 above) for a description. The prohibition on share-cropping was, at least at first, not very successful. Because share-cropping arrangements worked to the benefit of both black (property-less) and white (propertied) farmers, they remained in wide-spread use. However, the prohibition did have another, less obvious but in practical terms very serious, effect: it meant that, in cases where white farmers reneged on share-cropping agreements, black farmers could not, as they could previously, rely on the law to enforce the agreements.

Similarly, regulation of the South African fishing industry was introduced in the apartheid era that operated in such a way that subsistence fishing, which was previously operated legally on a large scale, was effectively prohibited.[90]

This violation of the duty to respect the right to food in apartheid South Africa has recently seen an interesting development. In 1998 the Marine Living Resources Act (MLRA)[91] was adopted. One of the purposes of the MLRA was to regularise the position of subsistence fishers through the so-called Individual Transferable Quotas (ITQ) system, by creating a system of licensing that included a category for subsistence fishers.[92]

Despite its laudable aims with respect to subsistence fishers, the MLRA's implementation has been beset with problems, to such an extent that it has caused interference with some subsistence fishers' existing capacity to acquire food from the sea. First, after an initial allocation of licenses for subsistence fishing, the annual allocation process, due to administrative backlogs, was postponed a number of times, with the result that no quotas were allocated for those years.[93] Second, due to a combination of factors, including influence peddling in the award of quotas; the relatively high costs and complex procedures involved in the application process; and government's tendency to favour access for larger commercial enterprises, people who have been subsistence fishers all their lives have been unable to obtain quota access.[94] This state of affairs can also arguably be characterised as a *prima facie* violation of the duty to respect the right to food, which the state would have to justify.

Mitigating the impact of interferences in the exercise of the right to food

It is unrealistic to argue that the duty to respect the right to food absolutely prohibits the state from interfering in existing access to food – very often it is necessary for the state to interfere in the entitlements that people have to food in order for it to achieve some other important public purpose. In such cases, the duty to respect

---

[90] Subsistence fishers operated in a legal vacuum – there was no quota category for subsistence fishing and subsistence fishers had to obtain recreational or commercial licences to operate legally. Both options were out of their reach; E Witbooi 'Subsistence fishing in South Africa: Implementation of the Marine Living Resources Act' (2002) 17 *International Journal of Marine and Coastal Law* 431 432. As with the prohibition of share-cropping (n 89 above) this meant both that subsistence fishers operated illegally and that they could not rely on the law to protect their fishing against interference. Subsistence fishing is currently a form of direct entitlement to food for a small but significant proportion of South Africa's population: 30 000 fishers depend on subsistence fishing to survive, and at least another 30 000 depend on subsistence fishing in combination with seasonal commercial employment; J Sunde 'On the brink' (2003) 12 *SPC Women in Fisheries Information Bulletin* 30 30.
[91] Act 18 of 1998.
[92] M Isaacs 'Subsistence fishing in South Africa: Social policy or commercial micro-enterprise?' (2001) 3(2) *Commons Southern Africa* 20.
[93] Although exemptions from the regulatory scheme were awarded for those years, this happened only after fishers resorted to civil disobedience; n 92 above, 21-22. See also Witbooi (n 90 above) 436-437.
[94] Sunde (n 90 above) 31.

requires that an effort be made to mitigate the effect of the interference in the exercise of the right to food.

The security of tenure laws referred to above again provide a good example of how this constitutional duty has been translated into a statutory entitlement of sorts. The laws, in some instances, require courts to consider to what extent suitable alternative land is available for evictees before granting an eviction order and an eviction order can be denied if such an alternative is absent.[95] Suitable alternative land is in one instance defined as land that is suitable with respect to the needs of occupiers for both residential *and agricultural use*.[96] In this way, the laws seek to give expression also to the duty of the state, there where it is impossible to avoid interfering with people's existing access to food, to mitigate that interference by providing alternative modes of access to food.

Removing obstacles in the way of the exercise of the right to food

The duty to respect the right to food is also violated if the state makes it difficult or impossible for people to gain access to food or to enhance their existing access to food. The recent Constitutional Court case of *Mashava v The President of the Republic of South Africa*[97] provides an example. In this case, the Constitutional Court confirmed a High Court order invalidating a presidential proclamation[98] assigning the administration of the Social Assistance Act (SAA)[99] to provincial governments.

Mr Mashava, an indigent, permanently disabled person, had applied for a disability grant to the Limpopo provincial Department of Health and Welfare in October 2000. After more or less four months he was told that he had been awarded the grant and could start collecting it from the Department's payment offices. However, despite him trying to do so for a considerable period of time, the grant was never paid to him. Only after he brought legal pressure to bear on the Department was the grant finally paid out for the first time on 25 January 2002. Even then, the Department failed to pay out the full amount of back pay owed.[100] Mr Mashava contended that, had it not been for the assignment of the administration of the SAA to the provinces, his grant would have been approved and paid out to him within a reasonable time, as the payment of the grant would then have depended on efficient, standardised and adequately resourced administration at national level rather than the administrative incapacity of the Limpopo provincial Department of Health and

---

[95] In respect of ESTA (n 84 above), see secs 9(3)(a), 10(2) & (3) & 11(3); in respect of PIE (n 85 above), see sec 6(3)(b).
[96] See ESTA (n 84 above), the definition of 'suitable alternative accommodation' in sec 1.
[97] *Mashava v The President of the Republic of South Africa* 2004 12 BCLR 1243 (CC).
[98] Proclamation R7 of 1996, *Government Gazette* 16992 GN R7, 23 February 1996. The assignment was made in terms of sec 235 of the interim Constitution.
[99] Act 59 of 1992.
[100] This background is set out in the *Mashava*-judgment (n 97 above) para 9.

Welfare and 'potential demands for the reallocation of social assistance monies to other [provincial] purposes'.[101]

The validity of the proclamation was challenged on the argument that the President, in terms of the transitional arrangements in the interim Constitution and the allocation of legislative and executive powers between provinces and national government, was not competent to make the assignment, without reliance on any constitutional right.[102] Nevertheless, the case was very much about Mr Mashava's constitutional rights – his right to have access to social assistance, and particularly his right to food. He and his dependents relied on the regular and efficient payment of his disability grant for their 'daily sustenance and well-being'.[103] In the absence of the possibility of earning an income through employment, the disability grant was their only entitlement with which to acquire food and the administrative inefficiency that bedevilled its payment constituted an obstacle in the way of their exercise of the right to food.[104] In effect, the decision of the Constitutional Court is a decision that the state must give effect to the duty to respect, amongst other rights, the right to food, by removing an impediment to its effective exercise.

3.2.2 The duty to protect the right to food

The duty to protect the right to food requires the state to protect the existing enjoyment of this right, and the capacity of people to enhance their enjoyment of this right or newly to gain access to the enjoyment of this right, against third party interference.

Legislative and executive measures

The most obvious way for the state to give effect to the duty to protect the right to food is for the elected branches of government to regulate, through legislation or executive/administrative decisions, the manner in which private entities participate in the production, storage and transfer of food. The aim should be for the state to regulate these activities in such a way that, in balance with other important constitutional principles such as freedom and equality, access to food for everyone is optimised.

The first example of such regulation that usually comes to mind is price regulation, where the state either sets a maximum price that

---

[101] n 100 above, para 10.
[102] n 100 above, para 1.
[103] n 100 above, para 9.
[104] The extent to which access to a social assistance grant and access to food is directly linked and lack of access to a social assistance grant, particularly for the rural poor in South Africa, translates into lack of access to food, has been demonstrated by a number of studies; see M Chopra *et al* 'Poverty wipes out health care gains' (2001/02) 6(4) *Children First* 16. It has also been estimated that social assistance grants close the 'poverty gap' (the gap between household income and the subsistence income line) by an average of 23%; Department of Social Development *Transforming the present – Protecting the future: Report of the Commission of Inquiry into a Comprehensive System of Social Security for South Africa* (the 'Taylor Commission') 59.

may be charged by private producers and retailers for basic foodstuffs to ensure that basic foodstuffs remain reasonably affordable, or introduces other measures to ensure food price stability.[105] The price of standard bread used to be regulated in this way in South Africa, but a general drive for liberalisation of agricultural markets has seen this fall away.[106]

Another way in which the state can protect access to adequate food against the depredations of profit-oriented free market players is through standard setting in respect of the safety and nutritional value of food. An example of this kind of regulation in South Africa is the Foodstuffs, Cosmetics and Disinfectants Act (FCDA),[107] which is intended to regulate fungicide and pesticide residue and additive and preservative levels in food, by setting minimum and maximum standards and creating mechanisms for the monitoring of these levels in foodstuffs. South Africa has also recently introduced mandatory micronutrient fortification of certain basic foodstuffs.

Finally, an important way in which the state currently seeks to give effect to its duty to protect the right to food is through protection of informal tenure rights. All three laws discussed above in the context of the state's duty to respect the right to food[108] - PIE,[109] ESTA[110] and the Labour Tenants Act[111] - protect informal rights to land as a resource for food production also against private interference in the same way as it protects these rights against the state: by making eviction more difficult than it would otherwise be through imposing additional procedural and substantive safeguards that have to be met before an eviction order can be granted by a court. In this way people's access to land, which for a small but significant group of people in South Africa constitutes their only entitlement to have access to food, is protected.[112]

---

[105] Measures to introduce or maintain stability in food prices include stock-piling of food reserves, and direct interventions in the food trade sector, such as requiring grain traders to report regularly on realised and planned imports, which, combined with accurate systems of crop estimate could contribute to stabilising food markets; Food Pricing Monitoring Committee (n 3 above) 31.

[106] Watkinson & Makgetla (n 75 above) 4 & 13. Watkinson & Makgetla point out that in the absence of regulation, there has been a 'hidden price rise' in bread – although the price per loaf in rand remained relatively stable in the period 1990 to 2001, both the weight and quality of the standard loaf deteriorated to such an extent that the real price per gram rose 293% in the same period.

[107] 54 of 1972.

[108] See sec 3.2.1 above.

[109] n 85 above.

[110] n 84 above.

[111] n 85 above.

[112] Six hundred thousand people in South Africa depend on farming as their main source of food. A further one million use farming to supplement other means of obtaining food; Watkinson & Makgetla (n 75 above) 2. See also sec 67(c) of the Magistrates' Courts Act 32 of 1944, which prohibits the attachment and sale in execution to satisfy a judgment debt of the 'stock, tools and agricultural implements of a farmer' and so protects the capacity of a subsistence farmer to produce food against interference from creditors.

It is important to note that the duty of the state to protect the right to food through the regulation of private conduct does not only require it to create a regulatory framework, but also to implement and enforce that framework effectively.[113] Concerns have, for example, recently been raised about the extent to which the FCDA is effectively enforced, with indications that the required monitoring is not taking place and that the standards created in the Act are not applied.[114] Similarly, the effectiveness of security of tenure legislation has been questioned, particularly in rural areas, where the link between tenure security and access to food is manifest.

Citing complicity between magistrates, police, and private landowners; disregard of the law by landowners; and the absence of legal aid in rural areas as causes, critics point out that evictions are still possible and happen regularly, and that farm workers or labour tenants who are evicted and fail to find alternative accommodation on farms rarely find recourse in municipal housing projects or other available land distribution programmes.[115] Such failures to implement regulatory measures intended to protect people's rights to food can also constitute *prima facie* violations of the duty to protect the right.

The judiciary

In addition to the legislative and executive branches of government, the courts have an important role to play in giving effect to the duty to protect the right to food, in two ways. In the first place, courts can protect the right to food by adjudicating constitutional and other challenges to state measures that are intended to advance the right to food. This protective role of courts has been illustrated in South Africa with respect to the right to have access to adequate housing in *Minister of Public Works v Kyalami Ridge Environmental Association*,[116] but with respect to the right to food it is best

---

[113] This is true for any measure devised to give effect to a socio-economic right. See *Grootboom* (n 63 above) para 42 where the Constitutional Court held that '[a]n otherwise reasonable programme that is not implemented reasonably will not constitute compliance with the state's obligations'.

[114] Watkinson & Makgetla (n 75 above) 5. They attribute also the deterioration in the weight and quality of standard bread (see n 106 above) partly to the lack of effective enforcement of regulations; 4.

[115] E Lahiff 'Land reform in South Africa: Is it meeting the challenge?' (2001) 1 *PLAAS Policy Brief* 2.

[116] 2001 3 SA 1151 (CC). In this case a state decision, taken in exercise of the constitutional duty to provide access to adequate housing, temporarily to house destitute flood victims on the grounds of a prison outside Johannesburg, was challenged by surrounding property owners as in violation of administrative justice rights. The Court rejected the challenge, albeit without any direct reliance on the state's duty to protect the right to have access to adequate housing. See also *City of Cape Town v Rudolph* (n 88 above) where a constitutional challenge to the security of tenure law PIE (n 85 above) was rejected by the Cape High Court, holding that, although the law infringed property rights, this could be allowed as the state had enacted it because the Constitution required it or at least authorised it to do so. See in this respect G Budlender 'Justiciability of socio-economic rights: Some South African experiences' in YP Ghai & J Cottrell (eds) *Economic, social and cultural rights in practice. The role of judges in implementing economic, social and cultural rights* (2004) 33 36.

illustrated by a decision of the German Federal Constitutional Court.[117]

In this case, legislation regulating the price and sale of drinking milk in Germany was challenged. This legislation - intended to keep the price of drinking milk at an affordable level and to ensure that the dairy industry is sustained in circumstances of serious over-production - both restricted the price of drinking milk and determined that drinking milk produced in a certain region could only be sold to a dairy within that region, that the dairy in question was obliged to buy all the drinking milk produced in that region and that drinking milk could then again only be bought from that dairy. The price of processed dairy products was not similarly restricted and milk intended for processed dairy products could be sold and bought freely across Germany. The effect of increasing surplus production of milk in this unequally regulated industry was that prices for processed dairy products were significantly lower than prices for drinking milk. To offset this disadvantage for suppliers and dairies selling milk for processed dairy products, suppliers and dairies selling drinking milk were required to pay a special tax. These suppliers and dairies challenged the regulation of the regulatory scheme on the basis that it infringed their freedom of competition.

The German Constitutional Court rejected the challenge, holding that, as milk was a basic foodstuff, it was in the general interest that its price be kept at an affordable level and that, as the sustenance of the agricultural sector and particularly the dairy sector, as a national asset essential to meeting basic needs, was in the general interest, the control of the sale of milk and the imposition of the special tax was also saved, in spite of its admitted restriction of the freedom of competition. In effect, the Court held that the state was giving effect to a constitutional duty to ensure that people's basic food needs are met on a sustainable basis through its regulation of the dairy industry, and that this saved the regulatory framework.[118]

Courts also have a duty to protect the right to food in a second way - through the exercise of their law-making activity in interpreting legislation and developing the rules of common law. South African courts are constitutionally obliged when interpreting legislation or developing rules of common law to do so in such a way that the 'spirit, purport and objects' of the Bill of Rights are promoted.[119] This requires courts to infuse legislation and the common law with the value system underlying the Constitution - to read the rights in the Bill of Rights and the values underlying them into the existing law. Because, as Amartya Sen has pointed out, access to food in a private ownership economy is so centrally determined by 'a system of legal relations (ownership rights, contractual obligations, legal exchanges, etc)', because, quite literally, 'the law stands between food

---

[117] 18 BverfGE 315, 1965 (n 6 above).
[118] See E de Wet 'Can the social state principle in Germany guide state action in South Africa in the field of social and economic rights?' (1995) 11 *South African Journal on Human Rights* 30 38 for a discussion.
[119] See sec 39(1) of the Constitution.

availability and food entitlement',[120] the constitutionally informed law-making role of courts is potentially an extremely important way in which the protection of the right to food can be advanced.

Courts can do so first by interpreting legislation regulating access to resources for the production of food or to food itself in such a way that entitlements to food are protected. In an indirect fashion, there are numerous examples where this has already happened in South Africa. The most obvious such example again relates to the tenure security laws referred to above.[121] Courts have, in cases decided on the basis of both ESTA and the Labour Tenants Act, extended the scope of protection afforded by these laws by finding that various forms of interference with food production activities such as crop cultivation and cattle rearing, and not only interference in the residential occupation of land, constitute evictions that have to comply with the stringent procedural and substantive safeguards imposed by these laws.

In *Ntshangase v The Trustees of the Terblanché Gesin Familie Trust*,[122] the Land Claims Court held that when a property owner prevents an occupier from accessing grazing lands and a watering hole on his property that she had previously used for her cattle, that constitutes an eviction for purposes of ESTA.[123]

In respect of the Labour Tenants Act,[124] the Land Claims Court, in *Van der Walt v Lang*,[125] held that where a property owner had previously allowed an occupier to graze a certain number of cattle on his land, a subsequent restriction of the number of cattle allowed constituted an eviction subject to the Act's safeguards. Also, in *Zulu v Van Rensburg*,[126] the Court held that impounding the cattle of an occupier constituted an eviction that had to comply with the Act's safeguards.[127]

An interesting possibility for further court driven development of the statutory law to protect the right to food came to light in the recent Constitutional Court case of *Jaftha v Schoeman*.[128] In this case the Court considered the constitutionality of provisions of the Magistrates' Courts Act[129] that allowed, either where sufficient movables could not be found, or where a court, on good cause shown, ordered it, the sale in execution of the immovable property, including

---

[120] Sen (n 39 above) 166.
[121] See secs 3.2.1 & 3.2.2 above.
[122] n 86 above, para 4.
[123] n 84 above.
[124] n 85 above.
[125] n 86 above, para 13.
[126] n 86 above, 1259.
[127] See also the range of decisions of the Land Claims Court interpreting the term 'rights in land' in the Restitution of Land Rights Act (n 83 above) to include also 'beneficial occupation', so that the long term use of land for grazing and cultivation purposes also constitutes such a right in land that can be reclaimed; eg *In re Kranspoort Community* (n 83 above).
[128] *Jaftha v Schoeman; Van Rooyen v Stoltz* 2005 1 BCLR 78 (CC).
[129] n 112 above. See sec 66(1)(a).

the home, of a debtor to satisfy a judgment debt. To protect the right of everyone to have access to adequate housing, the Court, through a combination of interpretation and of reading words into the Act, changed the Act in such a way that a judgment debtor's home can now only be sold in execution if a court has ordered it after considering all relevant circumstances.[130]

Jaftha involved only the protection of a judgment debtor's home and right to have access to adequate housing against sale in execution. However, in future cases where a creditor seeks the sale in execution of immovable property that a judgment debtor uses to produce food, courts can certainly extend the Constitutional Court's reasoning so that the fact that the immovable property is the debtor's means with which to exercise the right to food must also be considered relevant to the decision whether or not to allow its sale in execution. In this way courts could develop the law to protect judgment debtors' right to food against interference from creditors.

The judgment in *Jaftha* certainly leaves scope for this. For one thing, the Court explicitly stated that the factors that it listed to take account of when considering whether to allow sale in execution of immovable property were not the only ones that could play a role and that a court would have to consider any other factor that, on the facts of the case before it, is relevant.[131] In addition, the Court emphasised that the factor that drove it to conclude that the Magistrates' Courts Act as it stood violated the right to have access to adequate housing was the severe impact that the execution process could have on the human dignity of a judgment debtor and on a judgment debtor's capacity to have access to the basic necessities of life.[132] Certainly, the impact on an indigent person's human dignity and basic survival interests of the attachment and sale in execution of immovable property that the person uses to produce food for own use, in the absence of any other major source of access to food, is comparable to the impact of the sale in execution of such a person's home.

Courts can of course also protect the right to food through the exercise of their powers to develop the common law. Regrettably,[133] there has been little development in our law along this front. In the one case in which the Supreme Court of Appeal was approached to develop the common law rules of contract so as better to protect the right to have access to health care services, the Court rejected the

---

[130] *Jaftha* (n 128 above) paras 61-64 & 67.
[131] n 130 above, para 60. The factors that the Court lists that should considered are: 'the circumstances in which the debt was incurred; ... attempts made by the debtor to pay off the debt; the financial situation of the parties; the amount of the debt; whether the debtor is employed or has a source of income to pay off the debt *and any other factor relevant to the ... facts of the case ...*' (my emphasis).
[132] As above, paras 21, 25-30, 39 & 43.
[133] Regrettably, both because the development of the common law to give effect to socio-economic rights is especially important, as common law background rules of contract and property and exchange so centrally determine access to basic resources; and because one would expect courts to be more comfortable to utilise this avenue of enforcement of socio-economic rights rather than others, as the development of the common law has always been their task.

invitation to do so.[134] However, the courts have been fairly active in the development of the common law rules of eviction – something that, because access to land importantly determines access to food, is directly relevant to protection of the right to food. The common law rules of eviction hold that a property owner is entitled to an eviction order on a showing she is indeed owner of the land in question and that the person occupying it is doing so unlawfully. Where this showing is made, a court has no discretion whether or not to award the order.[135]

Section 26(3) of the Constitution could be read to change this rule: It determines that eviction from a home may only take place in terms of a court order granted *after all relevant circumstances had been considered*. The tenure security laws referred to above, all of which require courts to consider all relevant circumstances before granting an eviction order, give effect to section 26(3).[136] However, conflicting decisions in the High Courts raised uncertainty over whether the tenure security laws, particularly PIE, applied also to cases of so-called 'holding over' - cases where initially lawful occupation subsequently became unlawful.[137] As a result, courts had to consider whether section 26(3) changed the common law rules of eviction in those cases where PIE does not apply and the common law by default does. In *Ross v South Peninsula Municipality*,[138] the Cape High Court found that it did, so that an applicant for an eviction order, in addition to the common law showing, had to raise relevant circumstances that would entitle the court to grant the order.[139] However, a decision of the Witwatersrand High Court, *Betta Eiendomme (Pty) Ltd v Ekple-Epoh*,[140] contradicted *Ross*.

This conflict reached the Supreme Court of Appeal in *Brisley v Drotsky*,[141] where the Court held that the section 26(3) 'relevant circumstances' could only be *legally* relevant circumstances, that the only circumstances legally relevant to the question whether an eviction should be allowed were whether the evictor was owner of the land in question and the evictee was occupying it unlawfully and, consequently, that section 26(3) did not change the rules of common law as found in *Ross*.[142] As a result, all evictions from residential

---

[134] *Afrox Health Care (Pty) Ltd v Strydom* 2002 6 SA 21 (SCA) (argument that common law rule that contractual terms contrary to the public interest are unenforceable should be developed in the light of sec 27(1)(a) of the Constitution in such a way that disclaimers in admissions contracts to private hospitals are unenforceable rejected).
[135] *Graham v Ridley* 1931 TPD 476.
[136] ESTA (n 84 above), PIE and the Labour Tenants Act (n 85 above). See sec 3.2 above for a discussion of these laws.
[137] The question was specifically whether PIE applied to such evictions. See eg *Ellis v Viljoen* 2001 4 SA 795 (C) (PIE does not apply); and *Bekker v Jika* [2001] 4 B All SA 573 (SE) (PIE does apply).
[138] *Ross v South Peninsula Municipality* 2000 1 SA 589 (K).
[139] n 138 above, 596H.
[140] *Betta Eiendomme (Pty) Ltd v Ekple-Epoh* 2000 4 SA 486 (W). The Court, at 473A-B, held that sec 26(3) only applied to evictions by the state and not to evictions by natural or juristic persons.
[141] *Brisley v Drotsky* 2002 4 SA 1 (SCA).
[142] As above, para 42.

property where the occupant was 'holding over' remained subject to the old common law rule, which afforded a court no discretion in deciding whether to grant an eviction order.

This position soon changed. In *Ndlovu v Ngcobo; Bekker v Jika*,[143] the Supreme Court of Appeal held that PIE applied to evictions in cases of 'holding over' – in effect that section 26(3) extended to these evictions through PIE.[144] This negated *Brisley* – also in cases of 'holding over' a court would now, in terms of PIE, have a discretion, exercised in the light of all relevant circumstances, whether to grant an eviction order.

The holding in *Ndlovu* is potentially very important for people who access food through small-scale agricultural production. Increasingly in South Africa, the kind of property at issue in cases like *Ndlovu* is used not only for residential purposes but also to produce food at the very least to supplement other forms of access to food[145] – indeed, through various measures, the state encourages the cultivation of food gardens on residential plots as a way for people to enhance their access to food.[146] The protection afforded the security of tenure of occupiers of such property after the *Ndlovu* decision does not only protect their right to have access to adequate housing, but also their right to food.

However, the refusal of the Supreme Court of Appeal in *Brisley* to develop the common law of eviction in this respect could come back to haunt it. At the end of 2003, prompted by lobbying efforts from banks and large property management concerns, the Department of Housing published for public comment a draft amendment Bill to PIE[147] purporting to change the definition of an unlawful occupier so that cases of 'holding over' would once again be excluded from PIE's scope. Should this Bill be adopted,[148] the situation would again revert to that after *Brisley* – when faced with an application for an eviction order in cases of 'holding over', a court will then again not be able to take account of the impact which that eviction would have on the capacity of the evictee to have access to food. The Court's reticence in *Brisley* would then have denied the development of a potentially important tool for the protection of the right to food.

---

[143] *Ndlovu v Ngcobo; Bekker & Another v Jika* 2003 1 SA 113 (SCA).
[144] n 143 above, para 23.
[145] De Klerk *et al* (n 2 above) 54-58 note that food gardens in both urban and rural areas make a significant contribution to food security. Importantly, they point out that the biggest obstacle to the establishment and maintenance of food gardens is access to land and security of tenure.
[146] See eg the Department of Social Development's Poverty Relief Programme.
[147] The Draft Prevention of Illegal Eviction from and Unlawful Occupation of Land Bill, 2003, *Government Gazette* No 25391, GN 2276 of 2003, 27 August 2003.
[148] The status of the Bill is currently unclear.

3.2.3 The duty to promote and fulfil the right to food

The duty to promote and fulfil[149] the right to food requires the state to 'adopt appropriate legislative, administrative, budgetary, judicial, promotional and other measures'[150] so that those that do not currently enjoy access to food can gain access and so that existing access to food is enhanced.

The Constitutional Court has, in terms that closely track the description of the state's duty to fulfil the right to food in international law,[151] described the nature and extent of the duty to fulfil socio-economic rights in four cases, dealing with the rights to have access to adequate housing,[152] to health care[153] and to social assistance.[154] If applied to the right to food, it amounts to this:

- The state must devise and implement measures to give effect to the right to food.[155] Although the speed with and extent to which the state can fulfil the right to food through its legislative and other measures are obviously determined by the resources at its disposal and although this can happen only progressively,[156] the state must be able to show that it has such measures in place and that it is in the process of implementing them. In addition the state must be able to show progress in its implementation of these measures – any deliberate retrogression would constitute a *prima facie* violation of the right to food, which will require a particularly convincing justification.[157]
- These measures must be reasonably capable of achieving the purpose of the right to food[158] – of creating and maintaining for every man, woman and child in South Africa '[t]he availability of food in a quantity and quality sufficient to satisfy the dietary

---

[149] I discuss the duties to promote and fulfil here as one. Liebenberg has suggested that the duty to promote requires the state to undertake educational measures in respect of a right – to educate people about the nature and content of a right and the tools and opportunities with which to access it; S Liebenberg 'The interpretation of socio-economic rights' in M Chaskalson *et al Constitutional law of South Africa* (2003) (2nd ed, original service, 12-03) 33-1 33-6. Budlender (n 116 above) 37 describes it as a duty of executive and administrative agencies 'to have proper regard' to the advancement of socio-economic rights in their decision making. Both these meanings are included in my discussion of the 'duty to promote and fulfil' the right to food.

[150] Committee on ESCR General Comment No 14 *The right to the highest attainable standard of health (art 12 of the Covenant)* para 33.

[151] See General Comment No 12 (n 32 above) paras 21-28.

[152] *Grootboom* (n 63 above)

[153] *Soobramoney* (n 67 above) and *Treatment Action Campaign* (n 64 above). *Treatment Action Campaign* can also be characterised as dealing with the duty to respect the right to health care.

[154] *Khosa* (n 65 above).

[155] General Comment No 12 (n 32 above) para 21.

[156] See sec 27(2) of the Constitution: 'The state must take reasonable legislative and other measures, *within available resources*, to achieve the *progressive realisation* of [this] right ...' (my emphasis).

[157] *Grootboom* (n 63 above) para 45. See also Committee on ESCR General Comment No 3 (n 49 above) para 9 (a deliberate retrogression would require full justification 'by reference to the totality of rights ... in the Covenant and in the context of the full use of the maximum available resources').

[158] *Grootboom* (n 63 above) para 41.

needs of individuals, free from adverse substances, and acceptable within a given culture; [and] [t]he accessibility of such food in ways that are sustainable and that do not interfere with the enjoyment of other human rights'.[159] To be judged as reasonable in this sense, the state's measures must meet at least the following basic standards:
- They must be comprehensive and co-ordinated, clearly allocating responsibilities to different spheres within government.[160]
- Financial and human resources to implement them must be available.[161]
- They must be both reasonably conceived and reasonably implemented.[162]
- They must be 'balanced and flexible', capable of responding to intermittent crises and to short-, medium- and long-term food needs.[163]
- They may not exclude 'a significant segment of society'.[164]
- They may not 'leave out of account the degree and extent of the denial' of the right to food and must respond to the extreme levels of food insecurity of people in desperate situations – that is, the state's measures must make provision both for access to food being *facilitated* for those who are able to make use of opportunities for themselves and for access to food being *provided* to those who are in desperate conditions and cannot make do for themselves.[165]
- They must be transparent in the sense that they must be made known both during their conception and once conceived to all affected.[166]

---

[159] General Comment No 12 (n 32 above) para 8.
[160] *Grootboom* (n 63 above) para 39. See also General Comment No 12 (n 32 above) paras 22 & 25.
[161] *Grootboom* (n 63 above) para 39. See also General Comment No 12 (n 32 above) para 21.
[162] *Grootboom* (n 63 above) para 42.
[163] n 162 above, para 43.
[164] As above. See also General Comment No 12 (n 32 above) para 26.
[165] *Grootboom* (n 63 above) para 44. See also General Comment No 12 (n 32 above) para 28.
[166] *Treatment Action Campaign* (n 64 above) para 123. See also General Comment No 12 (n 32 above) paras 23 & 24.

As yet, the duty to fulfil the right to food has not been the basis of a court decision in South Africa.[167] In the absence of such direct indication of what this duty means, a useful way in which to illustrate the concrete legal entitlements and duties that the duty to fulfil the right to food entails is to consider to what extent the state's existing measures to realise this right indeed meet constitutional requirements and particularly to point out possible constitutional failures in this respect. I focus on three elements of the duty to fulfil the right: The duty to have in place a national strategy with which to fulfil the right to food, the duty to ensure that such a national strategy be reasonable, and the duty to avoid any deliberate retrogression in the progressive fulfilment of the right to food.

Having a national strategy

Until relatively recently, it was difficult to draw up the South African government's constitutional scorecard on the duty to fulfil the right to food. Then, no coherent policy framework directed specifically at giving effect to the right to food existed in South Africa. In fact, it seemed that government simply had no 'national strategy' to fulfil the right to food as it is required to have both in terms of international law[168] and in terms of the Constitutional Court's *Grootboom* jurisprudence.[169] This in itself constituted at the time a *prima facie* violation of the right to food.

This very basic structural constitutional problem has over the last three years largely been overcome. Prompted in part by the national outcry over the sharp rises in food prices in 2001[170] and the resultant further erosion of food security amongst the poor, government has both introduced a range of new measures to address specific aspects of food insecurity and has made a significant effort to develop and publicise a coherent national strategy, focused on addressing food insecurity in South Africa.

Policies relating to the fulfilment of the right to food are currently co-ordinated in terms of a cross-departmental policy framework, the Integrated Food Security Strategy for South Africa (IFSS), driven by the Department of Agriculture.[171] This document sets out a broad policy framework for measures aimed at enhancing food security in

---

[167] The right to food indirectly did make a brief, but unsuccessful appearance in *Treatment Action Campaign* (n 64 above): Treatment Action Campaign argued that government should be ordered to provide, as part of a comprehensive package to prevent mother-to-child transmission of HIV, breast milk substitutes free of charge and on demand to HIV positive mothers who give birth at public health facilities. The Court declined to do so, arguing that the complex nature of the question whether or not substitutes are appropriate militated against the Court making a binding order in this respect and that such decisions are best left to health professionals; para 128.

[168] General Comment No 12 (n 32 above) para 21.

[169] *Grootboom* (n 63 above) para 39.

[170] In the year up to June 2002, the food price index rose 16.7% whilst non-food inflation was only 7.2%. In the same period, the price of a bag of maize meal doubled; Watkinson & Makgetla (n 75 above). For a full assessment of the extent and nature of the food price volatility in 2001/2002, see Food Pricing Monitoring Committee (n 3 above) 5-8.

[171] Department of Agriculture (n 2 above).

South Africa and is intended to 'streamline, harmonise and integrate diverse food security sub-programmes'.[172] To this end, The IFSS calls for a cross-departmental and cross-sectoral management structure.[173] It also identifies a number of key focus areas for policy development and implementation.[174]

Ensuring that the national strategy is reasonable

As explained above, whatever measures the state chooses to take in order to fulfil the right to food must be reasonable in the light of the test that the Constitutional Court developed in *Grootboom*, *Treatment Action Campaign*, and, most recently, *Khosa*. Again, as recently as two years ago, government's existing measures to address food insecurity *prima facie* failed this reasonableness test in at least two respects. In the first place, the lack of co-ordination in government efforts to promote and fulfil the right to food was then such that I argued at the time that it rose to the level of constitutional violation – that the measures were not sufficiently focused and co-ordinated to pass the reasonableness test set by the Constitutional Court in *Grootboom*.[175] No specific government department at national, provincial or local level focused in the first instance on the right to food in the way that, for instance, the Department of Health is dedicated primarily to realising the right to have access to health care services. Partly as a result, measures intended to foster food security developed in a piece-meal fashion, with different aspects – and sometimes the same aspects – of nutritional policy addressed by different departments.[176] Also, any attempt to provide an overview and assessment of state measures to fulfil the right to food was confounded by the difficulty in making overall sense of a loose patchwork of policies and programmes. In the light of the constitutional requirement of transparency in policy formulation and

---

[172] n 171 above, 11.
[173] An Inter-Ministerial Committee, chaired by the Minister of Agriculture, heads the IFSS at political level. It is managed and implemented by a National Co-ordinating Unit, with corollaries at provincial level (Provincial Co-ordinating Units), which oversee the work of District Food Security Officers and, at local level, Food Security Officers. The IFSS also envisages the establishment of a National Food Security Forum (NFSF), with membership drawn from the public sector, the private sector and civil society and with corollaries at provincial level (Provincial Food Security Forums), at district level (District Food Security Forums) and local level (Local Food Security Action Groups). The role of the NFSF is to provide 'strategic leadership and advisory services on food security' and to set standards and recommend policy options; n 171 above, 34.
[174] These are increasing household food production and trading; improving income generation and job creation; improving nutrition and food safety; increasing safety nets and food emergency systems; improving analysis and information management systems; providing capacity-building and holding stakeholder dialogue; n 171 above, 6.
[175] D Brand 'Between availability and entitlement: The Constitution, *Grootboom* and the right to food' (2003) 7 *Law, Democracy and Development* 1 22. See *Grootboom* (n 63 above) para 39.
[176] This problem has been acknowledged by government; Department of Agriculture (n 2 above) 11.

implementation referred to above, this lack of transparency in food-related policy was in itself constitutionally problematic.[177]

Both these potential violations of the right to food have since been adequately addressed. The IFSS referred to above is explicitly intended to co-ordinate measures to achieve food security. The Department of Agriculture is also now clearly identified as the lead department with respect to the fulfilment of the right to food. The production of a single coherent policy framework with respect to the fulfilment of the right to food has also greatly enhanced the transparency of government's measures. In addition, efforts to adopt right to food framework legislation are ongoing, which, if successful, would further enhance the focus, co-ordination and transparency of measures to fulfil the right to food.[178]

However, despite these important advances, there are two general problems with government's national strategy to fulfil the right to food. The first of these relates to the comprehensiveness of the strategy, the second to its implementation. The different measures co-ordinated within the IFSS come close to constituting the kind of 'comprehensive' programme,[179] that addresses 'critical issues and measures in regard to *all* aspects of the food system', as required by the Constitutional Court's reasonableness test and at international law.[180]

Government has instituted a range of measures to engender access to food. A number of programmes *facilitate access* to food, making it possible for reasonably self-sufficient people to gain access to food for themselves. One thinks here of programmes that enable people to produce food for consumption or to generate income with which to buy food, such as the Department of Agriculture's Food Security and Rural Development Programme,[181] the Departments of Agriculture and Land Affairs' Land Redistribution for Agricultural Development Programme,[182] the Department of Public Works' Community-Based Public Works (CBPW) Programme,[183] and the Department of Social Development's Poverty Relief Programme (PRP).[184]

---

[177] *Treatment Action Campaign* (n 64 above) para 123. See also General Comment No 12 (n 32 above) paras 23 & 24.

[178] See in this respect S Khoza 'Protecting the right to food in South Africa. The role of framework legislation' (2004) 5(1) *ESR Review* 3.

[179] *Grootboom* (n 63 above) para 39.

[180] For a more comprehensive overview of these measures, see D Brand 'Budgeting and service delivery in programmes targeted at the child's right to basic nutrition' in E Coetzee & J Streak (eds) *Monitoring child socio-economic rights in South Africa: Achievements and challenges* (2004) 87 93-101; E Watkinson 'Overview of the current food security crisis in South Africa' SARPN, available at http://www.sarpn.org.za/documents/doooo222/watkinson/index.php 7 (accessed 31 October 2004).

[181] Agricultural starter-packs and information packs to enable food production for own consumption are provided to food insecure rural households; Brand (n 180 above) 95.

[182] Financial support is provided for farmers from previously disadvantaged communities to enable them to buy land and agricultural implements; n 180 above, 96.

[183] Jobs are created by involving poor rural communities in public works projects; n 180 above.

[184] The department establishes communal rural food production clusters (food gardens, poultry houses, pig units); n 180 above.

A variety of measures also *provide access* to food to those who cannot make use of existing opportunities to obtain access to food. The bulk of these measures are special needs social assistance cash grants that enable certain especially vulnerable groups of people to acquire food.[185] There are also two permanent programmes in terms of which food and nutritional supplementation is provided directly to children: the Primary School Feeding Scheme (PSFS)[186] and the programme targeting children with acute protein energy malnutrition (the PEM programme),[187] both managed by the Department of Health. In 2002, government also introduced short-term crisis measures in response to rising food prices in the form of a programme to provide food parcels and agricultural starter packs to destitute families (to run for three years).[188]

Government's measures also take account of the need to ensure the availability of food. The Department of Agriculture (through appropriate production policies) and the Department of Trade and Industry (through appropriate food import strategies) have programmes in place and currently manage to maintain an adequate national food supply and so ensure national food security.[189] Different departments and institutions within government also run programmes to monitor different aspects of national and household food security in South Africa and to enhance nutritional status through nutritional education and micronutrient fortification of foodstuffs. An important recent addition to these programmes was the appointment of the Department of Agriculture's National Food Pricing Monitoring Committee to investigate and advise government on food prices in South Africa.[190]

---

[185] The State Old Age Pension; the Child Support Grant; the Foster Child Grant; the Disability Grant; the War Veteran's Grant; the Care Dependency Grant; and Grant-in-Aid. See also the Social Relief in Distress Grant, which, although narrowly tailored, is not a special needs grant; n 180 above, 98.

[186] In terms of the PSFS a nutritious meal is provided once every school day to primary school learners at school. For an analysis of this programme from a right to food perspective, see Brand (n 180 above) 104-116. See also, in general, McCoy *et al* (n 76 above).

[187] The PEM programme provides treatment in hospitals and clinics to severely malnourished children and discharges them when they have recovered. For a description and evaluation, see Chopra *et al* (n 104 above).

[188] In addition to the provision of food parcels and agricultural starter packs, government announced that it would increase a variety of social assistance grants (ranging from an increase of 2% in the Foster Child Grant to an increase of 8% in the Child Support Grant). For a critique of the effectiveness of these measures to address the effects of the 2001/2002 food pricing crisis, see E Watkinson & K Masemola 'The food crisis: More action needed' (2002) November *NALEDI Policy Bulletin* 4.

[189] See n 2 above.

[190] The Committee was appointed for a period of one year. It has completed its work and has submitted its final report to the Department of Agriculture. See n 3 above.

However, government's national strategy to fulfil the right to food does have one important gap: it fails to make any sustainable provision for the food needs of a substantial number of people who are in food crisis. The Constitutional Court, as part of its reasonableness test, has fashioned a requirement of reasonable inclusion, which holds that a policy should 'respond to the needs of those most desperate',[191] take into account the 'amelioration of the circumstances of those in crisis',[192] and may not exclude 'a significant segment of society'.[193] This requirement is closely linked to a requirement of flexibility, which holds that a measure must 'make appropriate provision for attention to ... crises and to short-, medium- and long-term needs'.[194] The requirements of reasonable inclusion and flexibility are also echoed in international law: The Committee on ESCR states in its General Comment No 12 that a national strategy to fulfil the right to food must include measures of an immediate nature, to address food crises[195] and must include measures to 'ensure the satisfaction of, at the very least, the minimum essential level required to be free from hunger'.[196]

Many South Africans do not even meet *basic essential* levels of access to food, let alone enjoy a fully adequate nutritional status. Their nutritional status is desperate, or in crisis, in the sense that they suffer the 'daily terrorism of hunger' and face serious and permanent health risks as a result.[197] Although this situation is evident from a wide variety of statistics – both food intake data and anthropometric indicators[198] – it is most dramatically shown by the fact that 43% of South African households live in food poverty (their monthly income is not enough for them to afford even a basic, low cost nutritionally adequate diet)[199] and that, in 1999, 52% of households nationally experienced hunger on a regular basis.[200] This crisis is not one of a passing nature, caused by some aberrant event such as a natural disaster or a period of unusual food market volatility. It is an 'endemic crisis', a long-term crisis caused indirectly by deep structural economic factors that result in wide-spread income poverty and lack of access to basic resources.[201]

Those South Africans who fall below basic essential levels of enjoyment of the right to food are, in *Grootboom*'s terms, 'desperate', 'in crisis' and 'living in intolerable conditions'. Children

---

[191] *Grootboom* (n 63 above) para 44.
[192] n 191 above, para 64.
[193] n 191 above, para 43.
[194] As above.
[195] General Comment 12 (n 32 above) para 16.
[196] n 195 above, para 17.
[197] Phrase used by Constitutional Court Justice Tolakele Madala in an address to the International Seminar on the Right to Food, January 2002, Centre for Human Rights, University of Pretoria (unpublished).
[198] For a recent overview of the available food intake data and anthropometric indicators showing this crisis, see Watkinson (n 180 above) 1-6.
[199] De Klerk *et al* (n 2 above) 25.
[200] n 199 above, 28 (citing Labadarios (n 4 above)).
[201] In fact, not only are the same people who were in a food crisis ten years ago still in a food crisis – the situation has worsened; Watkinson (n 180 above) 5.

who waste away because of lack of food and do not grow to their full physical and mental potential because of under- and malnourishment, and people who go hungry every day of their lives, exhibit the same urgent, immediate need with respect to the right to food as the community in *Grootboom* exhibited with respect to the right to have access to adequate housing. The case law suggests that government is obliged, in whichever measures it institutes to fulfil the right to food, to take account of the needs of such people. The current national food security strategy does not.

Against the background of a general focus on longer term capacity building interventions that focus on facilitating access to food for reasonably self-sufficient people government's food policy scheme of course makes quite substantial provision for the direct transfer of food, or the means with which to acquire food. Examples are the Primary School Feeding Scheme, the PEM programme and the various social assistance grants. However, all of these efforts are in some way targeted to special needs only. The Primary School Feeding Scheme benefits only children at primary school. The PEM programme benefits only severely malnourished children treated at public health facilities. The Child Support Grant, when fully extended, will only benefit children under 14, the state Old Age Pension only men older than 65 and women older than 60 and the Disability Grant only disabled persons. The result is that if you are older than 14 years of age and younger than 60 (for women) or 65 (for men), physically and mentally able, not in foster care and not a war veteran, however bad your nutritional situation is, there is no regular state assistance to meet even the most basic of your food needs.[202]

The only state assistance that is available for such persons is Social Relief in Distress and the current emergency food parcel programme. Both these programmes provide only temporary relief: Social Relief in Distress is provided monthly for a maximum of three months at a time and food parcels are handed out for three months in any given year and the programme is only in place until 2005. As such, neither of these crisis responses addresses the endemic nature of South Africa's food security crisis. In addition, the coverage of both these programmes is very low.[203] In this respect, the constitutionality of the national strategy to address food insecurity seems to be highly questionable.

A second requirement posed by the duty to fulfil the right to food, as interpreted by the Constitutional Court, deals with implementation. Although in none of the cases so far has this

---

[202] According to the Taylor Commission (n 104 above) 59, more than half of poor South Africans, or 11 840 597 people (the majority of whom would presumably also be those in a food crisis) fall within this social assistance vacuum.

[203] The implementation of the Social Relief of Distress Grant is notoriously patchy. Recently, eg, in the matter of *Kutumela v Member of the Executive Committee for Social Services, Culture, Arts and Sport in the North West Province* Case 671/2003 23 October 2003 (B), legal action was taken against the North West provincial government for its failure to take adequate steps to implement Social Relief of Distress. The case was settled, resulting in a wide-ranging order requiring the provincial government to take adequately resourced steps to ensure that those entitled to the grant do in fact get it. See the discussion of this case below, text accompanying notice 209.

requirement played a role in the Constitutional Court's decision, the Court has emphasised that it is not enough for the state simply to conceive a reasonable national strategy - it must also implement it reasonably.[204] In addition, the Court has said that a programme must be reasonably resourced: In its planning, regard must be had to the human, financial and institutional resources that will be required for its implementation and once adopted, those resources must be made available for and used for its implementation.[205]

The South African government's national strategy to fulfil the right to food suffers seriously from problems of implementation. The number of beneficiaries reached through government's various food access facilitation programmes (a rough figure of 120 300 by 2001)[206] is only a very small percentage of the nutritionally needy in South Africa. The same can be said of government efforts to provide food or the means through which to acquire food. The uptake rate of the different social assistance grants, despite significant annual gains, remains relatively poor - the Child Support Grant, for instance, currently enjoys an uptake rate of only 2,5 million children, whilst there are an estimated 6,1 million children between the ages of six and 15 alone who live below the poverty line and therefore presumably require social assistance.[207]

Two court cases, one an ongoing Indian matter and another a recent South African case, illustrate how the 'reasonable implementation' element of the duty to fulfil the right to food can be used as a practical legal tool - how, once the state has adopted measures to address food insecurity, it must ensure that they are implemented and particularly that they are adequately resourced.

In the case of *People's Union for Civil Liberties v Union of India*,[208] the Indian Supreme Court was approached with an application that in part was directed at obtaining an order that existing national measures to address food insecurity and famine be adequately resourced and implemented at state level so that it can effectively reach intended beneficiaries. In broad terms the complaint alleged that, although massive food reserves existed in India, and although measures existed both on an ongoing basis to address the food insecurity of poor households and in specific instances to address famines, these measures were failing to reach intended beneficiaries due to administrative inefficiency or complacency and because state governments routinely diverted funds from national government, intended to implement these programmes, to other needs.

The case has resulted in a series of interim orders requiring, among other things, that the identification of beneficiaries qualifying for state assistance be standardised and completed; that the effectiveness of the current public distribution system for food be

---

[204] *Grootboom* (n 63 above) para 42.
[205] n 204 above, para 39. See also General Comment No 12 (n 32 above) para 21
[206] Brand (n 180 above) 102.
[207] As above.
[208] n 6 above. For a discussion of this case, see KB Mahabal 'Enforcing the right to food in India: The impact of social activism' (2004) 5(1) *ESR Review* 7.

enhanced and that corruption in the process be rooted out; and that funds allocated from national level to state governments for use in public distribution of food and famine measures in fact be used for those purposes. The case is ongoing.

The recent *Kutumela* case[209] in South Africa provides a similar example. In this case, the plaintiffs were a number of indigent people from the North West Province who had applied for the Social Relief of Distress Grant, but despite clearly qualifying in terms of the criteria set for the grant, did not receive it. The complaint alleged that although, in terms of the Social Assistance Act and its regulations, provincial governments were required to provide the grant to eligible individuals upon application, the North West Province had not dedicated for its implementation the necessary human, institutional and financial resources. As a result, the grant was available on paper but not in practice.

The case was settled between the parties, but the settlement agreement was made an order of court. This order is particularly wide-ranging. Apart from certain relief specific to the parties, it provides for various forms of general relief. Specifically, it requires the North West provincial government to acknowledge its legal responsibility to provide Social Relief of Distress effectively to those eligible for it; to devise a programme to ensure the effective implementation of Social Relief of Distress, which will enable it to process applications for Social Relief of Distress on the same day that they are received, will enable its officials appropriately to assess and evaluate such applications and will enable the eventual payment of the grant; and to put in place the necessary infrastructure for the administration and payment of the grant, *inter alia* by training officials in the welfare administration in the province. In addition, to deal with the absence of uniform standards and processes across the Republic with regard to Social Relief of Distress, the National Department of Social Development was ordered to develop uniform standards and procedures. Finally, provincial government was ordered effectively to make the availability of Social Relief of Distress known to the public.

Avoiding retrogression

A final manner in which the duty to promote and fulfil the right to food can operate as a concrete legal tool, is in preventing retrogressive measures in the state's progressive realisation of the right to food. The duty to fulfil the right to food requires the state to 'avoid retrogressive measures'.[210] Any deliberate retrogression in the fulfilment of the right to food will constitute a *prima facie* violation of the right to food and will require rigorous justification. This element of the duty to fulfil socio-economic rights has been

---

[209] n 203 above.
[210] Liebenberg (n 149 above) 33-34.

emphasised by the Constitutional Court[211] and is also recognised at international law.[212]

Although as a rule there has been steady progress in government's efforts to fulfil the right to food in South Africa, a possible example of such a retrogressive measure presents itself in the form of the National Departments of Agriculture (NDA) and Land Affairs' (DLA) efforts to effect redistribution of agricultural land. Before 2001, the NDA redistributed agricultural land to farm workers and emerging farmers from previously disadvantaged groups with the explicit purpose of 'improv[ing] their livelihoods and quality of life'.[213] Land was redistributed through a system of state subsidy: Qualifying households would receive a Settlement/Land Acquisition Grant (SLAG) of R16 000 with which to buy land. In addition, municipalities were enabled to make communal land available to the urban and rural poor for grazing and cultivation use through the Grant for the Acquisition of Municipal Commonage. A focus in the redistribution process at this stage was clearly enabling, through providing access to agricultural land, people to produce food for their own food needs and additional income.

Partly as a result of a range of problems in the redistribution process, but also because greater emphasis was later placed on promoting equitable access for emergent black farmers into commercial agriculture,[214] the programme was reconsidered in 2000, resulting in the development of a new programme – Land Redistribution for Agricultural Development (LRAD) – in 2001. In LRAD the focus had clearly shifted. LRAD is aimed not so much at improving livelihoods and quality of life as at enabling access to the commercial agriculture sector for 'those aspiring to become full-time, medium to large-scale commercial farmers'.[215] This focus is reflected in LRAD's structure. To qualify for a SLAG subsidy, a recipient household had to fall under a maximum monthly income of R1 500. To qualify for a grant under LRAD, a recipient has to make a minimum own contribution to the acquisition of land of R5 000. As Edward Lahiff has pointed out, this clearly excludes the poorest of the poor from the benefit of the programme and dramatically reduces the extent to which it can make a contribution to the fulfilment of the right to food.[216] As such, the change in direction in redistribution policy is a *prima facie* violation of the right to food.

---

[211] *Grootboom* (n 63 above) para 45.
[212] General Comment No 3 (n 49 above) para 9.
[213] Department of Land Affairs *White paper on land policy* (1997) 56.
[214] Lahiff (n 115 above) 4.
[215] As above.
[216] The shift in strategy had also another much more direct retrogressive effect. Lahiff (n 115 above) 4 points out that, when the Department of Land Affairs was reconsidering its land redistribution measures during 2000, a moratorium on new projects was introduced. The result was that capital expenditure for land redistribution dropped from R358 million in 1998/99 to R173 million in 1999/2000 and to R154 million in 2000/01. As a consequence, the Medium Term Expenditure Framework allocations for land redistribution dropped with 23% in the period 1999/2001.

4 Conclusion

Jean Drèze and Amartya Sen, writing about the role of law in creating and maintaining, but perhaps also protecting against hunger and malnutrition, say the following:[217]

> When millions of people die in a famine, it is hard to avoid the thought that something terribly criminal is going on. The law, which defines and protects our rights as citizens, must somehow be compromised by these dreadful events. Unfortunately, the gap between law and ethics can be a big one. The economic system that yields a famine may be foul and the political system that tolerates it perfectly revolting, but nevertheless there may be no violation of our lawfully recognised rights in the failure of large sections of the population to acquire enough food to survive.
>
> The point is not so much that there is no law against dying of hunger. That is, of course, true and obvious. It is more that the legally guaranteed rights of ownership, exchange and transaction delineate economic systems that can go hand in hand with some people failing to acquire enough food for survival.
>
> ...
>
> In seeking a remedy to this problem of terrible vulnerability, it is natural to turn towards a reform of the legal system, so that rights of social security can be made to stand as guarantees of minimal protection and survival.

The reform of the legal system that Drèze and Sen refer to has begun in South Africa – our Constitution recognises a justiciable right to food. Still, even here it is often difficult to translate the feeling that 'something terribly criminal is going on' into concrete legal terms that would enable one to take meaningful legal action. This is so because, as they point out, failures in food security – starvation, hunger and malnutrition – are all too easily attributable and are all too often attributed to 'natural' causes that cannot be controlled by the state or society. In this way legal responsibility for those failures is masked. This is also the case because, particularly in a society such as ours, violations of the right to food are often hidden behind violations of other rights and instances of the exercise of the right to food appear as instances of the exercise of other rights.

In this chapter I provide an overview, necessarily slight, of the extent to which the constitutional right to food has led to a 'reform of the legal system' in South Africa, and has created 'rights of social security that can be made to stand as guarantees of minimal protection and survival'. I have pointed to food-related legal duties and entitlements that have developed in the context of legislation regulating access to land and security of tenure and of case law regulating access to social assistance. I have also speculated about the possibilities of challenging aspects of government's measures to address food insecurity in South Africa through direct reliance on the right to food. There is already a lot there, but clearly much further development is required.

---

[217] Drèze & Sen (n 38 above) 20.

Six / The right to water

Anton Kok*
Malcolm Langford**

1 Introduction

Water, an essential part of the human diet and integral to survival, has been recognised as a right in the Constitution of the Republic of South Africa.[1] Since access to water in South Africa has largely been conditional upon land ownership and wealth (and race), the majority of South Africans have struggled to secure the right to water. Few international standard-setting documents give separate recognition to the right of (access to) water, although there are some significant and notable exceptions.[2]

The right to water is also an indispensable element of other rights, particularly the rights to adequate food or nutrition,[3] to health and a clean and/or healthy environment[4] and water conservation.

---

*   I thank Bronwen Morgan, Centre for Socio-Legal Studies, Oxford, for her helpful comments on an earlier draft of this chapter.
** I thank the Lionel Murphy Foundation for funding earlier research on the right to food and water.

[1] Constitution of the Republic of South Africa, 1996 (1996 Constitution).

[2] Eg, the Convention on the Elimination of Discrimination Against Women (1979) (CEDAW) and the Convention on the Rights of the Child (1979) (CRC). Other principal documents include the 1977 Mar del Plata Declaration and the recent General Comment on the Right to Water by the UN Committee on Economic, Social and Cultural Rights (General Comment No 15 *The right to water (arts 11 & 12 of the Covenant)* (29th session, 2002) [UN Doc E/C 12/2002/11]). See sec 2 of this chapter.

[3] Water forms a multidimensional relationship with the right to food: It is a liquid food, a component of semi-liquid foods and it is necessary for the preparation and production of food. See the discussion in M Vidar & MA Mekouar *Water, health and human rights. World Water Day* http://www.worldwaterday.org/2001/thematic/hmnrights.html (accessed 30 June 2004).

[4] See UNICEF *Strategies in water and environmental sanitation* (http://www.unicef.org/programme/wes/pubs/sp/spen.pdf) which states at B6: '[H]uman health and wellbeing depend on a healthy environment, including clean water, sanitary waste disposal and an adequate supply of food.' Also see para B35 of Item 14(a) (Social and human rights questions: Advancement of women) of the provisional agenda of the Economic and Social Council E/1999/66-A/54/123: 'Water is both a basic human need and an important productive resource. It *helps to improve domestic hygiene and health* and enhances child care as well as crop and/or animal care' (our emphasis). Compare I Woolard & C Barberton 'The extent of poverty and inequality' in C Barberton *et al* (eds) *Creating action space: The challenge of poverty and democracy in South Africa* (1998) 31: 'Access to water, electricity and sanitation impact directly on quality of life. Access to clean water and sanitation has the most obvious and direct consumption benefits in reducing mortality and poor health and increasing the productive capacity of the poor. For example, the poor (especially women) must commit large shares of their income or time to obtaining water and firewood. This time would be better used in child care or income-generating activities.'

Other human rights, such as housing and education, may also protect specific aspects of the right to water.[5] Therefore, legal documents that give expression to these rights indirectly protect the right of access to sufficient water.

While the right to water purportedly provides the normative and ethical framework for recent South African legislation in the water sector, only a small number of judgments have addressed the constitutional right to have access to sufficient water. This chapter therefore firstly provides an overview of the international and comparative right to water standards, which may guide constitutional interpretation, as well as an analysis of the constitutional right itself. A brief comment is also made on the important and related right to sanitation.

2 International, regional and comparable national law

2.1 International law

The right to water does not enjoy wide-ranging explicit recognition at international level. The right to water, or the right to have access to water is mentioned by name in only a few, albeit important, international documents. Where the right is explicitly mentioned, it is in most cases restricted to access to water for drinking and other domestic purposes.[6] Nevertheless, it is important to remember that other internationally recognised human rights, for example food or a healthy environment, may entitle an individual to water for other purposes.

Because of the close link between water, food (nutrition), health and hygiene, international documents that protect these rights are also relevant.

Article 11(1) of the International Covenant on Economic, Social and Cultural Rights (CESCR) proclaims:

> The States Parties to the present Covenant recognise the right of everyone to an *adequate standard of living* for himself and his family, including adequate food, clothing and housing ...

In November 2002, the body responsible for the oversight of the Covenant, the United Nations (UN) Committee on Economic, Social

---

[5] Eg the Committee on Economic, Social and Cultural Rights commented that the right to housing includes the right to sustainable household access to facilities for obtaining water, and the right to education implies the presence of drinking facilities within schools. See General Comment No 4 *The right to adequate housing (art 11(1) of the Covenant)* (6th session, 1991) [UN Doc E/1992/23] para 8(b) and General Comment No 13 *The right to education (art 13 of the Covenant)* (21st session, 1999) [UN Doc E/C 12/1999/10] para 6(a) of the Committee.

[6] Gleick states: 'Moreover, several of the explicit rights protected by international rights conventions and agreements, specifically those guaranteeing the rights to food, human health, and development, cannot be attained or guaranteed without also guaranteeing access to basic clean water.' PH Gleick 'The human right to water' (1999) 5 *Water Policy* 487-503 (available at http://www.pacinst.org 4 (accessed 30 June 2004)).

and Cultural Rights (Committee on ESCR or Committee), interpreted this article to include an independent right to water for personal and domestic uses. After noting that the listed rights in the article (ie, food, clothing and housing) are non-exhaustive due to the use of the word 'including', the Committee stated:

> The right to water clearly falls within the category of guarantees essential for securing an adequate standard of living, particularly since it is one of the most fundamental conditions for survival.[7]

In support of its interpretation, the Committee referred to other international documents and its own long history in monitoring steps taken by states to ensure all persons in their jurisdiction had access to water. The General Comment – an authoritative but not legally binding interpretation – also provides an extensive interpretation of the implications of the right to water for state parties in terms of the duties incumbent upon them to realise the right.

The Committee also appears to derive the stand-alone right to water from health provisions of CESCR. Article 12(1) provides for the right of everyone to the highest attainable standard of health,[8] and article 12(2)(c) obliges state parties to aim for the prevention, treatment and control of epidemic, endemic, occupational and other diseases. In an earlier General Comment, the Committee had only stated that the underlying determinants of the right to health include potable water.[9] Moreover, the Committee in General Comment No 15 elaborated on a number of other aspects of water under the right to health, beyond those of direct access to water for personal and domestic needs. Article 12(2)(b) provides that state parties to the treaty must aim to improve all aspects of environmental and industrial hygiene. The Committee notes that this duty 'encompasses taking steps on a non-discriminatory basis to prevent threats to health from unsafe and toxic water conditions'.[10]

Article 14(2)(h) of the Convention on the Elimination of Discrimination Against Women (1979) (CEDAW) obliges state parties to ensure to rural women the right to enjoy adequate living conditions, particularly in relation to housing, sanitation, electricity and water supply, transport and communications.

Articles 24(1) and (2)(c) of the Convention on the Rights of the Child (1989) (CRC) oblige state parties to implement children's rights to health by taking appropriate measures to combat disease and malnutrition within the framework of primary health care. It specifically requires that readily available technology should be applied, and that adequate nutritious food and clean drinking water

---

[7] See para 3 of General Comment No 15 (n 2 above).
[8] The title of the General Comment includes the right to health, along with the right to an adequate standard of living, and the Committee states: 'The right to water is also inextricably related to the right to the highest attainable standard of health' (see General Comment No 15 (n 2 above) para 3).
[9] See paras 11, 12, 15, 34, 36, 40, 43 & 51 of the Committee on ESCR's General Comment No 14 *The right to the highest attainable standard of health (art 12 of the Covenant)* (22nd session, 2000) [UN Doc E/C 12/2002/4].
[10] General Comment No 15 (n 2 above) para 8. See also General Comment No 14 (n 9 above) para 15.

should be provided, taking into consideration the dangers and risks of environmental pollution.

International humanitarian law provides extensive protection during armed conflict with respect to water. Sufficient drinking water is to be supplied to prisoners of war and other detainees.[11] They are to be provided with shower and bath facilities as well as water, soap and other facilities for their daily personal toilet and washing requirements.[12] The Additional Protocols to the Geneva Conventions of 1977 also prohibit the destruction of 'objects indispensable to the survival of the civilian population, such as food-stuffs, agricultural areas for the production of food-stuffs, crops, livestock, drinking water installations and supplies and irrigation works'.[13]

A number of international conferences on international environmental issues and/or water have taken place. The Preamble to the Mar del Plata Declaration of the 1977 United Nations Water Conference states:

> [A]ll peoples, whatever their stage of development and their social and economic conditions, have the right to have access to drinking water in quantities and a quality equal to their basic needs.

In 1991 the UN General Assembly adopted the United Nations Principles for Older Persons.[14] The Principles are divided into five sections that correlate closely with the rights recognised in CESCR. The section entitled 'Independence' *inter alia* states that 'older persons should have access to adequate food, water, shelter, clothing and health care'.[15] Access should be brought about 'through the provision of income, family and community support and self-help'.[16]

The 1992 Dublin Statement on Water and Sustainable Development[17] recognised 'the basic right of all human beings to have access to clean water and sanitation at an affordable price'.[18]

Action programmes adopted by states at such conferences, such as the 1992 Agenda 21 and the Programme of Action of the 1994

---

[11] See arts 21, 25 & 46 Geneva Convention III; arts 89 & 127 Geneva Convention IV; and art 5 Additional Protocol II.
[12] See art 29 Geneva Convention III and art 85 Geneva Convention III.
[13] See art 54 Additional Protocol I and art 14 Additional Protocol II.
[14] The principles were adopted as part of General Assembly Resolution 46/91 of 16 December 1991, entitled 'Implementation of the International Plan of Action on Ageing and Related Activities'.
[15] Also see para 5 of the Committee on ESCR's General Comment No 6 *The economic, social and cultural rights of older persons* (13th session, 1995).
[16] Also see para 32 of General Comment No 6 (n 15 above).
[17] The statement was issued by government-designated experts from 100 countries and representatives of 80 international, intergovernmental and non-governmental organisations at the International Conference on Water and the Environment.
[18] Principle No 3, The Dublin Statement on Water and Sustainable Development, International Conference on Water and the Environment (1992).

International Conference on Population and Development, have likewise included the right to water.[19]

As stated earlier, the right to water could be derived from other human rights. Article 25(1) of the Universal Declaration of Human Rights (Universal Declaration) states that 'everyone has the right to a standard of living *adequate* for the *health* and well-being of himself and his family, including *food* ...'.[20]

The World Health Organisation (WHO) and the UN Children's Fund (UNICEF) have developed concrete standards to give meaning to the right to have access to 'adequate' water. The WHO and UNICEF prescribe at least 20 litres safe drinking water per person per day that must be located within a reasonable distance from the household.[21]

2.2 Regional law

The European Social Charter, ratified by the majority of the members of the Council of Europe, does not explicitly refer to a right to nutrition or water. Article 11 states that contracting parties to the Charter should, either directly or in co-operation with public or private organisations, *inter alia* remove as far as possible the causes of ill-health and prevent as far as possible epidemic, endemic and other diseases. This obligation clearly links with a need to ensure proper sanitation and a clean water supply.[22] Similar logic can be applied to article 31 of the Revised European Charter, currently accepted by eight member states, where state parties are obliged to 'promote access to housing of an adequate standard' to ensure the 'effective exercise of the right to housing'. This obligation is enforced by means of a reporting and collective complaints mechanism.

---

[19] See para 18.47, Agenda 21, *Report of the United Nations Conference on Environment and Development* (1992) and Principle No 2, Programme of Action of the United Nations International Conference on Population and Development.

[20] Our emphasis.

[21] WHO/UNICEF *Global Water Supply and Sanitation Assessment 2000 Report* (2000) 77. The Pan-American Health Organisation has interpreted 'reasonable distance' as 'in an urban environment ... at a distance not farther than 200 meters from a house or to a public stand post. In rural areas, the definition is more flexible and may vary with the topography of the area.' See 'Mid-decade evaluation of water supply and sanitation in Latin America and the Caribbean', conference held by the Pan-American Health Organisation and WHO in Washington DC, 1997, available at http://www.cepis.org.pe/muwww/fulltext/aguabas/mideca/mideca.html (accessed 30 June 2004). The World Bank has defined 'reasonable access' as 'in the home or within 15 minutes' walking distance'. A proper definition should be adopted taking local conditions into account: in urban areas; a distance of not more than 200 metres from a house to a public stand post may be considered reasonable access; in rural areas, reasonable access implies that the housewife does not have to spend a disproportionate part of the day fetching water for the family's needs. See http://poverty.worldbank.org/files/ 4237_annex_s.pdf (accessed 30 June 2004).

[22] See the WHO definition of environmental sanitation: '(a) the promotion of hygiene and (b) the prevention of disease and other consequences of ill-health, relating to environmental factors'.
See WHO *What is environmental sanitation?* (2004) available at http://www.who.int/docstore/ water_sanitation_health Environmental_sanit/envindex.htm (accessed 7 September 2004).

In any case, the Committee of Ministers of member states of the Council of Europe have recognised that:[23]

> [E]veryone has the right to a sufficient quantity of water for his or her basic needs. International human rights instruments recognise the fundamental right of all human beings to be free from hunger and to an adequate standard of living for themselves and their families. It is quite clear that these two requirements include the right to a minimum quantity of water of satisfactory quality from the point of view of health and hygiene. Social measures should be put in place to prevent the supply of water to destitute persons from being cut off.

Article 11 of the American Convention on Human Rights in the Area of Economic, Social and Cultural Rights of 1988 states that 'everyone shall have the right to live in a healthy environment and to have access to basic public services'.

Article 16(2) of the African Charter on Human and Peoples' Rights (African Charter or Charter) proclaims that state parties to the Charter must take the necessary measures to protect the health of their people. Access to water is not explicitly mentioned, but the obligation to protect the health and environment of its citizens would imply that a state party must ensure that its subjects enjoy basic water and sanitation services. The African Commission on Human and Peoples' Rights (African Commission) has previously derived rights such as food and housing from the right to health and other Charter rights.[24] Further, in *Free Legal Assistance Group & Others v Zaire*,[25] the Commission held that the 'the failure of the government to provide basic services such as safe drinking water and electricity and the shortage of medicine as alleged in Communication 100/93 constitutes a violation of article 16 [right to health]'.[26]

Article 14(1) of the African Charter on the Rights and Welfare of the Child provides that every child has the right 'to enjoy the best attainable state of physical, mental and spiritual health'. Article 14(2)(c) is explicit in its protection of the right:

> States Parties to the present Charter shall undertake to pursue the full implementation of this right and in particular shall take measures to ensure the provision of adequate nutrition and *safe drinking water* (our emphasis).

Article 15 of the Protocol to the African Charter on Human and Peoples' Rights on the Rights of Women in Africa states that:

> States Parties shall ensure that women have the right to nutritious and adequate food. In this regard, they shall take appropriate measures to:
> (a) provide women with *access to clean drinking water*, sources of domestic fuel, land, and the means of producing nutritious food;
> (b) establish adequate systems of supply and storage to ensure food security (our emphasis).

---

[23] Para 5, Recommendation Rec (2001) 14 of the Committee of Ministers to Member States on the European Charter on Water Resources. See also para 19.
[24] *SERAC and CESR v Nigeria*, Communication 155/96, decision made at the 30th ordinary session, Banjul, The Gambia, from 13 to 27 October 2001.
[25] (2000) AHRLR 74 (ACHPR 1995).
[26] Para 47 of the English version. (The French version is more detailed and contains more paragraphs (64 paragraphs versus 48 paragraphs.)

2.3 Comparable national law

The right to water has also been recognised in national constitutions. Supplying potable water is an obligation or directive principle in many constitutions, while numerous constitutions protect the related rights to health and environmental health.[27] In a number of countries the right to water has been derived from other constitutional rights.[28]

The right to drinking water has been tested in national courts, including India and Brazil.[29] In *FK Hussain v Union of India*,[30] the High Court of Kerala found that the extraction and pumping of groundwater on the Lakshadweep islands must not threaten water needed for drinking. Finding that the 'right to sweet water, and the right to free air, are attributes of the right to life, for these are the basic elements which sustain life itself', the Court ordered that the authorities submit their plans for pumping groundwater to the Ministries for Environment and Science for approval. If the pumping was to proceed, an agency should be established to monitor the project to make sure it complied. In Brazil, the Special Jurisdiction Appellate Court of Paraná found that the disconnection of a water supply, even for non-payment, violated constitutional rights to essential services.[31]

3 South African law

3.1 Recognition of the right in section 27

3.1.1 'Sufficient'

Section 27(1)(b) of the 1996 Constitution states that 'everyone has the right to have access to ... sufficient ... water'. Section 27(2), according to the Constitutional Court, qualifies this right: 'The state must take reasonable legislative and other measures, within its available resources, to achieve the progressive realisation of each of these rights.'[32]

---

[27] The right to water is explicitly protected in the Constitutions of The Gambia, Uganda and Zambia. A number of draft constitutions (eg Kenya) also contain the right. For a comprehensive overview, see (forthcoming) M Langford *et al Legal resources for the right to water: National and international standards* COHRE 2004; http://www.cohre.org/water (accessed 30 June 2004).

[28] See eg Arrêt n°36/98 du 1 Avril 1998, Commune de Wemmel, Moniteur belge, 24/4/98, where a Belgian Court of Arbitration recognised the right of everyone to a minimum supply of drinking water utilising art 23 of the Constitution (the right to the protection of a healthy environment): See H Smets 'Le Droit à l'eau' *Rapport de l'Académie de l'eau* 2002'; http://www.oieau.fr/ academie/gege/DroitAlEau_01.PDF (accessed 30 June 2004).

[29] For jurisprudence from other countries, see Langford *et al* (n 27 above) 31.

[30] OP 2741/1988 (1990-02-26).

[31] Bill of Review 0208625-3.

[32] *Minister of Health & Others v Treatment Action Campaign & Others (No 2)* 2002 5 SA 721 (CC) (*TAC*).

The Constitution does not provide explicit guidance as to the meaning of 'sufficient' water, and in particular does not prescribe the quantity and quality of water each individual is entitled to access. The meaning of 'sufficient' is yet to be considered by a South African court. Little guidance can be derived from judicial rulings in this respect since South African courts, notably the apex court, have shied away from (or neglected) examining the precise content of economic and social rights.[33] Yet, the issue is critical for evaluating programmes and policy and the crafting of appropriate court orders (for example in disconnection cases).

The use of the word 'everyone' in section 27(1)(b) suggests that 'sufficient' should be interpreted in a universalist fashion – in other words, access to water for uses and purposes relevant to all individuals. This accords with one of the purported central requirements for asserting a human right, namely that the claimed right can be universally enjoyed.[34]

The Committee on ESCR has adopted such a universalist or individualist approach. It states that:

> The water supply for each person must be sufficient and continuous for personal and domestic uses.[35] These uses ordinarily include drinking, personal sanitation, washing of clothes, food preparation, personal and household hygiene. The quantity of water available for each person should correspond to World Health Organisation (WHO) guidelines.[36]

The final version of the General Comment (as opposed to an earlier draft made public) does not define precise quantities, although it references scholarship from the WHO and other experts which suggests that the above uses require approximately 50 litres per person per day or the minimum essential level (approximately 20 litres) where the state party is suffering from resource constraints.[37]

---

[33] See critique by D Bilchitz 'Towards a reasonable approach to the minimum core: Laying the foundations for future socio-economic rights jurisprudence' (2003) 19 *South African Journal on Human Rights* 1.

[34] See M Cranston *What are human rights?* (1973) as discussed in A Devereux 'Australia and the right to adequate housing' (1991) 20 *Federal Law Review* 232-233. According to Cranston, the other two tests for an alleged human right is that the right is of paramount importance and can be ensured in practical terms. Also see an analysis of different possible approaches in M Langford 'The right to water and the International Covenant on Economic, Social and Cultural Rights' available at http://www.cohre.org/water (accessed 30 June 2004).

[35] 'Continuous' means that the regularity of the water supply is sufficient for personal and domestic uses – fn 12 to para 12 of General Comment No 15 (n 2 above).

[36] See paras 12 & 37(a) of General Comment No 15 (n 2 above). The footnoted references (in fn 14 to the paragraph) are J Bartram & G Howard 'Domestic water quantity, service level and health: What should be the goal for water and health sectors' WHO 2002; and PH Gleick 'Basic water requirements for human activities: Meeting basic needs' (1996) 21 *Water International* 83-92.

[37] General Comment No 15 (n 2 above) para 12. Gleick (n 6 above) states that 'some basic amount of clean water is necessary to prevent death from dehydration, to reduce the risk of water-related diseases, and to provide for basic cooking and hygienic requirements' (p 5 of the internet version). Gleick has recommended 25 litres per person per day with an additional 15 litres for bathing and 10 litres for cooking. The Comprehensive Assessment of the Freshwater Resources of the World prepared for the Commission on Sustainable Development of the UN provides a qualitative assessment: '[A]ll people require access to adequate amounts of clean water, for such basic needs as drinking, sanitation and hygiene ...' (available at http://www.un.org/esa/sustdev/ freshwat.htm (accessed 30 June 2004)).

This interpretation generally accords with, but slightly extends, prior WHO and UNICEF guidelines. These organisations have recommended that individuals should be able to secure a certain quantity and quality of water for meeting basic domestic needs. WHO has recommended 20 litres per person per day.[38]

Neither the Committee nor WHO prescribe exact standards for quality, but only require that the water should be safe for each purpose.[39] This may mean that the required quality of water may vary depending on the purpose for which it is to be used. In the case of drinking water a very high standard is required. The Committee also states that water must 'be of an acceptable colour, odour and flavour'.[40] This latter requirement may not be necessary for health, but it is certainly consistent with the notion of human dignity contained in section 1 of the Constitution.

However, the above approach is subject to the criticism that it suffers from a Western or urban bias. In certain rural areas, particularly water for livestock, for example, may be more important than water for sanitation where water-based systems may not be utilised. This objection is not significant if we consider that the definitions above are flexible enough to allow for cultural variation. From a theoretical perspective, water for more situational needs, such as livelihoods, could be claimed under other rights such as the right of access to sufficient food. This latter approach was adopted in the General Comment on the right to water where it states: 'The Committee notes the importance of ensuring sustainable access to water resources for agriculture to realise the right to adequate food.'[41]

The Water Services Act of South Africa[42] recognises the right to access to a basic water supply,[43] which could include a range of fundamental needs. The Act defines 'basic water supply' as 'the prescribed minimum standard of water supply services necessary for the reliable supply of a sufficient quantity and quality of water to households, including informal households, to support life and personal hygiene'. The relevant regulation[44] provides that:

> The minimum standard for basic water supply services is ... a minimum quantity of potable water of 25 litres per person per day or six kilolitres per household per month at a minimum flow rate of not less than 10 litres per minute; within 200 metres of a household; and with an effectiveness

---

[38] WHO/UNICEF (n 21 above).
[39] The WHO does not propose a health-based guideline value for taste and odour, turbidity, aluminium, ammonia, chloride, hardness, hydrogen sulphide, iron, dissolved oxygen, pH, sodium, sulphate, total dissolved solids or zinc. Health-based guidelines values are proposed for manganese, toluene, xylenes, ethyl benzene, styrene, monochlorobenzene, dichlorobenzene, trichlorobenzene, synthetic detergents and chlorine. See WHO *Guidelines for drinking water quality* (2003) para 10.
[40] General Comment No 15 (n 2 above) para 12(b).
[41] See para 7 of General Comment No 15 (n 2 above).
[42] 108 of 1997.
[43] Sec 3(1).
[44] *Government Gazette* 22355, 8 June 2001, Government Notice R509, Regulation 3.

such that no consumer is without a supply for more than seven full days in any year.[45]

The National Water Act[46] covers water for other purposes, such as livelihoods, and a system of licences has been established for securing access to water.[47]

3.1.2 'Access'

The manner in which the right has been framed makes it clear that the state is not obliged to provide every inhabitant of South Africa with a *free* water supply. The state's duty towards those individuals who have the ability to pay for water services entails that the state must create the conditions and opportunity to ensure that those individuals have 'access' to sufficient water.[48]

'Access' to water entails economic and physical access.[49] With regard to *economic* access, the Committee on ESCR has commented that 'water, and water facilities and services, must be affordable for all' and state parties must adopt:[50]

> [T]he necessary measures that may include, *inter alia*: (a) use of a range of appropriate low-cost techniques and technologies; (b) appropriate pricing policies such as free or low-cost water; and (c) income supplements. Any payment for water services has to be based on the principle of equity, ensuring that these services, whether privately or publicly provided, are affordable for all, including socially disadvantaged groups. Equity demands that poorer households should not be disproportionately burdened with water expenses as compared to richer households.

---

[45] L Niklaas & R Stein 'Negotiating the rights of access to sufficient water through the courts' 2nd WARFSA/WaterNet Symposium: Integrated Water Resources Management - Theory, practice, cases, Cape Town, 30-31 October 2001 268 question whether this blanket allocation is sufficient to meet the demands of the Constitution. They point out that poor households often consist of more than eight people and that the allocation of free water should depend on the number of people per household. They concede this approach has practical difficulties and suggest that people who cannot afford and prove that they cannot afford to pay for water must be exempt from water cut-offs. The new Strategic Framework for Water Services (released 1 October 2003, available at http://www.dwaf.gov.za (accessed 30 June 2004)) uses 25 litres per person per day for communal water sources (standpipes) as a standard for basic service, and six kilolitres per formal household per month (yard or house connections).

[46] 36 of 1998.

[47] In general, see secs 27-31 and 39-55 of the Act. In issuing a licence, the responsible authority must *inter alia* take into account factors such as the need to redress the results of past racial and gender discrimination, efficient and beneficial use of water in the public interest and the resource quality objectives of the water resource. The responsible authority may attach conditions to a licence *inter alia* relating to the protection of the water resource, water management, return flow and discharge or disposal of waste.

[48] In *Government of the Republic of South Africa v Grootboom* 2001 1 SA 46 (CC) para 36, the Constitutional Court described this obligation as having to 'unlock the system' by *inter alia* providing a legislative framework.

[49] General Comment No 15 (n 2 above) para 12.

[50] As above, paras 12 & 27. *Grootboom* (n 48 above) paras 35-37 is less generous in that it does not explicitly recognise subsidised or free services for those who cannot afford it. The Court (merely) states that the state must 'create the conditions for access to adequate housing *at all economic levels of our society*', that 'issues of *development* and *social welfare* are raised in respect of those who cannot afford to provide themselves with [services]' and that 'the poor are particularly vulnerable and their needs require *special attention*' (our emphasis).

Regarding *physical* access, the Committee states that water must be within the 'safe and physical reach' of everyone,[51] meaning 'within, or in the immediate vicinity, of each household, educational institution and workplace'.[52] Special attention should also be paid to those persons who face particular difficulties in physically accessing water.[53]

The conditions for access can be created by, for example:

- building the necessary infrastructure and effectively maintaining facilities and equipment;
- subsidising existing water services or ensuring that water services are affordable to poverty-stricken South African inhabitants;[54]
- ensuring that drinking water is unpolluted;
- ensuring that water resources are not monopolised by powerful groups; and
- ensuring an equitable allocation of water.

---

[51] General Comment No 15 (n 2 above) para 8.

[52] n 51 above, para 12(c)(i). See also General Comment No 4 (n 5 above) para 8(b), General Comment No 13 (n 5 above) para 6(a) and General Comment No 14 (n 9 above) paras 8(a) & (b). 'Household' includes a permanent or semi-permanent dwelling, or a temporary halting site.

[53] The Committee comments in para 16 of General Comment No 15 (n 2 above) that attention should also be given to those who face difficulty in physically accessing adequate drinking water, including people with disabilities, older persons, children, women, persons in detention, victims of natural disasters, persons living in disaster-prone areas, and those living in arid and semi-arid areas, or on small islands. The statutory framework in South Africa also facilitates attention to a variety of access difficulties: Sec 9(2) of the Water Services Act allows national standards on water service provision to differentiate between different users as well as different geographic areas, the latter on both socio-economic and physical grounds; and sec 9(3) subjects such differentiation to, *inter alia*, an obligation to consider the need for equitable access to water services. Sec 10 allows analogous approaches in the case of setting tariffs.

[54] Compare para 3 of the Committee on ESCR's General Comment No 1 (*Reporting by state parties* (3rd session, 1989) [UN Doc E/1989/22]) that notes that special attention must be given to 'any worse-off regions' and to 'any specific groups or subgroups' which appear to be particularly vulnerable or disadvantaged. Para 9 of General Comment No 2 (*International technical assistance measures (art 22 of the Covenant)* (8th session, 1990) [UN Doc E/1990/23]) requires that the goal of protecting the right of the poor and vulnerable should become a basic objective of economic adjustment. Para 12 of General Comment No 3 (*The nature of state parties' obligations (art 2, para 1 of the Covenant)* (5th session, 1990) [UN Doc E/1991/23]) notes that even in times of severe resource constraints (eg as a result of an economic recession), the vulnerable members of society must be protected. This comment was reiterated in para 10 of General Comment No 5 (*Persons with disabilities* (11th session, 1994)) and para 17 of General Comment No 6 (n 15 above). Para 13 of General Comment No 12 (*The right to adequate food (art 11 of the Covenant)* (20th session, 1999) [UN Doc E/C 12/21999/5]) notes that socially vulnerable people such as landless persons and other particularly impoverished segments of the population may need attention through special programmes. Para 28 of the same Comment states that measures should be undertaken to ensure that the right to adequate food is especially fulfilled for vulnerable population groups and individuals. The same should apply in the context of access to water. Limburg Principle 14 notes that special attention should be given to measures to improve the standard of living of the poor and other disadvantaged groups. In a South African context, this would especially be black rural women. (Compare para 20 of the Maastricht Guidelines.) The Maastricht Guidelines have been published in (1998) 20 *Human Rights Quarterly* 691-701 and the Limburg Principles are available at http://www.law.uu.nl/ english.sim/specials/no-20/20-10.pdf (accessed 30 June 2004). Also see para 27 of General Comment No 15 (n 2 above).

3.1.3 Obligations of the state

At the very least, the state may not interfere with existing access to water. The state may not prevent people from using their own available resources to satisfy their individual water needs. The state must also ensure that individuals do not deny other individuals their right to have access to adequate water.

The Constitution permits the progressive realisation of the right, but does not permit inaction - expeditious and effective steps must be taken to realise the right.[55] The state should develop:

- clear goals;
- realistic strategies for the achievement of these goals;[56]
- time-related benchmarks to measure progress;[57]
- monitoring and review mechanisms by which progress in the realisation of the right may be measured.[58]

The right to have access to water will be violated if the state's water policy leads to a deliberate decline in the provision of water to South African inhabitants.[59]

The duty to realise progressively the right of access to sufficient water in section 27(2) is limited by the phrase 'within its available resources'. The Committee on ESCR has interpreted this qualification to include resources existing within a state as well as resources available from the international community through international assistance and co-operation.[60] The Constitutional Court has indicated that it will be slow in interfering with budgetary decisions and

---

[55] Sec 27(2) 1996 Constitution. The term 'progressive realisation' was borrowed from international documents. According to para 9 of General Comment No 3 of the Committee (n 54 above), this phrase should be interpreted to oblige a state to 'move as expeditiously and effectively as possible' towards the full realisation of the particular right. The Constitutional Court held that this interpretation is in harmony with the demands of the South African Constitution in *Grootboom* (n 48 above) para 45. Gleick (n 6 above) has noted the following: 'The specific number [of the required minimum standard of water] is less important than the principle of setting a goal and implementing actions to reach that goal' (p 9 of the internet version).

[56] Para 4 of General Comment No 1 of the Committee on ESCR (n 54 above) speaks of 'principled policy-making'.

[57] Compare para 6 of General Comment No 1 (n 54 above) of the Committee on ESCR. The Committee notes that global benchmarks are of limited use in this regard and that national or other more specific benchmarks can provide an 'extremely valuable' indication of progress. The Department of Water Affairs has a variety of time-related targets, including some that are sensitive to distribution across rural and urban areas.

[58] Compare sec V of General Comment No 15 (n 2 above).

[59] A deliberately retrogressive measure that reduces the extent to which the right to access to sufficient water is guaranteed will violate the right according to para 14(e) of the Maastricht Guidelines (n 54 above). Para 9 of General Comment No 3 (n 54 above) of the Committee on ESCR states that 'any deliberately retrogressive measures ... would require the most careful consideration and would need to be fully justified ...'

[60] Compare para 13 of General Comment No 3 (n 54 above) of the Committee on ESCR. In para 18 of General Comment No 15 (n 2 above), the Committee makes the observation: 'Realisation of the right should be feasible and practicable, since all States Parties exercise control over a broad range of resources, including water, technology, financial resources and international assistance, as with all other rights in the Covenant.'

allocation of resources by the state,[61] although recent cases suggest the Court is willing to be more intrusive.[62]

Section 7(2) of the 1996 Constitution provides that '[t]he state must respect, protect, promote and fulfil the rights in the Bill of Rights'.

The duty to *respect* entails that the state must refrain from interfering with the right of access to sufficient water.[63] This would mean that the state must refrain from arbitrarily depriving people of their right of access to sufficient water, or denying or obstructing the right of access to sufficient water, or unfairly discriminating when allocating water resources.

The obligation to respect has been tested in at least two High Court decisions dealing with the disconnection of existing water services. In *Manqele v Durban Transitional Metropolitan Council*[64] the applicant, an unemployed woman who occupied premises with seven children, sought a declaratory order that the discontinuation of water services to the premises was unlawful. She argued that the by-laws in terms of which the water service was disconnected were *ultra vires* the Water Services Act. The applicant relied on her right to a basic water supply as referred to in the Act and did not rely on the Constitution. The respondent argued that as no regulations have been promulgated to give meaning to the right to a 'basic' water supply, the right the applicant relied on had no content. The Court agreed with the respondent's argument. De Visser notes that the decision was 'regrettable', and had constitutional arguments been advanced, the Court would have been confronted with assessing the scope of the right to basic water supply under the Act.[65]

In *Residents of Bon Vista Mansions v Southern Metropolitan Local Council*,[66] the applicants sought interim relief on an urgent basis for the reconnection of their water supply. The applicants relied directly on the Constitution in this matter. The Court held that the obligation

---

[61] *Soobramoney v Minister of Health, Kwazulu-Natal* 1998 1 SA 765 (CC) para 29. The judgment contains few safeguards against government decisions: the decision must be 'rational' and must be taken 'in good faith'. If these requirements are met, courts will not interfere with a particular decision. The state will not act rationally if it allocates grossly inadequate or no resources to the realisation of a particular socio-economic right, but barring such extreme examples, the state has a free hand in the allocation of resources.

[62] See *Grootboom* (n 48 above) and *TAC* (n 32 above). In *Grootboom* para 68, the Court states that the national government must provide *adequate* budgetary support, which appears to be a more stringent test than rationality. *TAC* para 38 held that the state has to take *reasonable* measures that may have *budgetary* implications. This statement could be read to indicate that the state must provide *reasonable budgetary support*, which also sets a more stringent test than mere rationality.

[63] P de Vos 'Pious wishes or directly enforceable human rights?: Social and economic rights in South Africa's 1996 Constitution' (1997) 13 *South African Journal on Human Rights* 67 79-81. Compare para 6 of the Maastricht Guidelines and para 15 of General Comment No 12 of the Committee on ESCR (both n 54 above).

[64] 2001 JOL 8956 (D); 2002 6 SA 423 (D); referred to by Niklaas & Stein (n 45 above) 267.

[65] See J de Visser 'Disconnection of water supply' (2001) 3(1) *Local Government Law Bulletin*. 'Basic water supply' has since been given statutory content – see nn 41-44 above.

[66] 2002 6 BCLR 625 (W), referred to by Niklaas & Steyn (n 45 above) 266.

to respect existing access entails that the state may not take any measures that result in the denial of such access. By disconnecting the water supply, the council had *prima facie* breached the applicants' existing rights. The Court referred to the Water Services Act and noted that the Act provides that a water service provider may set conditions under which water services may be discontinued. The Act states further that the procedure according to which water services may be discontinued must be fair and equitable and must provide for reasonable notice of the intention to discontinue the service and must provide for an opportunity to make representations. Where a person proves to the satisfaction of the relevant water services provider that he or she is unable to pay for basic services, the service may not be discontinued. The Court held that a *prima facie* violation of a local council's constitutional duty occurs if a local authority disconnects an existing water service, and that such disconnection therefore requires constitutional justification. The *Bon Vista* decision appears more consistent with international jurisprudence.[67]

Interference with water supplies in some situations may require a court order in advance. If the disconnection, denial or limitation of access to water services or supplies amounts to a constructive eviction - a resident is forced to leave his or her home as a result - then it is arguable that this cannot occur without a court order. Under section 26(3) of the Constitution, an eviction cannot proceed without judicial sanction. The Land Claims Court has suggested that restricting the use of land may amount to an eviction.[68]

We submit that the duty to *protect* the rights in the Bill of Rights also entails that the state must prevent violations of the right of access to sufficient water by third parties.[69] For instance, if a farmer unreasonably and arbitrarily cuts off the access to water of lawful occupiers of his property, the state must act to restore access to sufficient water to the occupiers.

---

[67] The Committee on ESCR states in para 56 of General Comment No 15 (n 2 above): 'Before any action that interferes with an individual's right to water is carried out by the State party, or by any other third party, the relevant authorities must ensure that such actions are performed in a manner warranted by law, compatible with the Covenant, and that comprises: (a) opportunity for genuine consultation with those affected; (b) timely and full disclosure of information on the proposed measures; (c) reasonable notice of proposed actions; (d) legal recourse and remedies for those affected; and (e) legal assistance for obtaining legal remedies (see also General Comments No 4 (n 5 above) and No 7 (*The right to adequate housing (art 11.1 of the Covenant): Forced evictions* (16th session, 1997)). Where such action is based on a person's failure to pay for water, their capacity to pay must be taken into account. Under no circumstances shall an individual be deprived of the minimum essential level of water.'

[68] See *Van der Walt v Lang* 1999 1 SA 189 (LCC) and *Dhladhla v Erasmus* 1999 1 SA 1065 (LCC) as cited and referred to in S Liebenberg & K Pillay (eds) *Socio-economic rights in South Africa: A resource book* (2000).

[69] Compare para 6 of the Maastricht Guidelines (n 54 above).

Likewise, water services operated by private operators must be sufficiently regulated by the government to ensure the right to water is not interfered with.[70] The previous discussion of rights arising in the event of disconnection by government actors applies equally to such actions by private actors.

In the context of the right of access to sufficient water, the state's duty to *promote* the rights in the Bill of Rights would *inter alia* mean the promotion of educational and informational programmes designed to enhance awareness and understanding of the right of access to sufficient water.[71]

The government's duty to *promote* a right also provides a shield against claims arising from other legal provisions or constitutional rights.[72] In *Minister of Public Works and others v Kyalami Ridge Environmental Association & Others*,[73] for example, the right to adequate housing assisted the national government in defending its right to create temporary housing for flood victims, despite assertions by neighbouring residents that property values would fall and their peaceful environment would be disturbed. In the case of water, such protection is buttressed by section 25(8) of the Constitution:

> No provision of this section may impede the state from taking legislative and other measures to achieve land, *water and related reform*, in order to redress the results of past racial discrimination ... (our emphasis).

In order to *fulfil* the rights in the Bill of Rights, the state must take appropriate legislative, administrative, budgetary, judicial and other measures towards the full realisation of the right.[74] It also means that the state carries a duty to facilitate and provide access to sufficient water. The state must proactively engage in activities intended to strengthen people's access to and utilisation of resources and means to ensure their livelihood. When an individual or a group is unable to procure sufficient water, the state has a duty to fulfil the right directly.[75]

---

[70] Compare para 24 of General Comment No 15 (n 2 above): 'Where water services (such as piped water networks, water tankers, access to rivers and wells) are operated or controlled by third parties, States Parties must prevent them from compromising equal, affordable, and physical access to sufficient, safe and acceptable water. To prevent such abuses, an effective regulatory system must be established, in conformity with the Covenant and this General Comment, which includes independent monitoring, genuine public participation and imposition of penalties for non-compliance.'

[71] Compare para 3(a) of General Comment No 10 of the Committee on ESCR (*The role of national human rights institutions in the protection of economic, social and cultural rights* (19th session, 1998) [UN Doc E/C 12/1998/25]). Also see Madala J's comment in *Soobramoney* (n 61 above) para 49: 'Perhaps a solution may be to embark upon a massive education campaign to inform the citizens generally ...'

[72] See G Budlender 'The justiciability of the right to housing: The South African experience' available at http://www.lrc.org.za/4Pub/Papers/delhi%20paper.pdf (accessed 30 June 2004).

[73] 2001 3 SA 1151 (CC).

[74] Compare para 6 of the Maastricht Guidelines (n 54 above).

[75] See para 25 of General Comment No 15 (n 2 above). This would of course be subject to the slightly more nuanced analysis of maximum available resources in paras 17-19 of General Comment No 15 and more particularly as presented in General Comment No 3 of the Committee.

The Constitutional Court has held that sections 26(2) and 27(2) qualify the section 7 obligations in the context of socio-economic rights.[76] The obligation to respect, protect, promote and fulfil the right of access to sufficient water must therefore be read subject to the internal qualifiers discussed above. The obligation to 'respect' is, however, primarily a negative obligation and it is difficult to imagine what role the internal limitations in sections 26(2) and 27(2) will play in qualifying this obligation.

Further, the Constitutional Court has interpreted section 27(2) to qualify the section 27(1) right in that the two subsections must be read together in defining the scope of the positive rights that everyone has.[77] In *Minister of Health v Treatment Action Campaign (TAC)*, the Court rejected an argument that section 27(1) confers an individual right to a minimum core entitlement to which every person in need is entitled.[78]

3.2 Interrelationship with other rights

As stated earlier, an obvious link exists between adequate food or nutrition, a clean and healthy environment, water conservation and water. The sections in the 1996 Constitution dealing with these rights, therefore, also have direct relevance when discussing access to water.

Section 28(1)(c) states that every child has the right to 'basic nutrition', which arguably includes sufficient water for drinking, food preparation and even food production. This right differs from the socio-economic rights listed in sections 26 and 27 in that the state immediately has to respect, protect, promote and fulfil it.[79] The Constitutional Court held in *Grootboom* that, in the context of access to housing, sections 28(1)(b) and 28(1)(c) must be read together and that the obligations set out in section 28(1)(c) primarily rest on the parents or family of the child and only alternatively on the state, for example in the case where children are removed from their families.[80] In *TAC*,[81] in the context of providing health care, the Court made it clear that the state would carry a primary obligation to ensure that children born to mothers who are indigent and unable to gain

---

[76] *TAC* (n 32 above) para 39.
[77] *Grootboom* (n 48 above) para 34; *TAC* (n 32 above) para 39.
[78] The first and second *amici's* argument to this effect was rejected on the flimsiest of grounds – in effect the Court said that the *amici's* interpretation could not be accepted as it did not accord with the Constitutional Court's interpretation in *Grootboom*, but the *amici* expressly argued that the Court's interpretation in *Grootboom* was wrong. Also see Bilchitz (n 33 above) 6.
[79] Sec 28 does not contain a qualifier similar to secs 26(2) & 27(2).
[80] *Grootboom* (n 48 above) paras 76-79.
[81] Para 79.

access to private treatment which is beyond their means, enjoy basic health care services. Applying these guidelines by analogy to the right of access to sufficient water would mean that parents carry the primary obligation to provide access to sufficient water to children in their care, but where they are financially unable to do so, the state would have to step into the breach.

Section 35(2)(e) proclaims that everyone who is detained, including every sentenced prisoner, has the right to 'conditions of detention that are consistent with human dignity, including at least exercise and the provision, *at state expense*, of *adequate* accommodation, *nutrition*, reading material and medical treatment' (our emphasis).[82]

Section 24 states that everyone has the right to an environment that is not harmful to their health or well-being and to have the environment protected through reasonable legislative and other measures that prevent pollution and ecological degradation; promote conservation and secure ecologically sustainable development and use of natural resources while promoting justifiable economic and social development. Clean and clear water links closely with an environment that is not harmful[83] and the need to prevent pollution.[84]

Other relevant rights include the rights to equality,[85] dignity,[86] life[87] and administrative justice.[88]

3.3 General guidelines

On the basis of the above, the following general guidelines may be laid down:

- Every South African inhabitant should have access to water. The state should prioritise improvement of access to water in those areas where the greatest need exists.
- Every inhabitant should have access to enough water to meet basic needs.
- Such water should be of adequate quality.
- Water sources should be as close as possible to households.
- Water should be available on a daily basis.

---

[82] Sec 35(2)(e) is the only section in the Constitution dealing with socio-economic rights that explicitly obliges the state to provide the rights listed in this subsection at its own cost.
[83] Sec 24(a).
[84] Sec 24(b)(i).
[85] Sec 9.
[86] Sec 10.
[87] Sec 11. However, according to the Constitutional Court's judgment in *Soobramoney* (n 61 above), sec 11 should be read subject to the specific formulation of the socio-economic rights in secs 26 & 27. According to the Constitutional Court's approach, sec 11 has almost nothing to add to the interpretation of the socio-economic rights.
[88] Sec 33. Niklaas & Stein (n 45 above) argue that local authorities must provide an opportunity to defaulting consumers to make representations before their water supply is discontinued.

- Water provision services must be easily maintainable, effective, reliable and must be flexible enough to upgrade easily.
- Water should be as affordable as possible, especially to the disadvantaged and vulnerable members of South African society.
- Adequate policy measures must be developed and monitored to prevent pollution of water resources and to encourage water conservation.
- Water use must be managed and controlled adequately.
- The state must monitor the right to water and provide, as far as possible, effective remedies for violations.

4   Basic sanitation

The right to basic sanitation is not mentioned explicitly in the South African Bill of Rights. The right to an amount of water for sanitation purposes is included in the right to water as discussed above. Moreover, a right to sanitation could be derived from section 24(a) (the right to a clean environment) read with the right of access to adequate water.[89] Failure to control sanitary excreta disposal is one of the major causes of environmental pollution and water diseases. The WHO guidelines prescribe 'sanitary excreta disposal' to be the isolation and control of faeces from both adults and children so that they do not come into contact with water sources, food or people. The Committee on ESCR has noted the importance of sanitation for the right to water and considers it an element of the rights of housing and health.[90]

5   Conclusion

The measure of neglect of the right to water in international and national jurisprudence stands in contrast to the severity of the plight of the millions without proper access to water. However, lately this gross deprivation has resulted in the increased conceptualisation of water access issues in human rights terms. This in turn has led to new international and national legal standards about access to water being developed. On this basis a right to water jurisprudence is fast developing, both in international and regional law, and within domestic jurisdictions such as South Africa.

---

[89] Sec 3 of the Water Services Act 108 of 1997 recognises every South African inhabitant's right of access to basic water supply and basic sanitation. 'Basic sanitation' is defined as 'the prescribed minimum standard of services necessary for the safe, hygienic and adequate collection, removal, disposal or purification of human excreta, domestic waste water and sewage from households, including informal households'. This definition recognises the state's obligation to the poorest and most vulnerable members of South African society.

[90] See para 29 of General Comment No 15 (n 2 above): 'Ensuring that everyone has access to adequate sanitation is not only fundamental for human dignity and privacy, but is one of the principal mechanisms for protecting the quality of drinking water supplies and resources. In accordance with the rights to adequate housing and health ... States Parties have an obligation to progressively extend safe sanitation services, particularly to rural and deprived urban areas, taking into account the needs of women and children.'

Seven / The right to social security and assistance

Linda Jansen van Rensburg
Lucie Lamarche

1 Introduction

Section 27(1)(c) of the South African Constitution[1] provides that everyone has the right to have access to social security, including, if they are unable to support themselves and their dependants, appropriate social assistance. Section 27(2) in turn requires the state to take reasonable legislative and other measures, within its available resources, to achieve the progressive realisation of this right. Section 28(1)(c) further grants every child the right to basic social services.

In this chapter we describe and analyse these rights. In section 2, we describe the two foundational terms 'social security' and 'social assistance'. In sections 3 and 4 we provide an overview of the extent to and manner in which the right to social security and assistance is entrenched in international and regional human rights instruments. Finally, against that background, in section 5 we turn to the provisions in the South African Constitution, analysing and describing them in the light of recent jurisprudence and current policy and practice regarding social security and assistance in South Africa.

2 Social security, social assistance and social protection

Although the concepts of social security and social assistance are referred to in the Constitution, no clear definition of these concepts has been established in South Africa and the terms are sometimes used interchangeably with each other and with other terms such as 'social protection', 'social welfare' and 'social insurance'.[2]

---

[1] Constitution of the Republic of South Africa of 1996 (the Constitution).
[2] White Paper for Social Welfare, General Notice 1108 in *Government Gazette* 18166 of 8 August 1997 (White Paper for Social Welfare) para 45.

For purposes of this chapter, social security and social assistance can be described as two different means of promoting the ultimate goal of social protection.[3] The Commission of Inquiry into a Comprehensive System of Social Security for South Africa[4] defines social protection as follows:[5]

> Comprehensive social protection is broader than the traditional concept of social security, and incorporates [all] *developmental strategies and programmes designed to ensure, collectively, at least a minimum living standard for all citizens*. It embraces the traditional measures of social insurance, social assistance and social services, but it goes beyond that to focus on causality through an integrated policy approach including many of the developmental initiatives undertaken by the State (our emphasis added).

Social security as one possible form of social protection refers to contributory schemes of social protection, in terms of which benefits for a variety of possible contingencies are 'earned' through the payment of contributions.[6] Social security schemes can be privately run schemes in terms of which, for instance, private employers and employees pay regular contributions to pension or provident funds, or private persons buy social insurance covering other unexpected events.[7] Social security schemes can also be public, in the sense that employers and employees and sometimes also the state itself contribute to a state-run scheme for social protection.[8]

A current South African example of a public social security scheme is the Unemployment Insurance Fund,[9] which pays out benefits to contributors and their dependants in the event of unemployment, illness, maternity and adoption. Employers and employees contribute on an equal basis to the Fund with practically no state contribution. Compensation for employment injuries and diseases is paid to employees and their dependants out of the Compensation Fund, to which employers contribute on the basis of industry-based risk assessments.[10]

---

[3] L Lamarche 'Social security as a human right' in D Brand & S Russel (eds) *Exploring the core content of socio-economic rights: South African and international perspectives* (2002) 109 120.

[4] The Taylor Commission (so called after its chairperson, Prof Vivienne Taylor). This Commission was appointed on the basis of a decision by the South African Cabinet and charged with developing recommendations on the establishment of a comprehensive social security system for South Africa.

[5] Department of Social Development *Transforming the present - Protecting the future: Report of the Commission of Inquiry into a Comprehensive System of Social Security for South Africa* (2002) 41.

[6] M Scheinin 'The right to social security' in A Eide et al *Economic, social and cultural rights: A textbook* (1995) 159.

[7] Private social security schemes are sometimes called *social insurance* schemes, to distinguish them from public social security schemes.

[8] White Paper for Social Welfare (n 2 above), ch 7 para 2.

[9] Established in terms of the Unemployment Insurance Act 30 of 1966.

[10] Established in terms of the Compensation for Occupational Injuries and Diseases Act 130 of 1993.

Social assistance schemes as forms of social protection, on the other hand, are schemes in terms of which individuals or groups receive 'need-based assistance from public funds' without themselves ever having contributed directly to the scheme.[11] The current social assistance programme in South Africa covers the following contingencies: the state Old Age Pension; the Disability Grant; the Child Support Grant, Foster Child Grant and the Care Dependency Grant.[12] In terms of the number of beneficiaries, the state Old Age Grant, Child Support Grant and the Disability Grant are the largest social assistance programmes within the government funded social security system. These are all special needs-based social assistance grants – they are intended to benefit only especially vulnerable groups in society. An example of a social assistance scheme that is universally needs-based would be the Basic Income Grant that has been proposed by the Taylor Commission.[13]

Traditionally, the concept of social protection, whether in the form of social security or social assistance, is seen to refer to a specific list of benefits provided in the case of a specific variety of contingencies. The ILO Convention No (102) on Social Security (Minimum Standards) of 1952,[14] for instance, lists the classic branches of social protection as benefits paid in the event of sickness, maternity, employment injury, unemployment, invalidity, old age and death; the provision of medical care; and the provision of subsidies for families with children.[15] The Glossary to the White Paper on Social Welfare[16] lists old age, disability, child and family care, poverty relief, unemployment, ill-health, maternity, child-rearing, widowhood, disability and old age as contingencies for purposes of social protection.

---

[11] Scheinin (n 6 above) 159. Social assistance schemes are sometimes also referred to as social welfare schemes.

[12] See secs 2-4 of the Social Assistance Act 59 of 1992 as amended by the Welfare Laws Amendment Act 106 of 1997 and clauses 4-12 of the new Social Assistance Bill B57D-2003 as amended by the Select Committee on Social Services (first introduced in the National Assembly as a sec 76 Bill; explanatory summary of Bill published in *Government Gazette* 25340 of 8 August 2003.) The new Social Assistance Bill is aimed at consolidating legal requirements and provisions for social assistance in the Republic, and at creating uniform norms and standards, which can apply countrywide. The Bill makes provision for grants for the following categories of people: Child Support Grant, Care Dependency Grant, Foster Child Grant, Disability Grant, Older Persons' Grant, War Veteran's Grant and a Grant-in-Aid. The current system provides for exactly the same grants. The Department of Social Development, in briefing the Portfolio Committee on Social Development, indicated that it would not be making any policy shifts in the new Social Assistance Bill and that the Bill would be tabled to remove the assignment to the provinces as indicated in the memorandum.

[13] Department of Social Development (n 5 above) 42.

[14] ILO Convention (102).

[15] See International Labour Organisation *Introduction to social security* (1989) 3.

[16] n 2 above.

The concept of social protection that the Taylor Commission proposes is potentially much wider than an understanding of social protection limited to the usual list of contingencies. To limit social protection to only these traditional areas may leave insufficient room for development to provide new answers to new social problems that may arise.[17] Consistent with the idea in the White Paper for Social Welfare of a broader integrated, comprehensive and co-ordinated approach towards social protection, the Taylor Commission has developed 'minimum' requirements for a comprehensive social protection package. It remarks that comprehensive social protection requires a variety of mechanisms, embracing a package of social protection interventions and measures. These should include:

- measures to address 'income poverty' (provision of minimum income);
- measures to address 'capability poverty' (provision of certain basic services);
- measures to address 'asset poverty' (provision of income-generating assets); and
- measures to address 'special needs' (for example disability or child support).[18]

Key components of such a comprehensive social protection package are, according to the Taylor Commission, the (eventual) introduction of a Basic Income Grant; the gradual extension of the Child Support Grant, eventually to cover children under the age of 18; maintenance of the state Old Age Grant; and reform of the current Disability Grant, Foster Child Grant and Child Dependence Grant. Other elements of the proposed package, which perhaps are not traditionally seen as measures of social protection, include free health care (the Taylor Commission advocates the eventual introduction of a National Health Insurance system), free primary and secondary education, free water and sanitation (up to a certain basic level), free electricity (up to a certain basic level), access to affordable and adequate housing, access to jobs and skills training.[19]

For purposes of this chapter, our concept of social protection, and consequently our understanding of the form that both social security and social assistance programmes can take, accords with the Taylor Commission's broad approach. However, because it is the term that is most often used in the international arena, we will use the term 'social security' throughout as a collective term, referring to social protection in the broad sense.

---

[17] D Pieters *Introduction into the basic principles of social security* (1993) 1.
[18] Department of Social Development (n 5 above) 41-42.
[19] As above, 42-43. See also MP Olivier & L Jansen van Rensburg 'Addressing the alleviation of poverty through social welfare measures' (2002) Paper presented at the XVth World Congress of Sociology in Brisbane, Australia, 7-13 July 2002.

3 International law

Section 39(1)(b) of the Constitution compels a court, tribunal or forum, when interpreting the Bill of Rights,[20] to consider international law. In *S v Makwanyane and Another*,[21] the Constitutional Court held that, in the context of section 39(1)(b), the phrase 'public international law' refers both to international law that is binding on South Africa and to international law that South Africa is not bound to. In addition, the Court emphasised that both 'hard' and 'soft' international law must be considered by courts in their interpretation of the Bill of Rights.[22] International law of whatever kind is particularly important in the interpretation of socio-economic rights, such as the right to have access to social security and assistance, as there is a dearth of comparable jurisprudence from foreign domestic jurisdictions for our courts to draw on.[23] What follows is an overview of the body of international law that is most relevant to the interpretation of the right to social security and assistance in the South African Constitution.

3.1 United Nations binding instruments

3.1.1 The International Covenant on Economic, Social and Cultural Rights

On 3 October 1994 South Africa signed the United Nations' (UN) International Covenant on Economic, Social and Cultural Rights (CESCR).[24] However, South Africa is yet to ratify this treaty.

CESCR, in its article 9, entrenches a right to social security, recognising both the public and private components of the right. It enjoins state parties to 'recognise the right of everyone to social security, including social insurance'.[25] In addition to the provisions of article 9, article 11(1) requires that states guarantee an adequate standard of living to everyone.[26] The right to an adequate standard of living can be interpreted to mean that a state must at the very least

---

[20] ch 2 of the Constitution.
[21] 1995 3 SA 391 (CC).
[22] As above, para 35. 'Soft' international law consists of imprecise standards, generated by declarations adopted by diplomatic conferences or resolutions of international organisations, that are intended to serve as guidelines to states in their conduct, but which lack the status of 'law'. See J Dugard *International law. A South African perspective* (2000) 36.
[23] In *Government of the Republic of South Africa v Grootboom* 2000 11 BCLR 1169 (CC) para 26, the Court makes the following observation: 'The relevant international law can be a guide to interpretation but the weight to be attached to any particular principle or rule of international law will vary. However, where the relevant principle of international law binds South Africa, it may be directly applicable.'
[24] GA Res 2200A (XXI), UN GAOR Supp (No 16) 49, Doc A/6316 (1966) UNTS, entered into force 3 January 1976.
[25] Art 9: 'The States Parties to the present Covenant recognise the right of everyone to social security, including social insurance.'
[26] Art 11(1): 'The States Parties to the present Covenant recognise the right of everyone to an adequate standard of living for himself and his family.'

provide social assistance and other needs-based forms of social benefits in cash or in kind to anyone without adequate resources.[27] Articles 10(1) and (2) can also be read to refer to social security and assistance in specific contexts. These sections recognise the family as the natural and fundamental group unit of society, worthy of the widest possible protection and assistance.[28] Pregnant mothers are to be afforded special protection and should be provided with paid maternity leave or leave with adequate social security benefits.[29]

The right to social security in article 9, and the other social protection-related rights in articles 10 and 11, like the other rights found in CESCR, are qualified by article 2(1), which determines that they need be implemented only *progressively* and *to the maximum of available resources*.[30] The enforcement of the rights is entrusted to a reporting system, in terms of which state parties to CESCR have to report on a regular basis to the UN Committee on Economic, Social and Cultural Rights (Committee on ESCR).

The provisions dealing with social security in the Covenant are general. As a result, the Committee on ESCR has, in its interpretation of the Covenant, relied on the well-developed standard-setting and implementation procedure under the auspices of the International Labour Organisation (ILO).[31]

---

[27] Lamarche (n 3 above) 126-127.
[28] Art 10(1) states that '[t]he widest possible protection and assistance should be accorded to the family, which is the natural and fundamental group unit of society, particularly for its establishment and while it is responsible for the care and education of dependent children'.
[29] Art 10(2): 'Special protection should be accorded to mothers during a reasonable period before and after childbirth. During such period working mothers should be accorded paid leave or leave with adequate social security benefits.'
[30] Art 2(1): 'Each State Party to the present Covenant undertakes to take steps, individually and through international assistance and co-operation, especially economic and technical, to the maximum of its available resources, with a view to achieving progressively the full realisation of the rights recognised in the present Covenant by all appropriate means, including particularly the adoption of legislative measures.'
[31] Scheinin (n 6 above) 162. See also E/CN.4/2001/62/add 2: *Report of the High Commissioner for Human Rights*, Addendum, *Report on the workshop on the justiciability of economic, social and cultural rights, with particular reference to the draft Optional Protocol to the International Covenant on Economic, Social and Cultural Rights*.

The approach of the Committee seems to be to complement the standard setting of the ILO through its interpretation of CESCR. This is evidenced by the guidelines for state reporting under the Covenant, in which the Committee requires states to provide information on social security based on all nine of the categories of benefits used in the ILO's Convention (102): medical care; sickness benefits; unemployment benefits; old age benefits; employment injury benefits; family benefits, maternity benefits; invalidity benefits; and survivors' benefits.[32] In the absence of a General Comment on the right to social security and assistance, the reliance of the Committee on ILO Convention (102) has been particularly important in the Committee's attempts to describe a minimum content of the right.[33]

Convention (102) does not provide a single definition of social security. This definition has to be construed from the various parts of the Convention, each addressing one of the nine social risks that it covers. To ratify Convention (102),[34] an ILO member state is obliged to comply, at the moment of ratification, with at least three of the following parts of the Convention: medical care, sickness benefits, unemployment benefits, old age benefits, worker's compensation benefits, family, invalidity, maternity and survival benefits. From amongst these parts, at least one part concerning either unemployment, old age, worker's compensation, invalidity or survival benefits must be accepted. Each part of the Convention provides for specific standards aimed at guaranteeing the benefit of social protection to certain persons described as protected classes of persons. Each part also provides for certain basic levels of benefits. In all cases, a ratifying member must comply with some general parts of the Convention, including Part XI, which provides for periodic

[32] Compilation of Guidelines on the Form and Content of Reports to be Submitted by State Parties to the International Human Rights Treaties E/C12/1991/1; Revised General Guidelines Regarding the Form and Contents of Reports to be Submitted by State Parties under arts 16 & 17 of the International Covenant on Economic, Social and Cultural Rights, paras 27 & 28 (CESCR Reporting Guidelines). The CESCR Reporting Guidelines were adopted by the Committee on ESCR at its 5th session in 1990. The consolidated guidelines for the initial part of the reports of state parties to be submitted under the various international human rights instruments, including the Covenant, are contained in document HRI/CORE/1 (see ch I of the present document), sent to state parties by *note verbale* G/SO 221 (1) of 26 April 1991.
[33] For a detailed analysis, see L Lamarche 'The right to social security as a human right guaranteed by the Covenant on Economic, Social and Cultural Rights - The time has come to think about it' in A Chapman & S Russell (eds) *Core obligations: Building a framework for economic, social and cultural rights* (2002) 82-108. Para 31 of the CESCR Reporting Guidelines provides as follows: 'Please indicate whether in your country there are any groups which do not enjoy the right to social security at all or which do so to a significantly lesser degree than the majority of the population. In particular, what is the situation of women in that respect? Please give particulars of such non-enjoyment of social security.
(a) Please indicate what measures are regarded as necessary by your government in order to realise the right to social security for the groups mentioned above.
(b) Please explain the policy measures your government has taken, to the maximum of its available resources, to implement the right to social security for these groups. Give a calendar and time-related benchmarks for measuring your achievements in this regard.
(c) Please describe the effect of these measures on the situation of the vulnerable and disadvantaged groups in point, and report the successes, problems and shortcomings of such measures.'
[34] Up to now, 40 states have ratified Convention (102).

payments of social security. Since the adoption of Convention (102), all subsequent international and regional social security instruments[35] revolve around these three basic goals: enlarging the protected classes of persons or workers; upgrading the level and duration of benefits; and guaranteeing, except in the case of medical care, periodic payments of social security.

The history of all social security conventions adopted by the ILO shows a constant tension between member states of the organisation and the Bureau of the ILO in respect of the definition of protected classes of persons. In the process of drafting a convention, the Bureau has always tried to expand the categories of persons covered in order to reach the ultimate goal of social security conventions, which is universal coverage. Member states for their part always succeeded in limiting the prescribed categories to a percentage of waged workers or residents.[36]

Since the beginning of the 1990s, the ILO Social Security division has been given a mandate by the International Labor Conference to search for solutions that can include 'other workers' than 'male waged workers' in a social protection device.[37] This effort culminated in the latest Social Security for All Campaign, launched in June 2003. The ILO experts proposed an inclusive definition of social security that addresses principles as well as needs. The model suggests the following characteristics as forming the essentials of social security in a universal context:

(a) the provision of benefits to households and individuals;
(b) through public or collective arrangements;
(c) aimed at protecting against low or declining living standards; and
(d) arising from a number of basic risks and needs.

As in the case of other rights guaranteed by CESCR, provision of the 'essential' or 'immediate' content of the right to social security cannot be delayed in the name of the progressive realisation commitment provided for in article 2 of CESCR. The ILO's proposal for immediate access to protection against basic social risks for all encompasses the immediate obligation of states according to CESCR. Although the Committee on ESCR's guidelines for reporting do not express an interpretation by the Committee of the right to social security, they capture the essence of the immediate obligation of the states with respect to this right by asking state members to report on

---

[35] Except for Convention (168) on Employment Promotion and Protection against Unemployment (1988). See below, subsec 3.2.

[36] See eg the discussion preceding the adoption of Convention (128) about the prescribed percentage of the population to be covered for the purpose of ratifying the Convention; Report V(I), 50th session, 1966 12-13 and Report V(2) 25-27. Those reports and discussions also illustrate clearly that even at the time, states preferred a system based on prescribed categories of workers to any other as it authorised them not to consider in their calculation atypical, marginal and part-time workers. But again, this strategy does not mean that social security schemes, in order to respect Convention (102) requirements, can only be designed to benefit workers.

[37] *Extending social security: Policies for developing countries*, ESS Paper No 13, ILO Social Policy and Development Branch; W van Ginneken 2003 *and social security: A new consensus* (2001).

the exclusionary effects of existing national social security schemes in the case of vulnerable groups and women.

It is clear that the process by which state members report on the implementation of the right to social security guaranteed by section 9 of CESCR would benefit from a closer collaboration between the ILO and the Committee, as well as from the adoption of a General Observation by the Committee. In the meanwhile, useful guidance can be taken from the ILO work and the recent Campaign on Social Security for All.

In addition, the interdependence of sections 9 and 11 of CESCR makes it clear that no state can pretend to respect the right to social security or even the essential content of this right if the national organisation of social security produces more social exclusion and poverty than it provides security to some workers. In some cases, the extension of the covered categories of workers will be needed, as in some others, a major tax-financed effort aimed at offering to all a protection against basic social risks will be more appropriate. But in no cases can a state delay the task of urgently providing basic security to all, if it has ratified CESCR.

3.1.2 Convention on the Rights of the Child

South Africa has ratified the UN Convention on the Rights of the Child (CRC).[38] This Convention contains a set of rights and freedoms to be enjoyed by all children. A child as defined in this Convention is any human being under the age of 18, unless a particular nation's laws set an earlier age for the attaining of majority status.[39] Article 23 explicitly states that every child has the right to benefit from social security, including social insurance, and that the state should take the necessary measures to achieve the full realisation of this right in accordance with national law. Social security benefits should be granted, taking into account the resources and the circumstances of the child and those responsible for the maintenance of the child.

Article 6 of the Convention places state parties under an obligation to ensure the survival and development of the child to the maximum extent possible.[40] Article 6 is understood by the Committee on the Rights of the Child (Committee on RC) as follows:[41]

---

[38] GA Res 44/25, Annex 44 UN GAOR Supp (No 49) 167, UN Doc A/44/49 (1989) entered into force 2 September 1990. (South Africa ratified the Convention on 16 June 1995, without entering any reservations.)
[39] According to the South African Constitution (sec 28(3)), 'child' means a person under the age of 18 years. This is also in line with the Social Assistance Act 59 of 1992, Welfare Laws Amendment Act 106 of 1997 and new Social Assistance Bill B57D-2003 that defines child as a person under 18 years.
[40] (1) States Parties recognise that every child has the inherent right to life.
(2) States Parties shall ensure to the maximum extent possible the survival and development of the child.
[41] CRC/C/5 entitled General Guidelines Regarding the Form and Content of Initial Reports to be Submitted by States Parties under art 44 para 1(a) of the Convention, which were adopted by the Committee on the Rights of the Child at its 22nd meeting (first session) on 15 October 1991 para 19.

Under this section States Parties are requested to provide relevant information, including the principal legislative, judicial, administrative or other measures in force; the institutional infrastructure for implementing policy in this area, particularly monitoring strategies and mechanisms; and factors and difficulties encountered and progress achieved in implementing the relevant provisions of the Convention, in respect of:
(a) survival and development (article 6, paragraph 2);
(b) disabled children (article 23);
(c) health and health services (article 24);
(d) social security and child care services and facilities (articles 26 and 18, paragraph 3);
(e) standard of living (article 27, paragraphs 1-3).

These provisions give rise to numerous derivative social security rights, such as the right to health care necessary for survival, and a standard of living that meets the needs for food, clothing, shelter and education.[42]

On 25 and 26 January 2000, the Committee on RC considered South Africa's first state report under CRC and adopted concluding observations on South Africa's compliance with the indicated Convention. In the first place the Committee noted that South Africa had not yet ratified CESCR. The Committee stressed that the ratification of CESCR would strengthen the efforts of the state party (ie South Africa) to meet its obligations in guaranteeing the rights of all children under its jurisdiction and encouraged South Africa to reinforce its efforts to finalise the ratification of this instrument.[43] Secondly, the Committee also made certain observations regarding socio-economic rights of children and the failures in the current system.[44] In the part described as 'Subjects of concern and recommendations of the Committee', it criticised the South African government on, among others issues, the lack of co-ordination between institutions implementing CRC;[45] the lack of prioritisation in budgetary allocations and distributions to ensure implementation of the economic, social and cultural rights of children; inadequacies in data collection regarding children's rights (the Committee recommended that such a system should cover all children up to the age of 18 years, with specific emphasis on those who are particularly vulnerable);[46] insufficient measures to guarantee for all children access to education, health care and other social services (particularly for especially vulnerable children); and inadequate levels of benefit of the Child Support Grant (which the Committee recommended must be expanded to include children up to the age of 18 years who are still in school).

---

[42] Department of Social Development (n 5 above) 50; L Jansen van Rensburg 'Die beregtiging van die fundamentele reg op toegang tot sosiale sekerheid' ('The adjudication of the fundamental right to access to social security') unpublished LLD thesis, Rand Afrikaans University, 2000 45.
[43] Committee on the Rights of the Child *Concluding Observations* 2000 CRC/C/15/Add.122 para 11.
[44] n 43 above, paras 12, 15, 24, 29 & 32.
[45] The same point of critique was made by the South African Human Rights Commission (SAHRC) *4th Annual Economic and Social Rights Report: 2000-2002* 29-30.
[46] This is annually done by the SAHRC; n 45 above, 171-234.

It is clear from the report that South Africa in major respects failed to comply with the provisions of CRC. The Committee indicated these deficiencies and recommended what still needs to be done. This approach assists South Africa in addressing these problems.

The South African Law Commission,[47] for instance, considered these observations and recommendations and made overall proposals in the drafting of the Children's Bill: For example, while the Commission acknowledged that means testing for purposes of determining eligibility for grants is not ideal, as the costs involved in conducting the means testing divert funds away from the actual recipients, it recommended that means testing be retained for all the grants except the Child Support Grant. The Commission reasoned that, given resource limitations, all the grants and subsidies should be targeted only at the poorest of the poor to enable those children to survive.

The Commission further observed that a significant problem facing South African children at present concerned the availability of financial support for children orphaned by HIV/AIDS, and especially those living in child-headed households. Unless they are aged under seven,[48] and living with a primary caregiver who can apply for a Child Support Grant, or placed in formal foster care in order for the Foster Child Grant to be payable, there is no monetary support available. Further, children who are HIV positive or have AIDS themselves are not regarded as able to qualify for the Care Dependency Grant.[49]

The Commission therefore recommended the introduction of the following social security scheme for children:

- a child grant;
- a foster care and court-ordered kinship care grant;
- an informal kinship care grant;
- an adoption grant;
- an emergency court grant;
- a subsidy to enable children with disabilities to obtain assistive devices;
- subsidies to NGOs contracted to the state to implement programmes and projects giving effect to this Act;
- fees to NGOs, FBOs and welfare organisations who carry out services on behalf of the state; and
- a subsidy to encourage the provision of early childhood development services.

Unfortunately, the proposed social security scheme for children by the Law Commission was not included in the new Children's Bill.[50] This Bill (the 'reintroduced Bill') contains part of the envisaged Children's Act. The Bill that was initially submitted to parliament

---

[47] Discussion Paper 103 Project 110 *Review of the Child Care Act* (2002) 333-338.
[48] Since the report, government has started a three-year process of extending the grant to children under the age of 14 years. Sec 4(1) of the Social Assistance Act as amended by the Welfare Laws Amendment Act. See R 460 in Government Gazette 24630 of 31/03/2003.
[49] Although adults with HIV above a certain cell count are able to qualify for the Disability Grant.

(referred to as 'the consolidated Bill') dealt with the full spectrum of protection of children in both national and provincial spheres and was to be dealt with in terms of section 76 of the Constitution (functional area of concurrent national and provincial legislative competence). It was later found to be a 'mixed' Bill, including elements to be handled in terms of both section 75 (functional area of national legislative competence) and section 76 of the Constitution. Due to its mixed character, the Deputy Speaker of the National Assembly requested the Executive to split the consolidated Bill, which has now been done. The provisions of the consolidated Bill that will apply to the provincial government have been removed and, consequently, the current Bill contains only matters which have to be dealt with in terms of section 75 of the Constitution.

As soon as the current Bill is enacted, an amendment Bill containing the matters which apply to the provincial government only ('the amendment Bill') will be introduced. The amendment Bill will have to be dealt with in terms of section 76 of the Constitution. The amendment Bill will complete the current Bill by inserting the provisions which deal with service delivery and further protection of families and children. The amendment Bill will insert the following chapters in the envisaged Act: Chapter 8 introduces a provision on the compulsory reporting by certain persons of children in need of care and protection, and addresses the child protection system, the provision of child protection services, the National Child Protection Register and measures relating to the health of children. Chapter 9 makes provision for prevention and early intervention as a first layer of services provided to children and families in need of assistance. Chapter 11 deals with contribution orders. Chapter 13 deals with foster care and care by family members.[51]

---

[50] Children's Bill B70 of 2003 as reintroduced in the National Assembly as a sec 75 Bill; "Explanatory summary of Bill" published in *Government Gazette* 25346 of 13/08/2003.
[51] See "Explanatory summary of Bill" published in *Government Gazette* 25346 of 13/08/2003.

3.1.3 Convention on the Elimination of All Forms of Discrimination Against Women

The UN Convention on the Elimination of All Forms of Discrimination Against Women (CEDAW)[52] has been ratified by South Africa. Article 11 of CEDAW requires the eradication of employment-related discrimination in social security and the loss of seniority or benefits due to pregnancy or marriage.[53] Article 13 guarantees for women the right of equality to family benefits and insurance.[54] Article 14[55] gives rural women the right to benefit directly from social security benefits, an area in which South Africa still needs to do more than is currently being done.[56] To accelerate *de facto* equality between men and women,[57] affirmative action is permitted by article 4.

Generally, the exclusion of certain categories of employees and non-employees from social insurance legislation can be seen as an indirect form of discrimination on the basis of gender. These include domestic workers,[58] casuals and informal sector workers. In this

---

[52] GA Res 34/180, 34 UN GAOR Supp (No 46) at 193, UN Doc A/34/46, entered into force 3 September 1981. (South Africa ratified the Convention on 15 December 1995, without entering any reservations.)

[53] Art 11(1)(e): 'States Parties shall take all appropriate measures to eliminate discrimination against women in the field of employment in order to ensure, on a basis of equality of men and women, the same rights, in particular the right to social security, particularly in cases of retirement, unemployment, sickness, invalidity and old age and other incapacity to work, as well as the right to paid leave.' An example of where South Africa might be in contravention of art 11 is found in sec 25 of the Basic Conditions of Employment Act 75 of 1997, which mandates employers to provide four months maternity leave to women, but does not require employers to continue remunerating employees during the four months maternity leave and also does not require employers to maintain their contributions to social security schemes while an employee is on maternity leave.

[54] Art 13(a)-(b): 'States Parties shall take all appropriate measures to eliminate discrimination against women in other areas of economic and social life in order to ensure, on a basis of equality of men and women, the same rights, in particular (a) the right to family benefits; (b) the right to bank loans, mortgages and other forms of financial credit.'

[55] Art 14(2)(c): 'States Parties shall take all appropriate measures to eliminate discrimination against women in rural areas in order to ensure, on a basis of equality of men and women, that they participate in and benefit from rural development and, in particular, shall ensure to such women the right to benefit directly from social security programmes.'

[56] In the area of social assistance, rural women can apply for the Old Age Grant if they are over 60 years or for child support if they meet the requirements. However, rural women will not qualify for social insurance because they are not permanently employed and do not contribute to the Unemployment Insurance Fund, except if they are domestic workers and they are totally excluded from the Occupational Injuries and Diseases Fund.

[57] Art 4(2): 'Adoption by States Parties of special measures, including those measures contained in the present Convention, aimed at protecting maternity shall not be considered discriminatory.'

[58] Domestic workers have recently been included in the Unemployment Insurance Fund. A domestic worker is defined as an employee who performs domestic work in the home of his or her employer, and includes (a) a gardener; (b) a person employed by a household as a driver of a motor vehicle; and (c) a person who takes care of any person in that home, but does not include a farm worker; sec 1 of the Unemployment Insurance Contributions Act 4 of 2002 and sec 1 of the Unemployment Insurance Act 63 of 2001. However, domestic workers are still excluded from the Compensation for Occupational Injuries and Diseases Act 130 of 1993 (sec 1).

regard, recommendations made by the CEDAW Committee are useful in the process of interpreting and applying CEDAW rights.

3.1.4 Convention on the Elimination of All Forms of Racial Discrimination[59]

Articles 2(1)(c) and (d) of the Convention on the Elimination of All Forms of Racial Discrimination (CERD) prohibits the perpetuation of racial discrimination in policies and legislation, while article 5(e)[60] refers to equality in the rights to unemployment benefits, housing and social security. The exclusion of certain categories of employees and non-employees, in particular domestic workers, casuals, and informal sector workers, from social insurance legislation can, under some circumstances, be seen as indirect discrimination on the basis of race.[61]

---

[59] 660 UNTS 195, entered into force 4 January 1969. (South Africa signed the Convention on 3 October 1994.)

[60] Art 5(e): 'In compliance with the fundamental obligations laid down in article 2 of this Convention, States Parties undertake to prohibit and to eliminate racial discrimination in all its forms and to guarantee the right of everyone, without distinction as to race, colour, or national or ethnic origin, to equality before the law, notably in the enjoyment of the following rights: economic, social and cultural rights, in particular: (i) the rights to work, to free choice of employment, to just and favourable conditions of work, to protection against unemployment, to equal pay for equal work, to just and favourable remuneration; (ii) the right to form and join trade unions; (iii) the right to housing; (iv) the right to public health, medical care, social security and social services; (v) the right to education and training; (vi) the right to equal participation in cultural activities.'

[61] The limited nature of protection in terms of the South African social security system has affected the poor as well as the informally employed and structurally unemployed among them, in particular. This stems from the fact that the social insurance system, notably unemployment insurance and compensation for work injuries and diseases, does not provide coverage to those outside formal employment. Social assistance measures seldom operate to the direct advantage of the poor and the informally employed among them. Due to the targeted nature of both social services and programmes, and of the various social grants (notably the Old Age Grant, the Disability Grant and the recently introduced Child Support Grant), many if not most of the persons falling within the categories mentioned remain part of the socially excluded population (MP Olivier & L Jansen van Rensburg 'The role and influence of international human rights instruments on South African poverty law' (2001) Paper presented at a seminar titled Law and Poverty IV - Moving towards international poverty law? Oñati, Spain, 3-4 May 2001 8). Because of South African demographics, casuals, domestic workers, informal sector workers and unemployed workers are mostly black. Although on the face of it racially neutral, the exclusion of these informal workers from benefits has a disproportionate racial impact and can be seen as indirect racial discrimination. See Department of Social Development (n 5 above) 15-33.

3.1.5 Treaties on the protection of refugees and stateless persons

There are several treaties in the area of the protection of refugees. Some of these treaties deal with social security issues. These are the Convention Relating to the Status of Refugees (Refugees Convention),[62] the Protocol Relating to the Status of Refugees,[63] the International Convention on the Protection of the Rights of all Migrant Workers and Members of Their Families[64] and the Convention Relating to the Status of Stateless Persons (Stateless Persons Convention).[65]

Both the Refugees Convention and the Stateless Persons Convention not only prohibit discrimination against refugees or other non-nationals on the basis of their status, but also require state parties to provide certain positive benefits to refugees on a par with nationals. An example is article 20 of the Refugees Convention that requires that where a rationing system exists for products in short supply for the population at large, refugees should be accorded the same treatment as nationals.[66] Under article 24 of the Refugees Convention, state parties are obliged to provide the same treatment as they provide to their own nationals in respect of social security, subject to stated limitations.[67] Similar provisions for the protection

---

[62] 189 UNTS 150, entered into force 22 April 1954 (South Africa acceded on 12 January 1996).
[63] 606 UNTS 267, entered into force 4 October 1967 (South Africa acceded on 12 January 1996).
[64] GA Res 45/158, Annex, 45 UN GAOR Supp (No 49A) 262, UN Doc A/45/49 (1990), entered into force 1 July 2003. Not yet signed or acceded to.
[65] 360 UNTS 117, entered into force 6 June 1960. Not yet signed or acceded to.
[66] Art 20: 'Where a rationing system exists, which applies to the population at large and regulates the general distribution of products in short supply, refugees shall be accorded the same treatment as nationals.'
[67] Art 24: '1. The Contracting States shall accord to refugees lawfully staying in their territory the same treatment as is accorded to nationals in respect of the following matters; (a) in so far as such matters are governed by laws or regulations or are subject to the control of administrative authorities: remuneration, including family allowances where these form part of remuneration, hours of work, overtime arrangements, holidays with pay, restrictions on home work, minimum age of employment, apprenticeship and training, women's work and the work of young persons, and the enjoyment of the benefits of collective bargaining; (b) social security (legal provisions in respect of employment injury, occupational diseases, maternity, sickness, disability, old age, death, unemployment, family responsibilities and any other contingency which, according to national laws or regulations, is covered by a social security scheme), subject to the following limitations: (i) There may be appropriate arrangements for the maintenance of acquired rights and rights in course of acquisition; (ii) National laws or regulations of the country of residence may prescribe special arrangements concerning benefits or portions of benefits which are payable wholly out of public funds, and concerning allowances paid to persons who do not fulfil the contribution conditions prescribed for the award of a normal pension. 2. The right to compensation for the death of a refugee resulting from employment injury or from occupational disease shall not be affected by the fact that the residence of the beneficiary is outside the territory of the Contracting State. 3. The Contracting States shall extend to refugees the benefits of agreements concluded between them, or which may be concluded between them in the future, concerning the maintenance of acquired rights and rights in the process of acquisition in regard to social security, subject only to the conditions which apply to nationals of the States signatory to the agreements in question. 4. The Contracting States will give sympathetic consideration to extending to refugees so far as possible the benefits of similar agreements which may at any time be in force between such Contracting States and non-contracting States.'

of stateless persons and migrant workers and members of their families are contained in the Stateless Persons Convention[68] and the International Convention on the Protection of the Rights of all Migrant Workers and Members of their Families.[69]

Apart from some exceptions for foreigners with permanent residence status, non-nationals are mostly excluded from South African social security. This applies for virtually all social assistance benefits,[70] as well as for certain branches of social security, such as the unemployment insurance scheme.[71]

In *Khosa v Minister of Social Development*,[72] the Constitutional Court addressed the constitutionality of certain provisions of the Social Assistance Act 59 of 1992 (as amended in some instances by the Welfare Laws Amendment Act 106 of 1997) and in effect addressed the requirements to qualify for some of the grants in the permanent grant administration process in South Africa. The applicants are permanent residents. They challenged certain sections of the Social Assistance Act that reserved grants for the elderly for South African citizens and thereby excluded otherwise eligible permanent residents, and that reserved child support grants and care dependency grants for South African citizens, again excluding otherwise eligible permanent residents, and particularly the children of permanent residents.

The Constitutional Court found these provisions to be unconstitutional, emphasising the fact that permanent residents are a vulnerable group and they need special constitutional protection. Because of the urgency of the matter, the Court decided that the most appropriate order to make was the 'reading-in' of the words 'permanent resident' in the challenged legislation.[73] While the Old Age Grant, Child Support Grant and Care Dependency Grant were in issue in the *Khosa* and *Mahlaule* cases, a consequence of the reading-in of the words 'permanent residents' in these sections of the Social

---

[68] Arts 24(1)(b)(i) & (ii): '1. The Contracting States shall accord to stateless persons lawfully staying in their territory the same treatment as is accorded to nationals in respect of the following matters: (b) Social security (legal provisions in respect of employment injury, occupational diseases, maternity, sickness, disability, old age, death, unemployment, family responsibilities and any other contingency which, according to national laws or regulations, is covered by a social security scheme), subject to the following limitations: (i) There may be appropriate arrangements for the maintenance of acquired rights and rights in course of acquisition; (ii) National laws or regulations of the country of residence may prescribe special arrangements concerning benefits or portions of benefits which are payable wholly out of public funds, and concerning allowances paid to persons who do not fulfil the contribution conditions prescribed for the award of a normal pension.'

[69] Arts 27, 45 & 54.

[70] In view of the fact that South African citizenship is in terms of sec 3(c) of the Social Assistance Act 59 of 1992 one of the eligibility criteria for accessing almost all social assistance benefits (such as old age and disability benefits, but not the Foster Child Grant); see also sec 12(1)(b)(i) of the Aged Persons Act 81 of 1967 for a similar restriction.

[71] Migrants are excluded from the operation of the Unemployment Insurance Act (UIA) if they have to be repatriated at the termination of their services; see now sec 3(1)(d) of the UIA 63 of 2001. Olivier & Jansen van Rensburg (n 19 above) 12.

[72] *Khosa v Minister of Social Development* 2004 6 SA 505 (CC).

[73] n 72 above, paras 92 & 95.

Assistance Act is that the Court has granted access to any social grant in South Africa to permanent residents.

While permanent residents are now entitled to the grant,[74] refugees, because of the fact that they do not have the necessary documentation, are still not eligible for social assistance grants.[75] This despite the fact that, according to the Refugee Act,[76] refugees enjoy full legal protection, which includes the enjoyment of the fundamental rights set out in the Bill of Rights.[77]

The exclusion of migrant workers raises serious questions of a constitutional nature.[78] Jurisprudentially the right to equal treatment has already in the area of employment been interpreted to imply that there is no basis to distinguish between foreigners who have obtained permanent resident status and South African citizens.[79] Furthermore, some of the present exclusions pertaining to non-citizens may be contrary to South Africa's treaty obligations – for example, the exclusion of foreign children from certain child grants.[80]

From a social security point of view this does not mean that all categories of non-citizen migrants would have to be treated alike. This may affect in particular the position of non-citizens who are *illegally* in the country. However, the White Paper on International Migration[81] recognises that there is no constitutional basis to exclude, *in toto*, the application of the Bill of Rights owing to the status of a person while in South Africa, including illegal immigrants.[82]

3.2 International Labour Organisation instruments

Under the UN system, the International Labour Organisation has been established to focus *inter alia* on social security rights. As a specialised agency, the ILO's standards manifest through recommendations and international labour conventions which have binding effect on those state parties who ratify them, since the conventions have the status of international treaties. However, recommendations are non-binding instruments, serving the purpose of clarifying matters dealt with by the conventions, but also performing

---

[74] As above.
[75] SAHRC (n 45 above) 216.
[76] Refugee Act 130 of 1998.
[77] Sec 27(b) of the Refugee Act 130 of 1998.
[78] Sec 27(1)(c) of the 1996 Constitution grants the 'right to access to social security' (inclusive of the right to access to social assistance) to 'everyone'. This right is underpinned by the fundamental right to equality, enshrined in sec 9.
[79] See *Larbi-Odam v Member of the Executive Council for Education (North-West Province)* 1998 1 SA 745 (CC) paras 30-31; see also *Baloro v University of Bophuthatswana* 1995 4 SA 197 (BSC).
[80] See art 9 of CRC, signed and ratified by South Africa; Olivier & Jansen van Rensburg (n 19 above) 12. See *Khosa* (n 72 above). The issue whether refugees must receive special protection as in the case of permanent residents was not addressed by the Constitutional Court. The Court did, however, reason that it might be reasonable to exclude citizens from other countries, visitors and illegal residents, who have only a tenuous link with the country. See para 59.
[81] Of 31 March 1999.
[82] White Paper on International Migration paras 2.2-2.4.

the important task of setting guidelines for national policy and action.[83]

The Social Security (Minimum Standards) Convention No 102 of 1952[84] is regarded as the most comprehensive standard. Not only does Convention No 102 insist on the periodicity and regularity of available cash benefits,[85] but it also provides for minimum standards in nine distinct branches of social security. These branches are medical care,[86] sickness,[87] unemployment,[88] old age,[89] employment injury,[90] family,[91] maternity,[92] invalidity,[93] and survivors' benefits.[94] At least three schemes from the above categories need to be established by member states to the Convention. One of these three schemes must be either an unemployment benefit, old age benefit, employment injury benefit or an invalidity or survivors' benefit. The scope of protection and benefits, including the amount thereof, is defined by the minimum standard provided by the Convention.

In order to provide for a higher degree of protection than Convention No 102, new instruments have been established to supplement or revise the conventions adopted before the Second World War. The aim is to improve the system gradually, dealing with the following particular branches:

- the Employment Injury Benefits Convention No 121 of 1964;[95]
- the Invalidity, Old-age and Survivors' Benefits Convention No 128 of 1967;[96]
- the Medical Care and Sickness Benefits Convention No 130 of 1969;[97] and
- the Maternity Protection Convention No 183 of 2000.[98]

Convention No 183 of June 2000 was adopted to provide for 14 weeks' maternity leave to all employed women, inclusive of those in atypical forms of dependent work. This was preceded by Convention No 102,

---

[83] Art 19 ILO Constitution.
[84] Not signed or ratified by South Africa.
[85] Sec 1(2) of the Convention 102 defines the term benefit in arts 10, 34 & 49 as either direct benefit in the form of care or indirect benefit consisting of a reimbursement of the expenses borne by the person concerned.
[86] Part II arts 7-12.
[87] Part III arts 13-18.
[88] Part IV arts 19-24.
[89] Part V arts 25-30.
[90] Part VI arts 31-38.
[91] Part VII arts 39-45.
[92] Part VIII arts 46-52.
[93] Part IX arts 53-58.
[94] Part X arts 59-64.
[95] Not ratified by South Africa.
[96] Not ratified by South Africa.
[97] Not ratified by South Africa.
[98] Not ratified by South Africa.

as was the right to maternity benefits, prescribed by the Maternity Protection Convention No 103 of 1952.[99]

The ILO has elaborated standards in accordance with the above-mentioned developments. These standards are applicable in all branches of social security, with particular relevance to migrant workers. Among these standards are:

- the Equality of Treatment (Social Security) Convention No 118 of 1962;[100]
- the Migration for Employment Convention (Revised) No 97 of 1949;[101] and
- the Migrant Workers (Supplementary Provisions) Convention No 143 of 1975.[102]

Equality of treatment to workers of other ratifying countries is granted by The Equality of Treatment (Social Security) Convention No 118 of 1962. This applies to all nine branches of social security, although the obligations of the Convention may be accepted as regards only one of those branches. This guarantees the payment of long-term benefits even when the worker resides abroad. This is not only available to nationals of the ratifying state, but also to nationals of any other state which has accepted the obligations of the Convention for the corresponding branch.[103] Children resident within the territory of one of the states having accepted the obligations of the Convention for such a branch are guaranteed access to family allowances.[104]

The Migration for Employment Convention (Revised) No 97 of 1949 applies to employment migrants. Various provisions are aimed at regulating conditions under which the migration of persons for employment shall take place, in such a manner that equality of treatment is ensured. Examples of such provisions are:

---

[99] Noting the need to revise the Maternity Protection Convention (Revised) 1952, to promote equality of all women in the workforce and the health and safety of the mother and child, in order to recognise the diversity in economic and social development of member states, as well as the diversity of enterprises, and the development of the protection of maternity in national law and practice the ILO decides to revise this Convention.

[100] Not ratified by South Africa.

[101] Not ratified by South Africa.

[102] Not ratified by South Africa.

[103] Art 5(1): 'In addition to the provisions of article 4, each Member which has accepted the obligations of this Convention in respect of the branch or branches of social security concerned shall guarantee both to its own nationals and to the nationals of any other Member which has accepted the obligations of the Convention in respect of the branch or branches in question, when they are resident abroad, provision of invalidity benefits, old age benefits, survivors' benefits and death grants, and employment injury pensions, subject to measures for this purpose being taken, where necessary, in accordance with article 8.'

[104] Art 6: 'In addition to the provisions of article 4, each Member which has accepted the obligations of this Convention in respect of family benefit shall guarantee the grant of family allowances both to its own nationals and to the nationals of any other Member which has accepted the obligations of this Convention for that branch, in respect of children who reside on the territory of any such Member, under conditions and within limits to be agreed upon by the Members concerned.'

- the information states shall make available to one another concerning migration;[105]
- the establishment of free assistance and information services for migrants;[106]
- facilities for the departure, journey and reception of migrants;[107]
- medical services for migrants and the members of their families;[108] and
- the obligation to apply, without discrimination in respect of nationality, race, religion or sex, to immigrants lawfully within their territory, treatment no less favourable than that which they apply to their own nationals in respect of certain matters.[109]

Recommendation No 86 supplements the Convention.

The Migrant Workers (Supplementary Provisions) Convention No 143 of 1975 obliges ratifying states to respect the basic human rights of all migrants for employment. This is accomplished by preventative and suppressive measures towards clandestine movements of migrants for employment and illegal employment of migrants. Ratifying states are also obliged to promote genuine equality of treatment in respect of

---

[105] Art 1: 'Each member of the International Labour Organisation for which this Convention is in force undertakes to make available on request to the International Labour Office and to other Members (a) information on national policies, laws and regulations relating to emigration and immigration; (b) information on special provisions concerning migration for employment and the conditions of work and livelihood of migrants for employment; (c) information concerning general agreements and special arrangements on these questions concluded by the Member.'

[106] Art 2: 'Each Member for which this Convention is in force undertakes to maintain, or satisfy itself that there is maintained, an adequate and free service to assist migrants for employment, and in particular to provide them with accurate information.'

[107] Art 4: 'Measures shall be taken as appropriate by each Member, within its jurisdiction, to facilitate the departure, journey and reception of migrants for employment.'

[108] Art 5: 'Each Member for which this Convention is in force undertakes to maintain, within its jurisdiction, appropriate medical services responsible for (a) ascertaining, where necessary, both at the time of departure and on arrival, that migrants for employment and the members of their families authorised to accompany or join them are in reasonable health; (b) ensuring that migrants for employment and members of their families enjoy adequate medical attention and good hygienic conditions at the time of departure, during the journey and on arrival in the territory of destination.'

[109] Art 6: '1. Each Member for which this Convention is in force undertakes to apply, without discrimination in respect of nationality, race, religion or sex, to immigrants lawfully within its territory, treatment no less favourable than that which it applies to its own nationals in respect of the following matters: (a) in so far as such matters are regulated by law or regulations, or are subject to the control of administrative authorities (i) remuneration, including family allowances where these form part of remuneration, hours of work, overtime arrangements, holidays with pay, restrictions on home work, minimum age for employment, apprenticeship and training, women's work and the work of young persons; (ii) membership of trade unions and enjoyment of the benefits of collective bargaining; (iii) accommodation; (b) social security (that is to say, legal provision in respect of employment injury, maternity, sickness, invalidity, old age, death, unemployment and family responsibilities, and any other contingency which, according to national laws or regulations, is covered by a social security scheme), subject to the following limitations: (i) there may be appropriate arrangements for the maintenance of acquired rights and rights in course of acquisition; (ii) national laws or regulations of immigration countries may prescribe special arrangements concerning benefits or portions of benefits which are payable wholly out of public funds, and concerning allowances paid to persons who do not fulfil the contribution conditions prescribed for the award of a normal pension; (c) employment taxes, dues or contributions payable in respect of the person employed; and (d) legal proceedings relating to the matters referred to in this Convention.'

employment and occupation, social security, trade union and cultural rights, as well as individual collective freedoms of migrants. Article 8 of Convention 143 states as follows:

> (1) On condition that he has resided legally in the territory for the purpose of employment, the migrant worker shall not be regarded as in an illegal ...
> (2) Accordingly, he shall enjoy equality of treatment with nationals ...

Article 9 further provides that:

> [W]ithout prejudice to measures designed to control movements of migrants for employment by ensuring that migrant workers enter national territory and are admitted to employment in conformity with the relevant laws and regulations, the migrant worker shall, in cases in which these laws and regulations have not been respected and in which his position cannot be regularised, enjoy equality of treatment for himself and his family in respect of rights arising out of past employment as regards remuneration, social security and other benefits.

A distinction should be made between legal refugees, legal migrant workers and others for the purpose of underlying states' responsibility in the field of social security. This distinction is advisable for South Africa, keeping in mind that the Convention is supplemented by Recommendation No 151.

The Discrimination (Employment and Occupation) Convention No 111 of 1958 was ratified by South Africa on 5 March 1997.[110] This Convention requires each state party to declare and pursue a national policy designed to promote equality of opportunity and equal treatment in respect of employment and occupation.[111]

3.3 United Nations non-binding instruments

A wide range of UN non-binding instruments exists in the form of declarations, guidelines, standard minimum rules, etc - all dealing with the right to social security. Although these documents do not have legally binding effect, they serve a significant purpose in defining the obligations of states. UN Assembly Declarations can achieve the status of customary international law once they have been repeated in state practice.[112] Such would express the political will of a wide range of states, representative of the regions of the world,[113] and especially when adopted without discord.

It is widely accepted that the Universal Declaration of Human Rights[114] has attained the status of customary international law. Various judicial authorities have invoked its provisions, both in a domestic and legislative evolution of authoritative legal norms. The Preamble to the Universal Declaration expressly states that its

---

[110] This is the only ILO Convention with regard to social security that South Africa has ratified. South Africa ratified it on 5 March 1997.

[111] Art 2.

[112] In order for a rule to attain the status of international law, there must be consistent practice and *opinio juris* in respect of the rule.

[113] For more on how resolutions of the United Nations General Assembly can attain the status of customary international law, see Dugard (n 22 above) 32.

[114] GA Res 217A (III), UN Doc A/810 71 (1948).

purpose is to provide 'a common understanding' of the human rights and fundamental freedoms referred to in the UN Charter and to serve 'as a common standard of achievement for all peoples and all nations'. Article 22 of the Universal Declaration provides for the following:[115]

> Everyone, as a member of society, has the right to social security and is entitled to realisation, through national effort and international co-operation and in accordance with the organisation and resources of each state, of the economic, social and cultural rights indispensable for his dignity and the free development of his personality.

It also caters for other areas covered by the concept of social security. Specifically, it enshrines the right of everyone[116]

> to a standard of living adequate for the health and well-being of himself and of his family, including food, clothing, housing and medical care and necessary social services, and the right to security in the event of unemployment, sickness, disability, widowhood, old age or other lack of livelihood in circumstances beyond his control.

Mothers and children are given special recognition, as the Declaration guarantees their entitlement to 'special care and assistance', stating unambiguously that this applies to 'all children, whether born in or out of wedlock'.[117] Within the context of employment benefits, workers are also afforded 'the right to just and favourable remuneration ensuring for [themselves] and [their] famil[ies] an existence worthy of human dignity, and supplemented, if necessary, by other means of 'social protection'.[118]

For purposes of social security, other examples of soft law are the Limburg Principles of 1987[119] and the so-called Maastricht Guidelines of 1997.[120] These constitute the official commentary of the International Commission of Jurists in co-operation with other institutions. Contained in these instruments are a series of explanatory remarks on the nature, application and duties of state parties towards CESCR. The Copenhagen Declaration on Social Development and Programme of Action is yet another important

---

[115] See also Scheinin (n 6 above) 161.
[116] Art 25(1) Universal Declaration.
[117] Art 25(2) Universal Declaration.
[118] Art 23(3) Universal Declaration.
[119] The Limburg Principles on the implementation of the International Covenant on Economic, Social and Cultural Rights' (1987) 9 *Human Rights Quarterly* 122-135.
[120] The Maastricht Guidelines on violations of the International Covenant on Economic, Social and Cultural Rights' (1998) 20 *Human Rights Quarterly* 691-701.

example of soft law, adopted at the UN World Summit for Social Development in 1995[121] and renewed in 2000.[122] In the process, consensus was reached as to placing people at the centre of the concerns for sustainable development, pledged to eradicate poverty, promote full and productive employment, and foster social integration to achieve stable, safe and just societies for all.

4 Regional law

4.1 The African Charter on Human and Peoples' Rights

The African Charter on Human and Peoples' Rights (African Charter or Charter)[123] was approved by the Organisation of African Unity (OAU) in 1981 and came into force in 1986.[124] South Africa acceded to the Charter on 9 July 1996, following the growing trend in the international community of states towards the regional development, protection and adjudication of international human rights standards.[125]

The Charter does not guarantee the right to social security in a direct sense,[126] but reference is made indirectly to rights that are regarded as specific contingencies of social security, as illustrated in articles 16, 18(1) and 18(4). Article 16 states that every individual shall have the right to enjoy the best attainable state of physical and mental health, and that state parties are obliged to take the necessary measures to protect the health of their people and to ensure that they receive medical attention when they are sick.[127] Article 18(1) places a duty on state parties to protect the family as the natural unit and basis of society and to protect the physical health and morals of the family. Article 18(4) recognises the right of the aged

---

[121] 1995 UN Doc A/Conf.166/9 (1995).
[122] 2000 UN Doc A/55/L.40 adopted at the 55th session of the General Assembly of the United Nations Agenda Item 37 titled 'The Implementation of the Outcome of the World Summit for Social Development and of the Special Assembly in this regard'. South Africa was present at this session.
[123] 1981 OAU Doc CAB/LEG/67/3 (1990). (South Africa ratified the Convention on 7 January 2000.)
[124] F Viljoen 'Introduction to the African Commission and the regional human rights system' in C Heyns (ed) *Human rights law in Africa* (2000) 385; CA Odinkalu & C Christensen 'The African Commission on Human and Peoples' Rights: The development of its non-state communication procedure' (1998) 16 *Human Rights Quarterly* 235-280.
[125] L Lindholt *Questioning the universality of human rights - The African Charter on Human and Peoples' Rights in Botswana, Malawi and Mozambique* (1997) 3-10; L Jansen van Rensburg & MP Olivier 'International and supra-national law' in MP Olivier et al *Social security: A legal analysis* (2003) 619 632.
[126] Lindholt (n 125 above) 217; Jansen van Rensburg & Olivier (n 125 above) 634.
[127] Art 16, which guarantees the right to 'the best attainable state of mental and physical health', has been considered by the African Commission in Communications 25/89, 47/90, 56/91 & 100/93, *Free Legal Assistance Group & Others v Zaire* (2000) AHRLR 74 (ACHPR 1995) 19th Session of the African Commission, April 1996. In its decision, the Commission gave a generous interpretation to the right to health, holding that it places a duty on the government of Zaire to 'provide basic services such as safe drinking water and electricity', in addition to its basic obligation to supply adequate medicine.

and disabled to special measures of protection in keeping with their physical and moral needs.[128]

The African continent has a unique way of addressing social rights and in particular social security rights. The duties of the family and community are of paramount importance in the social protection of the most needy. This interdependence is reflected in the African Charter in the individual's obligation to maintain his or her parents in the event of need.[129] There is also an obligation on individuals to pay taxes in the interest of society.[130] Cobbah[131] describes the existence of the individual within the African community as follows:[132] 'I am because we are, and because we are, therefore I am.' This implies that the duty to provide social protection is not only that of the state alone, but also that of the individual as a member of society.

Such an approach was also amplified by the Constitutional Court in *Grootboom*,[133] in particular as far as the family context is concerned. The Court remarked that the primary responsibility to provide housing to children is that of the parents. Only when it is clear that the parents do not or cannot provide, may the state be called upon to provide support – as is the case with extremely vulnerable groups of our community who cannot afford any form of housing, in particular temporary shelter.[134]

4.2 The African Charter on the Rights and Welfare of the Child

The African Charter on the Rights and Welfare of the Child (African Children's Charter or Children's Charter)[135] addresses various contingencies of social security. Rights of the child which enjoy protection in terms of this document are the rights to survival, protection and development,[136] education,[137] health and health services[138] and the right not to be exploited economically.[139] The Children's Charter further contains a special provision regarding the social security rights of handicapped children.[140]

---

[128] Art 15 enshrines the right of every individual to work under equitable and satisfactory conditions, and declares that every worker shall receive equal pay for equal work. The Charter further assures the best attainable state of mental and physical health, and the obligation to take the necessary measures to protect the health of the people and to give medical attention to the sick.
[129] Art 29(1).
[130] Art 29(6).
[131] JAM Cobbah 'African values and the human rights debate: An African perspective' (1987) 9 *Human Rights Quarterly* 309 320.
[132] In the South African context this is known as the principle of *ubuntu*.
[133] n 23 above.
[134] n 23 above, para 77; Jansen van Rensburg & Olivier (n 125 above) 634.
[135] African Charter on the Rights and Welfare of the Child, 1990 OAU Doc CAB/LEG/ 24.9/49 (1990). (South Africa ratified the Convention on 7 January 2000.)
[136] Art 5.
[137] Art 11.
[138] Art 14.
[139] Art 15. See also Jansen van Rensburg & Olivier (n 125 above) 635.
[140] Art 13.

5 South African law

5.1 Introduction

The Constitution compels the state to ensure the 'progressive realisation' of social security. Section 27(1)(c) of the Constitution states that 'everyone has the right to have access to social security, including, if they are unable to support themselves and their dependants, appropriate social assistance'. Section 27(2) places an obligation on the state to ' ... take reasonable legislative and other measures, within its available resources, to achieve the progressive realisation of [this] right'. Section 28(1)(c) further grants every child the right to social services.

This right to access to social security is backed up by a host of other social security-related fundamental rights, such as the right to have access to health care services (section 27(1)(a)); the right to sufficient food and water (section 27(1)(b)); the right to adequate housing (section 26(1)); the right to education (section 29(1)); as well as the right of children to basic nutrition, shelter, basic health care services and social services (section 28(1)(c)). There are also other fundamental rights that evidently play a significant role in the context of South African social security, such as the right to equality (section 9),[141] the right to respect for and protection of everyone's inherent dignity (section 10),[142] the right to privacy (section 14), the right to property (section 25) and the right to administrative justice (section 33).[143] The state is obliged to respect, protect, promote and fulfil these fundamental rights[144] which, in the case of most of them, implies that it must incrementally give effect to them.[145]

---

[141] Section 9(3) prohibits direct or indirect unfair discrimination on a number of grounds, including race, gender, sex, pregnancy, marital status, ethnic or social origin, colour, sexual orientation, age, disability, religion, conscience, belief, culture, language and birth. For one way in which this prohibition can exert an influence in the field of social assistance, see *Khosa* (n 72 above) paras 40 & 44. In *Khosa*, the Court recognised that all rights are interdependent, mutually related and equally important and emphasised that this specific case concerned intersecting rights which reinforce one another at the point of intersection (para 40).

[142] See the discussion under subsec 4.3.2 - Underpinning values and aims of social security rights.

[143] The right to administrative action that is lawful, reasonable and procedurally fair, including the right to written reasons for decisions adversely affecting a person's rights.

[144] Sec 7(2).

[145] See secs 7(2) & 27(2) of the Constitution.

5.2 The constitutional scope of the right to social security

5.2.1 The wording of section 27(1)(c)

Section 27(1)(c) of the South African Constitution refers to the right to *have access to* social security and not purely to the 'right to social security'. The question must therefore be asked whether the term 'access to' can be interpreted as qualifying or indeed limiting the right to social security. Initially the distinction was understood as an attempt to avoid an interpretation that sections 26(2) and 27(2) create unqualified obligations on the state to guarantee the direct provision of social goods to everyone.[146] In *Grootboom*,[147] the Court reached a different conclusion, holding that the 'right to have access to housing' can be interpreted as broader than the 'right to housing'. The right does not only require the state to provide certain basic resources. It also imposes an obligation on the part of the state to create an infrastructure and the conditions to give an individual or group access to these facilities or services.

When the judgment of the court is made applicable to social security rights, the conclusion can be reached that 'access to' means more than a pure right to.[148] It suggests that the state will also have to provide, by way of legislative and other measures, that everyone has access to a range of measures aimed at the realisation of social security. An example is to create the necessary infrastructure and services in rural areas for the elderly poor to enable them to collect their old age grants.[149]

---

[146] D Davis *et al Fundamental rights in the Constitution – Commentary and cases* (1997) 345. See also B Majola 'A response to Craig Scott. A South African perspective' (1999) 1:4 *ESR Review* 6.

[147] Para 35: 'The right delineated in section 26(1) is a right of "access to adequate housing" as distinct from the right to adequate housing encapsulated in the Covenant. This difference is significant. It recognises that housing entails more than bricks and mortar. It requires available land, appropriate services such as the provision of water and the removal of sewage and the financing of all of these, including the building of the house itself.'

[148] This approach of the Court places a heavier burden on the resources of the state. It implies that the state will have to create effective policies to achieve the maximum output.

[149] An example of where currently in South Africa a basic resource (social assistance) is being provided by the state, but where the surrounding services necessary to facilitate access are lacking or inadequate, has to do with the Old Age Pension Grant. Beneficiaries of the Old Age Pension Grant wait for an average period of two hours at payout points before receiving their grants. However, 68% of payout points have no access to water, 64% have no toilet facilities and 79% have no facilities for persons with disabilities (SAHRC (n 45 above) 29).

5.2.2 Underpinning values and aims of social security rights

In various sections of the Constitution, reference is made to fundamental values that underpin the objectives and aims of the Constitution.[150] Courts, tribunals and forums are further compelled by the Constitution, when interpreting the Bill of Rights, to promote the values that underlie an open and democratic society based on human dignity, equality and freedom.[151] In *Grootboom*, the Court held:[152]

> There can be no doubt that human dignity, freedom and equality, the foundational values of our society, are denied those who have no food, clothing or shelter. Affording socio-economic rights to all people therefore enables them to enjoy the other rights enshrined in chapter 2. The realisation of these rights is also the key to the advancement of race and gender equality and the evolution of a society in which men and women are equally able to achieve their full potential.

The universal aim and basis for the existence of social security rights is to protect a person's right to human dignity.[153] Human dignity, thus, as a fundamental constitutional value[154] as well as a fundamental right[155] contained in the Bill of Rights, plays a very important role with regard to social security rights, and the equal treatment of those who are historically deprived.[156]

Without human dignity a person is excluded from society. A social security system aims to include an individual in society through measures or schemes implemented by the state and/or civil society to show solidarity towards such an individual.[157] A spin-off of such solidarity is the prevention of social exclusion - by way of social security measures a person can be placed in a position to fulfil his or her role in society with dignity.[158] The ILO[159] describes the importance of solidarity as follows:

> It is not possible to have social security, worthy of the name, without a consciousness of national solidarity and perhaps - tomorrow -

---

[150] Sec 1 of the Constitution states that the Republic of South Africa is one sovereign democratic state founded on the values of human dignity, the achievement of equality and advancement of human rights and freedoms, non-racialism and non-sexism. Sec 7(1) further states that the Bill of Rights is the cornerstone of democracy in South Africa. It enshrines the rights of all people in our country and affirms the democratic values of human dignity, equality and freedom.

[151] Sec 39(1)(a).

[152] n 23 above, para 23.

[153] R Ben-Israel 'Social security in the year 2000: Potentialities and problems' (1995) 16 *Comparative Labour Law Journal* 139 146; *Grootboom* (n 23 above) para 23.

[154] Secs 1 & 7(1) of the Constitution.

[155] Sec 10 of the Constitution reads as follows: 'Everyone has inherent dignity and the right to have their dignity respected and protected.'

[156] The South African courts have consistently stated that there is close correlation between the right to equality and the protection of a person's dignity: *Hoffmann v SA Airways* 2000 21 ILJ 2357 (CC); *Walters v Transitional Local Council of Port Elizabeth & Another* 2001 BCLR 98 (LC).

[157] Pieters (n 17 above) 7.

[158] J van Langendonck *Sociale zekerheid. Wat is dat eigenlijk?* ('Social security. What is that actually?') (1986) 1.

[159] International Labour Organisation *Into the twenty-first century: The development of social security* (1984) 115.

international solidarity. The effort of developing social security must therefore be accompanied by continuous effort to promote this crucial sense of shared responsibility.

For a variety of reasons, the consciousness of solidarity, which should support all our efforts towards social security, has tended to get weaker as the role of social security has widened.[160] In the development of a social security concept, a continuing effort must be made to promote this crucial sense of shared responsibility.[161] The aims of social security and social exclusion cannot be achieved if those who benefit from it do not play an active role in its development. It is essential for them to participate voluntarily in this process of change and to accept responsibility for the agencies created for them.[162]

Ubuntu[163] and nation building within the South African perspectives can contribute to a sense of shared responsibility. The White Paper for Social Welfare[164] describes the importance of *ubuntu* as follows:

> The principle of caring for each other's well-being will be promoted, and a spirit of mutual support fostered. Each individual's humanity is ideally expressed through his or her relationship with others and theirs in turn through a recognition of the individual's humanity. *Ubuntu* means that people are people through other people. It also acknowledges both the rights and the responsibilities of every citizen in promoting individual and societal well-being.

On this basis, it is clear that group solidarity is not a foreign principle within South African society. The respect for and promotion of the principle of *ubuntu* can guarantee the success of a comprehensive social security system. This in turn also emphasises the importance to be given to group protection in the fight against poverty and deprivation. In fact, upon analysing the Constitutional Court judgment in *Grootboom*, and comparing that judgment with the previous judgment in *Soobramoney*,[165] on the enforcement of socio-economic rights in the domain of social security, one is left with the clear impression that whenever the position of historically deprived and disadvantaged groups warrants judicial intervention, the courts will more readily come to assistance than in the case of an individual claiming assistance.

---

[160] International Labour Organisation (n 15 above) 6-7.
[161] International Labour Organisation (n 159 above).
[162] J Berghman *Basic concepts of social security in Europe* (1997) 8-9.
[163] Langa J describes *ubuntu* in *S v Makwanyane* 1995 3 SA 391 (CC), 1995 6 BCLR 665 (CC) para 224 as follows: 'The concept is of some relevance to the values we need to uphold. It is a culture which places some emphasis on communality and on the interdependence of the members of a community. It recognises a person's status as a human being, entitled to unconditional respect, dignity, value and acceptance from the members of the community such person happens to be part of. It also entails the converse, however. The person has a corresponding duty to give the same respect, dignity, value and acceptance to each member of that community. More importantly, it regulates the exercise of rights by the emphasis it lays on sharing and co-responsibility and the mutual enjoyment of rights by all.'
[164] n 2 above, ch 2 para 18.
[165] *Soobramoney v Minister of Health (KwaZulu-Natal)* 1997 12 BCLR 1696 (CC).

It can further be argued that the value of equality and the equality clause as contained in the Bill of Rights strive to repair the historical inequalities and injustices of the past. De Vos[166] remarks that the rights in the Bill of Rights are interrelated and mutually supportive.[167] He argues that there is a relationship between social and economic rights and the right to equality and that the transformative vision of the Constitution is one that is committed to remedying socio-economic inequality. The Court thus takes historical, socio-economic and political factors into account when giving content to socio-economic rights. The same assumption can be made with regard to the right to access to social security in particular. The conclusion can be made that the state cannot realise all socio-economic rights immediately, that the courts must keep this in mind, and that the material needs of those persons who are the most vulnerable ought to enjoy priority.

This approach is visible in the recent *Khosa* case, where the Court remarked:[168]

> There can be no doubt that the applicants are part of a *vulnerable group* in society and, in the circumstances of the present case, are worthy of constitutional protection. We are dealing, here, with *intentional, statutorily sanctioned unequal treatment* of part of the South African community. This has a strong stigmatising effect. Because both permanent residents and citizens contribute to the welfare system through the payment of taxes, the lack of congruence between benefits and burdens created by a law that denies benefits to permanent residents almost inevitably creates the impression that permanent residents are in some way inferior to citizens and less worthy of social assistance (our emphasis).

This exclusion is unfair, because permanent residents are cast to the margins of society and are deprived of exactly those rights, for example those recognised in section 27(1)(c), that may be essential for them to enjoy their other rights in the Constitution.[169]

---

[166] P de Vos '*Grootboom*, the right of access to housing and substantive equality as contextual fairness' (2001) 17 *South African Journal on Human Rights* 258-276.

[167] See also Jansen van Rensburg (n 42 above) 55-66. Leckie makes the following observation with regard to the interdependence, interrelatedness and mutual supportiveness of civil and political rights on the one hand and socio-economic rights on the other hand: 'Equality and non-discrimination form the basis of human rights law, and although generally associated with civil and political rights, these principles have always had pertinence to economic, social and cultural rights.' S Leckie 'Another step towards indivisibility: Identifying key features of violations of economic, social and cultural rights' (1998) 20 *Human Rights Quarterly* 81 104-105.

[168] *Khosa* (n 72 above) para 74.

[169] As above, para 77. See further para 81 where the Court remarked: 'The denial of access to social assistance is total, and for as long as it endures, permanent residents unable to sustain themselves or to secure meaningful support from other sources will be relegated to the margins of society and deprived of what may be essential to enable them to enjoy other rights vested in them under the Constitution. Denying permanent residents access to social security therefore affects them in a most fundamental way.'

5.2.3 The duty to respect, protect, promote and fulfil

Section 7(2) states that the state has a constitutionally entrenched duty to respect, protect, promote and fulfil the rights in the Bill of Rights and consequently the right to access to social security.[170] On a primary level, the duty to *respect* requires negative state action and the courts will only expect the state not to interfere unduly with a person's fundamental rights.[171] This is known as negative enforcement by the courts. The duty prohibits the state from acting in ways that undermine the rights. This can take the following forms:

- The state arbitrarily or unreasonably deprives people of the access that they enjoy to social security, for example by ceasing payment of a beneficiary's social security benefit/grant without justification.[172]
- A law or policy acts as a barrier which obstructs people from gaining access to social security, or children from enjoying social services, for example, if the state made the receipt of social security benefits subject to conditions which were impossible for beneficiaries to comply with.[173]

---

[170] P de Vos 'Pious wishes or directly enforceable human rights?: Social and economic rights in South Africa's 1996 Constitution' (1997) 13 *South African Journal on Human Rights* 67 78.

[171] As above, 83; *Grootboom* (n 23 above) para 34; *Minister of Health & Others v Treatment Action Campaign & Others* 2002 5 SA 72 (CC) para 46 (*TAC*).

[172] An example of this is the case of *Ngxuza & Others v The Permanent Secretary, Department of Welfare, Eastern Cape Provincial Government & Another* 2001 2 SA 609 (E). The appellants in this case approached the Court to reinstate the disability grants they had been receiving under secs 2(a) and 3(a) of the Social Assistance Act 59 of 1992, which the province had without notice to them wrongfully terminated. The Court ordered the province to concede the claims of the applicants, with payment of arrears and interest. See also *The Permanent Secretary, Department of Welfare, Eastern Cape Provincial Government & Another v Ngxuza & Others* 2001 4 SA 1184 (SCA). Another example is the case of *Maluleke v MEC, Health and Welfare, Northern Province* 1999 4 SA 367 (T), where the province had suspended payments of social pensions to some 92 000 people. The Court found the suspension of payments to be unlawful and invalid. In two other cases, that of *Mbanga v MEC, Health and Welfare, Eastern Cape & Another* 2002 1 SA 359 (SE) and *Mahambehlala v MEC, Health and Welfare, Eastern Cape & Another* 2002 1 SA 342 (SE), the provincial government failed to process claims for social grants within a reasonable time. Mr Mbanga applied for a pension grant on 8 March 1998 and met all the requirements, while Mrs Mahambehlala applied on 7 March 2000 for a disability grant, also meeting all the requirements. The Court held in both cases that the applicants' rights were infringed by the failure of the province to act within a reasonable time. The SAHRC (n 45 above) 28 also reported that Limpopo and the Eastern Cape were provinces where grant beneficiaries were most affected by arbitrary administrative action. In Limpopo, 92 000 welfare recipients of pension and disability grants were unfairly terminated by the province's welfare department. In the Eastern Cape, applications for social assistance were often lost without any trace and pensioners waited more than a year before they could receive financial assistance from government.

[173] For an example, see *Khosa* (n 72 above).

- A law or policy unfairly discriminates against certain groups (whether directly or indirectly) in providing access to social security, for example, if women or any other disadvantaged group were prohibited from applying for social security.[174]

On a secondary level, all fundamental rights require the state to *protect* citizens from political, economic and social interference with their stated rights.[175] It places a positive obligation on the state not to interfere in the political, civil, economic and cultural rights of its citizens. This obligation does not require the state to distribute money or resources to individuals, but requires a framework wherein individuals can realise these rights without undue influence from the state. The duty means that the state must provide effective legislative and common law remedies to protect people against violations of their rights by other individuals or groups in society. For example, the law should effectively prevent and prohibit unfair discrimination in the private insurance industry (medical aid schemes, life and disability insurance, etc) on the basis of race, gender, HIV/AIDS status, sexual orientation, etc.[176] The state should also ensure that private welfare organisations provide social services to children in a fair, non-discriminatory and effective manner, particularly where they are recipients of financial awards for these purposes.

At tertiary level, section 7(2) requires that the state *promote and fulfil* everyone's rights.[177] The beneficiary has the right to require positive assistance, or a benefit or service from the state. The nature and scope of these obligations placed on the state will depend on the exact wording or phrasing of the fundamental right.

Section 27(2) qualifies the positive obligation of the state to realise the right to have access to social security.[178] The state's obligation is delimited in three ways: The obligation is (a) to take 'reasonable legislative and other measures'; (b) 'to achieve the progressive realisation' of the right; and (c) 'within [the state's] available resources'.[179] Almost the same formulation is found in article 2(1) of CESCR.[180] In *Grootboom*,[181] the Court interpreted the meaning of

---

[174] The exclusion of individuals (and in particular children as a vulnerable group in society) on the basis of age can be used as an example in this case. The question may be asked whether the exclusion of children from the ages of (currently) 11 to 18 from the Child Support Grant infringes on their rights to social assistance (sec 27(1)(c)), human dignity (sec 10), life (sec 11) and equality (sec 9). See also *Khosa* (n 72 above).
[175] De Vos (n 166 above) 83.
[176] In terms of the Medical Schemes Act 131 of 1998, medical schemes may, as a rule, no longer refuse membership or differentiate between members of a scheme on the basis of age and medical history. Certain core medical services have to be covered by these schemes.
[177] De Vos (n 170 above) 86.
[178] As stated in *TAC* (n 171 above) para 32 with regard to sec 27(2), referring to *Grootboom* (n 23 above) para 21. In *TAC*, the Court expressly stated that sec 27(1) is not a self-standing right independent of sec 27(2) (para 28). These two subsections are textually linked. This was also confirmed in *Khosa* (n 72 above) para 43.
[179] *Grootboom* (n 23 above) para 38; J de Waal *et al The Bill of Rights handbook* (2002) 438.
[180] See sec 2.2.1 above.
[181] *Grootboom* (n 23 above) & *TAC* (n 171 above).

these different provisions in sections 26(2) and 27(2) and the manner in which the courts are prepared to enforce socio-economic rights.[182]

Reasonable legislative and other measures

In terms of article 2(1) of CESCR, each state has a duty to realise the rights in the Covenant to the 'maximum of their available resources'. The Committee on ESCR has said that, if the state is a developing country or is experiencing some economic difficulties, it must at least realise the minimum core obligations. The Committee on ESCR makes the following statement with regard to minimum core obligations:[183]

> The Committee is of the view that a minimum core obligation to ensure the satisfaction of, at the very least, minimum essential levels of each of the rights is incumbent upon every State Party.

The Committee further states that '[i]f the Covenant were to be read in such a way as to not establish such a minimum core obligation, it would largely be deprived of its *raison d'être*'. Failure by the state to provide for the basic subsistence needs of the population may be considered a *prima facie* violation of the Covenant.[184]

However, the Court in *Grootboom*[185] deviated from the international approach and stated that the real question in terms of the South African Constitution is whether the measures taken by the state to realise social rights are reasonable. Minimum core may be relevant when the Court considers reasonableness under section 27(2).[186] In *Grootboom*, the Court then went further and interpreted the relevant limitation by considering reasonableness. First of all, the Court stated that it would not enquire whether other more desirable or favourable measures could have been adopted, or whether public money could have been better spent.[187] When this is applied to the right of access to social security, it means that the Court will not enquire if the current social security system is appropriate for South Africa or ask if better measures should be put in place. For example, the Court will not replace the new Child Support Grant and reinforce the old Child Maintenance Grant or create new contingencies or branches of social security that currently do not exist.

The question would be whether the measures that have been adopted are reasonable. It is necessary to recognise that a wide range of possible measures could be adopted by the state to meet its obligations. Many of these would meet the requirement of reasonableness. Once it is shown that the measures do so, this

---

[182] This case raises the state's obligations under sec 26 of the Constitution, which gives everyone the right of access to adequate housing. Secs 26(2) & 27(2) have similar wording. Therefore the judgment of the Court will also be applicable to the interpretation of sec 27(2).
[183] General Comment No 3 *The nature of states parties' obligations (art 2, para 1 of the Covenant)* (5th session, 1990) [UN Doc E/1991/23] para 10.
[184] As above.
[185] *Grootboom* (n 23 above) para 33; *TAC* (n 171 above) para 34.
[186] *TAC* (n 171 above) para 34.
[187] *Grootboom* (n 23 above) para 41.

requirement is met.[188] Again, if applied to social security, this means that the Court will look at the social security system as a whole and the different measures to address the state's obligation. For example, is there a safety net for the most needy in society by way of social assistance measures? In our opinion the answer will be negative. Permanent social assistance grants in South Africa are highly categorised and only cover children from infancy to 14 years (Child Support Grant),[189] children in foster care (Foster Child Grant),[190] people with disabilities (Disability Grant),[191] children with disabilities (Care Dependency Grant),[192] the elderly (Old Age Grant).[193] In addition to the Old Age and Disability Grant, one can apply for a Grant-in-Aid.[194] This entire grant system is subject to a strict means test under the Social Assistance Act 59 of 1992.[195]

No provision is made by way of the permanent social assistance grant process for people without disabilities from the age of 14 to 60 or 65 (depending on gender). This implies that a large section of the population is still excluded from the social security programme which serves as the main safety net in South Africa, if one is not contributing to the Unemployment Fund or the Compensation for Occupational Sickness and Diseases Fund (Social Insurance) or to any private scheme. The only exception to the above is the temporary financial award an individual can apply for, called the Social Relief of Distress, aimed at being temporary financial material assistance, issued to people who are unable to meet their family's most basic needs.[196] Social Relief of Distress is defined as a means of alleviating the need of persons by means of the temporary rendering of material assistance

---

[188] As above.

[189] Sec 4(1) of the Social Assistance Act as amended by the Welfare Laws Amendment Act. The value of the Child Support Grant is currently R170. GN 409 in *Government Gazette* 26197 of 26/03/2004.

[190] Sec 4A(b) of the Social Assistance Act as amended by the Welfare Laws Amendment Act. The value of the Foster Child Grant currently amounts to R530. GN 409 in *Government Gazette* 26197 of 26/03/2004.

[191] Sec 3(a) of the Social Assistance Act as amended by the Welfare Laws Amendment Act. The value of grant is R740 available to women over 18 to 59 years and men over 18 to 64 years. GN 409 in *Government Gazette* 26197 of 26/03/2004.

[192] Sec 4B of the Social Assistance Act as amended by the Welfare Laws Amendment Act. The amount of the grant is R740 per month per child. GN 409 in *Government Gazette* 26197 of 26/03/2004.

[193] Sec 3(a) of the Social Assistance Act as amended by the Welfare Laws Amendment Act. The value of the grant is R740 available for women from 60 and men from 65 years. GN 409 in *Government Gazette* 26197 of 26/03/2004.

[194] Available for people who require full-time assistance by another person owing to his or her mental or physical disabilities who is not in care of an institution. The grant is R160. GN 409 in *Government Gazette* 26197 of 26/03/2004.

[195] See also http://www.welfare.gov.za/Documents/2003/Social%20Assistance/man.htm (accessed 30 June 2004). SAHRC (n 45 above) 27-28 reported that eligible beneficiaries of grants, eg the Child Support Grant, especially those in rural areas, found it difficult to access grants due to documentation requirements, such as identity documents and birth certificates and the minimal collaboration between the Department of Social Development and the Department of Home Affairs.

[196] Sec 5(2) of the Social Assistance Act 59 of 1992 as amended by sec 3 of the Welfare Laws Amendment Act 106 of 1997. Sec 5(2) of the Social Assistance Act reads as follows: 'The Director-General may, subject to the provisions of this Act, make a financial award to a person if he or she is satisfied that such person is in need of social relief of distress.'

to them. It is therefore intended for persons in such dire material need that they are unable to meet their or their family's most basic needs. It is designed to help persons and families over the crisis period.[197]

The Court in *Grootboom* remarked that:[198]

> Those whose needs are the most urgent and whose ability to enjoy all rights therefore is most in peril, must not be ignored by the measures aimed at achieving realisation of the right. It may not be sufficient to meet the test of reasonableness to show that the measures are capable of achieving a statistical advance in the realisation of the right.

From this it follows that regard must be given to historical disadvantage and particularly vulnerable groups and that they may not be neglected.[199] The social relief of distress award is highly questionable. It is submitted that this award does not address the material needs of those persons who are the most vulnerable and in desperate need of relief. Applying for social relief of distress is subject to a strict qualifying process, which requires, for example, that the applicant is not receiving assistance from any other organisation; that the applicant must not be awaiting permanent aid; that the applicant has not been affected by a disaster, and the area of the community in which he or she lives has not been declared a disaster area. The Department of Social Development further stresses that the rendering of Social Relief of Distress should not be seen as the sole responsibility of the state. Persons in need should, where possible, in the first instance be referred to churches, religious associations or welfare organisations.[200]

It could thus be argued that the more or less total exclusion of certain categories of the indigent population from the safety net of the permanent grant administration process renders the social security system of our country unreasonable. The principle behind this argument was illustrated in *Khosa*, where permanent residents were excluded from obtaining the Old Age, Child Support and Care Dependency Grants because of their non-citizenship.[201] The Court remarked that, when dealing with the issue of reasonableness, context is all-important. In considering whether the exclusion of permanent residents from the social security scheme is *reasonable*, the Court took the following factors into consideration: the purpose served by social security, the impact of the exclusion on permanent residents and the relevance of the citizenship requirement to that purpose. It is further necessary to have regard to the impact that this has on other intersecting rights. Where the right to social assistance is conferred by the Constitution on 'everyone' and permanent

---

[197] See http://www.welfare.gov.za/Documents/2003/Social%20Assistance/PDF Chap13.pdf (accessed 30 June 2004).
[198] *Grootboom* (n 23 above) para 44.
[199] It is thus commendable that the current system provides for the Child Support Grant, the Foster Child Grant, the Disability Grant, the Care Dependency Grant, the Old Age Grant and the Grant-in-Aid because these are all people who fall into vulnerable groups.
[200] n 197 above.
[201] *Khosa* (n 72 above).

residents are denied access to this right, the equality rights entrenched in section 9 are directly implicated.[202]

The Court referred to the stringent means test prescribed to comply with social grants and the fact that grants are made to those in need, especially targeting the *vulnerable*. The Court further referred to the testimony of the Director-General of the Department of Social Development who described the object of the social assistance legislation as a strategy to combat poverty, to realise the objectives of the Constitution and the Reconstruction and Development Plan and to comply with South Africa's international obligations.[203] The Court remarked that the aim of social security, and especially social assistance, is to ensure that society values human beings by providing them with their basic needs.[204] The Court came to the conclusion that to exclude permanent residents from the social assistance scheme because of the fact that they lack the citizenship requirement is not reasonable as set out in section 27(2) of the Constitution.[205] Excluding permanent residents limits their rights and fundamentally affects their dignity and equality.[206]

One way in which to rectify the exclusion of a large number of indigent South Africans from the social security net referred to above, would be to pay heed to the proposals made by the Taylor Commission[207] for a comprehensive social protection package, including a Basic Income Grant (BIG), income-generating opportunities and free basic services to those in need.[208]

---

[202] n 201 above, para 49.
[203] n 201 above, para 51.
[204] n 201 above, para 52.
[205] n 201 above, para 83.
[206] n 201 above, para 84.
[207] Department of Social Development (n 5 above) 42-43.
[208] In a recent newspaper article by M Merten ('Big could bust poverty' *Mail and Guardian* (13-06-2003) 37), reference was made to a case study done by the Programme for Land and Agrarian Studies at the University of the Western Cape. According to research among malnourished youngsters admitted to hospital, only four of the 54 children who qualified for the Child Support Grant in Mount Frere in the Eastern Cape received their grants and none of the 17 caregivers eligible for foster care received the grants. A senior researcher told the parliamentary committee that is currently reviewing the proposals made by the Taylor Commission that 'the worse off you were, the less likely you were actually to receive grants ... The existing allocation of grant is arbitrary.' It was also argued that the Basic Income Grant proposed by the Committee would dramatically reduce poverty, if and as long as administrative obstacles to the efficient implementation of the grant is resolved. The government has been extremely sceptical of the Basic Income Grant. It perceives the grant as dependency (hand-out) that would be created by government. According to the research done by the Programme for Land and Agrarian Studies, 'the Basic Income Grant would dramatically reduce poverty among the bottom third of households, lifting them into a situation where economic activity or subsistence farming was possible'. The statistics indicated that the poorest third of households in Mount Frere live on R32 per person or R234 a household a month. Income would rise to R974 a household with a universal Basic Income Grant for each household.

The Court in *Grootboom* stressed further that the policies and programmes must be reasonable both in their conception and their implementation.[209] This implies that the social security system must reach the people. In the cases of *Mbanga v MEC, Health and Welfare, Eastern Cape and Another*[210] and *Mahambehlala v MEC, Health and Welfare, Eastern Cape and Another*,[211] the provincial government failed to process claims for social grants within a reasonable time.[212] The Court held in both cases that the applicants' rights were infringed by the failure of the province to act within a reasonable time. This may be seen as a failure of the government to implement social security programmes.

Progressive realisation

The Committee on ESCR summarises the provision relating to the requirement of 'progressive realisation' of socio-economic rights as follows:[213]

> ... the phrase must be read in the light of the overall objective, indeed the *raison d'être*, of the Covenant, which is to establish clear obligations for States parties in respect of the full realisation of the rights in question. It thus imposes an obligation to move as expeditiously and effectively as possible towards that goal.

The Committee further mentions that:[214]

> Any deliberately retrogressive measures ... would require the most careful consideration and would need to be fully justified by reference to the totality of the rights provided for in the Covenant and in the context of the full use of the maximum available resources.

The Committee further stated that the ultimate objective of the Covenant is the 'full realisation' of the rights.[215] The fact that the 'full realisation' is subject to the condition of progressiveness is a recognition of the fact that the full realisation of all socio-economic rights will generally not be able to be achieved in a short period of time.[216]

In *Grootboom*,[217] the Court used the interpretation of the Committee on ESCR on the meaning of the phrase 'progressive realisation'. The Court stated that 'progressive realisation' shows that it was contemplated that the right could not be realised immediately, but that the goal of the Constitution is that the basic needs of all in our society be met effectively and the requirement of progressive realisation implies that the state must take steps to achieve this goal. When this statement of the Court is applied to the

---

[209] *Grootboom* (n 23 above) para 42.
[210] n 172 above.
[211] As above.
[212] See in general the discussion in n 172 above.
[213] General Comment No 3 (n 183 above) para 9.
[214] As above.
[215] MCR Craven *The International Covenant on Economic, Social and Cultural Rights: A perspective on its development* (1998) 128.
[216] n 215 above, 115; Maastricht Guidelines (n 120 above) guideline 8.
[217] *Grootboom* (n 23 above) para 45.

right to have access to social security, a twofold question arises. In the first place, what steps does the state take to keep the current social security system on track with inflation and the needs of the people receiving the benefits thereof? Secondly, what steps does the state take to broaden the current system to include a larger segment of the population and to address new and urgent contingencies?

With reference to the first question, it is encouraging to see that the state has increased the amounts of the permanent social assistance grants.[218] The age limit for the Child Support Grant is also currently being extended over a period from seven to 14.[219] Domestic workers[220] have also been included in the Unemployment Insurance Fund.[221] The inclusion of permanent residents in the social assistance system pursuant to *Khosa*[222] may also be seen as a positive step.

With reference to the second question, as already noted, permanent social assistance grants in South Africa are highly categorised. No provision is made by way of the permanent social assistance grant process for people without disabilities from the age of 14 to 60 or 65 (depending on gender). This implies that a large section of the population is still excluded from the social assistance programme which serves as the main safety net in South Africa, if one is not contributing to the Unemployment Fund or The Compensation for Occupational Sickness and Diseases Fund, or to any private scheme. Urgent contingencies such as financial support for children orphaned by HIV/AIDS, and especially those living in child-headed households, are not being addressed by the state.[223]

It can be argued that the state fails to meet the requirement of progressive realisation if it fails in the future to develop a more comprehensive and less categorised system of social security for South Africa, which would include indigent people without disabilities from the age of 15 to 60 or 65.

---

[218] However, it must be stressed that the Child Support Grant, eg, can be regarded as adequate only if it enables the primary caregiver to at least feed, clothe, shelter and acquire basic medicine for the child. It is highly questionable whether the present value of the grant is able to achieve this. The small benefit level of the grant does not appear to be linked to the needs of poor children and the cost of their support.

[219] Government is in the process of extending the Child Support Grant in phases to children under the age of 14 years over a period of three years. During the first phase, which lasted from 1 April 2003 to 31 March 2004, primary caregivers of children under the age of nine could apply for the grant. The second phase, from 1 April 2004 to 31 March 2005, currently allows primary caregivers of children under the age of 11 to apply. The final phase will extend from 1 April 2005 to 31 March 2006. Primary caregivers of children under the age of 14 will be able to apply for the Child Support Grant during this period. See R460 in *Government Gazette* 24630 of 31/03/2003.

[220] See n 61 above.

[221] Part of the social insurance system in South Africa.

[222] *Khosa* (n 72 above).

[223] See para 2.1.2 above. See also SAHRC (n 45 above) 28.

Within available resources

The Court in *Grootboom*[224] referred to the judgment in the case of *Soobramoney v Minister of Health (KwaZulu-Natal)*.[225] In *Soobramoney*, the meaning of the phrase 'available resources' was interpreted as follows:[226]

> What is apparent from these provisions is that the obligations imposed on the state by sections 26 and 27 in regard to access to housing, health care, food, water and social security are dependent upon the resources available for such purposes, and that the corresponding rights themselves are limited by reason of the lack of resources. Given this lack of resources and the significant demands on them that have already been referred to, an unqualified obligation to meet these needs would not presently be capable of being fulfilled.

In *Grootboom*,[227] the Court stressed that there is a balance between goal and means. The measures must be calculated to attain the goal expeditiously and effectively, but the availability of resources is an important factor in determining what is reasonable. The conclusion can thus be reached that the availability of resources is but one of the factors that have to be considered when determining whether there was an infringement of a right.[228] Another factor to be considered is the requirement of the Committee on ESCR that failure by the state to provide for the basic subsistence needs of the population may be considered a *prima facie* violation of the right to have access to social security.[229]

From the viewpoint that South Africa is currently (seemingly) in the process of ratifying CESCR, it is essential that the South African government should commence identifying minimum core content obligations for unique South African circumstances.

Regarding the argument about the availability of resources, the respondents in *Khosa* argued that the inclusion of permanent residents in the social grant system would impose an impermissibly high financial burden on the state.[230] The respondents indicated a progressive trend in government expenditure on social security. For example, in the last three years, the spending on social grants (including administrative cost) increased from R16,1 billion to R26,2 billion and a further increase to R44,6 billion is estimated in the following three years.[231] The respondents further estimated that there are about 260 000 permanent residents residing in the country. The respondents failed to furnish the court with statistical evidence

---

[224] *Grootboom* (n 23 above) para 46.
[225] *Soobramoney* (n 165 above).
[226] n 225 above, para 11.
[227] *Grootboom* (n 23 above) para 46.
[228] The National Department of Social Development reported to the SAHRC that even though there was no over- or underspending in 2000/2002, the budget allocation for the reporting period was not adequate to enable the Department to implement all its programmes and projects effectively. SAHRC (n 45 above) 28.
[229] General Comment No 3 (n 183 above) para 10.
[230] *Khosa* (n 72 above) paras 19 & 60.
[231] n 230 above, para 60.

on the number of permanent residents that might be eligible for social grants if the citizenship requirement is removed.[232]

In the absence of providing clear evidence of the additional cost in providing social grants to permanent residents, the respondents made some assumptions about the groups and numbers of eligible permanent residents, and came to the conclusion that this inclusion would additionally cost the state R243 million to R672 million per annum. The Court, taking the above numbers into account, came to the conclusion that the cost of including permanent residents in the system will only be a small portion of the cost compared with the whole budget spent on social grants.[233]

Another reason given by the respondents for excluding permanent residents from the social security scheme was the promotion of the immigration policy of the state, which seeks to exclude persons who may become a burden on the state and thereby to encourage self-sufficiency among foreign nationals.[234] The Court acknowledged that limiting the cost of the social welfare budget and excluding people who may become a burden on the state is permissible as long as it is done within the boundaries set by the rights and values in the Constitution.[235] The Court argued that through careful immigration policies, the state could ensure that those people who are admitted will not be a burden on it. The Court noted that in this particular case it is concerned with the aged and children,[236] and that they are unlikely to be able to provide for themselves and that the self-sufficiency argument does not hold up in this case.[237]

The Court held:[238]

> In my view the importance of providing access to social assistance to all who live permanently in South Africa and the impact upon life and dignity that a denial of such access has, far outweighs the financial and immigration considerations on which the state relies.

6 Conclusion

The importance of a comprehensive social security (protection) system for South Africa cannot be overemphasised. The Constitutional Court has recognised in *Grootboom*[239] that if the state had better social assistance programmes available for the poor, there would be less pressure on the other socio-economic rights. This includes, for example, that the state must, by means of a social assistance

---

[232] n 230 above, para 61.
[233] n 230 above, para 62.
[234] n 230 above, para 63.
[235] n 230 above, para 64.
[236] With respect to the Court, in the case of children it could be expected that their parents must be self-sufficient because it is the parents as primary care givers that are unable to support their children and as a consequence of that would apply for Child Support Grants.
[237] *Khosa* (n 72 above) para 65.
[238] n 237 above, para 82.
[239] Grootboom (n 23 above) para 30.

programme for children and parents who are unable to provide for themselves, assist them by means of, for example, child support grants.[240]

The idea of the Taylor Commission[241] of focusing on social protection as a means of implementing social security seems to be productive and in line with the evolution of international law standards. The social protection package gives to the courts and to policy makers a wider range of possible strategies aimed at promoting human dignity.[242]

In line with the views of the Taylor Commission, the South African Human Rights Commission also recommends the implementation of a Basic Income Grant:[243]

> It is recommended that the state introduce the BIG or any other measure, which will enable the poorest of the poor who are excluded from social security and social assistance to escape poverty and have some form of income. This income to households will enable everyone to meet basic subsistence needs and ... to live in accordance with human dignity.

The Basic Income Grant sets out that a sum of R100 per month be paid to everyone in the country, including children who are not in receipt of another grant like the Child Support Grant. The grant would thus be universal and avoid the costs and administrative burden associated with means testing. The grant would be retrieved from the tax system from middle-income earners and higher-income earners.[244]

South Africa has a high rate of poverty and inequality. Most South Africans live in poverty-stricken areas and do not have access to basic social services and social assistance. Poverty is one of the most serious challenges facing South Africa and this, to a large extent, was caused by past discriminatory and racial policies. The low wages earned by those employed deprive them of a decent standard of living in the midst of rampant unemployment. It is against this background that the Basic Income Grant was proposed as a measure to reduce poverty and afford human beings a decent standard of living.

---

[240] n 239 above, para 78.
[241] Department of Social Development (n 5 above) 41.
[242] Otherwise, we trap social security in a European debate (inclusion/exclusion of a specific scheme). It is not to say that some measures are not pure social insurance schemes and should not be looked at as such. But those measures are becoming the privilege of a working elite, notwithstanding the efforts of ILO to promote inclusive standards (part-time, migrants, homework, etc).
[243] SAHRC (n 45 above) 229.
[244] It has been argued that the Basic Income Grant proposed by the Taylor Commission would dramatically reduce poverty, if and as long as administrative obstacles to the efficient implementation of the grant are resolved. Compare n 208 above.

Eight / Environmental rights

Loretta A Feris
Dire Tladi

1   Introduction

Over the last two or three decades, the protection of the environment has become increasingly topical. Issues such as global warming, ozone depletion and biodiversity have dominated the international debate. In South Africa, public interest in the subject matter is reflected by, *inter alia*, concern with the health effects of pollution,[1] domestic consequences of threats to biodiversity and global warming. One report has estimated that two-thirds of all the species in the Kruger National Park could disappear within 48 years and that high-risk malaria areas in South Africa could double as a result of global warming.[2]

In this chapter, we focus on environmental rights. Our primary concern is the content of these rights. However, the question of content assumes the existence of rights. Unfortunately, the existence of environmental rights is not a foregone conclusion. Consequently, our discussion will contain references to the debate on the existence of environmental rights.[3]

We have organised our discussion into three main sections. First, we discuss environmental rights under the international system. Second, we briefly look at the regional systems and the protection they afford to environmental rights. Third, we look at the protection afforded to environmental rights under the South African Constitution.

---

[1]   In January 2003, for instance, it was reported that diesel fumes affected residents of a block of flats south of Durban after waste water from the Engen refinery flowed into the Stanvac canal in Merebank, Durban. The report is available at http://www.sabcnews.com/politics/the_provinces/ 0,1009,50849,00.html (accessed 28 May 2003).
[2]   B Jordan 'Most of our animals face extinction' *Sunday Times* (2002-06-30) 5.
[3]   A full discussion of this aspect in this chapter is neither possible nor useful. For contributions on the debate see JD van der Vyver 'The criminalisation and prosecution of environmental malpractice in international law' (1998) 23 *South African Yearbook of International Law* 23 *et seq*; G Handl 'Human rights and the protection of the environment: A mildly "revisionist" view' in AC Trindade (ed) *Human rights, sustainable development and the environment* (1992). See also generally the essays in AE Boyle & MR Anderson (eds) *Human rights approaches to environmental protection* (1996).

2 Conceptual debates on human rights and the environment

The issue of legal recognition of environmental rights is perhaps most complicated under the international system. First, does international law recognise environmental rights? Second, if such rights are recognised, in what form are they recognised? In other words, is there a general right to the environment or are environmental rights recognised merely as derivative of other existing rights? The third question involves the beneficiaries of the rights. Are environmental rights individual rights or group rights? Are future generations also beneficiaries of environmental rights? Even more difficult: Are the rights reserved exclusively for humans or are other species also entitled to the rights?

We do not propose to give a comprehensive and detailed analysis of all these issues, nor do we attempt to give final answers to the questions. All that we attempt to do is to provide an overview of the various debates and in the process to sketch a landscape of environmental rights under international law.

There are three main human rights approaches to the environment that one can take.[4] The first approach sees a right to the environment as a right in and of itself. This right may be an individual right, a group right, or both. It may benefit the present generation or future generations, or both. This approach, recognising a distinct right to the environment, is represented in the Proposed Legal Principles for Environmental Protection and Sustainable Development, adopted by the World Commission on Environment and Development (WCED) Experts Group on Environmental Law, which provides in Principle 1 that all human beings 'have the fundamental right to an environment adequate for their health and well-being'.[5] Similarly, Principle 2 of the Draft Principles on Human Rights and the Environment, adopted by the United Nations Commission on Human Rights, provides that all persons 'have the right to a secure, healthy and ecologically sound environment'.[6]

---

[4] See Van der Vyver (n 3 above) 8 *et seq.*
[5] See Proposed Legal Principles for Environmental Protection and Sustainable Development adopted by the WCED Experts Group on Environmental Law, reproduced in WCED *Our common future* (1987) 348. See also Principle 1, Draft Principles on Human Rights and the Environment in UN Sub-Commission on Prevention of Discrimination and Protection of Minorities *Human rights and the environment*, Final Report of the Special Rapporteur, UN Doc E/CN.4/Sub 2/1994 19.
[6] As above.

However, this first approach, apart from in the document referred to above, does not find much support under international law. A second approach does not recognise specific environmental rights, but sees a potential for protecting the environment under already existing and recognised rights, such as the rights to life, health, and dignity. This approach involves the reinterpretation of existing rights to give effect to environmental protection. It could be argued convincingly, for example, that the Koko incident[7] amounted to a violation of the right to health.[8] An example of such an approach to human rights and the environment is found in Principle 1 of the Declaration of the United Nations Conference on the Human Environment (Stockholm Declaration), which provides that humans have 'the fundamental right to freedom ... in an environment of a quality that permits a life of dignity'.[9] This is also the approach supported by the European Court of Human Rights.[10]

A third approach involves the use of procedural rights, such as access to information.[11] Indeed, these procedural rights have been said to be the key to environmental rights.[12] The idea is that if principles of democratic governance such as openness, accountability and civic participation are adhered to, then environmental standards will be maintained, or at least improved.

There appears to be reluctance on the part of some environmentalists to accept human rights approaches.[13] This

---

[7] The Koko incident involved the illegal dumping of hazardous wastes in Koko, Nigeria. It was one of the incidents that contributed to the rise in international prominence of the problem of hazardous waste trade. For a full discussion, see SF Liu 'The Koko incident: Developing international norms for the transboundary movement of hazardous wastes' (1992) *Journal of Natural Resources and Environmental Law* 121. For a brief discussion, see D Tladi 'The quest to ban hazardous wastes import into Africa: First Bamako and now Basel' (2000) 33 *Comparative and International Law Journal of Southern Africa* 210.

[8] In fact, the OAU ministers regarded the dumping of hazardous wastes from developed nations in Africa as a human rights abuse, terming it 'a crime against Africa and the African people'. See OAU Council of Ministers' Resolution on Dumping of Nuclear and Industrial Waste in Africa (1988), reproduced in C Heyns *Human rights law in Africa* (2004) 342; also reprinted in (1989) 28 *International Legal Materials* 568.

[9] n 4 above. See also the opinion of Weeramantry J in the *Case Concerning the Gabcikovo-Nagymaros Project (Hungary v Slovakia)* (1998) 37 *International Legal Materials* 162 206, where the judge recognised that the protection of the environment is a '*sine qua non* for numerous human rights'.

[10] See eg *López Ostra v Spain* (1995) ECHR Ser A 303-C.

[11] For a discussion, see A Eide *et al* (eds) *Economic, social and cultural rights: A textbook* (1995) 261 *et seq*. The authors discuss Communication 429/1990, *EW & Others v The Netherlands* as an example of how this may be achieved. See also in the South African context *Van Huyssteen NO v Minister of Environmental Affairs and Tourism* 1995 9 BCLR 1191 (C) where the court held that opponents to a proposed development had both *locus standi* and the right to access to information.

[12] Eide *et al* (n 11 above) 262, citing the 1990 European Community Directive on the Freedom of Access to Information on the Environment (90/313/EEC). See for further support Boyle & Anderson (n 3 above); S Douglas-Scott 'Environmental rights in the European Union: Participatory democracy or democratic deficit?' in Boyle & Anderson (n 3 above); J Cameron & R Mackenzie 'Access to environmental justice and procedural rights in international institutions' in Boyle & Anderson (n 3 above).

[13] See eg Handl (n 3 above); see also A d'Amato 'Do we owe a duty to future generations to preserve the global environment?' (1990) 84 *American Journal of International Law* 190; A d'Amato & SK Chopra 'Whales: Their emerging right to life' (1991) 85 *American Journal of International Law* 21; A Gillespie *International environmental law, policy and ethics* (1997).

scepticism can largely be explained with reference to the debate between ecocentric and anthropocentric approaches to the environment. Ecocentrists reject anthropocentrism (and by necessity any human rights approach) as flawed, because under such approaches the environment is protected, not because it has intrinsic value, but only for the sake of man.[14]

It can be argued that by embracing the concept of sustainable development, which is of necessity an anthropocentric concept, the international community has accepted anthropocentrism.[15] Moreover, according to Sands, the emergence of a body of rules of international law in the field of sustainable development represents an intersection of international environmental law, international economic law and international human rights law.[16] It is therefore helpful to look at the concept of sustainable development in international law.

Sustainable development is a relatively recent concept in international law discourse. While it is often thought that the Brundtland Commission coined this term in 1987,[17] there are indications that it appeared earlier than that.[18] The relationship between sustainable development and environmental rights is generally accepted. In the separate opinion of Weeramantry J in the *Gabcikovo case*,[19] sustainable development was defined as a right to development, which is limited by the need to preserve the environment.[20]

From the international instruments on sustainable development, one can deduce several elements of sustainable development. These are the principle of intergenerational equity, the principle of intragenerational equity and the principle of integration.

---

[14] For a detailed discussion of this debate, see D Tladi 'Of course for humans: A contextual defence of intergenerational equity' (2002) 9 *South African Journal of Environmental Law and Policy* 177. See also D Tladi 'Strong sustainability, weak sustainability, intergenerational equity and international law: Using the Earth Charter to redirect the environmental ethics debate' (2003) 28 *South African Yearbook of International Law* 200.

[15] The concept of sustainable development is central to modern international environmental law, having been at the centre of three United Nations conferences and permeating nearly all modern international environmental law instruments.

[16] P Sands 'International law in the field of sustainable development: Emerging legal principles' in W Lang (ed) *Sustainable development and international law* (1995) 53.

[17] WCED (n 5 above).

[18] Eg in 1980 the IUCN, UNEP and WWF published the World Conservation Strategy which contains several references to sustainable development. The introduction (sec 1) is titled 'Living resource conservation for sustainable development'. Similarly, para 10 of sec 1 provides that 'conservation and sustainable development are mutually dependant'.

[19] n 9 above.

[20] n 9 above, 206.

The principle of *intergenerational equity*, which has been made famous by Edith Brown Weiss, provides that the present generation owes a duty to future generations to preserve the environment.[21] Weiss argues that each generation receives a natural and cultural legacy in trust from previous generations and that there is an obligation on each generation to conserve the natural and cultural resource base for future generations.[22] This legacy imposes a set of planetary obligations upon members of each generation and also gives them planetary rights.[23] Support for the principle of intergenerational equity can be found in several modern international instruments for the protection of the environment. These include both binding[24] and non-binding instruments.[25]

The principle of intergenerational equity, which Weiss argues is an *obligatio erga omnes*,[26] has two implications for environmental rights discourse. In the first place, it implies that the future generations have a right to a clean environment. The idea that future generations (as a group) have rights against the present generation for a healthy environment is subject to procedural criticisms regarding standing. Since future generations do not have legal standing, the question that may be asked is, how would future generations claim their planetary rights? One argument can possibly be that it is in the interest of present generations to manage the environment in a sustainable manner – thereby also giving regard to the rights of future generations. However, Weiss goes further and advocates the

---

[21] See EB Weiss 'In fairness to future generations: International law, common patrimony and intergenerational equity' in P Hayden (ed) *The philosophy of human rights* (2001) 618. See also generally EB Weiss 'The planetary trust: Conservation and intergenerational equity' (1984) *Ecology Law Quarterly* 495; EB Weiss 'Our rights and obligations to future generations for the environment' (1990) 84 *American Journal of International Law* 198; L Gundling 'Our responsibility to future generations' (1990) 84 *American Journal of International Law* 207. See also the judgment in *Minors Oposa v Secretary of Department of Environment and Natural Resources* of Davide J in the Supreme Court of Philippines (reproduced in (1994) 83 *International Legal Materials* 173) in which the Court granted the petitioners' claim to a right to a balanced ecology, not only for themselves, but also for future Filipinos.
[22] Weiss (1989) (n 21 above) 2.
[23] n 22 above, 47-108. Planetary obligations refer to duties of use, such as the duty to conserve resources, avoid adverse impacts, prevent disasters and compensate for environmental harm. Planetary rights are linked to the conditions of the biosphere and those resources essential to the continued sustainability of the earth's ecosystem.
[24] See eg art 3(1) of the 1992 United Nations Framework Convention on Climate Change, reprinted in (1992) 31 *International Legal Materials* 851, which provides that 'parties should protect the climate system for the benefit of the present and future generations of humankind'. Similarly, the Preamble of the 1992 Biodiversity Convention, reprinted in (1992) 31 *International Legal Materials* 822, makes use of intergenerational equity. For earlier instruments, see the Preambles of the 1968 Convention on African Nature Conservation, reprinted in P Sands *et al Principles of international environmental law* Vol 2A: *Documents in international environmental law* 917 and the 1972 World Heritage Convention reprinted in Sands *et al* 746.
[25] See eg Principle 2 of the 1972 Declaration of the United Nations Conference on the Human Environment http://www.unep.org/Documents/Default (accessed 1 October 2001) which recognises the need to safeguard the environment against degradation 'for the benefit of present and future generations' and Principle 3 of the 1992 Rio Declaration on Environment and Development, reprinted in (1992) 31 *International Legal Materials* 876, which provides that the right to development should be fulfilled 'so as to equitably meet the developmental and environmental needs of present and future generations'.
[26] Weiss (1984) (n 21 above).

institution of a representative or a guardian *ad litem* for future generations. This, she argues, could take the role of an ombudsman who will have standing on behalf of future generations.[27]

The second implication of intergenerational equity for environmental rights discourse is captured in the judgment of Davide J in the *Minors Oposa* case:[28]

> Put a little differently, the minors' assertion of their right to a sound environment constitutes, at the same time, the performance of their obligation to ensure the protection of that right for generations to come.

Thus, when we enforce our environmental rights, we are simultaneously performing in terms of our intergenerational obligations.

The principle of *intragenerational equity* is concerned with the distribution of costs of environmental protection and benefits of developmental activities among members of the current generation. The intragenerational equity discourse finds expression in the popularly termed 'North-South' debate.[29] Intragenerational equity can be achieved by, *inter alia,* imposing fewer obligations on developing states, delaying compliance with obligations imposed or by transferring funds and/or technologies required to implement environmental protection.

Like the principle of intergenerational equity, the principle of intragenerational equity is expressed in several international law instruments.[30] In the context of environmental rights, intragenerational equity recognises the inherent right of peoples to development. This means therefore that any recognition of environmental rights must be balanced with the right to development. Integration of these two concepts requires that environmental concerns must be taken on board in developmental policy making and *vice versa*.

---

[27] Weiss (1989) (n 21 above) 86.
[28] *Minors Oposa* (n 21 above) 185.
[29] See on the North-South debate in the environmental context W Kempel 'Transboundary movement of hazardous wastes' in G Sjostedt (ed) *International environmental negotiations* (1993); J Ntambirweki 'The developing countries in the evolution of an international environmental law' (1991) *Hastings International and Comparative Law Review* 906. See more recently K Mickelson 'South, north, international environmental law and international environmental lawyers' (2002) *Yearbook of International Environmental Law* 52.
[30] For examples of intragenerational equity in non-binding instruments, see Principle 9 of the Stockholm Declaration and Principle 7 of the Rio Declaration. For examples in binding instruments, see the Preamble of the Vienna Convention for the Protection of the Ozone Layer, reprinted in (1987) 26 *International Legal Materials* 1516; see also the Montreal Protocol on Substances that Deplete the Ozone Layer, reproduced in BE Carter & PR Trimble (eds) *International law: Selected documents* (1991) 731 which delays the operation of the obligations for developing countries by 10 years and also provides for the establishment of financial mechanisms to assist developing countries to comply with their obligations. See also art 4(1) of the Climate Change Convention (n 24 above) and the Kyoto Protocol to the United Nations Framework Convention on Climate Change http://unfccc.int/resources/docs/convkp/html.pdf (accessed 19 February 2002) which does not impose substantive obligations on developing states.

Thus, Principle 4 of the Rio Declaration on Environment and Development (Rio Declaration) provides that to achieve sustainable development, 'environmental protection shall constitute an integral part of the developmental process'.[31] Using rights language, the principle of integration would require the balancing of the right to development with the right to environmental protection.

3   International law

There is no general, comprehensive international treaty on human rights and the environment. However, there are international instruments that proclaim environmental rights, most notably regional instruments.[32] The Stockholm Declaration,[33] adopted at the UN Conference on the Human Environment, is an important instrument along the path to recognition of a link between the environment and human rights. Principle 1 of the Stockholm Declaration provides that:

> Man has the fundamental right to freedom, equality and adequate conditions of life, in an environment of a quality that permits a life of dignity and well-being, and he bears a solemn responsibility to protect and improve the environment for present and future generations.

Surprisingly, both the Rio Declaration[34] and the Johannesburg Declaration on Sustainable Development (Johannesburg Declaration)[35] contain no references to environmental rights. Instead, Principle 1 of the Rio Declaration merely provides that human beings 'are at the centre of concerns for sustainable development'. The avoidance of environmental rights in the Rio and Johannesburg Declarations is probably indicative of the uncertainty of the place of human rights in international environmental and sustainable development law.[36]

---

[31] See also Principles 8, 10 & 13 of the Stockholm Declaration. See further WCED (n 5 above) 4 *et seq* & 326 *et seq*.
[32] See eg art 24 of the 1981 African Charter on Human and Peoples' Rights. At the international level, see art 12 of the 1966 Covenant on Economic, Social and Cultural Rights; art 24(2)(c) of the 1989 Convention on the Rights of the Child.
[33] UNEP, http://unep.org/Documents/Default (accessed 1 October 2001).
[34] 1992 Rio Declaration on Environment and Development reprinted in (1992) 31 *International Legal Materials* 876.
[35] The 2002 Johannesburg Declaration on Sustainable Development available at http://www.johanneburgsummit.org/html (accessed 29 November 2002).
[36] A Boyle 'The role of international human rights law in the protection of the environment' in Boyle & Anderson (n 3 above) 1. See also M Pallemaerts 'International environmental law from Stockholm to Rio: Back to the future?' in P Sands (ed) *Greening international law* (1993) which argues that the fact that this provision was not included in the instruments adopted at the Rio Conference on the Environment and Development (UNCED) is indicative of the unwillingness of the states participating at Rio to accept that individuals may be the bearers of environmental rights independent of any national legal system.

4 Regional systems

Perhaps the most significant document regionally which gives recognition to environmental rights is the 1981 African Charter on Human and Peoples' Rights (African Charter or Charter).[37] The significance of the Charter lies in that it was the first international instrument to recognise the right to the environment.[38] Another instrument that recognises environmental rights is the Additional Protocol to the American Convention on Human Rights in the Area of Economic, Social and Cultural Rights.[39]

It is interesting to note the differences in approach between the two instruments. While the African Charter proclaims that *peoples* have a right 'to a general satisfactory environment favourable to their development' (article 24), the Additional Protocol to the American Convention declares that *everyone* has the right to a healthy environment (article 11). Thus, the African Charter proclaims a collective right, while the Inter-American instrument proclaims an individual right.

The European Convention on Human Rights does not proclaim environmental rights. However, the European Court of Human Rights has adopted the indirect approach of fashioning environmental rights from already existing and generally accepted human rights. An example of the approach can be found in *Lopez Ostra v Spain*.[40] In that case, the Court ruled that the right to a private life under article 8 of the European Convention on Human Rights should be interpreted to imply for individuals guarantees against environmental pollution.[41]

---

[37] While the African system has the reputation of being the least effective regional system, there is hope that with the adoption of the 1998 Protocol to the African Charter on Human and Peoples' Rights Establishing the African Court on Human and Peoples' Rights (adopted in Ouagadougou, Burkina Faso) the system will gain some credibility. See eg AE Anthony 'Beyond the paper tiger: The challenge of a human rights court in Africa' (1997) *Texas International Law Journal* 512.

[38] Art 24. See M van der Linde 'African responses to environmental protection' (2002) 35 *Comparative and International Law Journal of Southern Africa* 99.

[39] (1980) 19 *International Legal Materials* 698.

[40] n 10 above.

[41] For other cases in which the European Court used environmental approaches to resolve human rights disputes, see *Fredin v Sweden* (1991) ECHR Ser A 192 and the dissenting opinion of Pettiti J in *Balmer-Schafroth & Others v Switzerland* (1998) 25 European Human Rights Reports 598. See also *Oneryildiz v Turkey* (2002) ECHR 491 available at http://hudoc.echr.coe.int/hudoc/default.asp?Cm=query (accessed 7 April 2004), especially at para 62 *et seq*, where the Court found that the failure of the Turkish government to remove a rubbish tip situated near a residential area violated the right to life enshrined in art 2 of the European Convention.

5 South African law

The notion of including an 'environmental right' in a domestic constitution is not novel in Africa. It is estimated that approximately two-thirds of African countries have incorporated a constitutional provision that ensures the right to a healthy environment.[42]

The environmental right under the South African Constitution is guaranteed in section 24, which provides as follows:

> Everyone has the right -
> (a) to an environment that is not harmful to their health or well-being; and
> (b) to have the environment protected, for the benefit of present and future generations, through reasonable legislative and other measures that
> (i) prevent pollution and ecological degradation
> (ii) promote conservation; and
> (iii) secure ecologically sustainable development and use of natural resources while promoting justifiable economic and social development.

Most of the problems that exist with environmental rights under the international and regional systems are absent under the domestic South African system. There is no question as to the existence of a right, as the Constitution expressly and unequivocally provides for a distinct environmental right. Thus, what is left for us to do under this section is to determine the aim of the provision, to whom the right applies, who the beneficiaries are and finally the nature and content of the right.

It can be argued that section 24 has two general aims. First, subsection (a) guarantees to everyone the right to live in an environment that will not cause him or her harm. Subsection (b) places a specific mandate on the state to take certain measures in order to realise the guarantee proclaimed in the first part of the section. Second, subsection (b) also places a negative obligation on the state to abstain from measures that may cause environmental degradation or that may generally impair the right guaranteed in subsection (a).[43]

The right under section 24, like all other rights in chapter 2, is first and foremost binding on the state. Section 8(1) makes the Constitution applicable to the legislature, the executive, the judiciary and all organs of state. In addition, section 24(b) places a specific duty on the state to regulate in favour of environmental protection. In this regard, the Bill of Rights adheres to the traditional view that a constitution should protect citizens against unwarranted interference by the state, and should as a result operate on the vertical plane. Section 8(2), however, deviates from this traditional

---

[42] See C Bruch *et al* 'Constitutional environmental law: Giving force to fundamental principles in Africa' (2001) 26 *Columbia Journal of Environmental Law* 131 145.
[43] J de Waal *et al The Bill of Rights handbook* (1999) 390 support the same argument and refer to *Ex Parte Chairperson of the Constitutional Assembly: In re Certification of the Constitution of the Republic of South Africa* 1996 10 BCLR 1253 (CC), where it was noted that socio-economic rights can be negatively protected from improper invasion; para 78.

view and provides that a provision of the Bill of Rights also binds natural and juristic persons if, and to the extent that, it is applicable, taking into account the nature of the right and of any duty imposed by the right.[44] The question is, to what extent does section 8(2) provide for horizontal application, and what is the effect of section 8(2) on the environmental right?

In determining whether a right applies on the horizontal plane, the court will have to consider the nature of the right and the nature of the duty imposed by the right. It can therefore be argued that this consideration, and not whether section 8(2) confers horizontality on the Bill of Rights, falls within the discretion of the court.[45] The common law and/or statutory recognition of these rights may furthermore support the notion that they are also suitable for horizontal application.[46] The common law principle of nuisance, as well as environmental laws such as the National Environmental Management Act (NEMA),[47] implicitly recognises the right to a healthy environment. It follows, therefore, that section 24(a) may be applicable to private disputes. This issue is important, since it is often private actors that cause massive environmental degradation. Environmentally harmful operations such as mines and factories as a rule are owned and operated by corporations. In the context of the environment, the power of private actors should therefore be limited by the Bill of Rights to ensure protection to more vulnerable groups.

The next question is: Who benefits under section 24? Is it a right for individuals or is it a group right? If it is a group right, does it confer benefits on the present or future generation, or on both?

In contrast to the way in which environmental rights have been formulated in international instruments, section 24 has been framed as an individual right and not as a collective one. Environmental degradation often affects groups of people, and it could consequently be argued that the right should protect groups and not just individuals. However, Gutto argues that since the Constitution opens a wider scope for representative, class and public interest litigation,

---

[44] For a discussion on the application clause in the final Constitution, see eg D Davis & S Woolman 'The last laugh: *Du Plessis v De Klerk*, classical liberalism, Creole liberalism and the application of fundamental rights under the interim and the final Constitutions' (1996) 12 *South African Journal on Human Rights* 361; JGW van der Walt 'Justice Kriegler's disconcerting judgment in *Du Plessis v De Klerk*: Much ado about direct horizontal application (read nothing)' (1996) 4 *Journal of South African Law* 732; H Cheadle & D Davis 'The application of the 1996 Constitution in the private sphere' (1997) 13 *South African Journal on Human Rights* 44; and C Sprigman & M Osborne 'Du Plessis is not dead: South Africa's 1996 Constitution and the application of the Bill of Rights to private disputes' (1999) 15 *South African Journal on Human Rights* 25.

[45] It has been noted that the nature of certain rights in the Constitution, such as the right to dignity and the right to an environment that is not harmful to health or well-being, is such that they may be capable of horizontal application; Cheadle & Davis (n 44 above) 57.

[46] As above.

[47] 107 of 1998. Sec 28(1) of NEMA, eg, places a duty of care and remediation of environmental damage on 'every person who causes, has caused or may cause significant pollution or degradation of the environment'. Similarly, sec 1 defines 'pollution' as follows: "'[P]ollution" means any change in the environment ... whether engaged in by any person or an organ of state, where that change has an adverse effect on human health or wellbeing ... or will have such an effect in the future.'

the rights of individuals may be exercised collectively.[48] Groups may therefore utilise the broadened standing provisions in section 38 of the Constitution to enforce the environmental right where the infringement is of a collective nature.

Having said that, one needs to take a closer look at section 24(b) to determine whether it in fact grants rights to groups. The section reads: 'Everyone has the right to have the environment protected, for the benefit of present and future generations ...' There are two ways that one can understand the subsection. First, it can mean simply that the present and future generations have the right to have the environment protected. In this sense it can be argued that the concept of generation refers to a group. As stated above, this would not present any problems of standing, as individuals would, under section 38, be entitled to enforce the right on behalf of the group. The other meaning is that the section confers the right only to individuals as members of present and future generations. In other words, the group (present and future generations) does not have a distinct right independent of the individual's. The last meaning appears to be grammatically more correct.[49] The difference in the approaches is not so significant and lies only in the fact that, under the first approach, the rights of the present and future generations are directly claimable, while under the second approach the rights would only be indirectly claimable.

When interpreting section 24, one has to determine the scope of the concept 'environment'. In line with the anthropocentric approach to the environment, the term 'environment' should not be limited to the non-human natural environment, but should be defined broadly, specifically to include the interrelationships between humans and the natural environment. Due respect should also be paid to the traditional rights, needs, values and dignity of indigenous cultures and communities.[50] An expanded definition of environment could, for example, be invoked to prevent the displacement and relocation of indigenous groups on the basis that the loss of culturally or historically significant sites violates section 24.[51]

The South African legislature has adopted an equally broad approach in statutory law. In the National Environmental Management Act,[52] for example, environment is defined as:

[t]he surroundings within which humans exist and that are made up of
(i) the land, water and atmosphere of the earth;
(ii) micro-organisms, plant and animal life;
(iii) any part or combination of (i) and (ii) and the interrelationships among and between them; and

---

[48] SBO Gutto 'Environmental law and rights' in M Chaskalson *et al* (eds) *Constitutional law of South Africa* (1998) 32-1 32-2.
[49] See De Waal *et al* (n 43 above) 310 and M van der Linde 'Introduction to a healthy environment in the South African Constitution' in L Mashava (ed) *A compilation of essential documents on the right to water and environment* (2000) 16.
[50] PD Glavovic 'Environmental rights as fundamental human rights' (1996) 3 *South African Journal of Environmental Law and Policy* 71 72.
[51] LA Feris 'The conceptualisation of environmental justice within the context of the South African Constitution' LLD thesis, University of Stellenbosch, 2000 199.
[52] 107 of 1998 (n 47 above).

(iv) the physical, chemical, aesthetic and cultural properties and conditions of the foregoing that influence human health and well-being.

The Environment Conservation Act[53] also defines environment widely as 'the aggregate of surrounding objects, conditions and influences that influence the life and habits of man or any other organism or collection of organisms'. These instances show that enough support exists for an inclusive interpretation of environment.[54]

The concepts 'health' and 'well-being' are central to the purpose of section 24. Health clearly relates to human health and generally incorporates both mental and physical integrity. Health has consequently been defined by the World Health Organisation as a 'state of complete physical, mental and social well-being'.[55] While there is no difficulty in understanding the implications of health, the implications of well-being are perhaps a little more difficult to grasp. While harm to well-being may include harm to physical or mental health, it clearly denotes something broader than only that. De Waal, Currie and Erasmus[56] suggest that the inclusion of well-being has the effect of widening the right to include aspects of the environment such as biodiversity, the degradation of which would not threaten health.

Glazewski[57] views well-being as inclusive of spiritual or psychological aspects, such as the individual's need to be able to communicate with nature. Human well-being therefore depends on conservation and the maintenance of wilderness areas and biodiversity. Over and above a spiritual and psychological meaning, well-being may also encompass social and economic dimensions.[58] Many indigenous groups, for example, depend on biodiversity as a source of nutrition and for its medicinal and cultural value. These groups would be able to argue that the destruction of biodiversity is harmful to their well-being. The concept of well-being could be useful to those individuals who wish to employ the right in situations where it is difficult to substantiate a claim that someone's health has been affected.[59] Since it is a broader concept, 'infringement of well-being' may be easier to substantiate.

Section 24(b) of the Constitution imposes a duty on the state to protect the environment for the benefit of both the present and future generations. The reference to future generations is in line with the notion of intergenerational equity. There is no constitutional duty on individuals, ie the present generation, to protect the environment, but it is contended that the state acts as a guarantor on behalf of the present generation to fulfil planetary obligations to future generations.[60] Such a duty is placed on the state in section 24(b).

---

[53] 73 of 1989.
[54] Feris (n 51 above) 200.
[55] World Health Organisation, Preamble of Constitution (1978).
[56] De Waal et al (n 43 above) 394.
[57] J Glazewski 'The environment and the new Constitution' (1994) 1 *South African Journal of Environmental Law and Policy* 3.
[58] Feris (n 51 above) 201.
[59] M Kidd *Environmental law: A South African guide* (1997) 36.

A welcome inclusion in section 24 is the concept of sustainable development. This provision brings the South African Constitution in line with international standards in that it notes the connection between human rights, the environment and development. Although developed in international law, the principle of sustainable development is one that needs to be interpreted, applied and achieved primarily at a national level.[61]

How do we interpret the concept of sustainable development within the context of the Constitution? The principles of the Rio Declaration[62] may serve as guidelines in the interpretation of section 24(b)(iii). Principles 3 and 4 form the core of the principle of sustainable development.[63] In terms of these principles a careful balance should be sought between individual rights of consumption and development and the wider interests of present and future generations. Development decisions should, therefore, not discard environmental considerations.

One way of ensuring this is for the legislature to provide for an Environmental Impact Assessment (EIA) for all developmental projects.[64] The Environment Conservation Act currently provides for such assessments.[65]

---

[60] Weiss (1989) (n 21 above) 86.
[61] AE Boyle & D Freestone 'Introduction' in AE Boyle & D Freestone (eds) *International law and sustainable development - Past achievements and future challenges* (1999) 7.
[62] UNEP http://www.unep.org/unep/rio.htm (accessed 7 July 2002). These principles refer among others to the right to development, poverty alleviation and capacity building (n 34 above).
[63] Principle 3: The right to development must be fulfilled so as equitably to meet developmental and environmental needs of present and future generations. Principle 4: In order to achieve sustainable development, environmental protection shall constitute an integral part of the development process and cannot be considered in isolation from it. Robinson (ed) *Agenda 21 and the UNCED proceedings* (1992) Vol 1 cxi.
[64] Boyle & Freestone (n 61 above) 10.
[65] See *Silvermine Valley Coalition v Sybrand Van der Spuy Boerderye & Others* 2001 (1) SA 478 (C). In that case, the Court considered the role of impact assessments under the Environmental Conservation Act 73 of 1989 and the National Environmental Management Act 107 of 1998. The Court (at 488) found that failure to perform an impact assessment where one is required under the statutes constitutes an unlawful act under the said statutes. However, the Court found under the relevant legislative framework that those failing to perform environmental impact assessments could not be compelled, subsequently, to perform an environmental impact assessment as a remedy for the unlawful act. See, however, *Hichange Investment (Pty) Ltd v Cape Produce Company & Others* Case No 1050/2001 Eastern Cape High Court (unreported), where the Court found that an environmental impact assessment could be ordered where a person is causing or has caused significant pollution. The Court distinguished *Silvermine* on the grounds that the applicant in *Silvermine* sought an impact assessment after the activity had been completed, whereas in the present case the polluting activity was continuing.

It may be argued that failure to implement EIAs may amount to a violation of the rights guaranteed in terms of section 24(b) of the Constitution, and in particular section 24(b)(iii). In addition, Principle 8 of the Rio Declaration refers to the need to 'reduce and eliminate unsustainable patterns of production and consumption'.[66] Sustainable development may therefore involve some limits on the utilisation of natural resources.[67] Article 2(4) of NEMA sets out factors to be considered in the understanding of this concept and specifies restrictions on natural resources use as one such factor.

For a truly integrated approach to sustainable development under the South African Constitution, the socio-economic rights protected, such as the housing rights,[68] will have to be used to give content to the concept of sustainable development as found in section 24. The Constitutional Court recently had an opportunity to give content to the concept of sustainable development in *Minister of Public Works & Others v Kyalami Ridge Environmental Association*.[69] After serious flood damage to homes in Alexandra Township, flood victims were accommodated (as a temporary solution) on a portion of state-owned land on which Leeuwkop Prison stands. A number of residents in the neighbouring area of Kyalami objected to the accommodation on several grounds, including their environmental rights under section 24.[70] This was a classic case involving the conflict between development (socio-economic) and environmental rights. There was apparently, on the one hand, the potential for environmental degradation,[71] but on the other hand, the social and economic plight of the flood victims was real. This was a perfect opportunity for the Constitutional Court to balance these two (seemingly) opposite needs. However, that opportunity was missed, as the Court proceeded to decide the case on the other grounds raised, for example whether the conduct of the applicants complied with just administrative action[72] and legality under several statutes.[73] While we believe the Court's decision was, in the final analysis, correct, the judgment could have been bolstered by a discussion of the requirements of sustainable development.

Section 24 determines that everyone has the right to have the environment protected through reasonable legislative and other measures.[74] In particular, the state is mandated to prevent pollution and ecological degradation, to promote conservation and to secure

---

[66] Rio Declaration (n 62 above).
[67] Boyle & Freestone (n 61 above) 9.
[68] Sec 26 South African Constitution.
[69] 2001 7 BCLR 652 (CC).
[70] n 69 above, para 57.
[71] n 69 above, para 71.
[72] Sec 33 of the Constitution grants the right to 'procedurally fair administrative action'.
[73] The relevant statutes are the Environmental Management Act 107 of 1998, the Environment Conservation Act 73 of 1989, the Peri-Urban Town Planning Scheme of 1975, the National Building Regulations and Building Standards Act 103 of 1977, and the Town Planning and Townships Ordinance (Gauteng) Ordinance 15 of 1986.
[74] Sec 24(b).

ecologically sustainable development and the use of natural resources while promoting justifiable economic and social development.[75]

To give effect to this provision, a regulatory framework needs to be in place. Environmental laws and regulations should provide not only for the substantive aspects of environmental protection, but also for related procedural safeguards such as standing, access to information and just administrative action.[76] It may also be argued that, to the extent that present legislation does not meet constitutional requirements, section 24 imposes an obligation on the state to bring current legislation in line with the Constitution. The reference to other measures includes those of an administrative, technical, financial and educational nature.[77]

NEMA is encouraging in this regard. Article 3 contains principles that not only provide a framework and guidelines for environmental policy making and implementation, but also aids in the interpretation of this Act as well as other environmental laws.[78] On a procedural level, a new *locus standi* regime in the Constitution provides a generous standing to approach the courts when rights are infringed.[79] In addition, NEMA contains a provision on access to information. Section 31 states that every person is entitled to have access to information held by the state relating to the environment, the state of the environment and threats to the environment.[80]

However, the obligation imposed on the state by section 24(b) is qualified by the concept of reasonableness. State actions will thus be measured by this standard to determine whether there has been an infringement of section 24. This becomes particularly significant where the state fails to take action. An applicant challenging state omission will have to prove that such failure to act was unreasonable. It is not clear when such an omission will be unreasonable. Arguably, the state may be able to rely on the lack of resources to justify a failure to prevent pollution or ecological degradation. Sections 26 and 27 of the Constitution, dealing with socio-economic rights, contain a specific proviso regarding *reasonable* measures relating to availability or resources. The Constitutional Court has indicated that these rights

---

[75] Secs 24(b)(i), (ii) & (iii).
[76] FZ Ksentini 'Human rights, environment and development' in S Lin & L Kurukulasuriya (eds) *UNEP's new way forward: Environmental law and sustainable development* (1995) 108.
[77] S Liebenberg 'Environment' in D Davis *et al* (eds) *Fundamental rights in the Constitution - Commentary and cases* (1997) 256.
[78] Secs 2(1)(b), (c) & (e).
[79] Sec 38 of the Constitution states: 'Anyone listed in this section has the right to approach a competent court, alleging that a right in the Bill of Rights has been infringed or threatened, and the court may grant appropriate relief, including a declaration of rights. The persons who may approach a court are - (a) anyone acting in their own interest; (b) anyone acting on behalf of another person who cannot act in their own name; (c) anyone acting as a member of, or in the interest of, a group or class of persons; (d) anyone acting in the public interest; and (e) an association acting in the interest of its members.' See also sec 32 of NEMA.
[80] Sec 31(1)(a) NEMA. For procedural rights enshrined in the Constitution, see sec 32 (right to information), sec 33 (right to administrative justice), sec 34 (access to courts) and sec 38 (*locus standi*).

are limited to the extent that they are only available in so far as state resources permit:[81]

> What is apparent from these provisions is that the obligations imposed on the state by sections 26 and 27 in regard to access to housing, health care, food, water and social security are dependent upon the resources available for such purposes, and that the corresponding rights themselves are limited by reason of the lack of resources. Given this lack of resources and the significant demands on them that have already been referred to, an unqualified obligation to meet these needs would not presently be capable of being fulfilled.

By the same token, if resources become available, the state will have to employ them to meet their obligations towards fulfilling its citizens' right to have the environment protected.[82]

6 Conclusion

There has been recognition of environmental rights in international law, regional systems and the South African legal system. However, this recognition is still in its infancy and the recognition of environmental rights continues to grow in all three systems.

While the international and regional systems are still grappling with the formulations of environmental rights, the South African Constitution clearly defines the right. However, even under the Constitution much development is required. This is so particularly in respect of the content of the concept of sustainable development. One can add that, while South Africa has benefited much from foreign and international jurisprudence on human rights since 1994, the potential exists for South Africa to benefit the international community by developing a strong environmental rights jurisprudence.

---

[81] *Soobramoney v Minister of Health (KwaZulu-Natal)* 1998 1 SA 765 (CC) para 11.
[82] De Waal *et al* (n 43 above) 423.

Table of cases

African Commission on Human and Peoples' Rights
Free Legal Assistance Group & Others v Zaire (2000) AHRLR 74 (ACHPR 1995) (Communications 25/89, 47/90, 56/91 and 100/93)	196, 231
Purohit and Moore v The Gambia (Communication 241/2000)	8
Social and Economic Rights Action Centre (SERAC) and the Centre for Economic and Social Rights v Nigeria (Communication 155/96)	8, 155, 165, 196

Belgium
Arrêt no 36/98 du 1 Avril 1998, *Commune* de Wemmel, Moniteur belge	197

Brazil
Marques v State of Parana (Bill of Review 0208625-3)	197

Canada
Eldridge v British Columbia (Attorney General) (1997), 151 DLR (4th) 577	7
Mahe et al v The Queen in the Right of Alberta et al (1990), 68 DLR (4th) 69	77

Colombia
Rights of sick persons/Aids patients (Constitutional Court, Judgment No T-505/92)	6

European Court of Human Rights
Balmer-Schafroth & Others v Switzerland (1998) 25 EHRR 598	256
Belgian Linguistic Case No. 1 (1967) Series A No. 5 1 EHRR 241	61
Belgian Linguistic Case No. 2 (1968) Series A No. 6 1 EHRR 252	61, 79
Fredin v Sweden (1991) ECHR Ser A 192	258
Kjeldsen, Busk Madsen & Pedersen (1976) ECHR Ser A 23	82
López Ostra v Spain (1995) ECHR Ser A 303	251, 256
Oneryildiz v Turkey (2002) ECHR 491	256

Germany
Milk and Butterfat Case 18 BverfGE 315, 1965	7, 154, 173

India
FK Hussain v Union of India OP 2741/1988 (1990-02-26)	197

(continued)

Francis Coralie Mullin v *The Administrator, Union Territory of Delhi* (1981) 2 SCR 516	6, 154
Paschim Banga Khet Mazdoor Samity & Others v *State of West Bengal & Another* (1996) AIR 2426 SC	6
People's Union for Civil Liberties v *Union of India* (Writ Petition [Civil] 196 of 2001 (1997) 1 SCC 301	17, 49, 154, 186
Unni Krishnan JP v *State of AP* AIR 1993 2178 SC	57

International Court of Justice

Hungary v *Slovakia (Case Concerning the Gabcikovo-Nagymaros Project)* (1998) 37 ILM 162	251, 252

Latvia

Case No 2000-08-0109 (Constitutional Court)	6

Philippines

Minors Oposa v *Secretary of Department of Environment and Natural Resources* (1994) 83 ILM 173	253, 254

South Africa

ABSA Bank Ltd v *Amod* 1999 2 All SA 423 (W), [1999] JOL 4735 (W)	95
Acting Superintendent-General of Education KwaZulu-Natal v *Ngubo & Others* 1996 3 BCLR 369 (N)	82
Afrox Health Care (Pty) Ltd v *Strydom* 2002 (6) SA 21 (SCA)	20, 41, 176
Antonie v *Governing Body, Settlers High School, and Others* 2002 (4) SA 738 (CPD), 2002 JOL 9663 (C)	72
August v *Electoral Commission* 1999 (3) SA 1 (CC), 1999 (4) BCLR 363 (CC)	55
B v *Minister of Correctional Services* 1997 6 BCLR 789 (C) (also cited as *Van Biljon* v *Minister of Correctional Services* 1997 (4) SA 441 (C), [1997] 2 All SA 574 (C), [1997] JOL 1281 (C)	16, 25, 43, 133, 134
Baartman v *Port Elizabeth Municipality* 2004 (1) SA 560 (SCA), 2003 JOL 11626 (SCA)	33
Baloro v *University of Bophuthatswana* 1995 (4) SA 197 (BSC), 1995 (8) BCLR 1018 (B)	225
Bel Porto School Governing Body v *Premier of the Western Cape Province* 2002 (3) SA 265 (CC), 2002 (9) BCLR 891, 2002 JOL 9413 (C)	45
Betta Eiendomme (Pty) Ltd v *Ekple-Epoh* 2000 (4) SA 468 (W), 2000 (3) All SA 403 (W)	24, 176
Brink v *Kitshoff* 1996 (4) SA 197 (CC), 1996 6 BCLR 752 (CC)	131

(continued)

Brisley v Drotsky 2002 (4) SA 1 (SCA) / 2002 12 BCLR 1229 (SCA), 2002 JOL 9693 (A)	19, 24, 25, 32, 41, 42, 95, 176, 177
Cape Killarney Property Investors (Pty)Ltd v Mahamba 2001 (4) SA 1222 (SCA), 2001 (4) All SA 479 (A)	15
Chetty v Naidoo 1974 (3) SA 13 (A)	94
Christian Education South Africa v Minister of Education 2000 (4) SA 757 (CC), 2000 10 BCLR 1051, 2000 JOL 7320 (CC)	72, 82
Christian Lawyers Association of South Africa & Others v Minister of Health & Others 1998 (4) SA 1113 (T), 1998 11 BCLR 1434 (T), 1998 JOL 3617 (T)	132
City Council of Pretoria v Walker 1998 3 BCLR 257 (CC) / 1998 (2) SA 363 (CC), 1998 JOL 2020 (CC)	29, 131
City of Cape Town v Rudolph 2004 (5) SA 39 (C), 2003 (11) BCLR 1236, (2003) 3 All SA 517 (C), 2003 JOL 11334 (C)	16, 31, 35, 39, 47, 55, 167, 172
Despatch Municipality v Sunridge Estate and Development Corporation (Pty) Ltd 1997 (4) SA 596 (SE) / 1997 8 BCLR 1023 (SE), 1997 2 All SA 283 (SE), 1997 JOL 1204 (SE)	32
Dhladhla & Others v Erasmus 1999 (1) SA 1065 (LCC), 1998 JOL 4151 (LCC)	204
Du Plessis v De Klerk 1996 5 BCLR 658 (CC)	18
Ellis v Viljoen 2001 (4) SA 794 (C), 2001 (5) BCLR 487 (CC), 2001 JOL 7923 (C)	24, 176
Ex parte Chairperson of the Constitutional Assembly: In re Certification of the Constitution of the Republic of South Africa, 1996 1996 (4) SA 744 (CC) ; 1996 10 BCLR 1253 (CC)	11, 22, 86, 92, 133, 257
Fose v Minister of Safety and Security 1997 (3) SA 786 (CC), 1997 (7) BCLR 851 (CC), (1998) JOL 1364 (CC)	54
Government of the Republic of South Africa v Grootboom and Others 2001 (1) SA 46 (CC) / 2000 11 BCLR 1169 (CC), 2000 JOL 7524 (CC)	7, 10, 15, 22, 23, 26, 27, 28, 35, 43, 44, 45, 46, 47, 48, 49, 50, 51, 52, 55, 56, 60, 62, 64, 65, 73, 74, 85, 86, 87, 88, 91, 92, 98, 99, 100, 101, 102, 104, 139, 140, 141, 142, 143, 162, 163, 172, 178, 179, 180, 181, 182, 184, 185, 186, 188, 200, 202, 203, 206, 213, 232, 234,

(continued)

Case	Pages
Government of the Republic of South Africa v Grootboom and Others 2001 (1) SA 46 (CC) / 2000 11 BCLR 1169 (CC), 2000 JOL 7524 (CC)	235, 236, 237, 238, 239, 240, 242, 244, 246, 247
Graham v Ridley 1931 TPD 476	24, 176
Grootboom v Oostenberg Municipality 2000 3 BCLR 277 (C), [2000] JOL 5991 (C)	55, 104
Harksen v Lane 1998 (1) SA 300 (300), 1997 11 BCLR 1489 (CC)	131
Hichange Investment (Pty) Ltd v Cape Produce Company & Others Case No 1050/2001 Eastern Cape High Court (unreported)	261
Hoffmann v SA Airways 2000 (1) SA 1 (CC), 2000(11) BCLR 1211 (C), 2000 JOL 7446 (CC), 2000 21 ILJ 2357 (CC)	235
In re Kranspoort Community 2000 (2) SA 124 (LCC), 2000 JOL 5882 (LCC)	40, 166, 174
In re The School Education Bill of 1995 (Gauteng) 1996 (3) SA 165 (CC), 1996 4 BCLR 537 (CC)	61, 77, 79, 80, 82
Jaftha v Schoeman 2005 (2) SA 140 (CC), 2005 1 BCLR 78 (CC)	10, 19, 26, 28, 32, 40, 41, 174, 175
Khosa v Minister of Social Development 2004 6 SA 505 (CC), 2004 (6) BCLR 569 (CC)	4, 5, 11, 19, 27, 28, 36, 44, 45, 46, 51, 52, 53, 54, 87, 162, 164, 178, 181, 224, 225, 233, 237, 238, 239, 242, 245, 246, 247
Khumalo & Others v Holomisa 2002 (5) SA 401 (CC), 2002 (8) BCLR 771 (CC)	19
Kutumela v Member of the Executive Committee for Social Services, Culture, Arts and Sport in the North West Province Case 671/2003, 23 October 2003 (B)	14, 48, 49, 185, 187
Larbi-Odam v Member of the Executive Council for Education (North West Province) 1998 (1) SA 745 (CC), 1997 (12) BCLR 1655 (CC)	225
Mahambehlala v MEC, Health and Welfare, Eastern Cape & Another 2002 (1) SA 342 (SE), 2001 (9) BCLR 899 (SE), 2001 JOL 8191 (SE)	238, 244
Maluleke v MEC, Health and Welfare, Northern Province 1999 (4) SA 367 (T), (1994) 4 B All SA 407, (1999) JOL 5495 (T)	238
Manqele v Durban Transitional Metropolitan Council 2002 (6) SA 423 (D), (2002) 2 All SA 39 (D), 2001 JOL 8956 (D)	203
Mashava v President of the Republic of South Africa 2004 12 BCLR 1243 (CC)	5, 36, 37, 169, 170
Matukane & Others v Laerskool Potgietersrus 1996 (3) SA 223 (WLD), 1996 1 All SA 468 (T)	67, 77, 81

(continued)

Case	Pages
Mbanga v MEC, Health and Welfare, Eastern Cape & Another 2002 (1) SA 359 (SE), 2001 (8) BCLR 821 (SE), 2001 JOL 8192 (SE)	238, 244
Mfolo & Others v Minister of Education, Bophuthatswana 1992 (3) SA 181 (BG), 1994 1 BCLR 136 (B)	81
Minister of Education v Harris 2001 (4) SA 1297 (CC), 2001 (11) BCLR 1157 (CC)	67
Minister of Health v Treatment Action Campaign and Others (TAC) 2002 (5) SA 721 (CC) / 2002 10 BCLR 1033 (CC)	11, 17, 20, 23, 25, 27, 28, 36, 43, 44, 45, 46, 49, 50, 51, 52, 53, 55, 62, 64, 86, 87, 88, 91, 98, 99, 100, 101, 105, 134, 138, 139, 141, 142, 143, 150, 162, 163, 178, 179, 180, 181, 182, 197, 203, 206, 238, 239, 240
Minister of Public Works & Others v Kyalami Ridge Environmental Association & Others 2001 (3) SA 1151 (CC) / 2001 7 BCLR 652 (CC), 2001 JOL 8289 (CC)	17, 38, 87, 172, 205, 262
Mkangeli v Joubert 2002 (4) SA 36 (SCA), 2002 (2) All SA 473 (A)	95
Modderfontein Squatters v Modderklip Boerdery (Pty) Ltd 2004 (6) SA 40 (SCA), 2004 (8) 821 (SCA), 2004 (3) All SA 169 (SCA)	26, 34, 35, 47, 55
Motala and Another v University of Natal 1995 3 BCLR 374 (D)	75
National Coalition of Gay and Lesbian Equality v Minister of Justice 1999 (1) SA 6 (CC) / 1998 12 BCLR 1517 (CC), 1998 JOL 3801 (CC), 1998 (2) SACR 556	131
Ndlovu v Ngcobo; Bekker & Another v Jika 2003 (1) SA 113 (SCA), (2002) 4 All SA 384	24, 25, 41, 95, 96, 177,
Ngxuza & Others v The Permanent Secretary, Department of Welfare, Eastern Cape Provincial Government & Another 2001 (2) SA 609 (E), 2000 (12) BCLR 1322 (E)	238
Ntshangase v The Trustees of the Terblanche Gesin Familie Trust [2003] JOL 10996 (LCC)	40, 167, 174
Permanent Secretary, Department of Welfare, Eastern Cape Provincial Government & Another v Ngxuza & Others 2001 (4) SA 1184 (SCA), 2001 (10) BCLR 1039 (A), 2001 JOL 8676 (A)	42, 238
Pharmaceutical Manufacturers Association of SA & Another: In re Ex Parte President of the Republic of South Africa & Others 1999 (4) SA 788 (T), 2000 (3) BCLR 241 (CC)	146
Port Elizabeth Municipality v Peoples Dialogue on Land and Shelter 2000 (2) SA 1074 (SEC), 2001 (1) All SA 381 (E)	95

(continued)

Port Elizabeth Municipality v Various Occupiers 2005 (1) SA 217 (CC), 2004 12 BCLR 1268 (CC), 2004 JOL 13007 (CC)	15, 26, 32, 33, 34, 35
President of the Republic of South Africa & Another v Hugo 1997 (4) SA 1 (CC) / 1997 6 BCLR 708 (CC), 1997 (1) SACR 867	27, 131
Prince v The President of the Law Society of the Cape of Good Hope 2002 3 BCLR 231 (CC), 2002 JOL 9305 (CC)	123
Prinsloo v Van der Linde 1997 (3) SA 1012 (CC), 1997 6 BCLR 759 (CC)	131
Residents of Bon Vista Mansions v Southern Metropolitan Local Council 2002 6 BCLR 625 (W), 2002 JOL 9513 (W)	16, 32, 203, 204
Ross v South Peninsula Municipality 2000 (1) SA 589 (C), 2000 (4) All SA 85 (C)	24, 32, 176
S v Makwanyane & Another 1995 (3) SA 391 (CC) / 1995 6 BCLR 665 (CC), 1995 (2) SACR 1	90, 136, 213, 236
S v Mhlungu 1995 (3) SA 867 (CC), 1995 (7) BCLR 793 (CC), 1995 (2) SACR 277	61, 74
S v Zuma 1995 (2) SA 642 (CC), 1995 (4) BCLR 401 (CC), 1995 (1) SACR 568	29
Silvermine Valley Coalition v Sybrand Van der Spuy Boerderye & Others 2001 (1) SA 478 (C), 2002 1 All SA 10 (C)	261
Soobramoney v Minister of Health, KwaZulu-Natal 1998 (1) SA 765 (CC) / 1997 12 BCLR 1696 (CC), 1998 (1) All SA 268 (CC)	4, 6, 22, 27, 32, 36, 43, 44, 52, 87, 89, 134, 135, 136, 137, 162, 178, 203, 205, 207, 236, 246, 264
Strydom v Minister of Correctional Services & Others 1999 3 BCLR 342 (W), 1999 JOL 4522 (W)	106
Treatment Action Campaign and Others v Minister of Health and Others 2002 4 BCLR 356 (T)	138
Van der Walt v Lang 1999 (1) SA 189 (LCC), 1998 JOL 3618	40, 167, 174, 204
Van Huyssteen NO v Minister of Environmental Affairs and Tourism 1996 (1) SA 283 (C), 1995 9 BCLR 1191 (C)	251
Walters v Transitional Local Council of Port Elizabeth & Another 2001 BLLR 98 (LC)	235
Witmann v Deutscher Schulverein, Pretoria & Others 1999 1 BCLR 92 (T)	82
Zulu v Van Rensburg 1996 (4) SA 1236 (LCC), (1996) 2 All SA 615 (LCC)	40, 167, 174

United Kingdom

R v Cambridge Health Authority, ex Pb (a minor) (QBD) 25 BMLR 5 — 137

United Nations Human Rights Committee

Arieh Hollis Waldman v Canada (1999) UN Doc CCPR/C/67/D/1996 — 80

EW & Others v The Netherlands Communication 429/1990 — 251

United States of America

Brown v Board of Education of Topeka 347 US 438 (1954) — 57

Goldberg v Kelly 397 US 254 (1970) — 7, 39

Newdow v United States Congress et al (2002) 292 F. 3d 597 — 82

Sniadach v Family Finance Corp 395 US 337 (1969) — 7

Tarasoff v Regents of the University of California (1976) 551 P 2d 334 — 124

Table of statutes

Bophuthatswana

18	1977	Bophuthatswana Constitution Act	81

Brazil

	1988	Constitution of the Federal Republic of Brazil (1998 Amendment) a 196	126

Canada

		Charter of Rights and Freedoms s 23	78

Chile

	1980	Constitution of Chile a 19	126

Gambia

	1970	Constitution	197

India

	1950	Constitution	57

Kenya

	2004	Draft Constitution	197

Latvia

	1922	Constitution s 109	6

South Africa

2	1975	Abortion and Sterilisation Act	131, 146
108	1991	Abolition of Racially Based Measures Act	128
27	1996	Admission Policy for Ordinary Schools Act s 19-25	73 73
81	1967	Aged Persons Act s 12(1)(b)(i)	224
75	1997	Basic Conditions of Employment Act s 25	221
92	1996	Choice on Termination of Pregnancy Act s 2(1)(a)	132, 145 145
130	1993	Compensation for Occupational Injuries and Diseases Act s 1	210 221

Table of statutes 275

(SA continued)

110	1983	Constitution of the Republic of South Africa		128
200	1993	Constitution of the Republic of South Africa (Interim Constitution)		1, 5, 37, 80, 128, 170
			s 7(2)	18
			8(3)(a)	76
			32	61
			32(a)	81
			32(b)	78
			32(c)	61, 79
			33(1)	29
			235	37, 169
108	1996	Constitution of the Republic of South Africa		1, 2, 7, 8, 12, 19, 22, 39, 46, 54, 60, 68, 72, 74, 76, 77, 78, 79, 80, 81, 82, 86, 87, 89, 91, 96, 97, 101, 104, 105, 127, 132, 137, 139, 142, 150, 154, 161, 163, 172, 173, 189, 191, 198, 200, 202, 203, 206, 209, 213, 233, 235, 237, 240, 243, 244, 247, 249, 257, 258, 261, 263, 264
			Preamble	61
			s 1	199, 235
			2	2
			7	143, 206
			7(1)	235
			7(2)	2, 6, 9, 30, 92, 98, 106, 138, 142, 159, 161, 162, 163, 203, 233, 238, 239
			8	18
			8(1)	18, 19, 257
			8(2)	18, 19, 92, 257, 258
			8(3)	18, 19
			9	4, 12, 81, 127, 131, 132, 164, 207, 225, 239, 243
			9(3)	4, 5, 19, 44, 45, 131, 233
			9(4)	5
			10	127, 138, 207, 233, 235, 239

(SA continued)

	11	4, 127, 135, 136, 207, 239
	12	126
	12(2)(a)	126, 132, 138
	12(2)(c)	126
	14	233
	15	81
	17	82
	22	63, 164
	23	164
	24	3, 164, 207, 257, 258, 259, 260, 261, 262, 263
	24(a)	126, 207, 208, 258
	24(b)	3, 13, 164, 257, 259, 260, 261, 262, 263
	24(b)(i)	207, 262
	24(b)(ii)	262
	24(b)(iii)	261, 262, 263
	25	15, 16, 31, 105, 164, 166, 233
	25(2)	31, 166
	25(3)	31, 166
	25(5)	2, 3, 13, 85, 88, 164
	25(6)	93, 164
	25(8)	205
	26	3, 22, 85, 87, 88, 92, 98, 101, 102, 104, 105, 127, 139, 164, 206, 207, 240, 246, 262, 263, 264
	26(1)	3, 4, 19, 40, 44, 49, 93, 98, 101, 102, 233, 234
	26(2)	2, 3, 13, 22, 28, 46, 49, 98, 101, 206, 234, 240
	26(3)	4, 15, 16, 19, 24, 25, 32, 33, 41, 42, 87, 93, 94, 95, 96, 97, 176, 177, 204

(SA continued)

27		3, 88, 101, 105, 108, 125, 126, 127, 131, 132, 138, 139, 141, 143, 148, 163, 197, 206, 207, 246, 263, 264
27(1)		3, 4, 19, 20, 44, 46, 92, 132, 135, 139, 143, 162, 206, 239
27(1)(a)		4, 131, 164, 176, 233
27(1)(b)		16, 153, 161, 162, 163, 197, 198, 233
27(1)(c)		15, 28, 44, 162, 164, 209, 225, 233, 234, 237, 239
27(2)		3, 13, 28, 43, 45, 46, 132, 135, 137, 139, 143, 151, 162, 178, 197, 202, 206, 209, 233, 234, 239, 240, 243,
27(3)		4, 32, 33, 36, 43, 44, 135, 136
28		64, 105, 140, 206
28(1)(b)		104, 206
28(1)(c)		3, 4, 44, 85, 88, 104, 126, 138, 139, 140, 153, 161, 206, 209, 233
28(2)		10
28(3)		85, 217
29		3, 59, 61, 81, 82, 164
29(1)		233
29(1)(a)		4, 59, 61, 62, 64, 65, 73
29(1)(b)		3, 59, 62, 74, 75
29(2)		77, 78
29(3)		79, 80, 81
29(4)		79, 80
32		12, 263
33		4, 5, 13, 164, 207, 233, 262, 263
34		263
35(1)		90

(SA continued)

		35(2)(e)	3, 4, 16, 85, 88, 105, 106, 126, 133, 134, 153, 161, 207
		36	28, 73, 131
		36(1)	18, 26, 27, 28, 29, 32, 43, 47, 163
		38	13, 42, 54, 86, 142, 259, 263
		39	6, 138
		39(1)	6, 39, 173
		39(1)(a)	61, 235
		39(1)(b)	89, 213
		39(2)	18
		75	220
		76	220
		167	54
		172(1)(a)	17, 142
		172(1)(b)(i)	54
		172(1)(b)(ii)	54
		184(3)	12
		195	138
		233	138
		237	138
67	1995	Development Facilitation Act	38
140	1992	Drugs and Drug Trafficking Act	
		s 4b	123
		Part III, Schedule 2	123
73	1989	Environment Conservation Act	260, 261, 262
63	1975	Expropriation Act	31, 166
62	1997	Extension of Security of Tenure Act	24, 31, 38, 40, 93, 166, 167, 171, 174, 176
		s 1	31, 167, 169
		2(1)	31, 166
		8(1)	13, 31, 167
		9(3)	167
		9(3)(a)	33, 169
		10(2)	33, 169
		10(3)	33, 169
		11(1)	13, 31, 167
		11(2)	13, 31, 167
		11(3)	13, 31, 33, 167, 169
54	1972	Foodstuffs, Cosmetics and Disinfectants Act	38, 171, 172
98	1998	Further Education and Training Act	74
		s 1	74
41	1950	Group Areas Act	128
63	1977	Health Act	129
101	1997	Higher Education Act	74, 76
		s 1	74
107	1997	Housing Act	15

Table of statutes 279

(SA continued)

31	1996	Interim Protection of Informal Land Rights Act	93
3	1996	Land Reform (Labour Tenants) Act	24, 31, 38, 40, 93, 166, 167, 171, 174, 175, 176
		s 1	31, 166, 167
32	1944	Magistrates' Courts Act	19, 26, 41, 175
		s 66(1)(a)	32, 40, 174
		67(c)	171
18	1998	Marine Living Resources Act	168
131	1998	Medical Schemes Act	147, 239
		s 24(2)(e)	147
		29(1)(n)	147
101	1965	Medicines and Related Substances Control Act	123
90	1997	Medicines and Related Substances Control Amendment Act	146, 147
		s 15	147
103	1977	National Building Regulations and Building Standards Act	262
27	1996	National Education Policy Act	65, 67
		s 3(4)(g)	66
107	1998	National Environmental Management Act	258, 259, 261, 263
		s 1	258
		2(1)(b)	263
		2(1)(c)	263
		2(1)(e)	263
		2(4)	262
		3	263
		28(1)	258
		31	263
		31(1)(a)	263
		32	263
61	2003	National Health Act	145, 148
56	1999	National Student Aid Scheme Act	76, 77
		s 3	76
		4	76
		14	76
		19	76
36	1998	National Water Act	200
		s 27-31	200
		39-55	200
57	1978	Patents Act	147
88	1997	Pharmacy Amendment Act	146
19	1998	Prevention of Illegal Eviction from and Unlawful Occupation of Land Act	15, 16, 24, 25, 31, 32, 33, 34, 38, 39, 94, 95, 96, 166, 176, 177
		s 4	31, 35, 97

(SA continued)

		4(1)	95
		4(6)	31, 94, 95, 167
		4(7)	31, 94, 95, 167
		5(1)(b)	31, 167
		6	31, 33, 166
		6(1)	31, 167
		6(3)	31, 167
		6(3)(b)	33, 169
		6(3)(c)	33
		6(4)	94
		7	31, 95, 166
		Schedule 1	32
52	1951	Prevention of Illegal Squatting Act	
		s 3B	32
		11(1)	32
4	2000	Promotion of Equality and Prevention of Unfair Discrimination Act	
		32	5
		34	5
		34(1)(a)	5
36	1919	Public Health Act	128, 129, 145
130	1998	Refugee Act	225
		s 27(b)	225
50	1999	Rental Housing Act	38, 93
22	1994	Restitution of Land Rights Act	40, 93, 166, 174
		s 2(2)	166
59	1992	Social Assistance Act	4, 5, 11, 13, 14, 19, 36, 37, 44, 46, 48, 169, 187, 217, 224, 241
		Preamble	15
		s 2-4	211
		2(a)	238
		3(a)	238, 241
		3(c)	19, 224
		4(b)(ii)	19
		4A(b)	241
		4B	241
		4B(b)(ii)	19
		4(1)	219, 241
		5(2)	241
9	2004	Social Security Agency Act	13
84	1996	South African Schools Act	63, 65, 66, 67, 68, 73
		3	74
		3(1)	63, 70
		5	67
		6(1)	78
		8	72
		9	72
		10	72
		34(1)	68
		35	66
		36	68

(SA continued)

		39	68
		39(4)	68
		40-41	68
		45	80
		46	80
		48	80
		61	68
30	1966	Unemployment Insurance Act	210
63	2001	Unemployment Insurance Act	
		s 1	221
		3(1)(d)	224
4	2002	Unemployment Insurance Contributions Act	
		s 1	221
108	1997	Water Services Act	16, 31, 32, 199, 203, 204
		s 3	208
		3(1)	199
		4(1)	16
		4(3)	16, 31
		9(2)	201
		9(3)	201
		10	201
		Reg 3	199
106	1997	Welfare Laws Amendment Act	211, 217, 219, 224, 241
		s 3	19, 241

Uganda

	1995	Constitution	197

United States of America

		Constitution Establishment Clause (First Amendment)	82
		US Public Law 105-277	147

Venezuela

	1961	Constitution	
		a 76	126

Zambia

	1991	Constitution	197

Further South African legislative material

GG	No			
24630	GN R460	31/03/2003	Amendment: Regulations Regarding Grants and Financial Awards to Welfare Organisations and to Persons in Need of Social Relief of Distress in terms of the Social Assistance Act 59 of 1992	219, 245
25346	GN 2200	13/08/2003	Children's Bill (Explanatory summary)	220
25391	GN 2276	27/08/2003	Draft Prevention of Illegal Eviction from and Unlawful Occupation of Land Bill 2003	177
19347	GN 1293	12/10/1998	Exemption of Parents from the Payment of School Fees Regulations	68
		1993	Higher Education White Paper 3	76
17944	GN 712	18/04/1997	Higher Education White Paper	76
26197	GN 409	26/03/2004	Increase in Respect of Social Grants	241
22824	R7203	09/11/2001	National Health Bill	145, 148
20372	GN 1926	10/08/1999	National Policy on HIV/AIDS for Learners and Educators in Public Schools and Students and Educators in Further Education and Training Institutions	73
19347	GN 2362	12/10/1998	Norms and Standards for School Funding	66, 80
18546	GN R1701	19/12/1997	Norms and Standards Regarding Language Policy in Public Schools	78, 79
		1975	Peri-Urban Town Planning Scheme	262
16992	GN R7	23/02/1996	Proclamation R7: Assignment to the Provinces of Acts of Parliament Relating to Welfare under Section 235 (8) of the Constitution of the Republic of South Africa, 1993	37, 169
22355	GN R509	08/06/2001	Regulations Relating to Compulsory National Standards and Measures to Conserve Water	199
15817	GN 657	01/07/1994	Rendering of Free Health Services	145
25340	GN 2173	08/08/2003	Social Assistance Bill (Explanatory summary)	211, 217
	15	1968	Town Planning and Townships Ordinance (Gauteng)	262
18166	GN 1108	18/18/1997	White Paper for Social Welfare	209, 210, 211, 212, 236
17910	GN 667	16/04/1997	White Paper for the Transformation of the Health System of South Africa	144
19920	GN 529	31/04/1999	White Paper on International Migration	225
		1997	White Paper on Land Policy	188

Table of international instruments

1988	Additional Protocol to the American Convention on Human Rights in the Area of Economic, Social and Cultural Rights (Protocol of San Salvador)	8, 256
a	10	110
	11	256
	12(1)	155
	13	58

1977	Additional Protocol to the Geneva Convention of 1977 I	194
a	54	194

1977	Additional Protocol to the Geneva Convention of 1977 II	194
a	5	194
	14	194

1981	African Charter on Human and Peoples' Rights	8, 155, 231, 232, 256
a	2	8
	4	8, 155
	14	8
	15	232
	16	8, 110, 155, 196, 231
	16(2)	196
	17	58
	18(1)	8, 231
	18(4)	231
	21	8
	22	155
	24	8, 255, 256
	29(1)	232
	29(6)	232

1990	African Charter on the Rights and Welfare of the Child	232
a	5	232
	11	58, 232
	11(3)(a)	70
	11(3)(b)	75
	11(3)(c)	75, 76
	13	232
	14	110, 232
	14(1)	196
	14(2)(c)	156, 196
	15	232

1988	American Convention on Human Rights in the Area of Economic, Social and Cultural Rights	
a	11	196

1948	American Declaration of the Rights and Duties of Man	
a	12	58

1992	Biodiversity Convention	
	Preamble	253

1992	Climate Change Convention (United Nations Framework Convention on Climate Change)	
a	3(1)	253
	4(1)	254

1989	Convention Concerning Indigenous and Tribal Peoples in Independent Countries	
a	25	109

1968	Convention on African Nature Conservation	
	Preamble	253

1979		Convention on the Elimination of All Forms of Discrimination against Women (CEDAW)	7, 90, 120, 124, 156, 191, 221, 222
	a	3, 10-14	7
		4	221
		4(1)	121
		4(2)	221
		10	58
		11	221
		11(1)(e)	221
		12	109, 120, 121, 122
		12(2)	156
		13	221
		13(a)	221
		13(b)	221
		14	221
		14(2)(c)	221
		14(2)(h)	193
1965		Convention on the Elimination of All Forms of Racial Discrimination (CERD)	90, 222
	a	1	121
		2(1)(c)	222
		2(1)(d)	222
		5(e)	222
		5(e)(iv)	109
1989		Convention on the Rights of the Child (CRC)	7, 90, 125, 155, 191, 217, 218, 219
	a	4, 6(2), 19, 20, 24, 26-29 & 31	7
		23(3), 23 (4), 28, 29	58
		6	217, 218
		18	218
		23	217, 218
		24	109, 218
		24(1)	193
		24(2)(c)	155, 163, 193, 255
		24(2)(e)	156, 163
		26	218
		27	218
		27(3)	156
		28	75
		28(1)(a)	70
		28(1)(b)	70
		28(c)	76
1951		Convention Relating to the Status of Refugees	90, 156, 223
	a	20	223
		24	223
1960		Convention Relating to the Status of Stateless Persons	223
	a	24(1)(b)(i)	224
		24(1)(b)(ii)	224
1950		European Convention for the Protection of Human Rights and Fundamental Freedoms	58, 155, 256
	a	2	61, 256
		8	256
1961		European Social Charter	8, 155, 195
	a	11	110, 195
		13	110
		31	195
1952		First Protocol of the European Convention on Human Rights	
	a	2	58, 82

1949	Geneva Convention Relative to the Treatment of Civilian Persons in Time of War (Geneva Convention IV)	
a	23	156
	55	156
	89	194
	127	194
1949	Geneva Convention Relative to the Treatment of Prisoners of War (Geneva Convention III)	
a	21	194
	25	194
	26	156
	29	194
	46	194
	51	156
	85	194
1952	ILO Convention No (102) on Social Security (Minimum Standards)	211, 215, 216, 226
a	1(2)	226
	10, 34, 39, 7-64	226
1988	ILO Convention No (168) on Employment Promotion and Protection against Unemployment	216
1958	ILO Discrimination (Employment and Occupation) Convention No 111	229
a	2	229
1964	ILO Employment Injury Benefits Convention No 121	226
1962	ILO Equality of Treatment (Social Security) Convention No 118	227
a	4	227
	5(1)	227
	6	227
	8	227
1967	ILO Invalidity, Old-age and Survivors' Benefits Convention No 128	216, 226
1952	ILO Maternity Protection Convention 103	227
2000	ILO Maternity Protection Convention 183	226
1969	ILO Medical Care and Sickness Benefits Convention No 130	226
1949	ILO Migration for Employment Convention (Revised) No 97	227
a	1	228
	2	228
	4	228
	5	228
	6	228
1975	ILO Migrant Workers (Supplementary Provisions) Convention No 143	227, 228
a	8	229
	9	229
1990	International Convention on the Protection of the Rights of All Migrant Workers and Members of their Families	223
a	27	224
	28	109
	45	224
	54	224
1968	International Covenant on Civil and Political Rights (CCPR)	114, 155
a	6	109, 155
	7	110

1968		International Covenant on Economic, Social and Cultural Rights (CESCR)	7, 8, 9, 91, 97, 100, 107, 112, 113, 114, 117, 118, 120, 122, 123, 124, 139, 140, 151, 154, 161, 193, 194, 204, 213, 215, 216, 217, 218, 230, 240, 244, 246,
	a	2	113, 216
		2(1)	112, 113, 159, 214, 239, 240
		2(2)	114
		2(3)	114
		3	122
		4	122
		9	213, 214, 217
		10	214
		10(1)	214
		10(2)	214
		11	157, 161, 214, 217
		11(1)	154, 163, 192, 213
		11(2)	154
		12	108, 109, 112, 113, 114, 115, 116, 118, 255
		12(1)	193
		12(2)(b)	193
		12(2)(c)	193
		13	58, 62, 65, 75
		13(1)	65
		13(2)	65
		13(2)(a)	62, 63, 65, 70
		13(2)(b)	63, 70, 75
		13(2)(c)	63, 75, 76
		13(3)	65
		13(4)	65
		14	58, 70
		16	124
1992		Kyoto Protocol to the United Nations Framework Convention on Climate Change	254
1987		Montreal Protocol on Substances that Deplete the Ozone Layer	254
1967		Protocol Relating to the Status of Refugees	223
1998		Protocol to the African Charter on Human and Peoples' Rights Establishing the African Court on Human and Peoples' Rights	256
2003		Protocol to the African Charter on Human and Peoples' Rights on the Rights of Women in Africa	
	a	15	196
1998		Rome Statute of the International Criminal Court	
	a	8(2)(b)(xxv)	156
1957		Standard Minimum Rules for the Treatment of Prisoners	156
	a	22-26 & 82	109
		20(1)	156
1945		Statute of the International Court of Justice	
	a	38(1)	90

1960	UNESCO Convention Against Discrimination in Education	58
a	1	81
1948	Universal Declaration of Human Rights	1, 7, 107, 110, 111, 112, 154, 229
	Preamble	112, 229
a	22-26	7
	22	230
	25	109, 111, 154
	25(1)	195, 230
	25(2)	230
	25(3)	230
	26	58
	26(1)	70
1974	Universal Declaration on the Eradication of Hunger and Malnutrition (UDEHM)	154
1985	Vienna Convention for the Protection of the Ozone Layer Preamble	254
1972	World Heritage Convention Preamble	253

Other international documents

European Community

Directive on the Freedom of Access to Information on the Environment (90/313/EEC)	251
Recommendation Rec (2001) 14 of the Committee of Ministers to Member States on the European Charter on Water Resources	196

International Labour Organisation

Extending social security: Policies for developing countries (ESS Paper No 13)	216
Recommendation No 86	228
Recommendation No 151	229
Report V(1)	216
Report V(2)	216

Organisation of African Unity / AU

Resolution on Dumping of Nuclear and Industrial Waste in Africa (1988)	251

United Nations

Agenda 21, Report of the United Nations Conference on Environment and Development (1992)	195
Beijing Platform: Beijing Declaration and Platform of Action of the Fourth World Conference on Women (Report of the Fourth World Conference on Women, 1995)	110, 118
Beijing Plus Five (Report of the Ad Hoc Committee of the Whole of the Twenty-Third Session of the General Assembly, 2000)	110, 118
Cairo Programme: Programme of Action of the International Conference on Population and Development (Report of the International Conference on Population and Development, 1994)	110, 117, 118, 195
Cairo Plus Five (Key actions for the further implementation of the programme of action of the International Conference on Population and Development, 1999)	110, 118, 119
'Comprehensive Assessment of the Freshwater Resources of the World' (Commission on Sustainable Development of the UN)	198
Copenhagen Declaration on Social Development and Programme of Action, 1995 (UN Doc A/Conf.166/9)	230
Declaration of the United Nations Conference on the Human Environment (1972)	251, 253, 253
Declaration on the Rights of Persons Belonging to National or Ethnic, Religious and Linguistic Minorities (1992)	80
General Assembly Resolution 2816(XXVI) (1971)	156
General Assembly Resolution 36/225 (1981)	156

(continued)

Habitat Agenda (1996)	91
Implementation of the Outcome of the World Summit for Social Development and of the Special Assembly in this regard (GA Agenda Item 37), 2000 (UN Doc A/55/L.40)	231
Johannesburg Declaration on Sustainable Development	255
Limburg Principles on the Implementation of the International Covenant on Social, Economic and Cultural Rights (UN Doc E/CN4/1987/17)	8, 100, 113, 122, 201, 230
Maastricht Guidelines on Violations of Economic, Social and Cultural Rights (reprinted in (1998) 20 *HRQ* 691)	8, 9, 113, 117, 118, 201, 202, 203, 204, 230, 244
Principles for Older Persons (GA Res. 46/91, 16 Dec. 1991)	194
Rio Declaration on Environment and Development (1991)	253, 254, 255, 261, 262
Standard Minimum Rules for the Treatment of Prisoners (1955)	105
Stockholm Declaration (Declaration of the United Nations Conference on the Human Environment) (1972)	256, 257

UN Commission on Human Rights

CESCR Reporting Guidelines (UN Doc HRI/CORE/1)	215
Compilation of Guidelines on the Form and Content of Reports to be Submitted by State Parties to the International Human rights Treaties (UN Doc E/C12/1991/1)	215
Report of the High Commissioner for Human Rights, Addendum, Report on the workshop on the justiciability of economic, social and cultural rights, with particular reference to the Draft Optional Protocol to the International Covenant on Economic, Social and Cultural Rights (UN Doc E/CN 4/2001/62/add 2)	214
Resolution 1998/33 (UN Doc E/CN 4/1999/49)	65
Resolution 2003/18 (UN Doc E/CN.4/RES/2003/18)	8
Resolution on Forced Evictions (Resolution 1993/77)	97

UN Committee on Economic, Social and Cultural Rights

Concluding Observations on the Congo (UN Doc E/C 12/1/Add 45)	124
General Comment No 1 (UN Doc E/1989/22)	201, 202
General Comment No 2 (UN Doc E/1990/23)	201
General Comment No 3 (UN Doc E/1991/23)	26, 58, 65, 74, 91, 100, 101, 113, 114, 117, 159, 178, 188, 201, 202, 205, 240, 244, 246
General Comment No 4 (UN Doc E/1992/23)	97, 102, 192, 201, 204

(continued)

General Comment No 5 (UN Doc E/1995/22)	201
General Comment No 6 (UN Doc E/1996/22)	110, 194, 201
General Comment No 7 (UN Doc E/1998/22)	97, 204
General Comment No 10 (UN Doc E/1999/22)	205
General Comment No 11 (UN Doc E/C 12/1999/4)	58, 70
General Comment No 12 (UN Doc E/2000/22)	9, 48, 156, 157, 158, 159, 160, 161, 164, 178, 179, 180, 182, 184, 186, 201, 203
General Comment No 13 (UN Doc E/C 12/1999/10)	58, 63, 65, 66, 74, 75, 76, 80, 192, 201
General Comment No 14 (UN Doc E/C 12/2000/4)	9, 10, 42, 48, 108, 115, 117, 118, 125, 140, 143, 178, 193, 201
General Comment No 15 (UN Doc E/C 12/2002/11)	9, 48, 191, 193, 198, 199, 200, 201, 202, 204, 205, 208
Preliminary Report of the Special Rapporteur on the Right to Education (UN Doc E/CN 4/1999/49)	65
Right to Adequate Food and to be Free from Hunger (UN Doc E/CN 4/Sub 2/1999/12)	154
Right to Education: Report submitted by the Special Rapporteur (UN Doc E/CN 4/2004/45)	71

UN Committee on the Elimination of Discrimination Against Women

General Recommendation 24 (UN Doc A/54/38 Rev. 1)	120, 121, 125
General Recommendation 25 (UN Doc CEDAW/C/2004/1/WP1/Rev.1)	122

UN Committee on the Rights of the Child

General Comment No 3 (UN Doc CRC/GC/2003/3)	125
General Comment No 4 (UN Doc CRC/GC/2003/4)	125
General Guidelines Regarding the Form and Content of Initial Report to be Submitted by States Parties under art 44 para 1(a) of the Convention (UN Doc CRC/C/5)	217
Observations on South Africa's Initial Report on the Implementation of the CRC (UN Doc CRC/C/15/Add.122)	70, 218

UN Development Programme

Human Development Report 1996	150

UN Economic and Social Council

Social and human rights questions: Advancement of women (Provisional Agenda, E/1999/66-A/54/123) — 191

UN Human Rights Committee

Concluding Observations: Peru (UN Doc CCPR/C/79/Add 72) — 110

General Comment No 6 (UN Doc HRI\GEN\1\Rev.1) — 155

UN Sub-Commission on Human Rights / UN Sub-Commission on Prevention of Discrimination and Protection of Minorities

Draft Principles on Human Rights and the Environment (UN Doc E/CN.4/Sub 2/1994) — 250

Resolution on Forced Evictions (Resolution 1992/14) — 96

World Health Organisation

12th WHO Model List of Essential Medicines (2002) — 117

Alma Ata Declaration (1978) — 117, 144

Constitution (1948) — 108, 109, 260

Global Water Supply and Sanitation Assessment Report (2000) — 195

Guidelines for drinking water quality (2003) — 199

Primary health care: Report of the International Conference on primary health care (1978) — 117

Reproductive health indicators for global monitoring: Report of the Second Interagency meeting (2001) — 119

Twenty-five questions and answers on health and human rights (2002) — 111

Other documents

Bangalore Declaration and Plan of Action (1995) — 8

Dublin Statement on Water and Sustainable Development (1992) — 194

Istanbul Declaration on Human Settlements (1996) — 91

Mar del Plata Declaration (2002) — 191, 194

Proposed Legal Principles for Environmental Protection and Sustainable Development (1987) — 250

Rome Declaration on Food Security (1996) — 156

World Conservation Strategy (1980) — 252

World Declaration on Education for All (1990) — 63

World Food Summit Plan of Action (1996) — 156

Subject index

A
abortion   110, 119, 121, 131-132, 145-146
absolute rights *see* basic socio-economic rights
acceptability
    of education   65, 71-72
    of food   160
    of health care   115, 116
access/accessibility
    to courts   263
    economic   67, 68, 76, 99, 116, 158
    to education   65, 67, 68, 76, 81
    to food   157, 158
    to health care   115, 116
    to housing   103
    to information   251, 263
    meaning of   3, 102, 200, 234
    physical   67, 116, 158
    to social security and assistance   234
    to water   200, 201
accommodation, right to   85, 105
adaptability
    of education   65, 73
adequate food
    culturally   159
    nutritionally   159
    and right to water   163, 191, 196, 199, 206
adequate housing   102-103
    culturally   103
adequate medical treatment   16-17, 25, 126, 133
administrative inefficiency as obstacle to access to rights   17, 36, 170, 186
administrative justice rights   4, 5, 164, 207, 233, 263
adult basic education   61, 62, 63, 73
affirmative action
    and access to health care   121
    and access to social security and assistance   221
affirmative obligations   116
African Commission on Human and Peoples' Rights   8, 155, 165, 196, 231
apartheid
    and education   60, 70, 75, 76
    and food   165, 167, 168
    and health care   127, 128, 129, 131, 144, 151
    and land and housing   30, 85, 96, 165, 167
availability
    of education   65, 66
    of food   157, 158, 187
    of health care   115, 116
    of housing   102
available resources   52, 58, 74, 114, 115, 137, 161, 202, 205, 246

B
Basic Income Grant   211, 212, 243, 248
basic nutrition   161, 163
basic socio-economic rights   4, 28, 64
biodiversity   249, 260
bodily and psychological integrity, right to   126, 132, 138

C
Care Dependency Grant   13, 183, 211, 219, 224, 241, 242
Child Support Grant   13, 163, 183, 185, 186, 211, 212, 218, 219, 222, 224, 239, 240, 241, 242, 243, 245, 247, 248
children
    interpretation of socio-economic rights of   88, 104, 140, 206, 207, 232

    of non-citizens   224, 225, 227
    right to basic health care of   140
    right to shelter of   104
    right to social security and assistance of   217, 218, 219, 220
    right to water of   206, 207
    socio-economic rights of   28
    standard of scrutiny applying to socio-economic rights of   43, 104, 105, 140, 163, 206, 207
citizenship
    and social assistance   224, 243, 244, 247
common law
    and the duty to protect socio-economic rights   10, 38-42, 172-177, 239
    courts' duty to develop the   10, 18, 20, 24, 25, 39, 40, 41, 96, 173, 175, 176, 177
    direct constitutional challenge to the   19
    environmental rights and the   258
    right to food and the   173, 175, 176, 177
    right to health care and the   41
    rules of eviction   24, 25, 94, 95, 96, 176, 177
    rules of standing   42
corporal punishment   72
culture
    in education   61, 67, 72, 77, 79, 80
customary international law   90, 229

D

damages   35, 41
detainees
    standard of scrutiny applying to breaches of rights of   43, 163
dignity   28, 41, 45, 51, 63, 69, 88, 89, 99, 105, 126, 127, 131, 138, 143, 148, 162, 175, 199, 207, 230, 235, 236, 243, 247, 248, 251, 255, 258, 259
directive principles of state policy   6, 57
direct socio-economic rights *see* basic socio-economic rights
Disability Grant   13, 37, 42, 169, 170, 183, 185, 211, 212, 219, 222, 238, 241, 242
disadvantaged groups *see* vulnerable groups
discipline of learners   71, 72
disconnection of water services   16, 31, 32, 197, 198, 203, 204, 205
drinking water   102, 116, 193-197, 199, 201
duties
    negative   10-12, 21, 26-30, 47, 61, 92, 93, 116, 131, 136, 206, 238, 257
    of conduct   113, 115
    of result   113, 115
    positive   10-12, 22, 26-28, 43, 61, 92, 98, 132, 136, 239
    to fulfil   10, 11, 42-52, 54, 116, 159, 160, 178-188, 205
    to promote   10, 42, 178, 187, 205
    to protect   8, 10, 37-42, 115, 166, 170-177, 196, 204
    to respect   9, 10, 11, 28, 30-37, 47, 92,115, 165-170, 203, 206, 238

E

economic access *see* access
education, right to (general)   57-84
    basic education   61-66, 68, 69, 70, 71, 73
    compulsory education   63
    free education   68, 70
    primary education   62, 63, 65, 70
effectiveness
    as standard of scrutiny   23, 27, 45, 53, 113
    of remedies   54, 55
emergency medical treatment   32-33, 36, 43, 44, 126, 135, 136
environmental rights (general)   249-266
    anthropocentric approach to the environment   252, 259

Subject index

ecocentric approach to the environment		252
equality		
	and food	164
	and social security and assistance	221, 222, 225, 227-229, 233, 235, 237, 239, 243
	and socio-economic rights	4-5, 7, 86, 88, 89, 164, 237
	and water	207
	in education	60, 70, 75, 80, 81
	in health care	116, 117, 120, 121, 122, 127, 128, 131-132, 149, 150-151
	in housing	88, 89, 97, 99
	substantive	5, 81, 99, 116, 117, 120, 121, 122, 127, 131-132, 149, 150-151
	unfair discrimination	5, 19, 36, 44, 61, 67, 70, 76, 80, 81, 114, 116, 120, 131, 132, 147, 148, 160, 164, 200, 221, 222, 223, 228, 233, 239
essential health care		36, 117
eviction		
	law regulating	16, 19, 24-25, 31, 32, 38, 39, 40, 42, 93-96, 96-97, 102, 166-167, 169, 171, 172, 174, 176-177, 204
	suitable alternative land in case of	33-36, 105, 169, 172
expropriation		31, 39, 166

F

family		
	care	104, 194, 206, 211, 214-215, 220, 221, 223, 226-232
	planning	120, 121, 144
famine		17, 186, 187, 189
food, right to (general)		153-190
Food and Agriculture Organisation		153, 156, 157
food prices		7, 154, 171, 180, 183
food security		
	definition	153, 157, 158, 160, 180, 196
	household	158, 183
	national	158, 183
foreign law		
	as interpretive source re socio-economic rights	6-9, 86, 89, 154
	and environmental rights	255
	and food	154
	and housing	86, 89
	and social security and assistance	213
Foster Child Grant		13, 211, 224, 241, 242
framework legislation		48, 160, 182
freedom from hunger		154, 156
freedom from torture		122
freedom of assembly		82
freedom of choice		59, 81-82, 164
freedom of expression		72
freedom to choose a trade, occupation or profession		63, 164
further education		62, 63, 73, 74-76

G

global warming	249
Grant-in-Aid	13, 183, 211, 241, 242

H

health, rights concerning (general)		107-152
health insurance		212
higher education *see* further education		
HIV/Aids		
	orphans	219, 245
	and education	73
	and nutrition	180
	and patient confidentiality	123, 124
	and the pharmaceutical industry	92

Subject index 295

and women	120
as disability	219
monitoring with respect to	124
mother-to-child transmission of	17, 23, 25, 36, 44, 50, 52
prisoners and	16, 133, 134, 138-142
state provision of anti-retrovirals	141, 150
unfair discrimination on the basis of	131, 239
holding over, practice of	24, 25, 95-96, 176-177
horizontal application of socio-economic rights	18-20, 205, 258
housing, right to (general)	85-106

I

impairment of access to socio-economic rights	10, 11, 13, 36, 37, 41, 74, 92 159, 165, 169, 243, 248, 257
independent educational institutions *see* private education institutions	
independent schools *see* private educational institutions	
indicators	118-119, 121, 122, 124, 149, 184
informal rights to land	38, 40, 166, 171
integration, principle of, with respect to environmental rights	252, 254, 255
interdependence, indivisibility and interrelatedness of rights	4-6, 57, 59, 88, 108, 111, 163-165, 191-192, 217, 232, 237
interference with the exercise of socio-economic rights	
by private parties	10, 32, 37-41, 65, 96, 98, 115, 155, 159, 162, 170, 171, 174, 175, 205, 239
by the state	9, 11, 15, 30, 32, 61, 65, 93, 96, 116, 131, 132, 155, 161, 165, 166, 168, 202, 203, 204, 238, 239
intergenerational equity	252-254, 260
internal limitation	27, 43, 73, 206
International Labour Organisation	9, 211, 214-217, 225-229, 235, 236, 248
interpretation	
contextual	60-61, 88-89, 99, 136
generous	136, 231
purposive	63, 118, 136
role of foreign law in	6-9, 86, 89, 154
role of international law in	6-9, 64, 89-91, 125, 138, 154, 192, 213
value driven	235
intragenerational equity	252, 254

J

justiciability of socio-economic rights	11, 20-22, 86, 91, 133, 143

L

Land Redistribution for Agricultural Development	182, 188
language	61, 71, 72, 77-81
life, right to	4, 6, 44, 109, 122, 135-136, 154, 155, 197, 217, 256
limitation of rights	26-30, 43, 73-74, 122-124, 131, 162, 163
local authorities	34, 57, 129, 207
locus standi see standing	

M

means-end scrutiny	23, 27, 45, 53
Medicines Control Council	45, 141
migrant workers	109, 223-225, 227-229
minimum core content	64, 65, 101, 115, 117, 118, 142, 143, 158, 206, 240, 246
monitoring	7, 38, 55, 58, 71, 108, 118, 121, 124-125, 139, 160, 171, 172, 183, 193, 202, 205, 218

N

National Health Insurance	212
negative duties *see* duties	

O

obligations *see* duties

P

permanent residents	4, 19, 28, 36, 44, 51, 53, 54, 162, 224-225, 237, 242-243, 245-247
pollution	103, 164, 194, 207-208, 249, 256, 257, 258, 261, 262, 263
pregnancy	36, 81, 110, 118, 119, 120, 121, 131, 132, 139, 141, 145, 146, 156, 221, 233
primary health care	101, 117, 144-145, 148, 193
Primary School Feeding Scheme	183, 185
prisoners *see* detainees	
privacy, right to	208, 233
medical or scientific experiments, right not to be subjected	126
private educational institutions	59, 79-81
private schools *see* private educational institutions	
progressive realisation	3, 4, 26, 27, 49, 62, 64, 74, 91, 98-100, 104, 105, 114, 162, 187, 202, 216, 233, 244-245
property, right to	16, 35, 38-40, 41, 85, 87, 93-97, 147, 157, 158, 166, 172, 174-177, 204, 205, 233
proportionality	27, 28, 32, 43, 45, 51, 162, 163
Protein Energy Malnutrition	183
provincial government	5-6, 14, 22, 37, 48-49, 52, 66, 129, 148-149, 169-170, 185, 187, 220, 238, 244

Q

qualified rights	28, 29, 47, 62

R

rationality	22, 27, 43, 44, 142, 162, 203
reasonableness review	5, 9, 22, 23, 27-29, 43-47, 49-51, 53, 64, 74, 76, 77, 100-101, 142, 162, 181-182, 184, 240-242, 263
refugees	223, 225, 229
religion	61, 72, 79, 81-82, 109, 114, 131, 228, 233
remedies	
appropriate relief	13, 54, 142, 263
declaratory order	55, 203
directory order	25, 55
effectiveness of	54
mandatory order *see* directory order	
structural interdicts	55, 56
supervisory interdicts *see* structural interdicts	
rental housing	38, 93
retrogressive measures	46, 47, 100, 178, 180, 187, 188, 202, 244
medical or scientific experiments, right not to be subjected	126

S

sanitation	61, 66, 67, 102, 108, 116, 117, 124, 144, 149, 191-196, 198, 199, 208, 212
school fees	68-71
security of tenure	24, 25, 31, 33, 34, 38, 39, 40, 93, 96, 102, 164, 166, 169, 172, 174, 176, 177, 189
separation of powers	9, 12, 14, 21, 22, 23, 132, 142
Settlement/Land Acquisition Grant	188
share-cropping	167, 168
shelter	15, 39, 40, 44, 85-89, 96, 98, 101, 102, 104, 105, 109, 115, 117, 139, 232, 235
social assistance, definition of	211
social insurance, definition of	210
social justice	1, 2, 5, 21, 39, 61, 87, 111, 131
social protection, definition of	210
Social Relief of Distress Grant	14, 48, 49, 185, 187, 241, 242
social security and assistance, right to (general)	209-248
social security, definition of	210

social solidarity	235, 236
South African Human Rights Commission	12, 73, 218, 238, 241, 246, 248
South African Law Commission	87, 219
squatting	32, 34-36
standard of scrutiny	12, 15, 26-28, 43-45, 47, 50-51, 77, 161, 162, 163
standing	13, 42, 82, 251, 253-254, 259, 263
statutory socio-economic rights	12-16, 23-25
subsistence farming	165, 166, 243
subsistence fishing	168
sufficiency *see* adequacy	
sustainable development	164, 194, 198, 207, 231, 250, 252, 255, 257, 261-263, 264

T

transformation	61, 75, 76, 127, 131, 132, 149, 151
transformative constitutionalism	1
transparency	51, 161, 181, 182

U

ubuntu	232, 236
Unemployment Insurance Fund	210, 221, 245
unqualified socio-economic rights *see* socio-economic rights	

V

vulnerable groups	58, 90, 94, 103, 104, 148, 151, 155, 160, 183, 188, 200, 201, 211, 217, 232, 236, 242, 258

W

War Veteran's Grant	13, 183, 185, 211
water, right to (general)	191-208
women	
discrimination against	88, 120, 121, 131, 132, 193, 196, 217, 221, 226, 227, 239
HIV-positive	36, 120, 141
World Health Organisation	108, 141, 144, 145, 198, 260

Bibliography

Addo, MK 'Justiciability re-examined' in Beddard, R & Hill, DM (eds) (1992) *Economic, social and cultural rights: Progress and achievement* London: St Martin's Press 93

Albertyn, C & Goldblatt, B 'Facing the challenge of transformation: The difficulties in the development of an indigenous jurisprudence of equality' (1998) 14 *South African Journal on Human Rights* 248

Albertyn, C & Kentridge, J 'Introducing the right to equality in the interim Constitution' (1994) 10 *South African Journal on Human Rights* 124

Alston, P & Quinn, G 'The nature and scope of state parties' obligations under the International Covenant on Economic, Social and Cultural Rights' (1987) 9 *Human Rights Quarterly* 156

Andrews, P & Ellmann, S (2001) *The post-apartheid constitutions: Perspectives on South Africa's basic law* Johannesburg: Witwatersrand University Press

An-Na'im, AA 'To affirm the full human rights standing of economic, social and cultural rights' in Ghai, YP & Cottrell, J (eds) (2004) *Economic, social and cultural rights in practice: The role of judges in implementing economic, social and cultural rights* London: Interights 7

Anthony, AE 'Beyond the paper tiger: The challenge of a human rights court in Africa' (1997) 12 *Texas International Law Journal* 511

Bakan, J 'What's wrong with social rights' in Schneiderman, D & Bakan, J (eds) (1992) *Social justice and the Constitution: Perspectives on a social union for Canada* Ottawa: Carleton University Press 85

Bandes, S 'The negative constitution: A critique' (1990) 88 *Michigan Law Review* 2271

Barberton, C; Blake, M & Kotze, H (eds) (1998) *Creating action space: The challenge of poverty and democracy in South Africa* Claremont: IDASA & David Philip

Baxter, L (1984) *Administrative law* Cape Town: Juta

Bekker, G (ed) (2000) *A compilation of essential documents on the rights to food and nutrition* Pretoria: Centre for Human Rights, University of Pretoria

Bekker, G (ed) (1999) *A compilation of essential documents on economic, social and cultural rights* Pretoria: Centre for Human Rights, University of Pretoria

Benatar, SR 'Health care reform in the new South Africa' (1997) 336 *The New England Journal of Medicine* 881

Ben-Israel, R 'Social security in the year 2000: Potentialities and problems' (1995) 16 *Comparative Labour Law Journal* 139

Berg, CJ; Atrash, HK; Koonin, LM & Tucker, M 'Pregnancy-related mortality in the United States 1987-1990'(1996) 88 *Obstetrics and Gynaecology* 161

Berger, J 'Taking responsibilities seriously: The role of the state in preventing transmission from mother to child' (2001) 2 *Law, Democracy and Development* 163

Berghman, J 'Basic concepts of social security in Europe' in Greve, B & Pieters, D (eds) (1999) *Social security in an interdisciplinary perspective* Antwerpen: Maklu 13

Bilchitz, D 'Towards a reasonable approach to the minimum core: Laying the foundations for future socio-economic rights jurisprudence' (2003) 19 *South African Journal on Human Rights* 1

Blyberg, A & Ravindram, DJ (2000) *Circle of rights: Economic, social and cultural rights activism: A training resource* University of Minnesota: Human Rights Resource Center

Boerefijn, I; Coomans, F; Goldschmidt, J; Holtmaat, R & Wolleswinkel, R (2003) *Temporary special measures: Accelerating de facto equality of women under article*

4(1) UN Convention on the elimination of all forms of discrimination against women Antwerpen: Intersentia

Bollyky, TJ 'R if C > P + B: A paradigm for judicial remedies of socio-economic rights violations' (2002) 18 (2) *South African Journal on Human Rights* 161

Botha, N 'International law and the South African interim Constitution' (1994) 9 *SA Publiek Reg / SA Public Law* 248

Boyle, AE 'The role of international human rights law in the protection of the environment' in Boyle, AE & Anderson, MR (eds) (1996) *Human rights approaches to environmental protection* Oxford: Clarendon Press 43

Boyle, AE & Anderson, MR (eds) (1996) *Human rights approaches to environmental protection* Oxford: Clarendon Press

Boyle, AE & Freestone, D 'Introduction' in Boyle, AE & Freestone, D (eds) (1999) *International law and sustainable development: Past achievements and future challenges* New York: Oxford University Press 1

Boyle, AE & Freestone, D (eds) (1999) *International law and sustainable development: Past achievements and future challenges* New York: Oxford University Press

Brand, D 'The proceduralisation of South African socio-economic right jurisprudence, or "What are socio-economic rights for?"' in Botha, H; Van der Walt, JGW & Van der Walt, AJ (2004) *Rights and democracy in a transformative constitution* Stellenbosch: SunMedia 33

Brand, D 'Budgeting and service delivery in programmes targeted at the child's right to basic nutrition' in Coetzee, E & Streak, J (eds) (2004) *Monitoring child socio-economic rights in South Africa: Achievements and challenges* Cape Town: IDASA 87

Brand, D 'Between availability and entitlement: The Constitution, *Grootboom* and the right to food' (2003) 7 *Law, Democracy and Development* 1

Brand, D 'Disclaimers in hospital admission contracts and constitutional health rights' (2002) 3 (2) *ESR Review* 17

Brand, D 'The minimum core content of the right to food in context: A response to Rolf Künneman' in Brand, D & Russel, S (eds) (2002) *Exploring the core content of socio-economic rights: South African and international perspectives* Pretoria: Protea Book House 99

Brand, D & Liebenberg, S 'The South African Human Rights Commission: The second economic and social rights report' (2000) 2 (3) *ESR Review* 12

Brand, D 'The South African Human Rights Commission: First economic and social rights report' (1999) 2 (1) *ESR Review* 18

Brand, D & Russel, S (eds) (2002) *Exploring the core content of socio-economic rights: South African and international perspectives* Pretoria: Protea Book House

Bruch, C; Coker, W & Van Arsdale, C 'Constitutional environmental law: Giving force to fundamental principles in Africa' (2001) 26 *Columbia Journal of Environmental Law* 131

Budlender, G 'Justiciability of socio-economic rights: Some South African experiences' in Ghai, YP & Cottrell, J (eds) (2004) *Economic, social and cultural rights in practice. The role of judges in implementing economic, social and cultural rights* London: Interights 33

Budlender, G 'The justiciability of the right to housing: The South African experience' http://www.lrc.org.za/4Pub/Papers/delhi%20paper.pdf

Cameron, J & Mackenzie, R 'Access to environmental justice and procedural rights in international institutions' in Boyle, AE & Anderson, MR (eds) (1996) *Human rights approaches to environmental protection* Oxford: Clarendon Press 129

Carstens, PA & Kok, JA 'An assessment of the use of disclaimers against medical negligence by South African hospitals in view of constitutional demands, foreign law and medico-legal considerations' (2003) 18 *SA Public Law* 430

Carter, BE & Trimble, PR (1991) *International law: Selected documents* Boston: Little Brown 731

Chapman, AR 'A "violations approach" for monitoring the International Covenant on Economic, Social and Cultural Rights' (1996) 18 *Human Rights Quarterly* 23

Chapman, AR 'Core obligations related to the right to health and their relevance for South Africa' in Brand, D & Russell, S (eds) (2002) *Exploring the core content of socio-economic rights: South African and international perspectives* Pretoria: Protea Book House 35

Chapman, AR & Russell, S (eds) (2002) *Core obligations: Building a framework for economic, social and cultural rights* New York: Intersentia

Chaskalson, A 'The third Bram Fischer memorial lecture: Human dignity as a foundational value of our constitutional order' (2000) 16 *South African Journal on Human Rights* 193

Cheadle, MH; Davis, DM & Haysom, NRL (eds) (2002) *South African Constitutional law: The Bill of Rights* Cape Town: Butterworths

Cheadle, MH 'Application' in Cheadle, MH; Davis, DM & Haysom, NRL (eds) (2002) *South African constitutional law: The Bill of Rights* Durban: Butterworths 19

Cheadle, MH & Davis, DM 'The application of the 1996 Constitution in the private sphere' (1997) 13 *South African Journal on Human Rights* 44

Chopra, M; Sogaula, N; Jackson, D; Sanders, D; Karaolis, N; Ashworth, A & Mc Coy, D 'Poverty wipes out health care gains' (2001/02) 6(4) *Children First* 16

Cobbah, JAM 'African values and the human rights debate: An African perspective' (1987) 9 *Human Rights Quarterly* 309

Cook, RJ; Dickens, BM & Fathalla, MF (2003) *Reproductive health and human rights: Integrating medicine, ethics and law* Oxford: Clarendon Press

Cook, RJ; Dickens, BM; Wilson, OAF & Scarrow, SE (2001) *Advancing safe motherhood through human rights* Geneva: Department of Reproductive Health and Research, World Health Organisation

Coomans, F 'In search of the core content of the right to education' in Brand, D & Russel, S (eds) (2002) *Exploring the core content of socio-economic rights: South African and international perspectives* Pretoria: Protea Book House 159

Corder, H; Kahanovitz, S; Murphy, J & Murray, C (1992) *A charter for social justice: A contribution to the South African Bill of Rights debate* Cape Town: Dept of Public Law, University of Cape Town

Cottrell, J & Ghai, YP 'The role of the courts in the protection of economic, social and cultural rights' in Ghai, YP & Cottrell, J (eds) (2004) *Economic, social and cultural rights in practice: The role of judges in implementing economic, social and cultural rights* London: Interights 58

Cranston, M (1973) *What are human rights?* New York: Taplinger

Craven, M 'Introduction to the International Covenant on Economic, Social and Cultural Rights' in Blyberg, A & Ravindram, DJ (2000) *Circle of rights. Economic, social and cultural rights: A training resource* Washington: International Human Rights Internship Programme 49

Craven, MCR (1998) *The International Covenant on Economic, Social and Cultural Rights: A perspective on its development* Oxford: Clarendon Press

D'Amato, A 'Do we owe a duty to future generations to preserve the global environment?' (1990) 84 *American Journal of International Law* 190

D'Amato, A & Chopra, SK 'Whales: Their emerging right to life' (1991) 85 *American Journal of International Law* 21

Dankwa, V; Flinterman, C & Leckie, S 'Commentary to the Maastricht Guidelines on violations of economic, social and cultural rights' (1998) 20 *Human Rights Quarterly* 705

Davis, DM 'The case against the inclusion of socio-economic demands in a bill of rights except as direct principles' (1992) 8 *South African Journal on Human Rights* 475

Davis, DM; Cheadle, MH & Haysom, N (1997) *Fundamental rights in the Constitution: Commentary and cases* Kenwyn: Juta

De Beer, C (1984) *The South African disease: Apartheid, health and health services* London: Catholic Institute for International Relations

De Villiers, B 'Social and economic rights' in Van Wyk, DH; Dugard, J; De Villiers, B & Davis, D et al (eds) (1994) *Rights and constitutionalism: The new South African legal order* Kenwyn: Juta 599

De Villiers, N 'Social grants and the Promotion of Administrative Justice Act' (2002) 18 *South African Journal on Human Rights* 320

De Visser, J 'Disconnection of water supply: Manquele v Durban Transitional Metropolitan Council' (2001) 3(1) *Local Government Law Bulletin* 15

De Vos, P 'The Promotion of Equality and Prevention of Unfair Discrimination Act and socio-economic rights' (2004) 5(2) *ESR Review* 5

De Vos, P '*Grootboom*, the right of access to housing and substantive equality as contextual fairness' (2001) 17 *South African Journal on Human Rights* 258

De Vos, P 'Pious wishes or directly enforceable human rights? Social and economic rights in South Africa's 1996 Constitution' (1997) 13 *South African Journal on Human Rights* 67

De Waal, J; Currie, I & Erasmus, G (2001) *The Bill of Rights Handbook* 4th ed, Cape Town: Juta

De Waal, J; Currie, I & Erasmus, G (1999) *The Bill of Rights Handbook* 2nd ed, Cape Town: Juta

De Wet, E 'Can the social state principle in Germany guide state action in South Africa in the field of social and economic rights?' (1995) 11 *South African Journal on Human Rights* 30

Devenish, GE 'The legal significance of the right to equality clause in the interim Constitution' (1996) 1 *Stellenbosch Law Review* 92

Devereux, A 'Australia and the right to adequate housing' (1991) 20 *Federal Law Review* 232

Devine, D 'The relationship between international law and municipal law in the light of the interim South African Constitution 1993' (1995) 44 *International and Comparative Law Quarterly* 1

Dlamini, C 'Culture, education and religion' in Van Wyk, DH; Dugard, J; De Villiers, B & Davis, D (eds) (1996) *Rights and constitutionalism: The new South African legal order* Oxford: Clarendon Press 573

Douglas-Scott, S 'Environmental rights in the European Union: Participatory democracy or democratic deficit?' in Boyle, AE & Anderson, MR (eds) (1996) *Human rights approaches to environmental protection* Oxford: Clarendon Press 109

Dreze, J & Sen, A (1989) *Hunger and public action* Oxford, UK: Clarendon Press

Dugard, J 'International law and the "final" Constitution' (1995) 11 *South African Journal on Human Rights* 241

Dugard, J (2000) *International law: A South African perspective* 2nd ed, Kenwyn: Juta

Dugard, J 'The role of international law in interpreting the Bill of Rights' (1994) 10 *South African Journal on Human Rights* 208

Du Plessis, LM & Corder, H (1994) *Understanding South Africa's transitional Bill of Rights* Kenwyn: Juta

Eide, A *The right to adequate food and to be free of hunger* (1999) E/CN 4/Sub 2/1999/12 paras 32-43 & 55-57

Eide, A 'Future protection of economic and social rights in Europe' in Bloed, A *et al* (eds) (1993) *Monitoring human rights in Europe: Comparing international procedures and mechanisms* Dordrecht: M Nijhoff 187

Eide, A; Krause, C & Rosas, A (eds) (1995) *Economic, social and cultural rights: A textbook* Dordrecht: M Nijhoff

Evans, T *et al* (eds) (2001) *Challenging inequities in health: From ethics to action* Oxford: Oxford University Press

Feris, LA (2000) *The conceptualisation of environmental justice within the context of the South African Constitution* (LLD Thesis) University of Stellenbosch: Dept of Public Law

Fitzpatrick, J & Slye, RC 'Republic of South Africa v Grootboom; Minister of Health v Treatment Action Campaign' (2003) 97 *The American Journal of International Law* 669

Flinterman, C 'Limburg Principles on the implementation of the International Covenant on Economic, Social and Cultural Rights' (1987) 9 *Human Rights Quarterly* 122

Freedman, F 'Understanding the right to equality' (1998) 115 *South African Law Journal* 243

Gillespie, A (1997) *International environmental law, policy and ethics* Oxford: Clarendon Press

Glavovic, PD 'The evolution and articulation of environmental rights as fundamental human rights' (1996) 3 *South African Journal of Environmental Law and Policy* 71

Glazewski, J 'The environment and the new Constitution' (1994) 1 *South African Journal of Environmental Law and Policy* 3

Gleick, PH 'Basic water requirements for human activities: Meeting basic needs' (1996) 21 *Water International* 83

Gleick, PH 'The human right to water' (1999) 5 *Water Policy* 487 http://www.pacinst.org

Goldblatt, B & Liebenberg, S 'Giving money to children: The State's constitutional obligation to provide child support grants to child headed households' (2004) 20 *South African Journal on Human Rights* 151

Gray, A 'Equity and the provision of pharmaceutical services' (1998) *South African Health Review* 103

Green, A (1992) *An introduction to health planning in developing countries* Oxford: Oxford University Press

Grimwood, A; Crewe, M & Betteridge D 'HIV/AIDS - Current issues' (2000) *South African Health Review 2000* 287

Gündling, L 'Our responsibility to future generations' (1990) 84 *American Journal of International Law* 207

Gutto, SBO 'Environmental law and rights' in Chaskalson, M; Kentridge, J; Klaaren, J; Marcus, G; Spitz, D & Woolman, S (1996) *Constitutional Law of South Africa* Lansdowne: Juta 32-1

Handl, G 'Human rights and the protection of the environment: A mildly "revisionist" view' in Cancado Trindade, AA (ed) (1992) *Human rights, sustainable development and environment* Costa Rica: Instituto Interamericano de Derechos Humanos

Hannum, H 'The UDHR in national and international law' (1998) 3(2) *Health and Human Rights* 145

Harrison, S & Qose, M 'Health legislation' (1998) *South African Health Review* 17

Haysom, N 'Constitutionalism, majoritarian democracy and socio-economic rights' (1992) 8 *South African Journal on Human Rights* 451

Heyns, CH & Van der Linde, M (2004) *Human rights law in Africa* Leiden: M Nijhoff

Heyns, CH & Brand, D 'Introduction to socio-economic rights in the South African Constitution' in Bekker, G (ed) (1999) *A compilation of essential documents on economic, social and cultural right / Economic and social rights series, Vol 1* Pretoria: Centre for Human Rights, University of Pretoria 1

Heyns, CH & Brand, D 'Introduction to socio-economic rights in the South African Constitution' (1998) 2 *Law, Democracy and Development* 153

Heyns, CH 'Extended medical training and the Constitution: Balancing civil and political rights and socio-economic rights' (1997) 30 *De Jure* 1

Isaacs, M 'Subsistence fishing in South Africa: Social policy or commercial micro-enterprise?' (2001) 3(2) *Commons Southern Africa* 20

Jansen van Rensburg, L (2000) *Die beregting van die fundamentele reg op toegang tot sosiale sekerheid* (LLD Thesis) Randse Afrikaanse Universiteit

Jansen van Rensburg, L & Olivier, MP 'International and supra-international law' in Olivier, MP; Smit, N & Kalula, ER (2003) *Social security: A legal analysis* Durban: Lexis Nexis Butterworths 619

Keightley, R 'The impact of the Extension of Security of Tenure Act on an owner's right to vindicate immovable property' (1999) 15 *South African Journal on Human Rights* 277

Kempel, W 'Transboundary movement of hazardous wastes' in Sjostedt, G (ed) (1993) *International environmental negotiation* Newbury Park: Sage

Khoza, S 'Protecting the right to food in South Africa. The role of framework legislation' (2004) 5 (1) *ESR Review* 3

Kidd, M (1997) *Environmental Law: A South African guide* Kenwyn: Juta

Kinney, ED 'The international human right to health: What does this mean for our nation and world?' (2001) 34 *Indiana Law Review* 1457

Klare, KE 'Legal culture and transformative constitutionalism' (1998) 14 *South African Journal on Human Rights* 146

Kollapen, J 'Monitoring socio-economic rights: What has the SA Human Rights Commission done?' (1999) 1(4) *ESR Review* 18

Kriel, R 'Education' in Chaskalson, M; Kentridge, J; Klaaren, J; Marcus, G; Spitz, D; Stein, A & Woolman, S (1996) *Constitutional Law of South Africa* 2nd ed, Original Service, Cape Town: Juta 38-1

Kseutini, FZ 'Human rights, environment and development' in Lin, S & Kurukulasuriya, L (eds)(1995) *UNEP'S new way forward: Environmental law and sustainable development*, Geneva: United Nations Environment Programme 108

Lahiff, E 'Land reform in South Africa: Is it meeting the challenge?' (2001) 1 *PLAAS Policy Brief* 2

Lamarche, L 'Social security as a human right' in Brand, D & Russel, S (eds) (2002) *Exploring the core content of socio-economic rights: South African and international perspectives* Pretoria: Protea Book House 109

Lamarche, L 'The right to social security as a human right guaranteed by the Covenant on Economic, Social and Cultural rights: The time has come to think about it' in Chapman, A & Russell, S (eds) (2002) *Core obligations: Building a framework for economic, social and cultural rights* New York: Intersentia

Langford, M; Khalfan, A; Faistein, C & Jones, H (2004)'Legal resources for the right to water: National and international standards' *COHRE* http://www.cohre.org/water

Langford, M 'The right to water and the International Covenant on Economic, Social and Cultural Rights' *COHRE* http://www.cohre.org/water

Leary, V 'The right to health in international human rights law' (1994) 1(1) *Health and Human Rights* 25

Leckie, S 'Another step towards indivisibility: Identifying key features of violations of economic, social and cultural rights' (1998) 20 *Human Rights Quarterly* 81

Liebenberg, S 'The protection of economic and social rights in domestic legal systems' in Eide, A; Krause, C and Rosas, A (2001) *Economic, social and cultural rights: A textbook* 2nd ed, Dordrecht: M Nijhoff 55

Liebenberg, S 'The right to social assistance: The implications of *Grootboom* for policy reform in South Africa' (2001) 17 *South African Journal on Human Rights* 232

Liebenberg, S & Pillay, K (eds) (2000) *Socio-economic rights in South Africa: A resource book* Bellville: Socio-Economic Rights Project, Community Law Centre, University of the Western Cape

Liebenberg, S 'Education' in Davis, DM; Cheadle, MH & Haysom, NRL (eds) (1997) *Fundamental rights in the Constitution: Commentary and cases* Kenwyn: Juta 294

Liebenberg, S 'Environment' in Davis, DM; Cheadle, MH & Haysom, NRL (eds) (1997) *Fundamental rights in the Constitution: Commentary and cases* Kenwyn: Juta 256

Liebenberg, S 'The interpretation of socio-economic rights' in Chaskalson, M; Kentridge, J; Klaaren, J; Marcus, G; Spitz, D; Stein, A & Woolman, S (1996) *Constitutional law of South Africa* 2nd ed, Original service, Cape Town: Juta 33-1

Liebenberg, S 'Social and economic rights: A critical challenge' in Liebenberg, S (ed) (1995) *The Constitution of South Africa from a gender perspective* Johannesburg: Thorold's Africana Books 79

Liebenberg, S 'The International Covenant on Economic, Social and Cultural Rights and its implications for South Africa' (1995) 11 *South African Journal on Human Rights* 359

Lindholdt, L (1997) *Questioning the universality of human rights: The African Charter on human and people's rights in Botswana, Malawi and Mozambique* Brookfield, Vt: Ashgate, Dartmouth

Liu, SF 'The Koko incident: Developing international norms for the transboundary movement of hazardous wastes' (1992) *Journal of Natural Resources and Environmental Law* 121

Madala, T (Jan 2002) *International seminar on the Right to Food* (Unpublished Address) Pretoria: Centre for Human Rights, University of Pretoria

Mahabal, KB 'Enforcing the right to food in India: The impact of social activism' (2004) 5(1) *ESR Review* 7

Majola, B 'A response to Craig Scott: A South African perspective' (1999) 1(4) *ESR Review* 6

Malherbe, EFJ 'Reflections on the background and contents of the education clause in the South African Bill of Rights' (1997) 1 *Tydskrif vir die Suid-Afrikaanse Reg* 85

Mbazira, C 'Reading the right to food into the African Charter on Human and Peoples' Rights' (2004) 5(1) *ESR Review* 5

McClain, CV 'The SA Human Rights Commission and socio-economic rights. Facing the challenges' (2002) 3(1) *ESR Review* 8

McCoy, D & Khosa, S 'Free health policies' (1996) 5 *South African Health Review* 157

Michelman, FI 'Formal and associational aims in procedural due process' in Pennock, JR & Chapman, JW (eds) (1977) *Due Process (Nomos XVII)* 126

Michelman, FI 'The constitution, social rights, and liberal political justification' (2003) 1 *International Journal of Constitutional Law* 13

Mickelson, K 'South, north, international environmental law and international environmental lawyers' (2002) *Yearbook of International Environmental Law* 52

Moellendorf, D 'Reasoning about resources: *Soobramoney* and the future of economic rights claims' (1998) 14 *South African Journal on Human Rights* 327

Molitor, MR (ed) (1991) *International environmental law: Primary materials* Boston: Kluwer Law and Taxation Publishers

Mureinik, E 'Beyond a charter of luxuries: Economic rights in the Constitution' (1992) 8 *South African Journal on Human Rights* 464

Ngwena, C 'Access to health care as a fundamental right: The scope and limits of section 27 of the Constitution' (2000) 25 *Journal for Juridical Science* 1

Ngwena, C 'Accessing abortion under the Choice on Termination of Pregnancy Act: Realising substantive equality' (2000) 25 *Journal for Juridical Science* 19

Ngwena, C 'AIDS in Africa: Access to health care as a fundamental right' (2000) 15 *SA Publiekreg/ Public Law* 1

Ngwena, C 'Substantive equality in South African health care: The limits of law' (2000) 4 *Medical Law International* 2

Ngwena, C 'The history and transformation of abortion law in South Africa' (1998) 30 *Acta Academica* 32

Nowak, M 'The right to education' in Eide, A; Krause, C & Rosas, A (eds) (2001) *Economic, social and cultural rights: A textbook* London: M Nijhoff 245

Ntambirweki, J 'The developing countries in the evolution of an international environmental law' (1991) 14 *Hastings International and Comparative Law Review* 905

Odinkalu, CA & Christensen, C 'The African Commission on Human and People's Rights: The development of its non-state communication procedure' (1998) 16 *Human Rights Quarterly* 235

Olivier, MP & Jansen van Rensburg, L (2002) *Addressing the alleviation of poverty through social welfare measures* Paper presented at the 'XVth World Congress of Sociology' Brisbane, Australia, 7-13 July 2002

Olivier, MP & Jansen van Rensburg, L (2001) *The role and influence of international human rights instruments on South African poverty law* Paper presented at a seminar titled *Law and Poverty IV - Moving towards international poverty law* Onati, Spain 3-4 May 2001

Pallemaerts, M 'International environmental law from Stockholm to Rio: Back to the future?' in Sands, P (ed) (1993) *Greening international law* London: Earthscan 1

Pieters, D (1993) *Introduction into the basic principles of social security* Boston: Kluwer Law & Taxation

Pieterse, M 'A different shade of red: Socio-economic dimensions of the right to life in South Africa' (1999) 15 *South African Journal on Human Rights* 372

Pieterse, M 'Towards a useful role for section 36 of the Constitution in social rights cases? *Residents of Bon Vista Mansions v Southern Metropolitan Local Council*' (2003) 120 *South African Law Journal* 41

Pillay, K 'Implementation of *Grootboom*: Implications for the enforcement of socio-economic rights' (2002) 6 *Law, Democracy and Development* 255

Pillay, K 'Implementing *Grootboom*: Supervision needed' (2002) 3(1) *ESR Review* 13

Pillay, K 'The rights to accommodation, housing and shelter in the South African Constitution' in Bekker, G (ed) (2000) *A compilation of essential documents on the rights to accommodation, housing and shelter* Pretoria: Centre for Human Rights, University of Pretoria 1

Porteus, K 'Education financing: Framing inclusion or exclusion' (2002) *EPU Quarterly Review of Education and Training in South Africa* 10

Price, M 'Health care as an instrument of apartheid policy in South Africa' (1986) 1(2) *Health Policy and Planning* 158

Quansah, EK 'Is the right to get pregnant a fundamental human right in Botswana?' (1995) 39 *Journal of African Law* 97

Robertson, RE 'Measuring state compliance with the obligation to devote the maximum available resources to realising economic, social and cultural rights' (1994) 16 *Human Rights Quarterly* 693

Robinson, NA (ed) (1993) *Agenda 21 & the UNCED Proceedings* New York: Oceana Publications, Inc

Roemer, R 'The right to health care' in Fuenzalida-Puelma, HL & Connor, SS (eds) (1989) *The right to health in the Americas: A comparative constitutional study* Washington DC: Pan American Health Organization 17

Roithmayr, D 'The constitutionality of school fees in public education' *ERP Issue Paper* 1, 17 http://www.law.wits.ac.za/cals/lt

Roux,T 'Legitimating transformation: Political resource allocation in the South African Constitutional Court' (2003) 10 *Democratization* 92

Roux, T 'Understanding *Grootboom* - A response to Cass R Sunstein' (2002) 12 (2) *Constitutional Forum* 41

Sabel, CF & Simon, WH 'Destabilisation rights: How public law litigation succeeds' (2004) 117 *Harvard Law Review* 1016

Sands, P 'International law in the field of sustainable development: Emerging legal principles' in Lang, W (ed) (1995) *Sustainable development and international law* London: Graham 53

Sands, P (1995) *Principles of international environmental law* Manchester: Manchester University Press

Savage, M & Benatar, SR 'An analysis of health and health services' in Schrire, RA (ed) (1990) *Critical choices for South Africa: An agenda for the 1990's* Cape Town: Oxford University Press 147

Scheinin, M 'Economic and social rights as legal rights' in Eide, A; Krause, C & Rosas, A (eds) (1995) *Economic, social and cultural rights: A textbook* Boston: M Nijhoff 41

Scheinin, M 'The right to social security' in Eide, A; Krause, C & Rosas, A (eds) (1995) *Economic, social and cultural rights: A Textbook* Boston: M Nijhoff 159

Schneiderman, D & Bakan, J (eds) (1992) *Social justice and the Constitution: Perspectives on a social union for Canada* Ottawa: Carleton University Press

Scott, C & Alston, P 'Adjudicating constitutional priorities in a transnational context: A comment on *Soobramoney's* legacy and *Grootboom's* promise' (2000) 16 *South African Journal on Human Rights* 206

Scott, C & Macklem, P 'Constitutional ropes of sand or justiciable guarantees? Social rights in a new South African Constitution' (1992) 141 *University of Pennsylvania Law Review* 1

Sen, A (1981) *Poverty and famines: An essay on entitlement and deprivation* Oxford: Clarendon Press

Shinn, C 'The right to the highest attainable standard of health: Public health's opportunity to reframe a human rights debate in the United States' (1999) 4 (1) *Health and Human Rights* 115

Shue, H (1980) *Basic rights: Subsistence, affluence and US foreign policy* Princeton, NJ: Princeton University Press

Simon, WH 'Rights and redistribution in the welfare system' (1986) 38 *Stanford Law Review* 1431

Sloth-Nielsen, J 'The child's right to social services, the right to social security and primary prevention of child abuse: Some conclusions in the aftermath of *Grootboom*' (2001) 17 *South African Journal on Human Rights* 210

Sprigman, C & Osborne, M 'Du Plessis is not dead: South Africa's 1996 Constitution and the application of the Bill of Rights to private disputes' (1999) 15 *South African Journal on Human Rights* 25

Steinberg, M et al 'HIV/AIDS: Facts, figures and the future' (2000) *South African Health Review 2000* 301

Sunde, J 'On the brink' (2003) 12 *SPC Women in Fisheries Information Bulletin* 30

Sunstein, CR 'Social and economic rights? Lessons from South Africa' (2001) 11(4) *Constitutional Forum* 123

Tladi, D 'Strong sustainability, weak sustainability, intergenerational equity and international law: Using the Earth Charter to redirect the environmental ethics debate' (2003) 28 *South African Yearbook of International Law* 200

Tladi, D 'Of course for humans: A contextual defence of intergenerational equity' (2002) 9 *South African Journal of Environmental Law and Policy* 177

Tladi, D 'One step forward, two steps back for constitutionalising the common law: Afrox Health Care v Strydom' (2002) 17 *SA Publiekreg/Public Law* 473

Tladi, D 'The quest to ban hazardous wastes import into Africa: First Bamako and now Basel' (2000) 33 *Comparative and International Law Journal of Southern Africa* 210

Toebes, B 'Towards an improved understanding of the international human right to health' (1999) 21 *Human Rights Quarterly* 661

Tomasevski, K (2003) *Education denied: Costs and remedies* New York: Zed Books

Tomasevski, K (2002) 'Free and compulsory education for all children: The gap between promise and performance' *Right to Education Primers*, No 2, 13 http://www.right-to-education.org

Tomasevski, K (2002) 'Human rights obligations: Making education available, accessible and adaptable' *Right to Education Primers*, No 3, 13-16; http://www.right-to-education.org

Tomasevski, K (2002) 'Removing obstacles in the way of the right to education' *Right to Education Primers* No 1, 8-9; http://www.right-to-education.org

Tomasevski, K (1998) 'Preliminary report of the Special Rapporteur on the Right to Education' submitted in accordance with the Commission on Human Rights Resolution 1998/33 Doc E/CN 4/1999/49; http://www.right-to-education.org

Trengove, W 'Judicial remedies for violations of socio-economic rights' (1999) 1(4) *ESR Review* 8

Vally, S 'Special needs education: Building an inclusive education and training system' (2001) *EPU Quarterly Review of Education and Training in South Africa* 7

Van Bueren, G 'Alleviating poverty through the Constitutional Court' (1999) 15 *South African Journal on Human Rights* 52

Van der Linde, M 'African responses to environmental protection' (2002) 35 *Comparative and International Law Journal of Southern Africa* 99

Van der Linde, M 'Introduction to a healthy environment in the South African Constitution' in Mashava, L (ed) (2000) *A compilation of essential documents on the rights to water and environment* Pretoria: Centre for Human Rights 16

Van der Merwe, D 'Land tenure in South Africa: A brief history and some reform proposals' (1989) *Journal for South African Law* 663

Van der Vyver, JD 'The criminalisation and prosecution of environmental malpractice in international law' (1998) 23 *South African Yearbook of International Law* 1

Van der Walt, AJ 'A South African reading of Frank Michelman's theory of social justice' in Botha, H; Van der Walt, AJ & Van der Walt, JC (eds) (2003) *Rights and democracy in a transformative constitution* Stellenbosch: SUN Press 163

Van der Walt, AJ 'Exclusivity of ownership, security of tenure and eviction orders: A critical evaluation of recent case law' (2002) 18 *South African Journal on Human Rights* 372

Van der Walt, AJ 'Exclusivity of ownership, security of tenure and eviction orders: A model to evaluate South African land-reform legislation' (2002) 2 *Journal of South African Law* 254

Van der Walt, AJ 'Sosiale geregtigheid, prosedurele billikheid en eiendom: Alternatiewe perspektiewe op grondwetlike waarborge (Deel Een)' ('Social justice, procedural fairness and property. Alternative perspectives on constitutional guarantees (Part One)') (2002) 13 *Stellenbosch Law Review* 59

Van der Walt, AJ 'Dancing with codes – Protecting, developing, and deconstructing property rights in a constitutional state' (2001) 118 *South African Law Journal* 258

Van der Walt, AJ 'Tentative urgency: Sensitivity for the paradoxes of stability and change in social transformation decisions of the Constitutional Court' (2001) 16 *SA Public Law* 1

Van der Walt, JWG 'Justice Kriegler's judgment in *Du Plessis v De Klerk*: Much ado about horizontal application (read nothing)' (1996) 4 *South African Law Journal* 732

Van Ginneken, W (2003) 'Extending social security: Policies for developing countries' *ESS Paper* No 13 Geneva, Switzerland: ILO

Van Hoof, GJH 'The legal nature of economic, social and cultural rights: A rebuttal of some traditional views' in Alston, P & Tomasevski, K (eds) (1984) *The right to food* SIM Boston: M Nijhoff 97

Van Langendonck, J (1986) *Sociale zekerheid: Wat is dat eigenlijk?* Antwerpen: Kluwer

Van Marle, K '"No last word" – Reflections on the imaginary domain, dignity and intrinsic worth' (2002) 13 *Stellenbosch Law Review* 307

Van Onselen, C (1996) *The seed is mine: The life of Kas Maine, a South African sharecropper, 1894-1985* New York: Hill and Wang

Van Rensburg, HCJ & Ngwena, C 'Health and health care in South Africa against an African background' in Cockeram, WC (ed) (2001) *The Blackwell companion to medical sociology* Oxford, UK: Blackwell 365

Van Rensburg, HCJ 'Health and health care in South Africa in transition' (1999) 31 *Acta Academica* 1

Van Rensburg, HCJ & Fourie, A 'Inequalities in South African health care, Part 1: The problem - manifestation and origins' (1994) 84 *South African Medical Law Journal* 95

Van Rensburg, HCJ & Benatar, SR 'The legacy of apartheid in health and health care' (1993) 24 *South African Journal of Sociology* 99

Van Rensburg, HCJ; Fourie, A & Pretorius, E (1992) *Health care in South Africa: Structure and dynamics* Pretoria: Academica

Van Rensburg, HCJ 'South African health care in change' (1991) 22 *South African Journal of Sociology* 1

Van Rensburg, HCJ & Fourie, A 'Privatisation of South African health care: In whose interest?' (1988) 11 *Curationis* 1

Vidar, M 'Towards voluntary guidelines on the right to adequate food' (2004) 5(1) *ESR Review* 11

Viljoen, F *The justiciability of socio-economic and cultural rights: Experiences and problems* Paper delivered at a conference on social, economic and cultural rights, organised by UNESCO, Addis Ababa, 10 March, 2005

Viljoen, F 'Children's rights: A response from a South African perspective' in Brand, D & Russel, S (eds) (2002) *Exploring the core content of socio-economic rights: South African and international perspectives* Pretoria: Protea Book House 201

Viljoen, F 'Introduction to the African Commission and the regional human rights system' in Heyns, CH (ed) (2000) *Human rights law in Africa* The Hague: Kluwer Law International

Watkinson, E & Masemola, K 'The food crisis: More action needed' (2002) Nov *Naledi Policy Bulletin* 4

Weiss, E B 'In fairness to future generations: International law, common patrimony and intergenerational equity' in Hayden, P (ed) (2001) *The philosophy of human rights* St Paul MN: Paragon House 618

Weiss, E B 'Our rights and obligations to future generations for the environment' (1990) 84 *American Journal of International Law* 198

Weiss, E B 'The planetary trust: Conservation and intergenerational equity' (1984) 11(4) *Ecology Law Quarterly* 495

Whitehead, M with Townsend, P & Davidson, N (eds) *Inequalities in Health: The Black Report/The Health Divide* (1992) New York: Penguin Books

Wildeman, RA 'School funding norms 2001: Are more learners benefiting?' (2001) *IDASA Budget Information Service* 7

Williams, LA 'Welfare and legal entitlements: The social roots of poverty' in Kairys, D (ed) (1998) *The politics of law: A progressive critique* 3rd ed, New York: Pantheon Books 569

Wilson, S 'Taming the Constitution: Rights and reform in the South African education system' (2004) 20 *South African Journal on Human Rights* 418

Windfuhr, M 'No masterpiece of political will: The last stage of negotiations on voluntary guidelines on the right to food' (2004) 5(4) *ESR Review* 16

Witbooi, E 'Subsistence fishing in South Africa: Implementation of the Marine Living Resources Act' (2002) 17 *International Journal of Marine and Coastal Law* 431

Woolard, I & Barberton, C 'The extent of poverty and equality' in Barberton, C; Blake, M & Kotze, H (eds) (1998) *Creating action space* Claremont: IDASA & David Philip Publishers 31

Woolman, S 'Application' in Chaskalson, M; Kentridge, J; Klaaren, J; Marcus, G; Spitz, D; Stein, A & Woolman, S (1996) *Constitutional Law of South Africa* 2nd ed, Original Service, Cape Town: Juta 10.1

Woolman, S & Davis, D 'The last laugh: *Du Plessis v De Klerk*, classical liberalism, Creole liberalism and the application of fundamental rights under the interim and the final Constitutions' (1996) 12 *South African Journal on Human Rights* 361

Yamin, A E & Maine, D P 'Maternal mortality as a human rights issue: Measuring compliance with international treaty obligations' (1999) 21 *Human Rights Quarterly* 574